DOES COCKSHUTT BEAT SANDY BALLS?

Simon Trewin is a drama graduate from Kent University and a lite
leading literary and talent agency – the Peters Fraser and Dunlop Group Ltd. He is the
co-author (with Tom Bromley and Michael Moran) of *Rock And Pop Elevens* (Michael O'Mara
2005), *The Encylopaedia Of Guilty Pleasures – 1001 Things You Hate To Love* (John Murray 2006)
and (with Tom Bromley, Michael Moran and Amanda Astill) of *Shopping While Drunk –
Confessions from Modern Life* (John Murray 2007). He has contributed to a number of books
including *Live 8 – The Official Book* (Century 2006) and *The Enlightened Bracketologist*
(Bloomsbury US 2007) and is currently working on *I Am Camera – me no Leica* (an anthology
of bad reviews from the stage, film, music and book worlds) and on *Please Stop Writing* – an
unconventional creative writing handbook (with Sarah Ballard). In his spare time he is
married to Helen and they have a son called Jack T.

www.myspace.com/thisissimon

Published by Random House Books 2007

2 4 6 8 10 9 7 5 3 1

First published in Great Britain in 2007 by
Random House Books
Random House, 20 Vauxhall Bridge Road,
London SW1V 2SA

www.rbooks.co.uk

Addresses for companies within
The Random House Group Limited can be found at:
www.randomhouse.co.uk/offices.htm

The Random House Group Limited Reg. No. 954009

A CIP catalogue record for this book is available from the British Library

ISBN 9781905211869

The Random House Group Limited makes every effort to ensure that the
papers used in its books are made from trees that have been legally sourced from
well-managed and credibly certified forests. Our paper procurement
policy can be found at: www.rbooks.co.uk/environment

Typeset by Palimpsest Book Production Limited,
Grangemouth, Stirlingshire
Printed and bound in Slovenia by
MKT Print d.d, Lubljana, Slovenia

Does Cockshutt Beat Sandy Balls?

. . . and other important questions
in the search for the best
of everything

Edited by
Simon Trewin
Designed by Nigel Holmes

rh
BOOKS

CONTENTS
Introduction

Congratulations on opening this book – you have already made a very important decision which will change your life forever. Pat yourself on the back, find a comfortable chair, maybe pour yourself a refreshing light beverage as well and settle down for an important session in self development. If you are in a shop and have yet to make that life-enhancing walk towards the till then ponder no longer and rush onwards – this could be the best £9.99 you ever spend. If, of course, this is in a clever 50% off promotion then don't skimp – buy TWO copies, give one to a mate and you'll have a friend for life.

What an opportunity.

But first, a plea – don't treat this book as a mere stocking filler or yet another addition to that festering pile of humour books in the smallest room in the house – this is more, much much more. Yes of course there are trivia books out there which will give you raw nuggets of knowledge to feed your fact-hunger and dazzle your nearest and dearest but they are mere fast food compared to the soul food you will find within. What we can offer here with *Does Cockshutt Beat Sandy Balls?* is an opportunity to think out loud and, through a terrifyingly simple series of intellectual leaps, to win most arguments. Think what power that will give you in the workplace or at home – no more feuds about the best goal ever scored in a World Cup tie, no more never-ending contretemps over the sexiest Bond Girl and a total cessation of linguistic battles over whether John Noakes was a better Blue Peter presenter than Peter Purves. If we could only impose this system on various diplomatic troublespots around the globe then we would be living in a world of peace, harmony and love. All we are saying is 'Give Bracketology A Chance'.

You may well be asking yourself at this point whether any book could really live up to this promise and look hype this effusive straight in the eye without blushing a bit? Oh yes. Truly. In fact I am so confident of these claims that if you feel in any sense that *Does Cockshutt Beat Sandy Balls?* fails to live up to these claims then I will enrol you free of charge in the University Of Bracketology Correspondence Scheme which will see me sending you an increasingly grumpy series of emails full of self-evident logic that will ultimately see you throwing your hands up in horror and shouting 'Cease, desist – I agree with you Simon'.

Onwards people – we have problems to solve and people to convince.

It's very simple, really. Bracketology is a way of breaking down every subject into a series of either/or questions. Whatever subject may be under discussion, all you need to do is line up your candidates and then systematically play them off against each other until you have one clear winner. It's a brilliantly simple method that can, of course, be applied to any question, and in *Does Cockshutt Beat Sandy Balls?* we're proud to have tackled 99 of the most burning questions of our time. Whether you want to find out the best advertising slogan or the most horrible smell, you can turn to the relevant page of this book, read down the first column of short-listed candidates, then follow them through a series of knock-out rounds until you get to the overall winner. I'm not going to deny that some of the decisions are contentious, and you may well find yourself tutting menacingly or even screaming your disapproval, but at the end of the book I'm confident you'll be converted to the charms of Bracketology.

Advertising Slogans

by SIMON TREWIN

There are supposed to be EU regulations in place that stop broadcasters including more than fifteen minutes of advertising per hour but frankly sometimes it feels like adverts dominate to a ridiculous extent. No doubt dramas are now being written with the frequency of ad breaks in mind – on Channel 4 there is frequently one after eight minutes of the programme. Once you strip out the opening credits, you hardly have the time to settle into the armchair, loosen your clothing and arrange a cat on your knee before the dramatic tension of *Lost* is thrown away and there are two women in a kitchen trying to sell you washing up liquid. Imagine if this practice was introduced into commercial theatre – although of course in Pinter plays they could fit the adverts into the pauses. Anyway, which of the following slogans help us Work, Rest and Play, and which make you feel as if you've just been Tangoed?

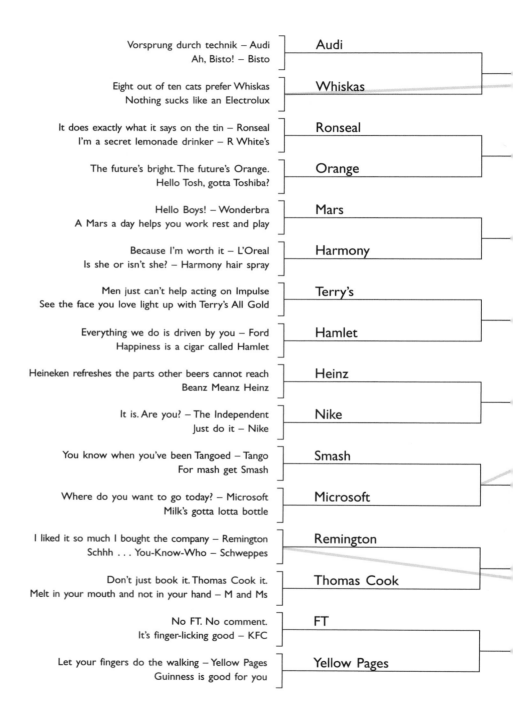

Vorsprung durch technik – Audi
Ah, Bisto! – Bisto

Audi

Eight out of ten cats prefer Whiskas
Nothing sucks like an Electrolux

Whiskas

It does exactly what it says on the tin – Ronseal
I'm a secret lemonade drinker – R White's

Ronseal

The future's bright. The future's Orange.
Hello Tosh, gotta Toshiba?

Orange

Hello Boys! – Wonderbra
A Mars a day helps you work rest and play

Mars

Because I'm worth it – L'Oreal
Is she or isn't she? – Harmony hair spray

Harmony

Men just can't help acting on Impulse
See the face you love light up with Terry's All Gold

Terry's

Everything we do is driven by you – Ford
Happiness is a cigar called Hamlet

Hamlet

Heineken refreshes the parts other beers cannot reach
Beanz Meanz Heinz

Heinz

It is. Are you? – The Independent
Just do it – Nike

Nike

You know when you've been Tangoed – Tango
For mash get Smash

Smash

Where do you want to go today? – Microsoft
Milk's gotta lotta bottle

Microsoft

I liked it so much I bought the company – Remington
Schhh . . . You-Know-Who – Schweppes

Remington

Don't just book it. Thomas Cook it.
Melt in your mouth and not in your hand – M and Ms

Thomas Cook

No FT. No comment.
It's finger-licking good – KFC

FT

Let your fingers do the walking – Yellow Pages
Guinness is good for you

Yellow Pages

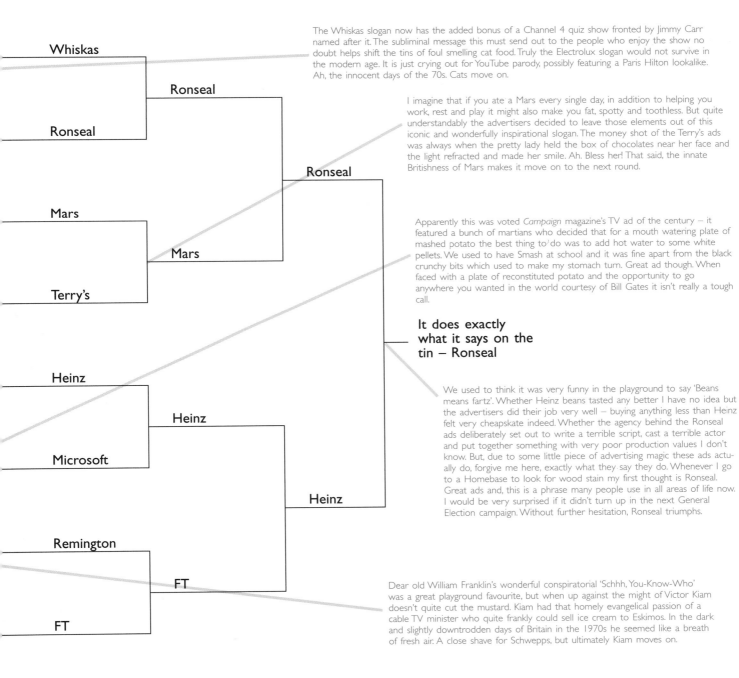

Whiskas

Ronseal

Ronseal

Ronseal

Mars

Mars

Terry's

Heinz

Heinz

Microsoft

Heinz

Remington

FT

FT

It does exactly what it says on the tin — Ronseal

The Whiskas slogan now has the added bonus of a Channel 4 quiz show fronted by Jimmy Carr named after it. The subliminal message this must send out to the people who enjoy the show no doubt helps shift the tins of foul smelling cat food. Truly the Electrolux slogan would not survive in the modern age. It is just crying out for YouTube parody, possibly featuring a Paris Hilton lookalike. Ah, the innocent days of the 70s. Cats move on.

I imagine that if you ate a Mars every single day, in addition to helping you work, rest and play it might also make you fat, spotty and toothless. But quite understandably the advertisers decided to leave those elements out of this iconic and wonderfully inspirational slogan. The money shot of the Terry's ads was always when the pretty lady held the box of chocolates near her face and the light refracted and made her smile. Ah. Bless her! That said, the innate Britishness of Mars makes it move on to the next round.

Apparently this was voted *Campaign* magazine's TV ad of the century – it featured a bunch of martians who decided that for a mouth watering plate of mashed potato the best thing to do was to add hot water to some white pellets. We used to have Smash at school and it was fine apart from the black crunchy bits which used to make my stomach turn. Great ad though. When faced with a plate of reconstituted potato and the opportunity to go anywhere you wanted in the world courtesy of Bill Gates it isn't really a tough call.

We used to think it was very funny in the playground to say 'Beans means fartz'. Whether Heinz beans tasted any better I have no idea but the advertisers did their job very well – buying anything less than Heinz felt very cheapskate indeed. Whether the agency behind the Ronseal ads deliberately set out to write a terrible script, cast a terrible actor and put together something with very poor production values I don't know. But, due to some little piece of advertising magic these ads actually do, forgive me here, exactly what they say they do. Whenever I go to a Homebase to look for wood stain my first thought is Ronseal. Great ads and, this is a phrase many people use in all areas of life now. I would be very surprised if it didn't turn up in the next General Election campaign. Without further hesitation, Ronseal triumphs.

Dear old William Franklin's wonderful conspiratorial 'Schhh, You-Know-Who' was a great playground favourite, but when up against the might of Victor Kiam doesn't quite cut the mustard. Kiam had that homely evangelical passion of a cable TV minister who quite frankly could sell ice cream to Eskimos. In the dark and slightly downtrodden days of Britain in the 1970s he seemed like a breath of fresh air. A close shave for Schwepps, but ultimately Kiam moves on.

Anagrams
by SIMON TREWIN

We are a nation of wordsmiths and there is something inherently pleasing about anagrams – a wonderful anagram looks up at you from the paper exuding an almost mathematical perfection that stimulates and excites all at once. When you realize that you can anagram 'To be or not to be: that is the question, whether its nobler in the mind to suffer the slings and arrows of outrageous fortune . . .' and get 'In one of the Bard's best-thought-of tragedies, our insistent hero, Hamlet, queries on two fronts about how life turns rotten' life seems somewhat better!

I'm a dot in place (Decimal point) — Hitler
Woman Hitler (Mother-in-law)

Ascend in Paris (Princess Diana) — ascend
Those surname counters (The census enumeration)

I can hear ten 'tens' (The centenarians) — adult
Adult novels (Love and lust)

Ensliced eats (Delicatessan) — IX
IX stand there (Six and three)

Docile, as a man tamed it (A domesticated animal) — docile
I herald a toss (Heads or tails)

Sun time (Minutes) — no hat
No hat, a smile (The Mona Lisa)

Elegant man (A gentleman) — elegant
Racing tipster (Starting price)

I'm an evil Tory bigot (Virginia Bottomley) — bigot
A miscreant list (State criminals)

No untidy clothes (The nudist colony) — clothes
Away! Hang him (A highwayman)

Here come dots (The Morse code) — positively
Positively (Is pity love?)

Price speeds mail vastly (Special delivery stamps) — price
Had met real loss (A motherless lad)

The classroom (Schoolmaster) — classroom
Home-arid desert (The dromedaries)

Deaths on these (The headstones) — evil
Evil's agent (Evangelist)

I'm her darned mate (The married man) — pithy
Pithy female braves fury (Buffy the Vampire Slayer)

It's your end (Our destiny) — grunt
Emit grunt (Muttering)

I'm Tory plan B (Tony Blair MP) — loonies
Loonies far up the Thames (The Houses of Parliament)

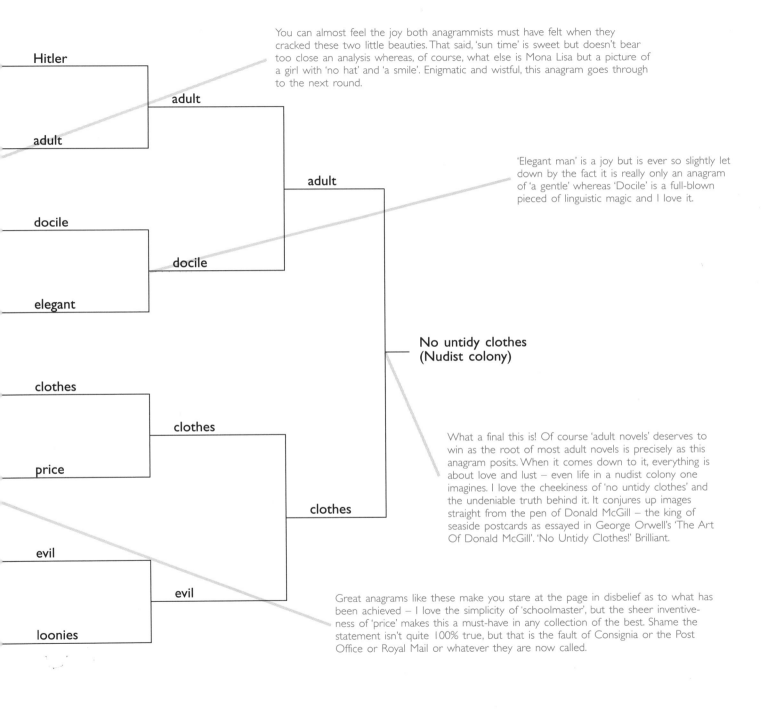

Hitler

adult

adult

docile

elegant

clothes

price

evil

loonies

adult

docile

clothes

evil

adult

clothes

**No untidy clothes
(Nudist colony)**

You can almost feel the joy both anagrammists must have felt when they cracked these two little beauties. That said, 'sun time' is sweet but doesn't bear too close an analysis whereas, of course, what else is Mona Lisa but a picture of a girl with 'no hat' and 'a smile'. Enigmatic and wistful, this anagram goes through to the next round.

'Elegant man' is a joy but is ever so slightly let down by the fact it is really only an anagram of 'a gentle' whereas 'Docile' is a full-blown pieced of linguistic magic and I love it.

What a final this is! Of course 'adult novels' deserves to win as the root of most adult novels is precisely as this anagram posits. When it comes down to it, everything is about love and lust — even life in a nudist colony one imagines. I love the cheekiness of 'no untidy clothes' and the undeniable truth behind it. It conjures up images straight from the pen of Donald McGill — the king of seaside postcards as essayed in George Orwell's 'The Art Of Donald McGill'. 'No Untidy Clothes!' Brilliant.

Great anagrams like these make you stare at the page in disbelief as to what has been achieved — I love the simplicity of 'schoolmaster', but the sheer inventiveness of 'price' makes this a must-have in any collection of the best. Shame the statement isn't quite 100% true, but that is the fault of Consignia or the Post Office or Royal Mail or whatever they are now called.

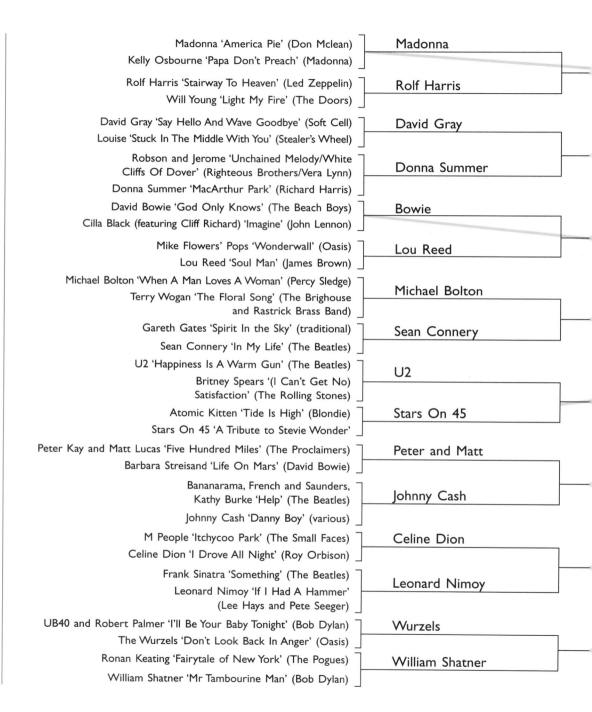

Awful Cover Versions

by SIMON TREWIN

Music has a way of instantly taking you back to a time and place in your life, whether it's the first time you heard The Beatles at your uncle's house on the occasion of your nephew's fourth birthday, that thirteenth birthday party when someone brought along a Bowie album and you heard the heart-stoppingly amazing 'Young Americans' or that time at university when you got dumped and every time you turned the radio on it was playing 'I Will Always Love You' by Whitney Houston. Cherished memories, all instantly triggered when you hear the song again. You can remember the orchestration in minute detail, every breath, every inflection and every lyric. Precious moments. Truly. So why, I ask, did someone have to go and spoil it all by inventing the notion of 'the cover version'? What did the world do to deserve classic songs being butchered to death? Obviously something truly terrible. I can't quite decide what is worse — an actor wandering into slightly unfamiliar territory by recording a favourite song (terribly) or a world class band or singer who really should know better. Time to find out.

Madonna 'America Pie' (Don Mclean)
Kelly Osbourne 'Papa Don't Preach' (Madonna)
Madonna

Rolf Harris 'Stairway To Heaven' (Led Zeppelin)
Will Young 'Light My Fire' (The Doors)
Rolf Harris

David Gray 'Say Hello And Wave Goodbye' (Soft Cell)
Louise 'Stuck In The Middle With You' (Stealer's Wheel)
David Gray

Robson and Jerome 'Unchained Melody/White Cliffs Of Dover' (Righteous Brothers/Vera Lynn)
Donna Summer 'MacArthur Park' (Richard Harris)
Donna Summer

David Bowie 'God Only Knows' (The Beach Boys)
Cilla Black (featuring Cliff Richard) 'Imagine' (John Lennon)
Bowie

Mike Flowers' Pops 'Wonderwall' (Oasis)
Lou Reed 'Soul Man' (James Brown)
Lou Reed

Michael Bolton 'When A Man Loves A Woman' (Percy Sledge)
Terry Wogan 'The Floral Song' (The Brighouse and Rastrick Brass Band)
Michael Bolton

Gareth Gates 'Spirit In the Sky' (traditional)
Sean Connery 'In My Life' (The Beatles)
Sean Connery

U2 'Happiness Is A Warm Gun' (The Beatles)
Britney Spears '(I Can't Get No) Satisfaction' (The Rolling Stones)
U2

Atomic Kitten 'Tide Is High' (Blondie)
Stars On 45 'A Tribute to Stevie Wonder'
Stars On 45

Peter Kay and Matt Lucas 'Five Hundred Miles' (The Proclaimers)
Barbara Streisand 'Life On Mars' (David Bowie)
Peter and Matt

Bananarama, French and Saunders, Kathy Burke 'Help' (The Beatles)
Johnny Cash 'Danny Boy' (various)
Johnny Cash

M People 'Itchycoo Park' (The Small Faces)
Celine Dion 'I Drove All Night' (Roy Orbison)
Celine Dion

Frank Sinatra 'Something' (The Beatles)
Leonard Nimoy 'If I Had A Hammer' (Lee Hays and Pete Seeger)
Leonard Nimoy

UB40 and Robert Palmer 'I'll Be Your Baby Tonight' (Bob Dylan)
The Wurzels 'Don't Look Back In Anger' (Oasis)
Wurzels

Ronan Keating 'Fairytale of New York' (The Pogues)
William Shatner 'Mr Tambourine Man' (Bob Dylan)
William Shatner

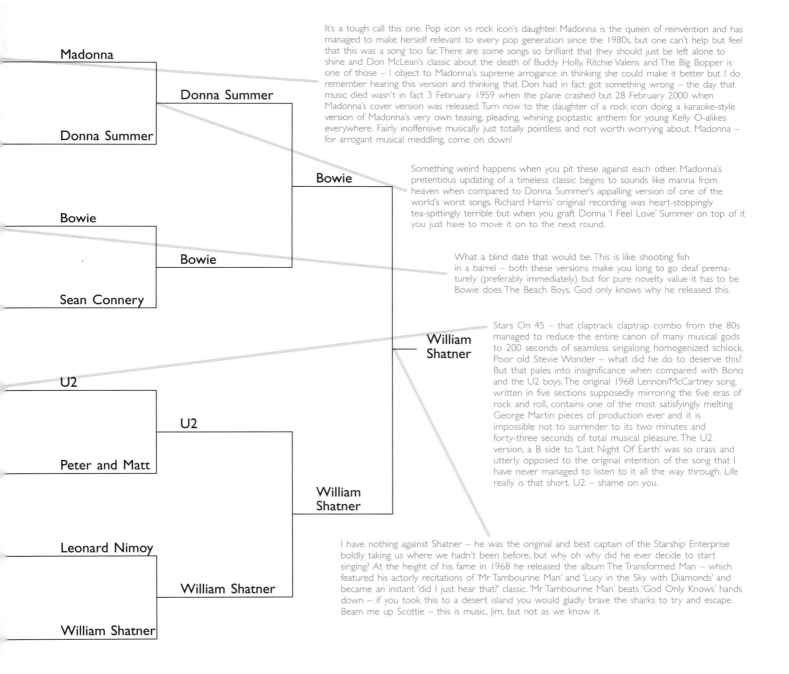

Madonna

Donna Summer

Donna Summer

Bowie

Bowie

Bowie

Sean Connery

William Shatner

U2

U2

Peter and Matt

William Shatner

Leonard Nimoy

William Shatner

William Shatner

It's a tough call this one. Pop icon vs rock icon's daughter. Madonna is the queen of reinvention and has managed to make herself relevant to every pop pop generation since the 1980s, but one can't help but feel that this was a song too far. There are some songs so brilliant that they should just be left alone to shine and Don McLean's classic about the death of Buddy Holly, Ritchie Valens and The Big Bopper is one of those – I object to Madonna's supreme arrogance in thinking she could make it better but I do remember hearing this version and thinking that Don had in fact got something wrong – the day that music died wasn't in fact 3 February 1959 when the plane crashed but 28 February 2000 when Madonna's cover version was released. Turn now to the daughter of a rock icon doing a karaoke-style version of Madonna's very own teasing, pleading, whining poptastic anthem for young Kelly O-alikes everywhere. Fairly inoffensive musically just totally pointless and not worth worrying about. Madonna – for arrogant musical meddling, come on down!

Something weird happens when you pit these against each other. Madonna's pretentious updating of a timeless classic begins to sounds like manna from heaven when compared to Donna Summer's appalling version of one of the world's worst songs. Richard Harris' original recording was heart-stoppingly tea-spittingly terrible but when you graft Donna 'I Feel Love' Summer on top of it you just have to move it on to the next round.

What a blind date that would be. This is like shooting fish in a barrel – both these versions make you long to go deaf prematurely (preferably immediately) but for pure novelty value it has to be Bowie does The Beach Boys. God only knows why he released this.

Stars On 45 – that claptrack claptrap combo from the 80s managed to reduce the entire canon of many musical gods to 200 seconds of seamless singalong homogenized schlock. Poor old Stevie Wonder – what did he do to deserve this? But that pales into insignificance when compared with Bono and the U2 boys. The original 1968 Lennon/McCartney song, written in five sections supposedly mirroring the five eras of rock and roll, contains one of the most satisfyingly melting George Martin pieces of production ever and it is impossible not to surrender to its two minutes and forty-three seconds of total musical pleasure. The U2 version, a B side to 'Last Night Of Earth' was so crass and utterly opposed to the original intention of the song that I have never managed to listen to it all the way through. Life really is that short. U2 – shame on you.

I have nothing against Shatner – he was the original and best captain of the Starship Enterprise boldly taking us where we hadn't been before, but why oh why did he ever decide to start singing? At the height of his fame in 1968 he released the album The Transformed Man – which featured his actorly recitations of 'Mr Tambourine Man' and 'Lucy in the Sky with Diamonds' and became an instant 'did I just hear that?' classic. 'Mr Tambourine Man' beats 'God Only Knows' hands down – if you took this to a desert island you would gladly brave the sharks to try and escape. Beam me up Scottie – this is music, Jim, but not as we know it.

Bad Lines by Great Poets

by ROBIN BROOKS

It's hard

To be a bard.

Even Homer nods, and great poets have off days. It's also hard to anticipate how your deathless verse might sound in a couple of centuries when usage has changed and form B, year 7 find you hysterical. Our poets are rightly revered (mostly – see Shelley) but reverence should not make us blind to those little moments of inattention or infelicity.

ROBIN BROOKS is a radio-playwright. He goes running with Simon Trewin sometimes, and always gets home first.

'Never, never, never, never, never.' – Shakespeare

'I wandered lonely as a cloud.' – Wordsworth

'Red lips are not so red, As the stained stones kissed by our English dead.' – Wilfrid Owen

'There was an Ancient Mariner, He stoppeth one of three.' – Coleridge

'What immortal hand or eye, can frame thy fearful symmetry?' – Blake

'They fuck you up, your Mum and Dad' – Larkin

'What, old Dad, dead?' – Tourneur

'"The curse is come upon me," cried the Lady Of Shallot.' – Tennyson

'Lady, three white leopards sat under a juniper tree.' – T. S. Eliot

Pretty much anything by Shelley

'Licence my roving hands to go, Before, behind, between, below.' – Donne

'Clothed in white samite, mystic, wonderful.' – Tennyson

'Lilies that fester smell far worse than weeds.' – Shakespeare

'His Captain's hand on his shoulder smote, "Play up, play up and play the game!"' – Henty

'We buried him darkly at dead of night, The sods with our bayonets turning.' – Wolfe

'Or if thy mistress some rich anger shows, Emprison her soft hand and let her rave, And feed deep, deep upon her peerless eyes.' – Keats

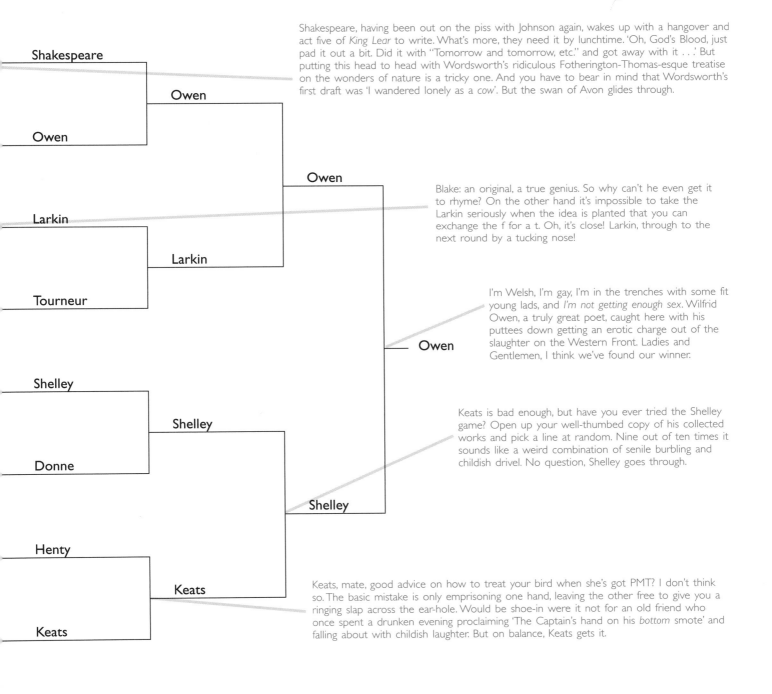

Shakespeare

Owen

Owen

Owen

Owen

Larkin

Larkin

Tourneur

Owen

Shelley

Shelley

Donne

Shelley

Henty

Keats

Keats

Shakespeare, having been out on the piss with Johnson again, wakes up with a hangover and act five of *King Lear* to write. What's more, they need it by lunchtime. 'Oh, God's Blood, just pad it out a bit. Did it with "Tomorrow and tomorrow, etc." and got away with it . . .' But putting this head to head with Wordsworth's ridiculous Fotherington-Thomas-esque treatise on the wonders of nature is a tricky one. And you have to bear in mind that Wordsworth's first draft was 'I wandered lonely as a *cow*'. But the swan of Avon glides through.

Blake: an original, a true genius. So why can't he even get it to rhyme? On the other hand it's impossible to take the Larkin seriously when the idea is planted that you can exchange the f for a t. Oh, it's close! Larkin, through to the next round by a tucking nose!

I'm Welsh, I'm gay, I'm in the trenches with some fit young lads, and *I'm not getting enough sex*. Wilfrid Owen, a truly great poet, caught here with his puttees down getting an erotic charge out of the slaughter on the Western Front. Ladies and Gentlemen, I think we've found our winner.

Keats is bad enough, but have you ever tried the Shelley game? Open up your well-thumbed copy of his collected works and pick a line at random. Nine out of ten times it sounds like a weird combination of senile burbling and childish drivel. No question, Shelley goes through.

Keats, mate, good advice on how to treat your bird when she's got PMT? I don't think so. The basic mistake is only emprisoning one hand, leaving the other free to give you a ringing slap across the ear-hole. Would be shoe-in were it not for an old friend who once spent a drunken evening proclaiming 'The Captain's hand on his *bottom* smote' and falling about with childish laughter. But on balance, Keats gets it.

Baldies
by SIMON TREWIN

The male members of my clan have never been much blessed with hair much beyond their 30s so I was hardly surprised when from my mid 20s on my face got bigger and bigger as my widow's peak retreated further and further towards my crown. Hairbrushes became a distant memory but, on the plus side, I have saved a fortune on trips to the barber. Luckily the 80s became the 90s and it became acceptable to shave your head – some may say it even became quite cool and hopefully people who have never known me with hair will think that my shining dome is a result of a style decision rather than a genetic accident. Luckily, I am not alone (and I am not just talking about National Front skinheads) – some of the coolest people in the world reach for the razor in the morning rather than the hairbrush. Here are thirty-two of them in their hairless glory but which one wins the Bracketology Comb Of Destiny?

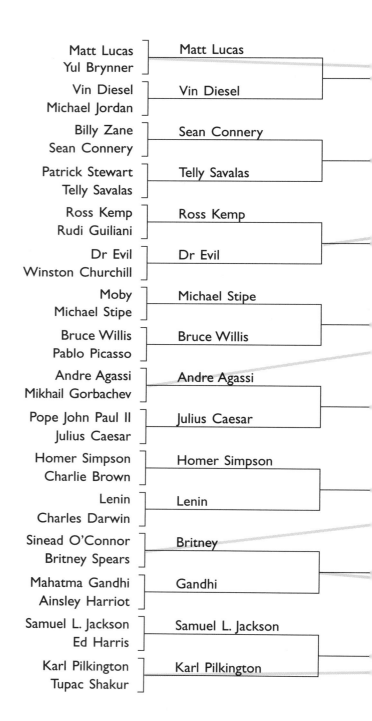

Matt Lucas
Yul Brynner — Matt Lucas

Vin Diesel
Michael Jordan — Vin Diesel

Billy Zane
Sean Connery — Sean Connery

Patrick Stewart
Telly Savalas — Telly Savalas

Ross Kemp
Rudi Guiliani — Ross Kemp

Dr Evil
Winston Churchill — Dr Evil

Moby
Michael Stipe — Michael Stipe

Bruce Willis
Pablo Picasso — Bruce Willis

Andre Agassi
Mikhail Gorbachev — Andre Agassi

Pope John Paul II
Julius Caesar — Julius Caesar

Homer Simpson
Charlie Brown — Homer Simpson

Lenin
Charles Darwin — Lenin

Sinead O'Connor
Britney Spears — Britney

Mahatma Gandhi
Ainsley Harriot — Gandhi

Samuel L. Jackson
Ed Harris — Samuel L. Jackson

Karl Pilkington
Tupac Shakur — Karl Pilkington

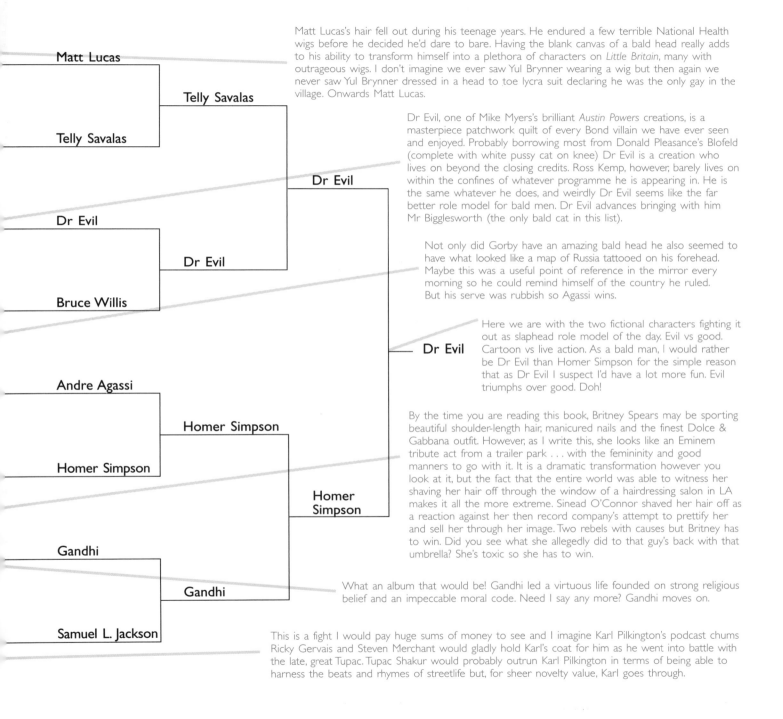

Matt Lucas

Telly Savalas

Telly Savalas

Dr Evil

Dr Evil

Dr Evil

Bruce Willis

Dr Evil

Andre Agassi

Homer Simpson

Homer Simpson

Homer Simpson

Gandhi

Gandhi

Samuel L. Jackson

Matt Lucas's hair fell out during his teenage years. He endured a few terrible National Health wigs before he decided he'd dare to bare. Having the blank canvas of a bald head really adds to his ability to transform himself into a plethora of characters on *Little Britain*, many with outrageous wigs. I don't imagine we ever saw Yul Brynner wearing a wig but then again we never saw Yul Brynner dressed in a head to toe lycra suit declaring he was the only gay in the village. Onwards Matt Lucas.

Dr Evil, one of Mike Myers's brilliant *Austin Powers* creations, is a masterpiece patchwork quilt of every Bond villain we have ever seen and enjoyed. Probably borrowing most from Donald Pleasance's Blofeld (complete with white pussy cat on knee) Dr Evil is a creation who lives on beyond the closing credits. Ross Kemp, however, barely lives on within the confines of whatever programme he is appearing in. He is the same whatever he does, and weirdly Dr Evil seems like the far better role model for bald men. Dr Evil advances bringing with him Mr Bigglesworth (the only bald cat in this list).

Not only did Gorby have an amazing bald head he also seemed to have what looked like a map of Russia tattooed on his forehead. Maybe this was a useful point of reference in the mirror every morning so he could remind himself of the country he ruled. But his serve was rubbish so Agassi wins.

Here we are with the two fictional characters fighting it out as slaphead role model of the day. Evil vs good. Cartoon vs live action. As a bald man, I would rather be Dr Evil than Homer Simpson for the simple reason that as Dr Evil I suspect I'd have a lot more fun. Evil triumphs over good. Doh!

By the time you are reading this book, Britney Spears may be sporting beautiful shoulder-length hair, manicured nails and the finest Dolce & Gabbana outfit. However, as I write this, she looks like an Eminem tribute act from a trailer park . . . with the femininity and good manners to go with it. It is a dramatic transformation however you look at it, but the fact that the entire world was able to witness her shaving her hair off through the window of a hairdressing salon in LA makes it all the more extreme. Sinead O'Connor shaved her hair off as a reaction against her then record company's attempt to prettify her and sell her through her image. Two rebels with causes but Britney has to win. Did you see what she allegedly did to that guy's back with that umbrella? She's toxic so she has to win.

What an album that would be! Gandhi led a virtuous life founded on strong religious belief and an impeccable moral code. Need I say any more? Gandhi moves on.

This is a fight I would pay huge sums of money to see and I imagine Karl Pilkington's podcast chums Ricky Gervais and Steven Merchant would gladly hold Karl's coat for him as he went into battle with the late, great Tupac. Tupac Shakur would probably outrun Karl Pilkington in terms of being able to harness the beats and rhymes of streetlife but, for sheer novelty value, Karl goes through.

Blue Peter Presenters
by SIMON TREWIN

There are two surefire ways to find out someone's age – first ask them who was presenting *Blue Peter* when they were little and secondly who was presenting *Top Of the Pops*. If, like with me, the answers are 'Valerie Singleton' and 'Jimmy Saville' then you're talking to a true Baby Boomer child of the sixties. My *Blue Peter* experiences were mainly black and white and certainly involved the *Blue Peter* garden being vandalised, the burying of the time capsule, massed bands of Dagenham Girl Pipers appearing through the huge scene dock doors at the back of the set, that elephant dumping on the floor of the studio and all of us sending in mounds of silver foil and bottle tops. The elephant dung was undoubtedly a good fertiliser but I could never work out precisely what the silver foil in the *Blue Peter* Appeal was going to be used for – maybe they were going to build a huge Dalek to tackle world poverty? In any event *Blue Peter* was as much essential viewing as *Crackerjack* and *Trumpton* and I loved my generation of presenters and that cheeky little Border collie – Shep. Aaah! Anyway – here's a bracket I made earlier.

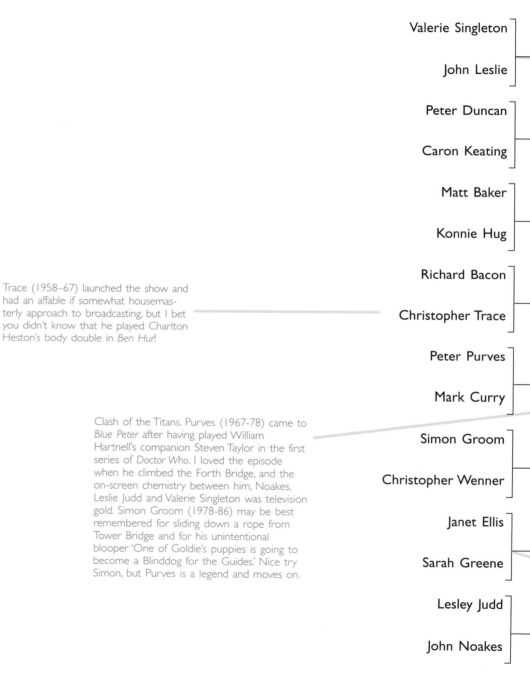

Trace (1958–67) launched the show and had an affable if somewhat housemasterly approach to broadcasting, but I bet you didn't know that he played Charlton Heston's body double in *Ben Hur*!

Clash of the Titans. Purves (1967-78) came to *Blue Peter* after having played William Hartnell's companion Steven Taylor in the first series of *Doctor Who*. I loved the episode when he climbed the Forth Bridge, and the on-screen chemistry between him, Noakes, Leslie Judd and Valerie Singleton was television gold. Simon Groom (1978-86) may be best remembered for sliding down a rope from Tower Bridge and for his unintentional blooper 'One of Goldie's puppies is going to become a Blinddog for the Guides.' Nice try Simon, but Purves is a legend and moves on.

Valerie Singleton

John Leslie

Peter Duncan

Caron Keating

Matt Baker

Konnie Hug

Richard Bacon

Christopher Trace

Peter Purves

Mark Curry

Simon Groom

Christopher Wenner

Janet Ellis

Sarah Greene

Lesley Judd

John Noakes

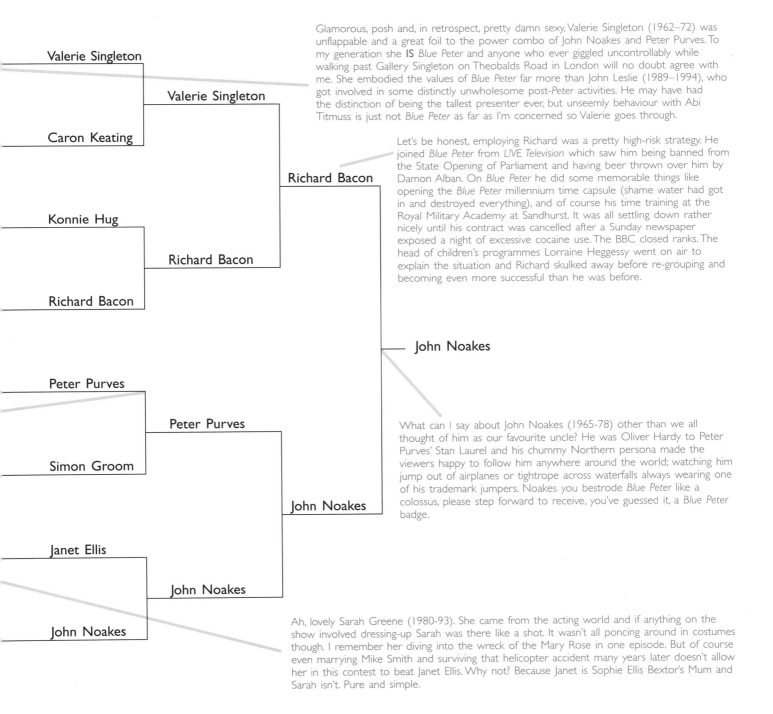

Valerie Singleton

Valerie Singleton

Caron Keating

Konnie Hug

Richard Bacon

Richard Bacon

Richard Bacon

Peter Purves

Peter Purves

Simon Groom

John Noakes

Janet Ellis

John Noakes

John Noakes

John Noakes

Glamorous, posh and, in retrospect, pretty damn sexy, Valerie Singleton (1962–72) was unflappable and a great foil to the power combo of John Noakes and Peter Purves. To my generation she **IS** *Blue Peter* and anyone who ever giggled uncontrollably while walking past Gallery Singleton on Theobalds Road in London will no doubt agree with me. She embodied the values of *Blue Peter* far more than John Leslie (1989–1994), who got involved in some distinctly unwholesome post-*Peter* activities. He may have had the distinction of being the tallest presenter ever, but unseemly behaviour with Abi Titmuss is just not *Blue Peter* as far as I'm concerned so Valerie goes through.

Let's be honest, employing Richard was a pretty high-risk strategy. He joined *Blue Peter* from *L!VE Television* which saw him being banned from the State Opening of Parliament and having beer thrown over him by Damon Alban. On *Blue Peter* he did some memorable things like opening the *Blue Peter* millennium time capsule (shame water had got in and destroyed everything), and of course his time training at the Royal Military Academy at Sandhurst. It was all settling down rather nicely until his contract was cancelled after a Sunday newspaper exposed a night of excessive cocaine use. The BBC closed ranks. The head of children's programmes Lorraine Heggessy went on air to explain the situation and Richard skulked away before re-grouping and becoming even more successful than he was before.

What can I say about John Noakes (1965-78) other than we all thought of him as our favourite uncle? He was Oliver Hardy to Peter Purves' Stan Laurel and his chummy Northern persona made the viewers happy to follow him anywhere around the world; watching him jump out of airplanes or tightrope across waterfalls always wearing one of his trademark jumpers. Noakes you bestrode *Blue Peter* like a colossus, please step forward to receive, you've guessed it, a *Blue Peter* badge.

Ah, lovely Sarah Greene (1980-93). She came from the acting world and if anything on the show involved dressing-up Sarah was there like a shot. It wasn't all poncing around in costumes though. I remember her diving into the wreck of the Mary Rose in one episode. But of course even marrying Mike Smith and surviving that helicopter accident many years later doesn't allow her in this contest to beat Janet Ellis. Why not? Because Janet is Sophie Ellis Bextor's Mum and Sarah isn't. Pure and simple.

Boring Museums
by SIMON TREWIN

Do you remember those school trips where you ate your packed lunch in the coach before it had left the school carpark and where the most important part of the day was the visit to the gift shop? Me too. The build-up was always incredibly exciting what with taking a note with the requisite integral tear-off slip home and getting special announcements in lessons promising a fully interactive visitors' centre which would thrill and bedazzle with its ingenuity and state of the art design? The reality of course was somewhat different, and after a three hour coach trip the museum was invariably cold and a bit chewed around the edges with a visitors' centre that consisted of three posters and a box of conifers. Compared to these little beauties, though, we obviously got off very lightly indeed . . .

Cumberland Pencil Museum in Keswick

Savings Bank Museum in Ruthwell

Scottish Mining Museum in Midlothian

Gasworks Museum in Biggar

Forge Mill Needle Museum in Redditch

Vacuum Cleaner Museum in Portland

Spam Museum of Minnesota

Pitch Drop Experiment at the University of Queensland

International Vinegar Museum in South Dakota

Tupperware Museum of Historical Food containers in Oregon

British Lawnmower Museum in Southport

Jerusalem's Tax Museum

Smalley's Hyde Park Miniature Museum in Houston

China's Comb Museum in Changzhou

Nima Sand Museum

Asphalt Museum in Sacramento

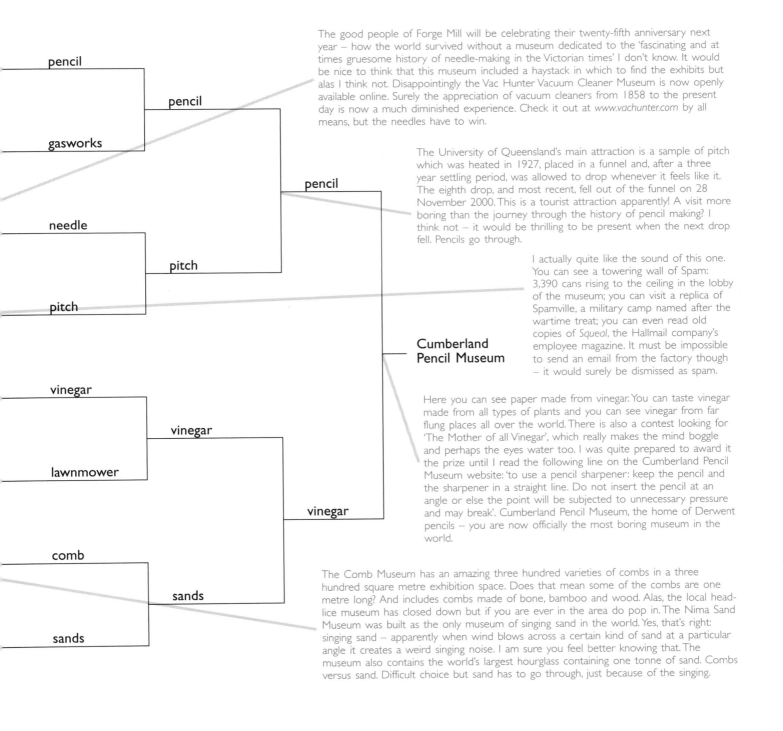

pencil

gasworks

needle

pitch

vinegar

lawnmower

comb

sands

pencil

pitch

vinegar

sands

pencil

vinegar

pencil

Cumberland Pencil Museum

The good people of Forge Mill will be celebrating their twenty-fifth anniversary next year – how the world survived without a museum dedicated to the 'fascinating and at times gruesome history of needle-making in the Victorian times' I don't know. It would be nice to think that this museum included a haystack in which to find the exhibits but alas I think not. Disappointingly the Vac Hunter Vacuum Cleaner Museum is now openly available online. Surely the appreciation of vacuum cleaners from 1858 to the present day is now a much diminished experience. Check it out at *www.vachunter.com* by all means, but the needles have to win.

The University of Queensland's main attraction is a sample of pitch which was heated in 1927, placed in a funnel and, after a three year settling period, was allowed to drop whenever it feels like it. The eighth drop, and most recent, fell out of the funnel on 28 November 2000. This is a tourist attraction apparently! A visit more boring than the journey through the history of pencil making? I think not – it would be thrilling to be present when the next drop fell. Pencils go through.

I actually quite like the sound of this one. You can see a towering wall of Spam: 3,390 cans rising to the ceiling in the lobby of the museum; you can visit a replica of Spamville, a military camp named after the wartime treat; you can even read old copies of *Squeal*, the Hallmail company's employee magazine. It must be impossible to send an email from the factory though – it would surely be dismissed as spam.

Here you can see paper made from vinegar. You can taste vinegar made from all types of plants and you can see vinegar from far flung places all over the world. There is also a contest looking for 'The Mother of all Vinegar', which really makes the mind boggle and perhaps the eyes water too. I was quite prepared to award it the prize until I read the following line on the Cumberland Pencil Museum website: 'to use a pencil sharpener: keep the pencil and the sharpener in a straight line. Do not insert the pencil at an angle or else the point will be subjected to unnecessary pressure and may break'. Cumberland Pencil Museum, the home of Derwent pencils – you are now officially the most boring museum in the world.

The Comb Museum has an amazing three hundred varieties of combs in a three hundred square metre exhibition space. Does that mean some of the combs are one metre long? And includes combs made of bone, bamboo and wood. Alas, the local head-lice museum has closed down but if you are ever in the area do pop in. The Nima Sand Museum was built as the only museum of singing sand in the world. Yes, that's right: singing sand – apparently when wind blows across a certain kind of sand at a particular angle it creates a weird singing noise. I am sure you feel better knowing that. The museum also contains the world's largest hourglass containing one tonne of sand. Combs versus sand. Difficult choice but sand has to go through, just because of the singing.

British Entrepreneurs
by PAUL TYRRELL

Do you wish you were an entrepreneur? Of course you do. Everyone does these days. Starting a business is now as sexy as releasing an album. It's creative, self-expressive, a mark of liberation from wage-slavery. And you don't need to be good-looking to make it happen.

But what is an entrepreneur? And what makes one great?

For most people, the term is synonymous with 'company founder'. Strictly though, it just means creating a new system for generating profit, while taking on some kind of personal risk. The prerequisite qualities include inspirational leadership, diligence and optimism. But by far the most important is 'pattern recognition'. An entrepreneur sees opportunities where others cannot. Indeed, if you're thinking of starting a business, a useful rule of thumb is to pursue markets that have generated very little published research. That way, your idea is more likely to be an untapped seam of riches (unless it's just plain awful – see 'optimism' above). Ultimately, an entrepreneur is someone with innate business talents, someone who could win customers regardless of product, service, brand or even industry. An ordinary business-person runs a single, moderately successful company. An entrepreneur is the sort of person you'd be glad to buy dentures from after they'd knocked out your teeth.

PAUL TYRRELL is a regular feature-writer for the *Financial Times*, where he specialises in entrepreneurship and innovation. If he could swap places with any British entrepreneur, it would be with one of the co-founders of the West Cornwall Pasty Company – brothers Aaron and Gavin Cocking, and Mark Christophers – who have earned vast sums by repackaging the world's oldest convenience food and still spend half their time surfing.

Karan Bilimoria, Cobra Beer
Perween Warsi, S&A Foods
— Karan Bilimoria

Christopher Evans, Merlin Biosciences
John Caudwell, Caudwell Group
— Christopher Evans

Alan Sugar, Amstrad
Peter Jones, Phones International
— Alan Sugar

Gordon Ramsay, Gordon Ramsay Holdings
Sahar Hashemi, Skinny Candy
— Gordon Ramsay

Simon Woodroffe, Yo! Sushi
Luke Johnson, numerous companies
— Luke Johnson

Stelios Haji-Ioannou, easyGroup
Duncan Bannatyne, Bannatyne Group
— Stelios Haji-Ioannou

Jacqueline Gold, Ann Summers
Mark Dixon, Regus
— Jacqueline Gold

Al Gosling, Extreme Group
Peter Cruddas, CMC Markets
— Peter Cruddas

Simon Fuller, 19 Entertainment
Felix Dennis, Dennis Publishing
— Felix Dennis

Lloyd Dorfman, Travelex
Deborah Meaden, numerous companies
— Lloyd Dorfman

Jane Cavanagh, SCi Entertainment
James Dyson, Dyson Group
— James Dyson

David Richards, Prodrive
Robert Braithwaite, Sunseeker
— David Richards

Charles Dunstone, Carphone Warehouse
Richard Branson, Virgin Group
— Richard Branson

Julian Richer, Richer Sounds
Anita Roddick, Body Shop
— Anita Roddick

Simon Nixon, moneysupermarket.com
Philip Green, Bhs and Arcadia Group
— Philip Green

Martha Lane-Fox, lastminute.com
Anthony Langley, Langley Holdings
— Anthony Langley

Bracket

- Christopher Evans
- Gordon Ramsay
  → **Christopher Evans**

- Stelios Haji-Ioannou
- Peter Cruddas
  → **Stelios Haji-Ioannou**

  → **Stelios Haji-Ioannou**

- Lloyd Dorfman
- James Dyson
  → **James Dyson**

- Richard Branson
- Philip Green
  → **Richard Branson**

  → **Richard Branson**

→ **Richard Branson**

Warsi is often called Britain's curry queen. S&A Foods, the Indian ready-meal brand she founded in 1986, has scooped numerous awards, created hundreds of jobs and still has a turnover of £57m. However, of all the many talented Asian entrepreneurs in the country, the one with the broadest range of skills has to be Karan Bilimoria. Founder and chief executive of Cobra beer, he has grown and diversified his brand continuously yet still found the time to become an active member of the House of Lords.

They're both foul-tempered, ruthlessly effective and hardened by working-class backgrounds. Sugar hosts *The Apprentice*, having built an £800m fortune from consumer electronics and property. Ramsay dispenses culinary and commercial advice via his *Kitchen Nightmares* series, having built a £55m fortune from top-drawer food service. If it ever came to blows, Sugar would simply outsource the fight to someone else, and Ramsay would end up having to taste his 'tartare of sea scallops in chilled basil consomme' through a straw. But the Englishman hasn't launched a hit product in years. It's the Scot who's in the ascendancy, with TV stardom in the US and restaurants opening worldwide.

Stelios is undoubtedly one of the world's best entrepreneurs. He set up the low-cost airline easyJet at the age of 28, turned Britain orange with many other 'easy' enterprises – from Internet cafés and cinemas to cruises and mobile telephones – and is now worth around £1.29bn. But Richard Branson is unstoppable. Already a *bona fide* British hero thanks to his eccentric PR stunts, he's now a leading 'green' investor, offering a $25m bounty for the solution to global warming. His Virgin brand, which encompasses every consumer industry you can imagine, has become a hallmark for quality and luxury and made him an estimated £3.1bn. Could any other entrepreneur really extend their airline into space so easily, and with quite such panache?

Mark Dixon is the archetypal 'serial entrepreneur'. He started out with a hotdog van, then manufactured hamburger buns, then set up a chain of serviced offices under the Regus brand. Regus suffered badly after the dotcom crash, but it still operates in 70 countries, employs 4,000 people and has a turnover of £680m. By contrast, Jacqueline Gold has remained UK-focused, turning her father's seedy sex shops into a £150m retail chain where post-feminist women can feel comfortable buying sex toys and lingerie. Dixon may have built the market for flexible workspace, but Gold has changed the sex-life of an entire nation.

Britain loves James Dyson because he used to be an underdog – when the world's leading home appliance manufacturers laughed at his idea for a bagless vacuum cleaner, he set up his own production line and promptly stole most of their customers. In spite of his decision to offshore that production line to Malaysia in 2002, he remains one of the country's leading lights of industrial design and innovation. However, at heart, he also remains a boffin. Richard Branson races balloons around the upper atmosphere and once signed the Sex Pistols to Virgin Records. No contest.

Felix Dennis may have shifted his focus from magazine publishing to writing bonkers poetry, but his legacy as a great entrepreneur and an even greater British eccentric is secure. Worth £750m, he is buying up thousands of acres of woodland in the Midlands to create and protect what he hopes will become the country's largest forest. Simon Fuller, by contrast, is the music mogul who brought us *Pop Idol*.

British Food
by SIMON TREWIN

Up until the age of thirteen I survived on a limited diet of jacket potatoes (without their jackets), grated cheese (cheddar mainly but Edam at a push), salad cream (but not mayonnaise), sausages (skinless) and cress (but not mustard). It doesn't seem to have done me much harm on the health front but I did realize when travelling around the UK in my early twenties what I had been missing out on in a cultural sense. The culinary diversity of the UK is much ignored and critics make sweeping statements saying that unlike the French, the Italians or the Greeks we have no national cuisine. How very wrong they are – we have plates and plates of wonderful dishes just crying out for proper recognition and, happily, their time has now come. Hopefully, reading this list will make your mouth water as much as it did mine compiling it. The quest here is to find one dish which we would happily put forward as quintessentially British.

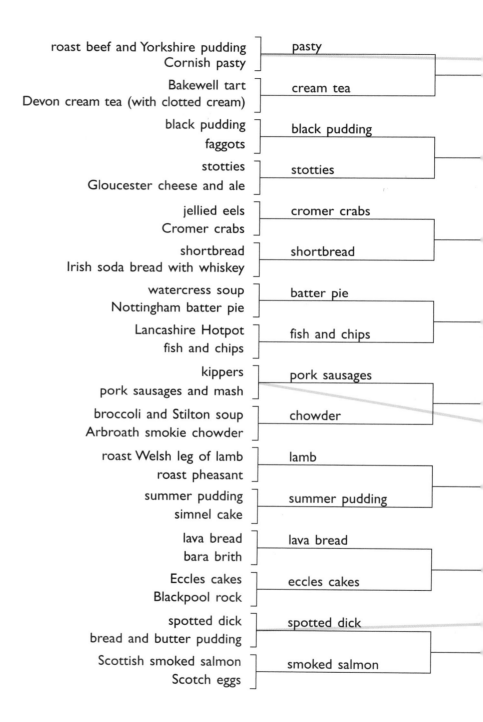

roast beef and Yorkshire pudding
Cornish pasty — pasty

Bakewell tart
Devon cream tea (with clotted cream) — cream tea

black pudding — black pudding
faggots

stotties — stotties
Gloucester cheese and ale

jellied eels — cromer crabs
Cromer crabs

shortbread — shortbread
Irish soda bread with whiskey

watercress soup — batter pie
Nottingham batter pie

Lancashire Hotpot
fish and chips — fish and chips

kippers — pork sausages
pork sausages and mash

broccoli and Stilton soup — chowder
Arbroath smokie chowder

roast Welsh leg of lamb — lamb
roast pheasant

summer pudding — summer pudding
simnel cake

lava bread — lava bread
bara brith

Eccles cakes
Blackpool rock — eccles cakes

spotted dick — spotted dick
bread and butter pudding

Scottish smoked salmon
Scotch eggs — smoked salmon

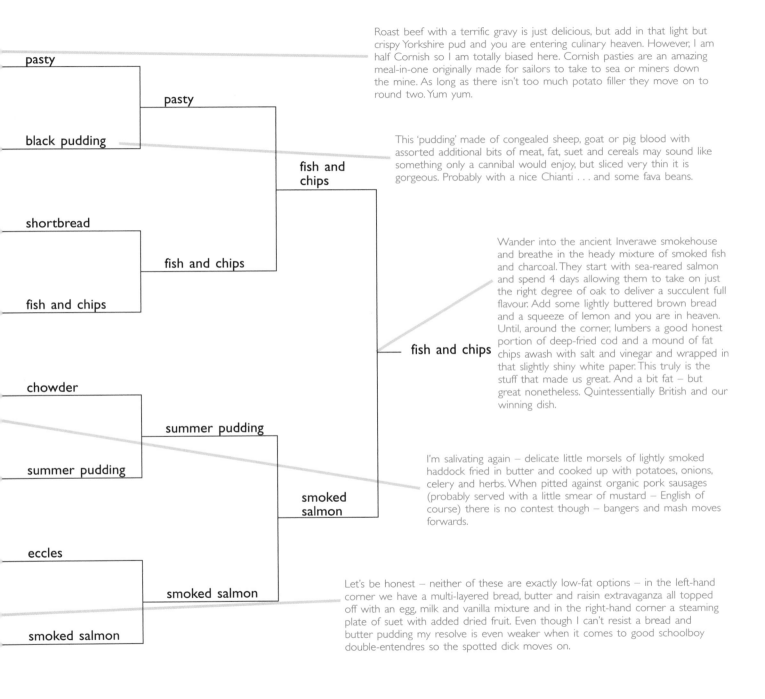

pasty

pasty

black pudding

fish and chips

shortbread

fish and chips

fish and chips

fish and chips

chowder

summer pudding

summer pudding

smoked salmon

eccles

smoked salmon

smoked salmon

Roast beef with a terrific gravy is just delicious, but add in that light but crispy Yorkshire pud and you are entering culinary heaven. However, I am half Cornish so I am totally biased here. Cornish pasties are an amazing meal-in-one originally made for sailors to take to sea or miners down the mine. As long as there isn't too much potato filler they move on to round two. Yum yum.

This 'pudding' made of congealed sheep, goat or pig blood with assorted additional bits of meat, fat, suet and cereals may sound like something only a cannibal would enjoy, but sliced very thin it is gorgeous. Probably with a nice Chianti . . . and some fava beans.

Wander into the ancient Inverawe smokehouse and breathe in the heady mixture of smoked fish and charcoal. They start with sea-reared salmon and spend 4 days allowing them to take on just the right degree of oak to deliver a succulent full flavour. Add some lightly buttered brown bread and a squeeze of lemon and you are in heaven. Until, around the corner, lumbers a good honest portion of deep-fried cod and a mound of fat chips awash with salt and vinegar and wrapped in that slightly shiny white paper. This truly is the stuff that made us great. And a bit fat – but great nonetheless. Quintessentially British and our winning dish.

I'm salivating again – delicate little morsels of lightly smoked haddock fried in butter and cooked up with potatoes, onions, celery and herbs. When pitted against organic pork sausages (probably served with a little smear of mustard – English of course) there is no contest though – bangers and mash moves forwards.

Let's be honest – neither of these are exactly low-fat options – in the left-hand corner we have a multi-layered bread, butter and raisin extravaganza all topped off with an egg, milk and vanilla mixture and in the right-hand corner a steaming plate of suet with added dried fruit. Even though I can't resist a bread and butter pudding my resolve is even weaker when it comes to good schoolboy double-entendres so the spotted dick moves on.

British Sitcoms
by SIMON TREWIN

Oh the torture of having to leave anything out of this category — where is *Ab Fab*, *Red Dwarf* and *Bless This House* or even *Love Thy Neighbour?* All of these and more are culturally significant not to mention great crowd-pleasers but something had to give — that is the nature of this game. Sitcoms are initially ephemeral, designed to fulfil a useful collapsing-on-the-sofa-with-half-an-hour-to-kill function, but ultimately they grow in importance as a yearning for yesteryear kicks in. I can certainly remember the texture of the carpet I grazed my knee on in my parents' sitting room when I was trying to copy Michael 'Ooh Betty!' Crawford's pratfalls and the sweets I used to eat on a Friday night when I was allowed to stay up to watch *Sykes*. It finished at 8.10, which seemed daringly late at the age of nine. Anyway here they all are with their unforgettable theme tunes, opening titles and wonderful performances. Modern day sitcoms don't quite cut the mustard in the same way but maybe that is my fault and not theirs.

Both these gems have impeccable performances and it's hard to choose between the masterful double-acts of Bewes and Bolam and Bramble and Corbett. Bewes' dull suburbanite was well balanced by Bolam's eternally up-for-it mischievous chancer, while in *Steptoe and Son* we saw two cunning schemers trying to outwit each other. *Likely Lads* inspired *Men Behaving Badly* and *Steptoe and Son* led to *Only Fools And Horses*. On balance *Steptoe* feels more classic to me and just has the edge.

Each episode of *The Good Life* felt like a one-act play worthy of Alan Ayckbourn. The casting was impeccable, from Penelope Keith's snooty Margot to Paul Eddington's slightly browbeaten (but devilish) Jerry, not forgetting Felicity Kendal and Richard Briers' proto-eco-warriors Barbara and Tom Good. Like *Fawlty Towers* or *Dad's Army* this still gets prime slots and viewing figures so it has clearly stood the test of time. Indeed, the green living issues it raises are all too relevant today. *George and Mildred*, on the other hand, is very much of its time. Faultless Brian Murphy and Yootha Joyce made this spin-off from *Robin's Nest* a must-see programme in its day but recently it has felt a little tired. So get your wellies on and let's go dig up some potatoes . . .

Apparently this is off to America to get the network television treatment. Fingers crossed — it is a national treasure and if the Church Of England really wanted to lure the millions back to swell their flagging congregations they could do worse than to offer Dawn French the job of Archbishop Of Canterbury.

Blackadder	Dad's Army
Dad's Army	
The Fall and Rise of Reginald Perrin	Father Ted
Father Ted	
Fawlty Towers	Fawlty Towers
Hancock's Half Hour	
I'm Alan Partridge	Alan Partridge
Men Behaving Badly	
Only Fools and Horses	Fools and Horses
One Foot in the Grave	
Porridge	Some Mothers
Some Mothers Do 'Ave Em	
Steptoe and Son	Steptoe and Son
The Likely Lads	
Open All Hours	Open All Hours
My Family	
Are You Being Served?	Are You Being Served?
Terry and June	
Gimme Gimme Gimme	Gimme Gimme
Rising Damp	
George and Mildred	The Good Life
The Good Life	
Butterflies	Birds Of A Feather
Birds of a Feather	
Red Dwarf	Hi-de-Hi
Hi-de-Hi	
Till Death Us Do Part	Till Death
It Ain't Half Hot Mum	
Keeping Up Appearances	Keeping Up
Mind your Language	
Vicar of Dibley	The Young Ones
The Young Ones	

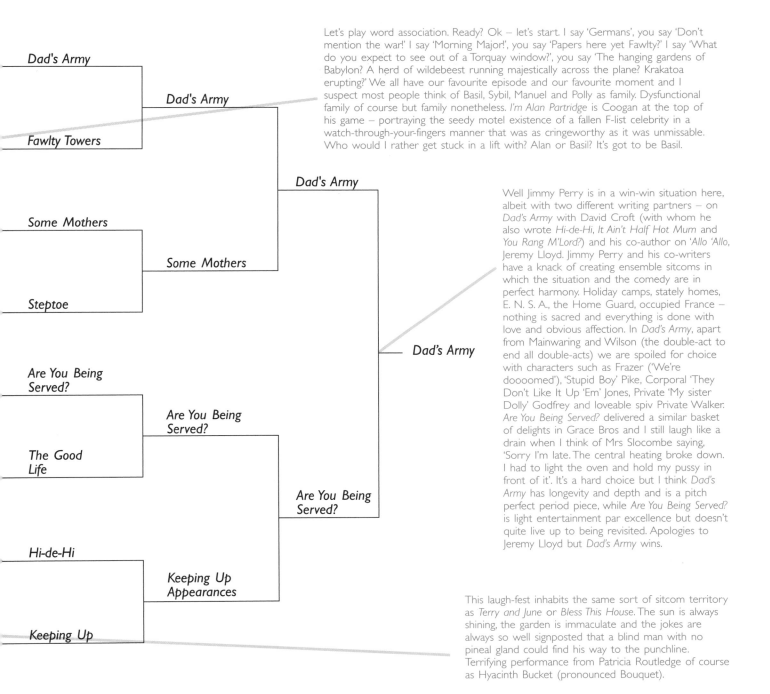

Dad's Army

Fawlty Towers

Dad's Army

Dad's Army

Some Mothers

Steptoe

Some Mothers

Dad's Army

Are You Being Served?

The Good Life

Are You Being Served?

Are You Being Served?

Hi-de-Hi

Keeping Up

Keeping Up Appearances

Let's play word association. Ready? Ok — let's start. I say 'Germans', you say 'Don't mention the war!' I say 'Morning Major!', you say 'Papers here yet Fawlty?' I say 'What do you expect to see out of a Torquay window?', you say 'The hanging gardens of Babylon? A herd of wildebeest running majestically across the plane? Krakatoa erupting?' We all have our favourite episode and our favourite moment and I suspect most people think of Basil, Sybil, Manuel and Polly as family. Dysfunctional family of course but family nonetheless. *I'm Alan Partridge* is Coogan at the top of his game — portraying the seedy motel existence of a fallen F-list celebrity in a watch-through-your-fingers manner that was as cringeworthy as it was unmissable. Who would I rather get stuck in a lift with? Alan or Basil? It's got to be Basil.

Well Jimmy Perry is in a win-win situation here, albeit with two different writing partners — on *Dad's Army* with David Croft (with whom he also wrote *Hi-de-Hi*, *It Ain't Half Hot Mum* and *You Rang M'Lord?*) and his co-author on *'Allo 'Allo*, Jeremy Lloyd. Jimmy Perry and his co-writers have a knack of creating ensemble sitcoms in which the situation and the comedy are in perfect harmony. Holiday camps, stately homes, E. N. S. A., the Home Guard, occupied France — nothing is sacred and everything is done with love and obvious affection. In *Dad's Army*, apart from Mainwaring and Wilson (the double-act to end all double-acts) we are spoiled for choice with characters such as Frazer ('We're doooomed'), 'Stupid Boy' Pike, Corporal 'They Don't Like It Up 'Em' Jones, Private 'My sister Dolly' Godfrey and loveable spiv Private Walker. *Are You Being Served?* delivered a similar basket of delights in Grace Bros and I still laugh like a drain when I think of Mrs Slocombe saying, 'Sorry I'm late. The central heating broke down. I had to light the oven and hold my pussy in front of it'. It's a hard choice but I think *Dad's Army* has longevity and depth and is a pitch perfect period piece, while *Are You Being Served?* is light entertainment par excellence but doesn't quite live up to being revisited. Apologies to Jeremy Lloyd but *Dad's Army* wins.

This laugh-fest inhabits the same sort of sitcom territory as *Terry and June* or *Bless This House*. The sun is always shining, the garden is immaculate and the jokes are always so well signposted that a blind man with no pineal gland could find his way to the punchline. Terrifying performance from Patricia Routledge of course as Hyacinth Bucket (pronounced Bouquet).

Bushisms

by SIMON TREWIN

In Richard Brindsley Sheridan's 1747 play *The Rivals* there was a character called Mrs Malaprop who would utter such phrases as 'He is the very pineapple of politeness.' and 'If I reprehend any thing in this world, it is the use of my oracular tongue, and a nice derangement of epitaphs!', so maybe George W. is carrying out an extensive literary joke by mimicking her. Or maybe he is just stupid. Real stupid. What worries me most is that he isn't just a Texan oilman or a captain of industry but this mangler of phrases, this two-left-footed linguist is THE MOST POWERFUL MAN IN THE WORLD. He could kill us all at the push of a button or the whisper of a word. It's a tough job being America's forty-third President and I am sure the hours are long and the stress levels high but what in the name of jumping Jehovah happens when Dubya's brain tries to connect with his mouth? Oh deary me. Difficult to choose between these classic Bushisms but choose we must.

'I want you to know. Karyn is with us. A West Texas girl, just like me.'
'Make no mistake about it, I understand how tough it is, sir. I talk to families who die.'

'The only way we can win is to leave before the job is done.'
'You teach a child to read, and he or her will be able to pass a literacy test.'

'I have opinions of my own. Strong opinions. But I don't always agree with them.'
'They misunderestimated me.'

'It's a very good question. Very direct. And I'm not going to answer it.'
'I don't know where bin Laden is. I have no idea and really don't care. It's not that important. It's not our priority.'

'I know the human being and fish can coexist peacefully.'
'Our enemies are innovative and resourceful, and so are we. They never stop thinking about new ways to harm our country and our people, and neither do we.'

'I'll be glad to reply to or dodge your questions, depending on what I think will help our election most.'
'One has a stronger hand when there's more people playing your same cards.'

'People say I'm indecisive, but I don't know about that.'
'If this were a dictatorship, it'd be a heck of a lot easier, just so long as I'm the dictator.'

'We shouldn't fear a world that is more interacted.'
'Families is where our nation finds hope, where wings take dream.'

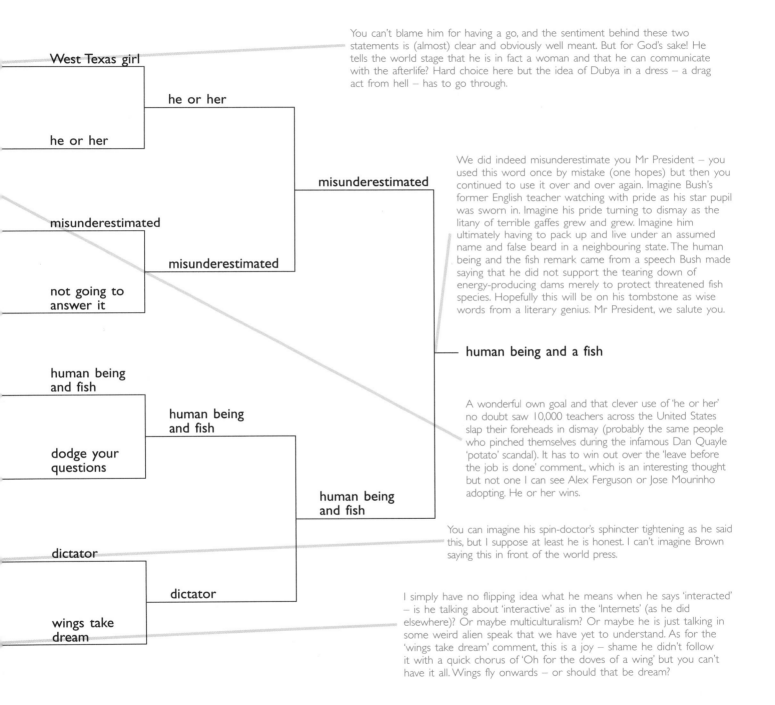

West Texas girl

he or her

he or her

he or her

misunderestimated

misunderestimated

not going to answer it

misunderestimated

human being and fish

human being and fish

dodge your questions

human being and fish

human being and fish

dictator

dictator

dictator

wings take dream

human being and a fish

You can't blame him for having a go, and the sentiment behind these two statements is (almost) clear and obviously well meant. But for God's sake! He tells the world stage that he is in fact a woman and that he can communicate with the afterlife? Hard choice here but the idea of Dubya in a dress – a drag act from hell – has to go through.

We did indeed misunderestimate you Mr President – you used this word once by mistake (one hopes) but then you continued to use it over and over again. Imagine Bush's former English teacher watching with pride as his star pupil was sworn in. Imagine his pride turning to dismay as the litany of terrible gaffes grew and grew. Imagine him ultimately having to pack up and live under an assumed name and false beard in a neighbouring state. The human being and the fish remark came from a speech Bush made saying that he did not support the tearing down of energy-producing dams merely to protect threatened fish species. Hopefully this will be on his tombstone as wise words from a literary genius. Mr President, we salute you.

A wonderful own goal and that clever use of 'he or her' no doubt saw 10,000 teachers across the United States slap their foreheads in dismay (probably the same people who pinched themselves during the infamous Dan Quayle 'potato' scandal). It has to win out over the 'leave before the job is done' comment., which is an interesting thought but not one I can see Alex Ferguson or Jose Mourinho adopting. He or her wins.

You can imagine his spin-doctor's sphincter tightening as he said this, but I suppose at least he is honest. I can't imagine Brown saying this in front of the world press.

I simply have no flipping idea what he means when he says 'interacted' – is he talking about 'interactive' as in the 'Internets' (as he did elsewhere)? Or maybe multiculturalism? Or maybe he is just talking in some weird alien speak that we have yet to understand. As for the 'wings take dream' comment, this is a joy – shame he didn't follow it with a quick chorus of 'Oh for the doves of a wing' but you can't have it all. Wings fly onwards – or should that be dream?

Cakes
by FIFI LE ROUX

Baking used to be thought of as dull: prosaic, utterly functional, a little bit too war-child making-and-mending. And then suddenly, bang! At some point in the late 90s it became hot and sexy, and glam happenings everywhere were fortified not just by cosmopolitans but by prettily-iced cupcakes, and baking as an activity not a necessity became as desirable a skill for the contemporary gal to possess as vintage dress-sourcing and naughty knicker-wearing. Somehow, it's survived the craze; after the hype there was no backlash, just a generation of women (for it is mostly women . . . I think) discovering the soul-lift to be found in stirring, mixing, icing (and eating). Ignore the misplaced arguments for/against its retrogressive implications of drudgery, and concentrate on the simple delight of sweet, unpoliticised domesticity, creating something out of nothing and feeling the magic alchemy that blossoms when you cradle your creation as it leaves the oven, closing your eyes for a second to pray that it's perfect. Of course, if one actually had to bake it wouldn't be nearly so fun . . . the decision to make a few brownies for supper instead of something more sensible is at least half the joy of a good cake.

FIFI LE ROUX is a baker by night, and is never happier than when wearing one of her pink vintage aprons over a little black dress. Her baking cupboard is always well-stocked, she has perfected the art of buttering and lining the tins with panache (though not the art of maintaining a tidy kitchen), and her biggest fear is running out of vanilla essence.

Both damp lemon cakelettes (usually in the more conventional form of a loaf, but I cannot resist cakes-in-miniature wherever possible) and egg-custard tarts are classic picnic nibbles. But the deciding factor is this: which best survives accidental splashes of rosé? The answer, by far, is the already wet cakelettes. As soon as they leave the oven, prick them with a cake fork (any other kind of fork is too forceful) all over and pour over a hot syrup of freshly squeezed lemon juice and icing sugar. The syrup will drip down the holes and imbue the whole cake with a sharp, sugary dampness that warmly welcomes any additional sauce, intentional or not.

Berry 'boy bait' deserves a rosette just for its name, no? Yet the sum of its yummy parts is not nearly as cheering or as remotely *well-hello-there*: it's an upside-down crumble, which is lovely enough but not prizewinning. Whereas Victoria sponge is plain in name but otherwise, utterly iconic – the sponge, the two-tone pale and deep-pink oozing middle, precariously almost-dripping from the sides. Begone modern-day reworkings that combine courgette and pistachio, use almond-blackcurrant icing to mimic a trifle, or even dare all with banana sponge and toffee syrup. The original is still uncontestedly the best – pale sponge, vanilla buttercream and raspberry jam filling (raspberry provides the tang that strawberry doesn't), icing sugar scattered over the top, preferably pushed through a doily for a gorgeous lacy effect. And absolutely nobody could tire of the taste: lip-lickingly sweet, with the salt of the buttercream (and hence why you must use slightly salted butter, regardless of what the recipe says) providing the perfect foil.

Pairing	Winner
blondies / millionaire's shortbread	**blondies**
brownies / syrup-spun profiteroles	**brownies**
YSL gold-leaf chocolate cake by Costes / *pain au chocolat* 'bread' pudding	**YSL gold-leaf**
molten chocolate babycakes/*moelleux au chocolat* / chocolate and Guinness cake	***moelleux au chocolat***
rosewater madeleines / Rocky Road	**rosewater madeleines**
Swedish cinnamon buns / cornflake crispies	**Swedish cinnamon buns**
damp lemon cakelettes / egg custard tarts	**damp lemon cakelettes**
Ladurée macaroons / bakewell tarts	**Ladurée macaroons**
raspberry meringue cake / Nigella's clementine cake	**raspberry meringue cake**
New York cheesecake / *galette des Rois*	**New York cheesecake**
old-fashioned apple pie / Mont Blanc	**old-fashioned apple pie**
red velvet cake / devil's food cake	**red velvet cake**
traditional trifle / Boston cream pie	**traditional trifle**
Victoria sponge / berry 'boy bait'	**Victoria sponge**
little key lime pies / *ricciarelli*	**little key lime pies**
cupcakes / strawberry shortcakes	**cupcakes**

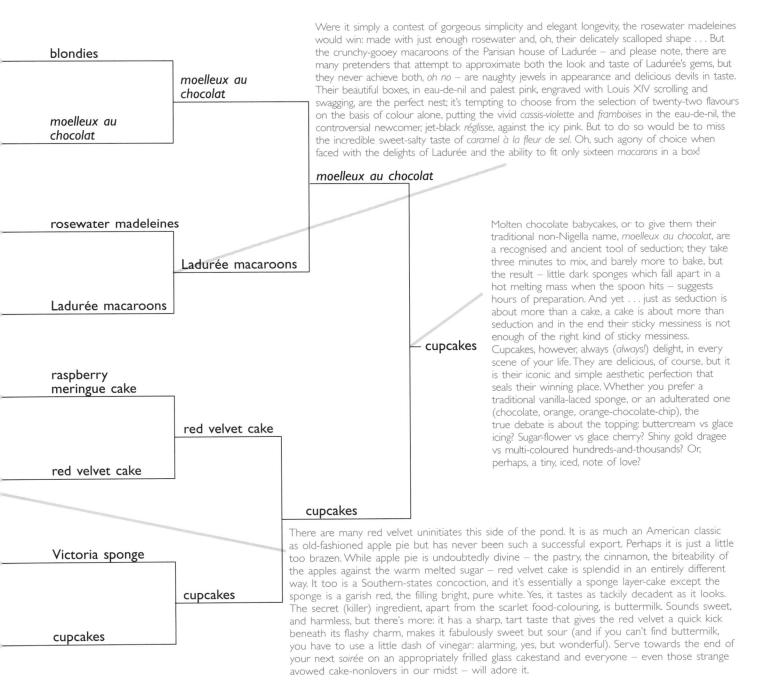

blondies

moelleux au chocolat

moelleux au chocolat

moelleux au chocolat

rosewater madeleines

Ladurée macaroons

Ladurée macaroons

raspberry meringue cake

red velvet cake

red velvet cake

cupcakes

Victoria sponge

cupcakes

cupcakes

— cupcakes

Were it simply a contest of gorgeous simplicity and elegant longevity, the rosewater madeleines would win: made with just enough rosewater and, oh, their delicately scalloped shape . . . But the crunchy-gooey macaroons of the Parisian house of Ladurée — and please note, there are many pretenders that attempt to approximate both the look and taste of Ladurée's gems, but they never achieve both, *oh no* — are naughty jewels in appearance and delicious devils in taste. Their beautiful boxes, in eau-de-nil and palest pink, engraved with Louis XIV scrolling and swagging, are the perfect nest; it's tempting to choose from the selection of twenty-two flavours on the basis of colour alone, putting the vivid *cassis-violette* and *framboises* in the eau-de-nil, the controversial newcomer, jet-black *réglisse*, against the icy pink. But to do so would be to miss the incredible sweet-salty taste of *caramel à la fleur de sel*. Oh, such agony of choice when faced with the delights of Ladurée and the ability to fit only sixteen *macarons* in a box!

Molten chocolate babycakes, or to give them their traditional non-Nigella name, *moelleux au chocolat*, are a recognised and ancient tool of seduction; they take three minutes to mix, and barely more to bake, but the result — little dark sponges which fall apart in a hot melting mass when the spoon hits — suggests hours of preparation. And yet . . . just as seduction is about more than a cake, a cake is about more than seduction and in the end their sticky messiness is not enough of the right kind of sticky messiness. Cupcakes, however, always (*always!*) delight, in every scene of your life. They are delicious, of course, but it is their iconic and simple aesthetic perfection that seals their winning place. Whether you prefer a traditional vanilla-laced sponge, or an adulterated one (chocolate, orange, orange-chocolate-chip), the true debate is about the topping: buttercream vs glace icing? Sugar-flower vs glace cherry? Shiny gold dragee vs multi-coloured hundreds-and-thousands? Or, perhaps, a tiny, iced, note of love?

There are many red velvet uninitiates this side of the pond. It is as much an American classic as old-fashioned apple pie but has never been such a successful export. Perhaps it is just a little too brazen. While apple pie is undoubtedly divine — the pastry, the cinnamon, the biteability of the apples against the warm melted sugar — red velvet cake is splendid in an entirely different way. It too is a Southern-states concoction, and it's essentially a sponge layer-cake except the sponge is a garish red, the filling bright, pure white. Yes, it tastes as tackily decadent as it looks. The secret (killer) ingredient, apart from the scarlet food-colouring, is buttermilk. Sounds sweet, and harmless, but there's more: it has a sharp, tart taste that gives the red velvet a quick kick beneath its flashy charm, makes it fabulously sweet but sour (and if you can't find buttermilk, you have to use a little dash of vinegar: alarming, yes, but wonderful). Serve towards the end of your next *soirée* on an appropriately frilled glass cakestand and everyone — even those strange avowed cake-nonlovers in our midst — will adore it.

Carry On Films
by SIMON TREWIN

Carry On films represent the essence of British comedy. Saucy, knowing and unashamedly mass-market they are seaside postcards brought to life and are (almost) never less than a joy. There is hardly an institution they haven't affectionately lampooned, from hospitals, schools, the police force, factory-workers and seaside resorts to package holidays and, of course, the Empire and beyond. Even when the jokes are at their most cringe-worthy they carry it off with such charm that you can forgive them anything. Watching one after a bit of a gap is like being reunited with a group of old friends and although you can see the gags coming a mile off and the budgets are so low that almost everything seems to be filmed in and around the confines of Pinewood none of this matters — they are a guilty pleasure incarnate. Just think of Sid's filthy laugh, Kenneth Williams' strangulated voice and Charles Hawtrey's terrible wigs — not to mention Barbara Windsor's cleavage — and it is impossible not to start sniggering.

This is an important film not just because it was the highest grossing British comedy until *Four Weddings And A Funeral* but also because it was the first foray into the hospital environment that would prove so fruitful later on. A charming film with a top rate British cast and a disgusting sight gag with a daffodil replacing a rectal thermometer. What more could you ask for?

There's nothing like a Jolly Roger on the Seven Seas with the *Carry On* team. Both these were set at sea — one historical and one contemporary — and both were real corkers. *Cruising* (the first colour film in the series), has Kenneth Connor at his fruitiest and has some glorious performances from the likes of Lance Percival (as the chef) and Ronnie Stevens (as the ever accommodating barman). Glorious production values and a beautifully scripted film. *Jack* is okay but with no Sid and no Hattie it doesn't splice my mainbrace. Missus.

Carry On Sergeant (1958)	Nurse
Carry On Nurse (1959)	
Carry On Teacher (1959)	Teacher
Carry On Constable (1959)	
Carry On Regardless (1961)	Cruising
Carry On Cruising (1962)	
Carry On Cabby (1963)	Jack
Carry On Jack (1963)	
Carry On Spying (1964)	Cleo
Carry On Cleo (1964)	
Carry On Cowboy (1965)	Screaming
Carry On Screaming! (1966)	
Carry On Don't Lose your Head (1966)	Camel
Carry On Follow that Camel (1967)	
Carry On Doctor (1967)	Doctor
Carry On Up the Khyber (1968)	
Carry On Camping (1969)	Camping
Carry On Again Doctor (1969)	
Carry On Up the Jungle (1970)	Jungle
Carry On Loving (1970)	
Carry On Henry (1971)	Henry
Carry On England (1976)	
Carry On Matron (1972)	Matron
Carry On Abroad (1972)	
Carry On Girls (1973)	Dick
Carry On Dick (1974)	
Carry On Behind (1975)	Convenience
Carry On At Your Convenience (1971)	
That's Carry On (1978)	Emmanuelle
Carry On Emmanuelle (1978)	
Carry On Columbus (1992)	What A Carry On!
What A Carry On! (1973)	

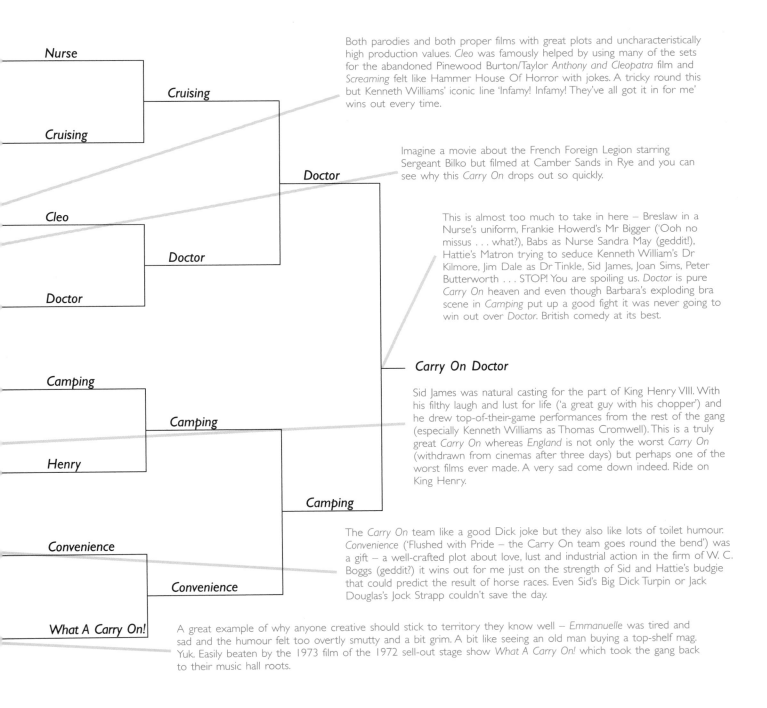

Nurse

Cruising

Cruising

Cleo

Doctor

Doctor

Doctor

Camping

Camping

Henry

Camping

Convenience

Convenience

What A Carry On!

Carry On Doctor

Both parodies and both proper films with great plots and uncharacteristically high production values. *Cleo* was famously helped by using many of the sets for the abandoned Pinewood Burton/Taylor *Anthony and Cleopatra* film and *Screaming* felt like Hammer House Of Horror with jokes. A tricky round this but Kenneth Williams' iconic line 'Infamy! Infamy! They've all got it in for me' wins out every time.

Imagine a movie about the French Foreign Legion starring Sergeant Bilko but filmed at Camber Sands in Rye and you can see why this *Carry On* drops out so quickly.

This is almost too much to take in here – Breslaw in a Nurse's uniform, Frankie Howerd's Mr Bigger ('Ooh no missus . . . what?), Babs as Nurse Sandra May (geddit!), Hattie's Matron trying to seduce Kenneth William's Dr Kilmore, Jim Dale as Dr Tinkle, Sid James, Joan Sims, Peter Butterworth . . . STOP! You are spoiling us. *Doctor* is pure *Carry On* heaven and even though Barbara's exploding bra scene in *Camping* put up a good fight it was never going to win out over *Doctor*. British comedy at its best.

Sid James was natural casting for the part of King Henry VIII. With his filthy laugh and lust for life ('a great guy with his chopper') and he drew top-of-their-game performances from the rest of the gang (especially Kenneth Williams as Thomas Cromwell). This is a truly great *Carry On* whereas *England* is not only the worst *Carry On* (withdrawn from cinemas after three days) but perhaps one of the worst films ever made. A very sad come down indeed. Ride on King Henry.

The *Carry On* team like a good Dick joke but they also like lots of toilet humour. *Convenience* ('Flushed with Pride – the Carry On team goes round the bend') was a gift – a well-crafted plot about love, lust and industrial action in the firm of W. C. Boggs (geddit?) it wins out for me just on the strength of Sid and Hattie's budgie that could predict the result of horse races. Even Sid's Big Dick Turpin or Jack Douglas's Jock Strapp couldn't save the day.

A great example of why anyone creative should stick to territory they know well – *Emmanuelle* was tired and sad and the humour felt too overtly smutty and a bit grim. A bit like seeing an old man buying a top-shelf mag. Yuk. Easily beaten by the 1973 film of the 1972 sell-out stage show *What A Carry On!* which took the gang back to their music hall roots.

Celebrity Chefs
by SIMON TREWIN

Difficult to know who the first celebrity chef was really – maybe it was Jesus with the whole loaves and fishes recipe? Or maybe that is just being facetious – in which case see you in hell at gas mark 400 (or if they use electric that is approximately 230,000°C). In any event, as the world becomes more and more obsessed with the cult of celebrity and access to high quality cooking ingredients improves it is inevitable that these two phenomena should collide and produce this breed of highly merchandiseable individuals. Their financial success has little directly to do with actually standing there wearing an apron, holding a spatula and stirring something in a saucepan and more to do with getting you to buy their branded aprons, spatulas, saucepans, flavour shakers – not to mention visiting their restaurants (probably more often than some of them do) to worship at their Aga. Anyway – who are the pot noodles among them and who are the Michelin monkeys? Step this way sir and madam. Your table is waiting and your maitre d' will be with you shortly.

Jamie Oliver Raymond Blanc	Jamie Oliver
Phil Vickery John Burton Race	John Burton Race
Delia Smith Antonio Carluccio	Delia Smith
Heston Blumenthal Michael Caines	Heston Blumenthal
Antony Worral Thompson Giorgio Locatelli	Antony W-T
Ainsley Harriot Richard Corrigan	Ainsley Harriot
Hugh Fearnley-Whittingstall Brian Turner	Hugh F-W
Nigel Slater Mary Berry	Nigel Slater
Rick Stein Keith Floyd	Rick Stein
Gary Rhodes Marcus Wareing	Gary Rhodes
Clarissa Dickson-Wright Michel Roux	Clarissa D-W
Graham Kerr (The Galloping Gourmet) Nigella Lawson	Nigella Lawson
Rose Gray and Ruth Rogers Anton Edelmann	Rose and Ruth
Madhur Jaffrey Sophie Grigson	Sophie Grigson
Ken Hom Gordon Ramsay	Gordon Ramsay
Fanny Craddock Richard Corrigan	Fanny Craddock

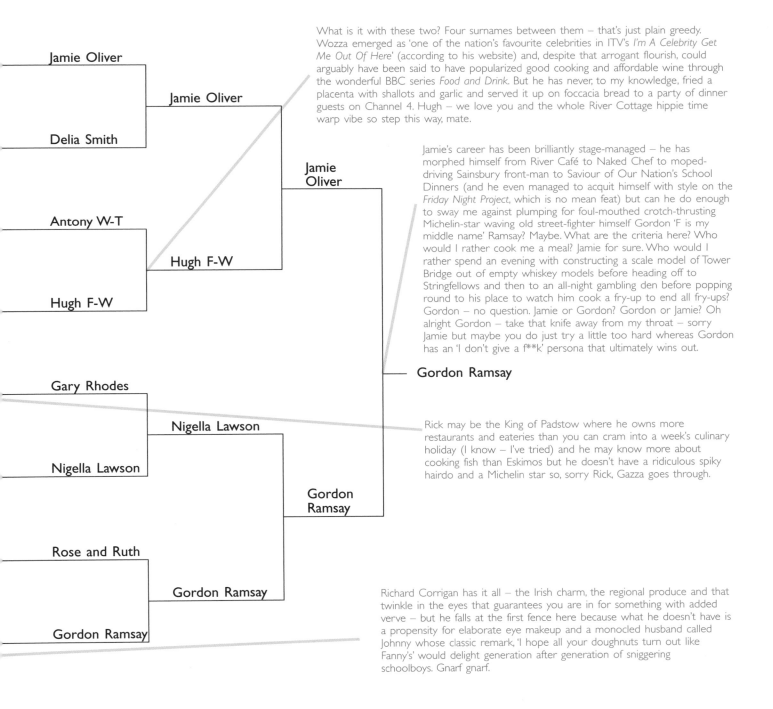

Jamie Oliver

Delia Smith

Jamie Oliver

Antony W-T

Hugh F-W

Hugh F-W

Jamie Oliver

Gary Rhodes

Nigella Lawson

Nigella Lawson

Gordon Ramsay

Rose and Ruth

Gordon Ramsay

Gordon Ramsay

Gordon Ramsay

What is it with these two? Four surnames between them — that's just plain greedy. Wozza emerged as 'one of the nation's favourite celebrities in ITV's *I'm A Celebrity Get Me Out Of Here*' (according to his website) and, despite that arrogant flourish, could arguably have been said to have popularized good cooking and affordable wine through the wonderful BBC series *Food and Drink*. But he has never, to my knowledge, fried a placenta with shallots and garlic and served it up on foccacia bread to a party of dinner guests on Channel 4. Hugh — we love you and the whole River Cottage hippie time warp vibe so step this way, mate.

Jamie's career has been brilliantly stage-managed — he has morphed himself from River Café to Naked Chef to moped-driving Sainsbury front-man to Saviour of Our Nation's School Dinners (and he even managed to acquit himself with style on the *Friday Night Project*, which is no mean feat) but can he do enough to sway me against plumping for foul-mouthed crotch-thrusting Michelin-star waving old street-fighter himself Gordon 'F is my middle name' Ramsay? Maybe. What are the criteria here? Who would I rather cook me a meal? Jamie for sure. Who would I rather spend an evening with constructing a scale model of Tower Bridge out of empty whiskey models before heading off to Stringfellows and then to an all-night gambling den before popping round to his place to watch him cook a fry-up to end all fry-ups? Gordon — no question. Jamie or Gordon? Gordon or Jamie? Oh alright Gordon — take that knife away from my throat — sorry Jamie but maybe you do just try a little too hard whereas Gordon has an 'I don't give a f**k' persona that ultimately wins out.

Rick may be the King of Padstow where he owns more restaurants and eateries than you can cram into a week's culinary holiday (I know — I've tried) and he may know more about cooking fish than Eskimos but he doesn't have a ridiculous spiky hairdo and a Michelin star so, sorry Rick, Gazza goes through.

Richard Corrigan has it all — the Irish charm, the regional produce and that twinkle in the eyes that guarantees you are in for something with added verve — but he falls at the first fence here because what he doesn't have is a propensity for elaborate eye makeup and a monocled husband called Johnny whose classic remark, 'I hope all your doughnuts turn out like Fanny's' would delight generation after generation of sniggering schoolboys. Gnarf gnarf.

Celebrity Child Names

by SIMON TREWIN

When I started at primary school in 1972, the register was read every morning by Mrs Bonicci and contained an endless litany of Marys, Johns, Peters, Williams and Janes. In the early 70s Lucy was about as exotic as it got. When I started four years later at Highgate Junior School there were people boarding from all over the world so things got a bit more interesting and we had a fair smattering of Ahmeds, Brads, Diegos and even a Padraic. The most impressive name, though, was Zak – a boy in my French set – although as his dad was the drummer of The Beatles and the possessor of the silliest name in the Fab Four we sort of expected nothing less. But goodness me Zak Starkey (now drummer for The Who) seems positively reserved compared to some of the names we are about to encounter. The only way any of these people survived a massive beating-up in the playground is because they came from famous homes – homes that everyone wanted to be invited to probably. Can you imagine naming your son Bunchester Tiddlefart McSqueak Häagen-Daz The Munga Smith and sending him happily off to the local comprehensive with a clear conscience? Thought not.

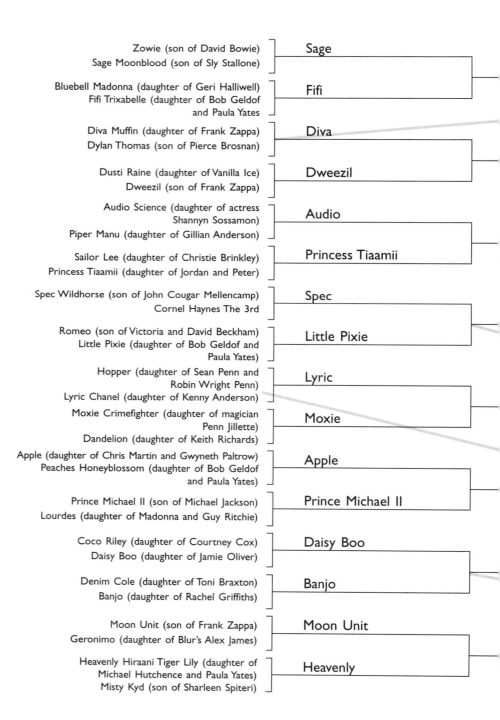

Zowie (son of David Bowie)
Sage Moonblood (son of Sly Stallone) — Sage

Bluebell Madonna (daughter of Geri Halliwell)
Fifi Trixabelle (daughter of Bob Geldof and Paula Yates) — Fifi

Diva Muffin (daughter of Frank Zappa)
Dylan Thomas (son of Pierce Brosnan) — Diva

Dusti Raine (daughter of Vanilla Ice)
Dweezil (son of Frank Zappa) — Dweezil

Audio Science (daughter of actress Shannyn Sossamon)
Piper Manu (daughter of Gillian Anderson) — Audio

Sailor Lee (daughter of Christie Brinkley)
Princess Tiaamii (daughter of Jordan and Peter) — Princess Tiaamii

Spec Wildhorse (son of John Cougar Mellencamp)
Cornel Haynes The 3rd — Spec

Romeo (son of Victoria and David Beckham)
Little Pixie (daughter of Bob Geldof and Paula Yates) — Little Pixie

Hopper (daughter of Sean Penn and Robin Wright Penn)
Lyric Chanel (daughter of Kenny Anderson) — Lyric

Moxie Crimefighter (daughter of magician Penn Jillette)
Dandelion (daughter of Keith Richards) — Moxie

Apple (daughter of Chris Martin and Gwyneth Paltrow)
Peaches Honeyblossom (daughter of Bob Geldof and Paula Yates) — Apple

Prince Michael II (son of Michael Jackson)
Lourdes (daughter of Madonna and Guy Ritchie) — Prince Michael II

Coco Riley (daughter of Courtney Cox)
Daisy Boo (daughter of Jamie Oliver) — Daisy Boo

Denim Cole (daughter of Toni Braxton)
Banjo (daughter of Rachel Griffiths) — Banjo

Moon Unit (son of Frank Zappa)
Geronimo (daughter of Blur's Alex James) — Moon Unit

Heavenly Hiraani Tiger Lily (daughter of Michael Hutchence and Paula Yates)
Misty Kyd (son of Sharleen Spiteri) — Heavenly

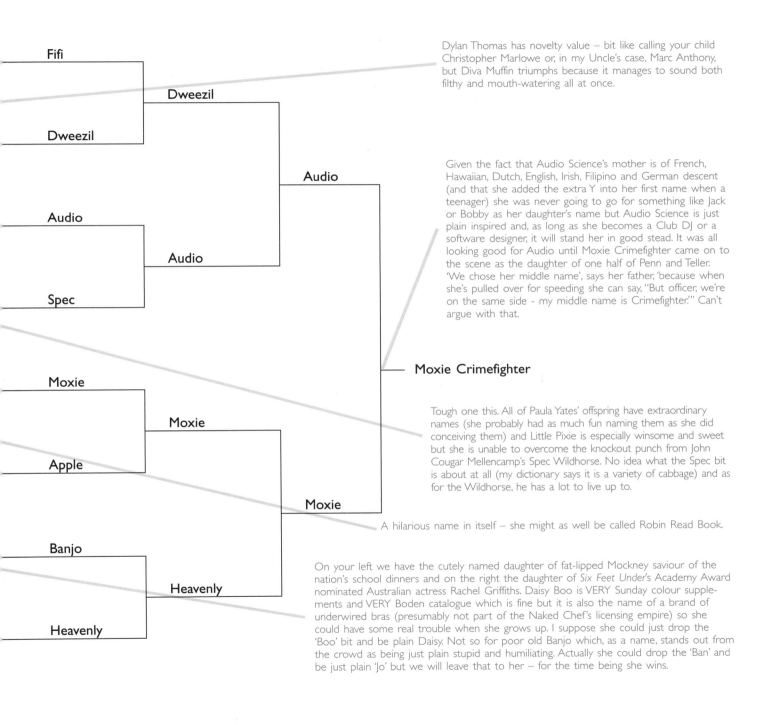

Fifi

Dweezil

Dweezil

Audio

Spec

Audio

Audio

Moxie

Apple

Moxie

Moxie

Banjo

Heavenly

Heavenly

Moxie

Moxie Crimefighter

Dylan Thomas has novelty value – bit like calling your child Christopher Marlowe or, in my Uncle's case, Marc Anthony, but Diva Muffin triumphs because it manages to sound both filthy and mouth-watering all at once.

Given the fact that Audio Science's mother is of French, Hawaiian, Dutch, English, Irish, Filipino and German descent (and that she added the extra Y into her first name when a teenager) she was never going to go for something like Jack or Bobby as her daughter's name but Audio Science is just plain inspired and, as long as she becomes a Club DJ or a software designer, it will stand her in good stead. It was all looking good for Audio until Moxie Crimefighter came on to the scene as the daughter of one half of Penn and Teller. 'We chose her middle name', says her father, 'because when she's pulled over for speeding she can say, "But officer, we're on the same side - my middle name is Crimefighter."' Can't argue with that.

Tough one this. All of Paula Yates' offspring have extraordinary names (she probably had as much fun naming them as she did conceiving them) and Little Pixie is especially winsome and sweet but she is unable to overcome the knockout punch from John Cougar Mellencamp's Spec Wildhorse. No idea what the Spec bit is about at all (my dictionary says it is a variety of cabbage) and as for the Wildhorse, he has a lot to live up to.

A hilarious name in itself – she might as well be called Robin Read Book.

On your left we have the cutely named daughter of fat-lipped Mockney saviour of the nation's school dinners and on the right the daughter of *Six Feet Under*'s Academy Award nominated Australian actress Rachel Griffiths. Daisy Boo is VERY Sunday colour supplements and VERY Boden catalogue which is fine but it is also the name of a brand of underwired bras (presumably not part of the Naked Chef's licensing empire) so she could have some real trouble when she grows up. I suppose she could just drop the 'Boo' bit and be plain Daisy. Not so for poor old Banjo which, as a name, stands out from the crowd as being just plain stupid and humiliating. Actually she could drop the 'Ban' and be just plain 'Jo' but we will leave that to her – for the time being she wins.

Cheesy Chat-Up Lines

by SIMON TREWIN

Being happily married for more than fifteen years now I truly can't remember what my chat-up line was to my wife Helen but I can categorically guarantee that it was none of the cringe-making little beauties lining up on the starting grid. If you believe Neil Strauss – the King of all PUA (pick-up artists) – (who laid the entire process bare in his extraordinary book *The Game*) there are some killer lines and 100% guaranteed routines out there. So once you have tried and failed with all thirty-two of my suggestions then please rush off and buy his excellent book (once you have been released from prison for sexual harassment or been discharged from casualty with your nose in plaster that is). Anyway – I'm sure I've met you somewhere before. Shall we slip over into that corner so that I can tell you all about it . . . ?

Your face or mine?
Did you hurt yourself when you fell from heaven?

fell from heaven

If I said you had a beautiful body would you hold it against me?
Do you have a map? I just keep on getting lost in your eyes.

beautiful body

Are you tired? Cause you've been running through my mind all day.
You have been very naughty. Go to my room.

go to my room

You look like a parking ticket – you've got fine written all over you.
My face is leaving in 15 minutes. Be on it.

face leaving

Is it hot in here or is it just you?
Is that a mirror in your pocket? I think I can see myself in your pants.

mirror

You must be Jamaican because you're Jamaican me crazy.
Can you phone your Mum and tell her you won't be home tonight?

phone your Mum

It's late – you'll do.
I lost my phone number – can I borrow yours?

phone number

I may not be the best looking man in here but I am the only one talking to you.
Can I buy you a drink or do you just want the money?

money

Is your dad a thief? Did he steal the stars out of the sky and place them in your eyes?
Winning the lottery doesn't mean much when you've got a weak heart like me.

lottery

Get your coat, love, you've pulled.
Do you know what would look good on you? Me.

coat

Do you believe in the hereafter? Well, then I guess you know what I'm here after.
I wanna melt in your mouth, not in your hands.

here after

What do you want for breakfast?
That's a lovely dress – can I talk you out of it?

breakfast

Is that a ladder in your tights or just the stairway to heaven?
Hi, I'm Mr. Right. Someone said you were looking for me.

stairway

'Can you be Wilma and I'll be Fred and we'll make the bed rock?'
Well I'm here – what are your two other wishes?

bed rock

You don't sweat much for a fat bird.
If you were a laser you would be set to stunning.

laser

Picture this: you, me, bubble baths, and a bottle of champagne.
If I could rearrange the alphabet, I'd put U and I together.

alphabet

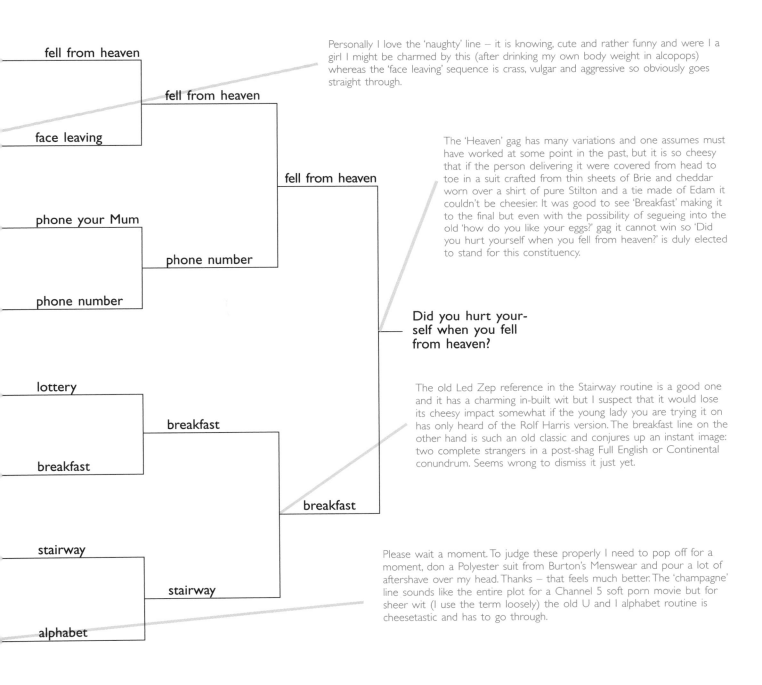

fell from heaven

fell from heaven

face leaving

fell from heaven

phone your Mum

phone number

phone number

lottery

breakfast

breakfast

stairway

stairway

alphabet

breakfast

Did you hurt your-
self when you fell
from heaven?

Personally I love the 'naughty' line – it is knowing, cute and rather funny and were I a girl I might be charmed by this (after drinking my own body weight in alcopops) whereas the 'face leaving' sequence is crass, vulgar and aggressive so obviously goes straight through.

The 'Heaven' gag has many variations and one assumes must have worked at some point in the past, but it is so cheesy that if the person delivering it were covered from head to toe in a suit crafted from thin sheets of Brie and cheddar worn over a shirt of pure Stilton and a tie made of Edam it couldn't be cheesier. It was good to see 'Breakfast' making it to the final but even with the possibility of segueing into the old 'how do you like your eggs?' gag it cannot win so 'Did you hurt yourself when you fell from heaven?' is duly elected to stand for this constituency.

The old Led Zep reference in the Stairway routine is a good one and it has a charming in-built wit but I suspect that it would lose its cheesy impact somewhat if the young lady you are trying it on has only heard of the Rolf Harris version. The breakfast line on the other hand is such an old classic and conjures up an instant image: two complete strangers in a post-shag Full English or Continental conundrum. Seems wrong to dismiss it just yet.

Please wait a moment. To judge these properly I need to pop off for a moment, don a Polyester suit from Burton's Menswear and pour a lot of aftershave over my head. Thanks – that feels much better. The 'champagne' line sounds like the entire plot for a Channel 5 soft porn movie but for sheer wit (I use the term loosely) the old U and I alphabet routine is cheesetastic and has to go through.

Children's Books
by SAM MILLS

Books that made you sneak-read under the covers as a child long after your parents had put the lights out; books you still continue to cherish as an adult for their imagination, insight and wonder. Some are over 50 years old, some are new, but all will live on for years to come . . .

SAM MILLS graduated from Oxford University before becoming a full-time novelist. Sam is the author of the teen novel *The Boys Who Saved the World* and the forthcoming *The Last Days of England*, an epic novel set a few years in the future when America invades England.

Holes by Louis Sachar
Harry Potter and the Prisoner of Azkaban by J. K. Rowling

Charlie and the Chocolate Factory by Roald Dahl
The Magic Faraway Tree by Enid Blyton

A Series of Unfortunate Events by Lemony Snicket
The Hungry Caterpillar by Eric Carle

The Bartlemeus Triology by Jonathan Stroud
His Dark Materials by Philip Pullman

The Curious Incident of the Dog in the Night-time by Mark Haddon
The Adventures of Huckleberry Finn by Mark Twain

Alice in Wonderland by Lewis Carroll
Peter Pan by J. M. Barrie

Paddington by Michael Bond
The Cat in the Hat by Dr Seuss

Goodnight Mister Tom by Michelle Magorian
How I Live Now by Meg Rosoff

Holes

Charlie and the
Chocolate Factory

Charlie and the
Chocolate Factory

A Series of
Unfortunate
Events

His Dark
Materials

Charlie and
the Chocolate
Factory

His Dark Materials

The Curious
Incident of the
Dog in the
Night-time

Alice in Wonderland

Charlie and the
Chocolate Factory

Alice in
Wonderland

Alice in
Wonderland

The Cat in
the Hat

Goodnight
Mister Tom

Goodnight
Mister Tom

The third Harry Potter is surely the best in the series – richly imaginative but succinct compared to the whoppers of the later books. The series has topped the list of banned books in the US due to the ridiculous charge that it encourages witchcraft amongst youngsters; J. K. responded with a quote from Ralph Waldo Emerson – 'Every burned book enlightens the world'.

Everlasting gobstoppers, hot cream for cold days and exploding candy for your enemies – just a few of the gloriously imaginative delights from Wonka's factory, the ultimate children's fantasy. It is now a legend that has sold thirteen million copies worldwide but when Dahl first wrote the book in the early 1960s his offbeat and utterly unique style caused UK publishers to reject it for years before its charm won out. A huge influence on children's books for decades to come, it laid the foundations for Harry P.

Alice flies through on the delightful nonsense of the Mad Hatter's tea party, the Cheshire Cat's smile and Twinkle, Twinkle Little Bat . . .

Marmalade and a delightfully English bear is beaten by the simple genius of the Cat. Dr Seuss and his publisher came up with a list of 250 words from which to write a book – he managed to write Cat using just 220.

Both books are set in wartime, both won *Guardian* fiction prizes, both are impossible to close without shedding tears – but *Goodnight Mister Tom*, the story of a boy evacuated in WWII and sent to live with the elderly, grumpy Mr Tom, is the most moving.

Chocolate Bars
by SIMON TREWIN

Next time you go to the British Museum, stop when you come to the statue of Hans Sloane, and remember what I am going to tell you. There is a little known connection between the British Museum and the proliferation of chocolate in the Western World. In 1689 a noted physician and collector (i.e. plunderer) going by the name of Hans Sloane was involved in the development of a chocolate drink in Jamaica. It was initially used by apothecaries to cure a number of ailments, but was later sold by the Cadbury brothers as an alternative to alcohol. The word 'chocolate' comes from the Nahuatl language of the Aztecs from Mexico, and is derived from the word *Xocalati,* which is a combination of *Xocolli* (meaning bitter) and *Alat* (meaning water). From its beginnings as an integral part of the Quakers' temperance movement to its current status as a multi-million pound industry, chocolate has been through many transformations. But it remains an incredibly naughty and unbeatably moreish treat. In the interests of science (and this book) I have scoured the sweetshops of the UK, bought boxes and boxes of chocolate, locked myself in my bedroom with only a looped compilation of Cadbury's Flake adverts for company and eaten half my bodyweight in cocoa. Here are my findings . . .

Rediscovering the Double Decker was a highly enjoyable experience – it is, as with all chocolate snacks, a mass of contradictions. The smoothness of the Cadbury's milk chocolate, the hardness of the crispy base and chewiness of the nougat topping, all add up to something you wouldn't give to anyone with false teeth. But how does it stack up against the Brunch Bar? There is something rather old-fashioned about the word 'brunch' – it all feels rather 80s. I have to say, so does the bar itself. Nice texture, easy to bite into, and with a neat feature whereby the top was covered in chocolate but on the sides you could look into the bar and see the rice crispies, cereals, raisins and oats. I think my problem with the Brunch Bar, and ultimately why the Double Decker wins out, is the Brunch Bar tries just a little too hard to be healthy with its muesli-in-a-chocolate-bar experience.

'Have a break, have a KitKat' – there is something almost sexual about how you can run your finger down the groove in the packaging, remove the outer layer of red and white wrapping and gently rub the surface of the silver paper to reveal the Cadbury's KitKat logo hiding beneath. It was also a wonderfully satisfying crack as you separate one bar from another, and that is before we experience the crunchy smooth taste sensation. The Dimebar I have an even more personal connection with. My wife starred in a series of Dimebar commercials for German TV including one where she ran across an airport terminal finding an empty telephone booth before mistakenly placing a Dimebar in the credit card slot of the phone. A great advert and we were grateful for the months of mortgage payments it gave us. On that basis and that basis alone the Dimebar has to go through.

I was never a big fan of Terry's Chocolate Orange – yes there was the fun to be had with tapping the orange, opening the foil and separating out the segments, but the combination of orange and chocolate flavours never really did it for me.

Double Decker
Brunch Bar — Double Decker

Boost
Toffee Crisp — Toffee Crisp

Dairy Milk
Snickers — Dairy Milk

Dime
Kit Kat — Dime

Crunchie
Flake — Flake

Galaxy
Bubble Bar — Bubble Bar

Milky Way
Mars Bar — Mars Bar

Lion
Hershey — Hershey

Curly Wurly
Peanut Butter Kit Kat — Curly Wurly

Topic
Fruit and Nut — Fruit and Nut

Drifter
Green and Black's — Green and Black's

Bounty
Terry's Chocolate Orange Bar — Bounty

Star Bar
Caramac — Caramac

Twix
Cadbury's Dairy Milk Turkish Delight — Twix

Aero
Texan — Texan

Fry's Orange Cream
Yorkie — Yorkie

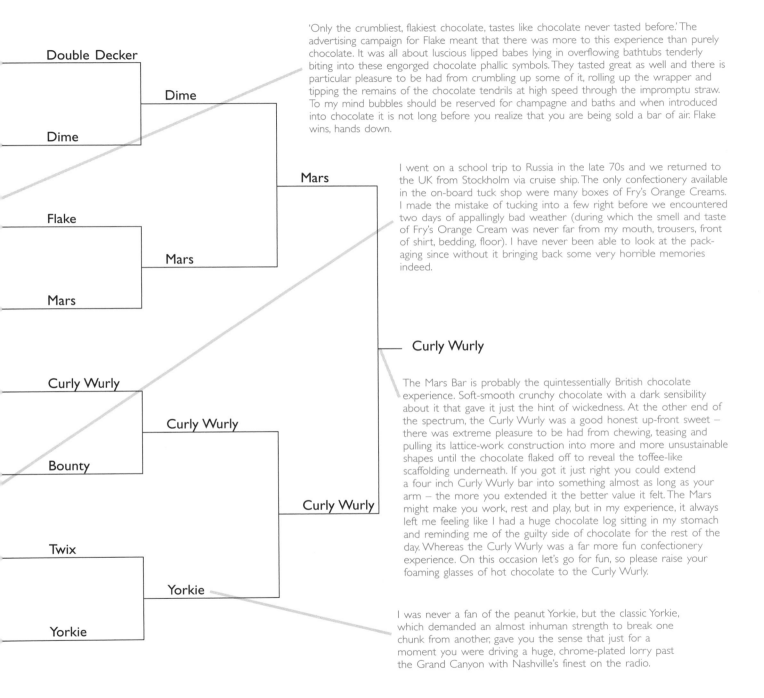

Double Decker

Dime

Dime

Dime

Flake

Mars

Mars

Mars

Curly Wurly

Curly Wurly

Bounty

Curly Wurly

Curly Wurly

Twix

Yorkie

Yorkie

Curly Wurly

'Only the crumbliest, flakiest chocolate, tastes like chocolate never tasted before.' The advertising campaign for Flake meant that there was more to this experience than purely chocolate. It was all about luscious lipped babes lying in overflowing bathtubs tenderly biting into these engorged chocolate phallic symbols. They tasted great as well and there is particular pleasure to be had from crumbling up some of it, rolling up the wrapper and tipping the remains of the chocolate tendrils at high speed through the impromptu straw. To my mind bubbles should be reserved for champagne and baths and when introduced into chocolate it is not long before you realize that you are being sold a bar of air. Flake wins, hands down.

I went on a school trip to Russia in the late 70s and we returned to the UK from Stockholm via cruise ship. The only confectionery available in the on-board tuck shop were many boxes of Fry's Orange Creams. I made the mistake of tucking into a few right before we encountered two days of appallingly bad weather (during which the smell and taste of Fry's Orange Cream was never far from my mouth, trousers, front of shirt, bedding, floor). I have never been able to look at the packaging since without it bringing back some very horrible memories indeed.

The Mars Bar is probably the quintessentially British chocolate experience. Soft-smooth crunchy chocolate with a dark sensibility about it that gave it just the hint of wickedness. At the other end of the spectrum, the Curly Wurly was a good honest up-front sweet – there was extreme pleasure to be had from chewing, teasing and pulling its lattice-work construction into more and more unsustainable shapes until the chocolate flaked off to reveal the toffee-like scaffolding underneath. If you got it just right you could extend a four inch Curly Wurly bar into something almost as long as your arm – the more you extended it the better value it felt. The Mars might make you work, rest and play, but in my experience, it always left me feeling like I had a huge chocolate log sitting in my stomach and reminding me of the guilty side of chocolate for the rest of the day. Whereas the Curly Wurly was a far more fun confectionery experience. On this occasion let's go for fun, so please raise your foaming glasses of hot chocolate to the Curly Wurly.

I was never a fan of the peanut Yorkie, but the classic Yorkie, which demanded an almost inhuman strength to break one chunk from another, gave you the sense that just for a moment you were driving a huge, chrome-plated lorry past the Grand Canyon with Nashville's finest on the radio.

Christmas Number Ones
by SIMON TREWIN

The mince pies are freshly baked, the children are pretending to be asleep upstairs, the turkey is stuffed, the tree is trimmed and the service of *Nine Carols and Lessons* is on the radio. Looking out of the window, I can see it's beginning to snow now and I'm sure I can hear sleighbells coming in from the east. This can mean only one thing – the nation has survived once again (as we knew it would) the annual battle to see who will become Christmas Number One. To be honest the heyday of this competition has long gone now and the inevitability of the X-Factor winner scooping the pool makes it all feel a bit lame. Let's roll back the carpet in the parlour, put on a silly paper hat, turn up the family's prized copy of *Now That's What I Call Christmas* and let the memories flood back. Which 'artiste' deserves the sixpenny piece in the Christmas pudding and who will get a hand-knitted jumper from Aunty Gladys – again?

Rolf Harris 'Two Little Boys'
Dave Edmunds 'I Hear You Knockin''

Two Little Boys

Benny Hill 'Ernie (The Fastest Milkman In The West)'
Little Jimmy Osmond 'Long Haired Lover From Liverpool'

Ernie

Slade 'Merry Xmas Everybody'
Whitney Houston 'I Will Always Love You'

Merry Xmas

Queen 'Bohemian Rhapsody'
Johnny Mathis 'When A Child Is Born'

When A Child Is Born

Wings 'Mull Of Kintyre/Girls School'
Boney M 'Mary's Boy Child/Oh My Lord'

Mary's Boy Child

Pink Floyd 'Another Brick In The Wall'
St Winifred's School Choir 'There's No One Quite Like Grandma'

There's No One

The Human League 'Don't You Want Me?'
Renee & Renato 'Save Your Love'

Save Your Love

The Flying Pickets 'Only You'
Band Aid 'Do They Know It's Christmas?'

Do They Know?

Shakin' Stevens 'Merry Xmas Everybody'
The Pet Shop Boys 'Always On My Mind'

Always On My Mind

Cliff Richard 'Mistletoe and Wine'
Mud 'Lonely This Christmas'

Lonely

Mr Blobby 'Mr Blobby'
East 17 'Stay Another Day'

Stay Another Day

Michael Jackson 'Earth Song'
Spice Girls 'Goodbye'

Earth Song

Westlife 'I Have A Dream/Seasons In The Sun'
Bob The Builder 'Can We Fix It?'

Can We Fix It?

Robbie Williams & Nicole Kidman 'Something Stupid'
Girls Aloud 'Sound Of The Underground'

Something Stupid

Michael Andrews featuring Gary Jules 'Mad World'
Band Aid 20 'Do they Know It's Christmas?'

Mad World

Shayne Ward 'That's My Goal'
Leona Lewis 'A Moment Like This'

A Moment Like This

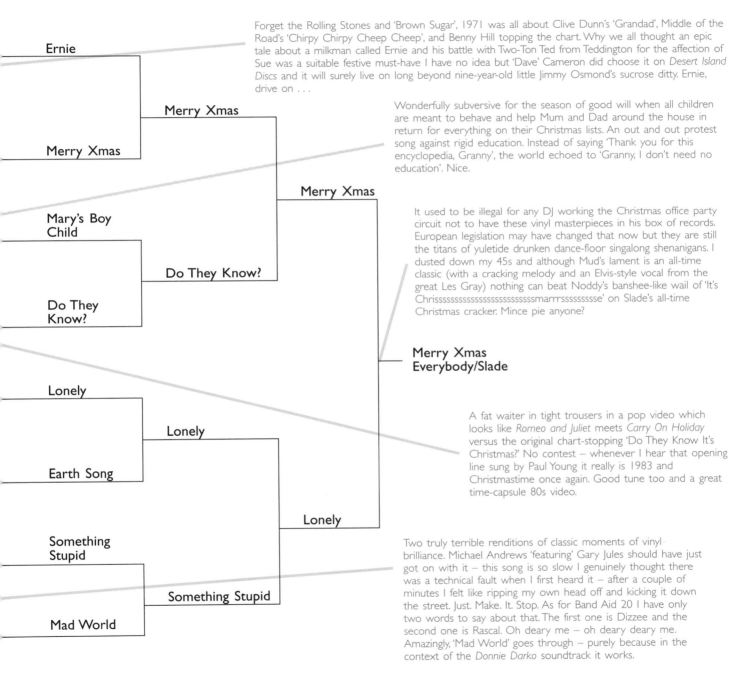

Ernie

Merry Xmas

Merry Xmas

Mary's Boy Child

Do They Know?

Do They Know?

Merry Xmas

Lonely

Lonely

Earth Song

Lonely

Something Stupid

Something Stupid

Mad World

Merry Xmas Everybody/Slade

Forget the Rolling Stones and 'Brown Sugar', 1971 was all about Clive Dunn's 'Grandad', Middle of the Road's 'Chirpy Chirpy Cheep Cheep', and Benny Hill topping the chart. Why we all thought an epic tale about a milkman called Ernie and his battle with Two-Ton Ted from Teddington for the affection of Sue was a suitable festive must-have I have no idea but 'Dave' Cameron did choose it on *Desert Island Discs* and it will surely live on long beyond nine-year-old little Jimmy Osmond's sucrose ditty. Ernie, drive on . . .

Wonderfully subversive for the season of good will when all children are meant to behave and help Mum and Dad around the house in return for everything on their Christmas lists. An out and out protest song against rigid education. Instead of saying 'Thank you for this encyclopedia, Granny', the world echoed to 'Granny, I don't need no education'. Nice.

It used to be illegal for any DJ working the Christmas office party circuit not to have these vinyl masterpieces in his box of records. European legislation may have changed that now but they are still the titans of yuletide drunken dance-floor singalong shenanigans. I dusted down my 45s and although Mud's lament is an all-time classic (with a cracking melody and an Elvis-style vocal from the great Les Gray) nothing can beat Noddy's banshee-like wail of 'It's Chrissssssssssssssssssssssssssssmarrrssssssssse' on Slade's all-time Christmas cracker. Mince pie anyone?

A fat waiter in tight trousers in a pop video which looks like *Romeo and Juliet* meets *Carry On Holiday* versus the original chart-stopping 'Do They Know It's Christmas?' No contest – whenever I hear that opening line sung by Paul Young it really is 1983 and Christmastime once again. Good tune too and a great time-capsule 80s video.

Two truly terrible renditions of classic moments of vinyl brilliance. Michael Andrews 'featuring' Gary Jules should have just got on with it – this song is so slow I genuinely thought there was a technical fault when I first heard it – after a couple of minutes I felt like ripping my own head off and kicking it down the street. Just. Make. It. Stop. As for Band Aid 20 I have only two words to say about that. The first one is Dizzee and the second one is Rascal. Oh deary me – oh deary deary me. Amazingly, 'Mad World' goes through – purely because in the context of the *Donnie Darko* soundtrack it works.

Cockney Rhyming Slang

by SIMON TREWIN

When Eastenders was launched on a grateful US public, legend has it that the broadcaster had to print a little booklet of Cockney-English translations to help the poor American viewers who were more than confused. They were no doubt very baffled indeed when Arthur or Pauline Fowler said that they would meet each other 'at the bottom of the apples and pears' and that Dot Cotton was going to get her 'Barnet sorted'. The mind boggles. I have a feeling that a lot of Cockney slang is made up to please middle-class etymologists and that when a couple of cheeky cockneys are together eating jellied eels, sewing more buttons on Pearly King and Queen outfits and discussing who came third at the last race at the Walthamstow Dog Track, they are as likely to start saying things like 'Fancy a pint of Nelson down the Nuclear?' as I am to don a velvet smoking jacket when I get home and start regaling my wife with tales of what a 'spiffing day I had at the office – don't you know?' It would be wrong to make any mention of Dick Van Dyke's accent as Bert The Chimney Sweep in the seminal movie Mary Poppins. That would be a cheap shot and unworthy of us. So without furver ado Maireeeee Poppins let's see wot we've got on the list. You're a toff and no mistakin . . .

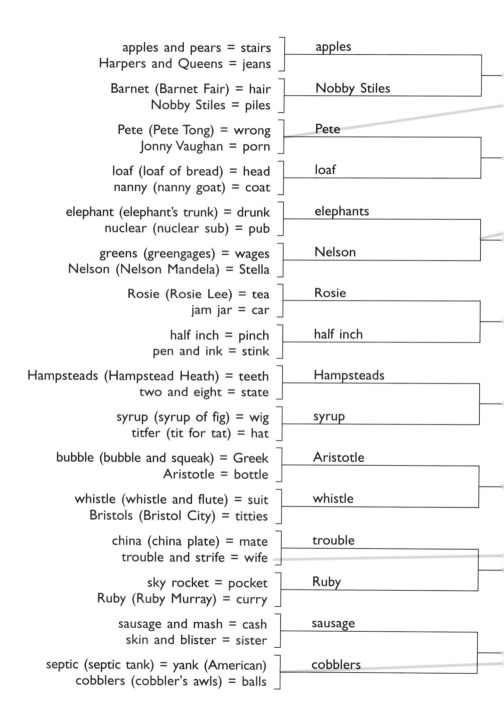

apples and pears = stairs
Harpers and Queens = jeans

Barnet (Barnet Fair) = hair
Nobby Stiles = piles

Pete (Pete Tong) = wrong
Jonny Vaughan = porn

loaf (loaf of bread) = head
nanny (nanny goat) = coat

elephant (elephant's trunk) = drunk
nuclear (nuclear sub) = pub

greens (greengages) = wages
Nelson (Nelson Mandela) = Stella

Rosie (Rosie Lee) = tea
jam jar = car

half inch = pinch
pen and ink = stink

Hampsteads (Hampstead Heath) = teeth
two and eight = state

syrup (syrup of fig) = wig
titfer (tit for tat) = hat

bubble (bubble and squeak) = Greek
Aristotle = bottle

whistle (whistle and flute) = suit
Bristols (Bristol City) = titties

china (china plate) = mate
trouble and strife = wife

sky rocket = pocket
Ruby (Ruby Murray) = curry

sausage and mash = cash
skin and blister = sister

septic (septic tank) = yank (American)
cobblers (cobbler's awls) = balls

apples
Nobby Stiles
Pete
loaf
elephants
Nelson
Rosie
half inch
Hampsteads
syrup
Aristotle
whistle
trouble
Ruby
sausage
cobblers

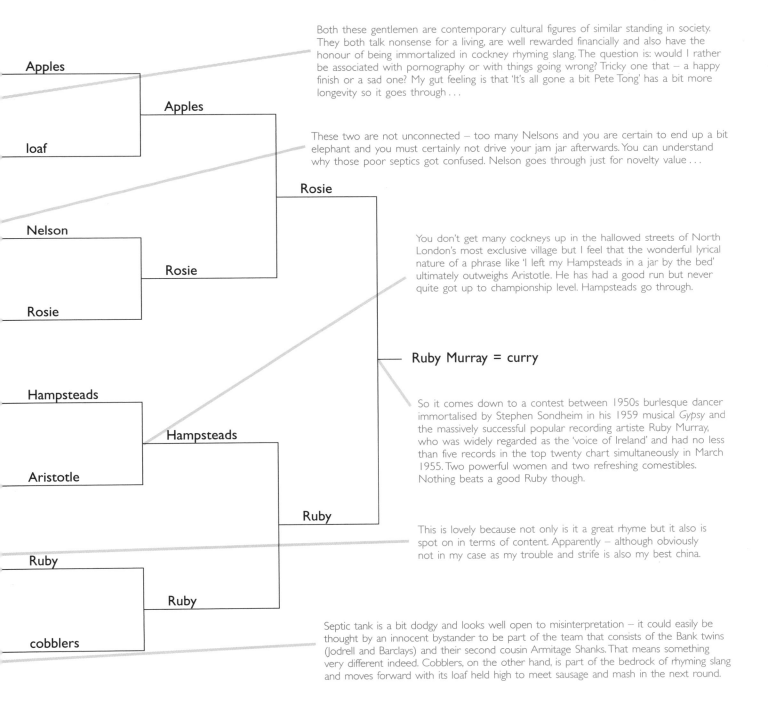

Apples

Apples

loaf

Rosie

Nelson

Rosie

Rosie

Ruby Murray = curry

Hampsteads

Hampsteads

Aristotle

Ruby

Ruby

Ruby

cobblers

Both these gentlemen are contemporary cultural figures of similar standing in society. They both talk nonsense for a living, are well rewarded financially and also have the honour of being immortalized in cockney rhyming slang. The question is: would I rather be associated with pornography or with things going wrong? Tricky one that – a happy finish or a sad one? My gut feeling is that 'It's all gone a bit Pete Tong' has a bit more longevity so it goes through . . .

These two are not unconnected – too many Nelsons and you are certain to end up a bit elephant and you must certainly not drive your jam jar afterwards. You can understand why those poor septics got confused. Nelson goes through just for novelty value . . .

You don't get many cockneys up in the hallowed streets of North London's most exclusive village but I feel that the wonderful lyrical nature of a phrase like 'I left my Hampsteads in a jar by the bed' ultimately outweighs Aristotle. He has had a good run but never quite got up to championship level. Hampsteads go through.

So it comes down to a contest between 1950s burlesque dancer immortalised by Stephen Sondheim in his 1959 musical *Gypsy* and the massively successful popular recording artiste Ruby Murray, who was widely regarded as the 'voice of Ireland' and had no less than five records in the top twenty chart simultaneously in March 1955. Two powerful women and two refreshing comestibles. Nothing beats a good Ruby though.

This is lovely because not only is it a great rhyme but it also is spot on in terms of content. Apparently – although obviously not in my case as my trouble and strife is also my best china.

Septic tank is a bit dodgy and looks well open to misinterpretation – it could easily be thought by an innocent bystander to be part of the team that consists of the Bank twins (Jodrell and Barclays) and their second cousin Armitage Shanks. That means something very different indeed. Cobblers, on the other hand, is part of the bedrock of rhyming slang and moves forward with its loaf held high to meet sausage and mash in the next round.

21

Cocktails

by SIMON TREWIN

In our naïve student days we thought it might be quite sophisticated and grand to hold a cocktail party – so we all dressed up and everyone brought a bottle of spirits. The hosts laid on lots of ice and cool cocktail glasses borrowed from the local pub and we even clubbed together and bought some of those natty little cocktail umbrellas in dayglo pink, green and yellow. I even recall some glace cherries and the odd little bowl of olives and associated nibbles. All was set for a lovely evening and it was indeed grand – someone even brought with them *The Savoy Cocktail Book* and we tasted everything from Champagne Cocktails to Pina Colada and Sea Breezes and Sidecars. After a while people danced and then we made the mistake of basically mixing everything that was left into a huge jug and then drinking and drinking and drinking until all decorum went out of the window. Some people were still drunk the following evening – the mistake we made was to venture off the path of properly balanced cocktail recipes into the murky hard-shoulder of 'well these two colours look nice together'. The experience also informed the section on hangover cures you will find later on in this volume. 'Nuff said.

Sea Breeze (vodka, cranberry juice, grapefruit juice)
Champagne Cocktail (champagne, sugar, Angostura bitters)

Champagne

Sangria (red wine, rum, orange juice, lemon juice, sugar)
Jack Rabbit (Jack Daniels, banana liqueur)

Jack Rabbit

Long Island Iced Tea (vodka, gin, tequila, rum, Southern Comfort, sour mix, Coke)
Screaming Orgasm (vodka, Bailey's, Kahlúa)

Orgasm

Pina Colada (pineapple juice, rum, coconut milk)
Pimm's (Pimm's, lemonade, fruit)

Pimm's

Rum Punch (pineapple juice, orange juice, lime juice, Angostura bitters)
Screwdriver (vodka, orange Juice)

Screwdriver

Moscow Mule (vodka, ginger beer)
Tequila Sunrise (tequila, Grenadine, orange juice)

Tequila

Black Russian (vodka, coffee liqueur)
White Russian (vodka, light cream, coffee liqueur)

White Russian

Strawberry Margarita (strawberries, tequila, Cointreau, lime juice)
Margarita (tequila, Cointreau, lime juice)

Margarita

Cuba Libre (rum, cola, lime)
Bloody Mary (vodka, tomato juice, Tabasco, Worcestershire sauce)

Cuba Libre

Sex On the Beach (vodka, peach schnapps, grapefruit, cranberry)
Sidecar (Cointreau, lemon juice, brandy)

Sex/Beach

Snowball (advocaat, lemonade, lemon)
Strawberry Daiquiri (frozen strawberries, lime juice, sugar, rum)

Snowball

Mojito (mint, sugar, lime juice, rum)
Caipirinha (sugar, rum, lime juice)

Mojito

Cheap Chocolate Milk (Irish cream, vodka, milk)
Cosmopolitan (Absolut citron, Cointreau, lime juice, cranberry juice)

Chocolate Milk

Rusty Nail (scotch and Drambuie)
Dr Pepper (amaretto and light beer)

Rusty Nail

Vodka Martini (vodka and dry vermouth)
Ball licker (vodka, cointreau, orange juice)

Martini

Alabama Slammer (Southern Comfort, amaretto, sloe gin, lemon juice)
Mind Eraser (Bailey's, Kahlúa, vodka)

Mind Eraser

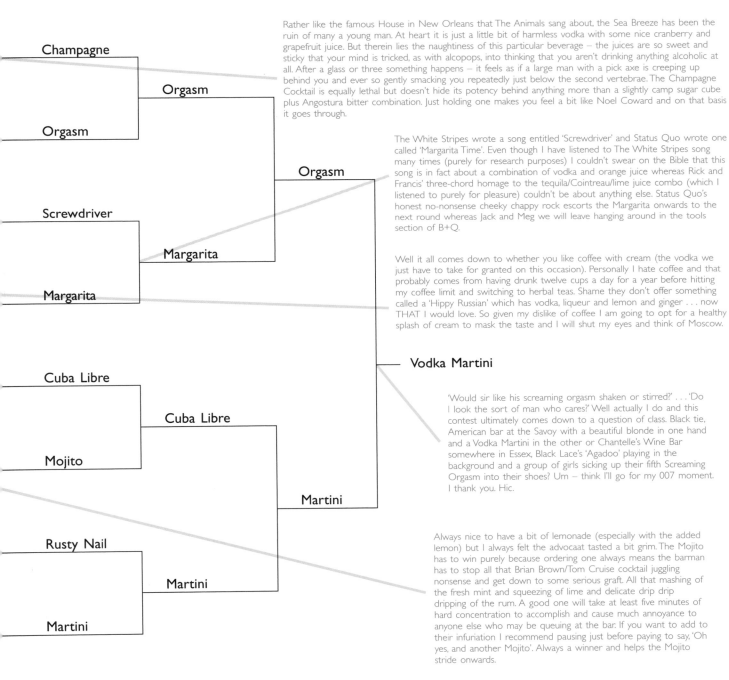

Champagne

Orgasm

Orgasm

Screwdriver

Margarita

Margarita

Cuba Libre

Cuba Libre

Mojito

Rusty Nail

Martini

Martini

Orgasm

Margarita

Cuba Libre

Martini

Orgasm

Vodka Martini

Rather like the famous House in New Orleans that The Animals sang about, the Sea Breeze has been the ruin of many a young man. At heart it is just a little bit of harmless vodka with some nice cranberry and grapefruit juice. But therein lies the naughtiness of this particular beverage – the juices are so sweet and sticky that your mind is tricked, as with alcopops, into thinking that you aren't drinking anything alcoholic at all. After a glass or three something happens – it feels as if a large man with a pick axe is creeping up behind you and ever so gently smacking you repeatedly just below the second vertebrae. The Champagne Cocktail is equally lethal but doesn't hide its potency behind anything more than a slightly camp sugar cube plus Angostura bitter combination. Just holding one makes you feel a bit like Noel Coward and on that basis it goes through.

The White Stripes wrote a song entitled 'Screwdriver' and Status Quo wrote one called 'Margarita Time'. Even though I have listened to The White Stripes song many times (purely for research purposes) I couldn't swear on the Bible that this song is in fact about a combination of vodka and orange juice whereas Rick and Francis' three-chord homage to the tequila/Cointreau/lime juice combo (which I listened to purely for pleasure) couldn't be about anything else. Status Quo's honest no-nonsense cheeky chappy rock escorts the Margarita onwards to the next round whereas Jack and Meg we will leave hanging around in the tools section of B+Q.

Well it all comes down to whether you like coffee with cream (the vodka we just have to take for granted on this occasion). Personally I hate coffee and that probably comes from having drunk twelve cups a day for a year before hitting my coffee limit and switching to herbal teas. Shame they don't offer something called a 'Hippy Russian' which has vodka, liqueur and lemon and ginger . . . now THAT I would love. So given my dislike of coffee I am going to opt for a healthy splash of cream to mask the taste and I will shut my eyes and think of Moscow.

'Would sir like his screaming orgasm shaken or stirred?' . . . 'Do I look the sort of man who cares?' Well actually I do and this contest ultimately comes down to a question of class. Black tie, American bar at the Savoy with a beautiful blonde in one hand and a Vodka Martini in the other or Chantelle's Wine Bar somewhere in Essex, Black Lace's 'Agadoo' playing in the background and a group of girls sicking up their fifth Screaming Orgasm into their shoes? Um – think I'll go for my 007 moment. I thank you. Hic.

Always nice to have a bit of lemonade (especially with the added lemon) but I always felt the advocaat tasted a bit grim. The Mojito has to win purely because ordering one always means the barman has to stop all that Brian Brown/Tom Cruise cocktail juggling nonsense and get down to some serious graft. All that mashing of the fresh mint and squeezing of lime and delicate drip drip dripping of the rum. A good one will take at least five minutes of hard concentration to accomplish and cause much annoyance to anyone else who may be queuing at the bar. If you want to add to their infuriation I recommend pausing just before paying to say, 'Oh yes, and another Mojito'. Always a winner and helps the Mojito stride onwards.

22

Comedy Catchphrases

by SIMON TREWIN

Catchphrases are a male preoccupation on the whole and the stuff of playground bonding and then, when you are a grown-up, of ice-breaking small talk at terrible dinner-parties and ghastly sales conferences. You can quickly judge whether someone is your kind of person depending on their knowledge of obscure *Monty Python* gags, early Alan Partridge or *The Goon Show* – catchphrases maketh the man. There are very few situations that can't be brightened up by throwing in a 'which was nice' from *The Fast Show*, a 'Nudge, Nudge, Wink Wink' from *Monty Python*, an ebullient 'Suits You Sir' (again from *The Fast Show*) or a saucy *Carry On*–style 'Ooh Matron'. Catchphrases have a habit of hanging around in the ether just waiting to land at the most appropriate or inappropriate time – but which one comes out on top? (As the actress said to the bishop.)

'How very dare you?' (*The Catherine Tate Show*)
'Nudge, nudge. Wink, wink. Say no more!' (*Monty Python*)

dare

'Am I bovverred?' (*The Catherine Tate Show*)
'I don't believe it!' (*One Foot In the Grave*)

bovverred

'And now for something completely different.' (*Monty Python*)
'I'm free!' (*Are You Being Served?*)

free

'Yeh but no but . . .' (*Little Britain*)
'What a fucking liberty.' (*The Catherine Tate Show*)

no but

'And it's goodnight from him.' (*The Two Ronnies*)
'You stupid boy.' (*Dad's Army*)

stupid boy

'That's Numberwang!' (*That Mitchell and Webb Look*)
'Listen very carefully, I shall say this only once.' (*'Allo 'Allo*)

Numberwang

'This week I have been mostly eating . . .' (*The Fast Show*)
'I have a cunning plan.' (*Blackadder*)

cunning plan

'Suits you, sir!' (*The Fast Show*)
'Drink! Feck! Arse! Gerls!' (*Father Ted*)

suits you

'This is a local shop for local people.' (*The League Of Gentlemen*)
'You are awful, but I like you.' (*The Dick Emery Show*)

like you

'I'm the only gay in the village.' (*Little Britain*)
'Don't mention the war!' (*Fawlty Towers*)

gay in the village

'Lovely, jubbly.' (*Only Fools And Horses*)
'Computer says no.' (*Little Britain*)

jubbly

'Can I do you now sir?' (*ITMA*)
'Ooh Matron!' (*Carry On Matron*)

Matron

'And on that bombshell . . .' (*I'm Alan Partridge*)
'You can't see the join.' (*Morecambe and Wise*)

see the join

'Are you having a laff?' (*Extras*)
'You just wouldn't let it lie.' (*Vic Reeves' Big Night Out*)

having a laff

'I want that one.' (*Little Britain*)
'It's all done in the best possible taste!' (*The Kenny Everett Television Show*)

possible taste

'You dirty old man.' (*Steptoe and Son*)
'We're doomed!' (*Dad's Army*)

dirty old man

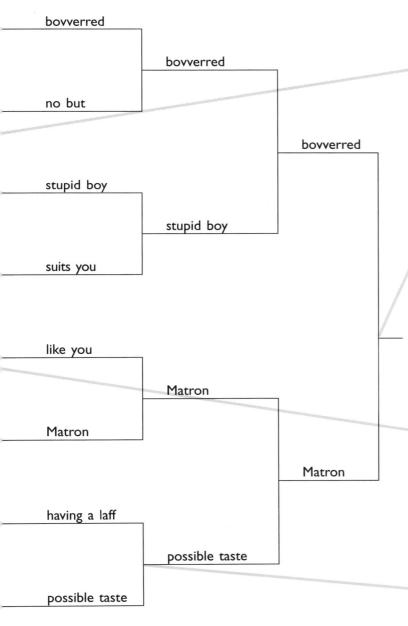

bovverred

bovverred

no but

bovverred

bovverred

stupid boy

stupid boy

suits you

Am I bovverred?

like you

Matron

Matron

Matron

Matron

having a laff

possible taste

possible taste

Unfortunate for these two classic lynchpins of post-war British comedy to go head to head in the early round of the competition. It is hard to choose between Captain Mainwaring's withering put-down of eager, nice-but-dim Private Pike and The Two Ronnies' eight-eyed smirking sign-off. But when push comes to shove 'stupid boy' has the edge and moves closer to comedy immortality.

No catchphrase competition is complete without cuddly Kenny Williams in his Doctor Tinkle persona and his saucy admonishment to Hattie Jacques's bestarched matron. In a parallel universe it would win hands down over Catherine Tate's truculent teenage ASBO-holding character's authority-challenging 'Am I bovverred?' (with or without Tony Blair performing it on Comic Relief 2007). Unfortunately, however, 'Ooh, Matron' was never actually uttered and is as false a film quote as Jimmy Cagney's 'You dirty rat' and Bogey's 'Play it again, Sam'. So for that reason alone Catherine Tate wins out. Not that I imagine she cares very much one way or the other.

Committed 'homosexualist' Daffyd lives in the Welsh town of Llanddewi Brefi, cavorts around in some extraordinarily figure-hugging lycra creations and takes great exception to anyone who 'likes a bit of cock' trespassing on his domain. A great comic creation and a great catchphrase but probably not one you are going to get a lot of everyday use out of . Unlike the *cri de coeur* of the ebullient sexual-terrorist Mandy – a mainstay of the Dick Emery comedy stable – who used to lean forward with false bosoms atremble and then push her subject very hard in the stomach before purring her iconic chat-up line. It's a hard act to beat. Mandy – please follow me to the next round.

An interesting bout this – Gervais created this anti-catchphrase for his character in *When The Whistle Blows*, the sitcom within the catchphraseless sitcom that highlights the vacuous nature of most British catchphrase-obsessed culture – it has of course backfired and become a huge catchphrase in itself. Cupid Stunt, Kenny Everett's huge-breasted bearded lady, used her elaborate leg-crossing to great effect and her catchphrase became a huge playground favourite which all those now grown-up schoolboys still bandy around today. Stunt goes through.

Cricket Dismissals

by TOM TOMASZEWSKI

There's no sport to equal cricket – it really is that simple. Football fans should be quietly put to sleep; rugby fans penned in cages on a remote Scottish isle. Perhaps there's room for lovers of badminton, but that's about it. The following selection of cricketing low points (English cricket, in particular, seems to thrive on its lows) encompasses all that's good, bad and embarrassing about the game. From the violent death of a seventeenth-century fielder to the slimming scandal of a twenty-first century icon, the ways in which cricketers have made their exits are frequently absurd.

TOM TOMASZEWSKI writes regularly for the *Independent on Sunday* and captains the University of Kent Cosmopolitans CC. His fiction has appeared erratically (www.tomazi.com).

Ian Botham (reckless leg-over)
9 Aug 1991, The Oval, England v W. Indies

Inzamam-ul-Haq (weighty roll-over)
6 Aug 2006, Headingley, Pakistan v England

Botham

Pakistan (hare-brained forfeit)
20 Aug 2006, The Oval, Pakistan v England

England (drawn test: boat leaving)
3–14 Mar 1939, Durban, England v S. Africa

Pakistan

Jasper Vinall (death by misadventure)
28 Aug 1624, Horstead in Sussex

Salman Butt (Trescothick's head)
12 Nov 2005, Multan, England v Pakistan

Vinall

Joey Solomon (theatre of hat)
2 Jan 1961, MCG, W. Indies v Australia

Colin Wells (fashion victim)
18 May 1980, Edgbaston, Sussex v Warwickshire

Wells

Andy Ducat (disintegrating bat)
4 Jul 1921, Headingley, England v Australia

Muralitharan (run out, being nice)
9 Dec 2006, Christchurch, Sri Lanka v New Zealand

Ducat

Michael Vaughan (unsporting appeal)
19 Dec 2001, Bangalore, England v India

Alvin Kalicharan (Greig crowd-pleaser)
3 Feb 1974, Trinidad, W. Indies v England

Kalicharan

Andrew Symonds (non-striker rebound)
13 Jan 2006, Melbourne, Australia v Sri Lanka

Shane Warne (mother's little helper)
12 Feb 2003, South Africa, World Cup

Warne

Conan Doyle (Spedegue's Dropper)
1880s, precise details a mystery

Andrew Flintoff (pedalo)
18 Mar 2007, St Lucia

Conan Doyle

While trying to hook Curtly Ambrose in the 1991 Oval test Botham's momentum carried him round on to the stumps. 'He just didn't quite get his leg over' BBC commentator John Agnew helpfully remarked as colleague Brian Johnston read through the English scorecard. Cue hysteria, helpless laughter and prolonged dead air. God knows how Johnners would have reacted to Inzamam's exit during the 2006 Headingley test. Sweeping Monty Panesar, the giant Pakistani lost his balance and ended up rolling over the stumps. Botham clearly wins out for reducing *Test Match Special* to a shambles.

In 1624, while trying to hit the ball a second time and defend his stumps, Edward Tye accidentally cracked Jasper Vinall on the head with his bat and killed him. In 2005 Salman Butt slogged Shaun Udal directly on to Marcus Trescothick's head – even more bizarrely, Geraint Jones caught the ball as it rebounded. Vinall wins, out of respect for the dead.

When Andy Ducat's bat exploded as he fended a ball from Ted McDonald in the 1921 Headingley test he was simultaneously caught and bowled: a splinter from the bat sailed on to the stumps, knocking off the bails, while the ball looped off into the slips. That dismissal pales to nothing, however, when compared to the result of the 2006 Oval test. After umpire Daryl Hare decided someone had been tampering with the ball, the fielding Pakistani side protested by remaining in their dressing room after tea. Although the Pakistanis soon declared they wanted to play on, the umpires farcically awarded the game to England. Utterly ridiculous and supremely unfortunate, there can be no other winner.

There's no room for sentiment in sport – ask an Australian – so Vinall makes way for Colin Wells. Standing at the non-striker's end during a Sunday league match in 1980, Wells was unlucky enough to be run out after a straight drive was deflected on to the stumps by the bowler's outrageously flared trousers.

For no clear reason Michael Vaughan brushed the ball away after missing a sweep shot in the 2001 Bangalore test. The Indians appealed and Vaughan joined the rare band of men dismissed for handling the ball – sad, but hardly as dramatic as Alvin Kalicharan being run out by Tony Greig during England's 1973–4 tour of the West Indies. Seeing Greig field the last ball of the day Kalicharan turned and started walking off the field. Greig, however, threw down the stumps and appealed for a run out. The umpires upheld the appeal – until the crowd threatened to riot and Kalicharan was reinstated (much to Greig's annoyance).

Shane Warne's early exit from the 2003 World Cup after failing a drug test because, he revealed, he'd taken a weight-loss pill recommended by his mum was nothing compared to author Conan Doyle's singular experience batting some time in the 1880s. Flailing wildly at a looping donkey-drop bowled by Bunny Lucas (it fell vertically from thirty feet above the wicket) he smashed his bat and two of the stumps, then saw the ball land on top of the remaining one. The incident inspired his short story, 'Spedegue's Dropper', about an asthmatic village cricketer with heart problems, whose habit of practising his bowling by lobbing a ball over a cord strung between two trees in the New Forest paid off when he was dramatically called into the Test team and bowled out the Australians in the deciding Ashes test.

Pakistan

Wells

Ducat

Conan Doyle

Pakistan

Ducat

Pakistan

Pakistan

24

Crosswordese
by TYLER HINMAN

Crossword puzzles have taken a decidedly modern leap in recent years, with greater emphasis on pop culture and modern words and phrases. However, the exigencies of crossword construction sometimes can only be eased by words with friendly letter patterns, and this ensures the eternal life of some words that would otherwise be doomed to obscurity. Thirty-two examples of crosswordese do battle here. Many more examples exist, but these make the cut for their frequent use and virtual unknowability to a puzzling novice.

TYLER HINMAN is an on-and-off crossword constructor. He is better known as the youngest champion in the history of the *American Crossword* Puzzle Tournament and one of the featured solvers in the 2005 documentary *Wordplay*. He received a degree in information technology from Rensselaer Polytechnic Institute (go Engineers!) in 2006. He is currently a bond trader in Chicago.

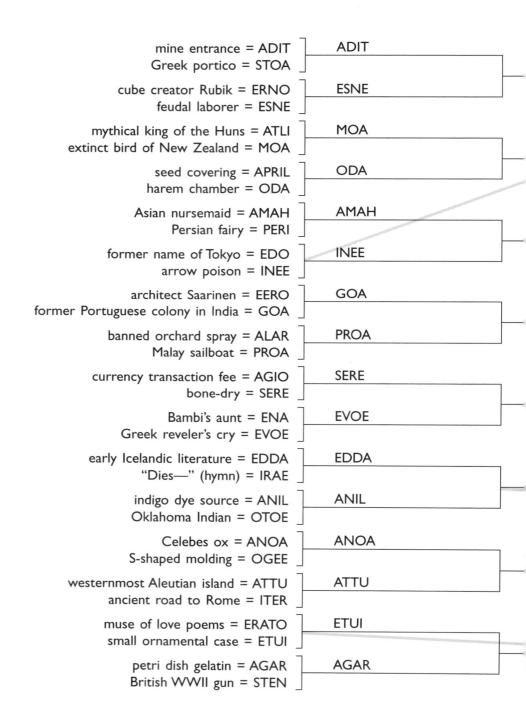

mine entrance = ADIT — ADIT
Greek portico = STOA

cube creator Rubik = ERNO — ESNE
feudal laborer = ESNE

mythical king of the Huns = ATLI — MOA
extinct bird of New Zealand = MOA

seed covering = APRIL — ODA
harem chamber = ODA

Asian nursemaid = AMAH — AMAH
Persian fairy = PERI

former name of Tokyo = EDO — INEE
arrow poison = INEE

architect Saarinen = EERO — GOA
former Portuguese colony in India = GOA

banned orchard spray = ALAR — PROA
Malay sailboat = PROA

currency transaction fee = AGIO — SERE
bone-dry = SERE

Bambi's aunt = ENA — EVOE
Greek reveler's cry = EVOE

early Icelandic literature = EDDA — EDDA
"Dies—" (hymn) = IRAE

indigo dye source = ANIL — ANIL
Oklahoma Indian = OTOE

Celebes ox = ANOA — ANOA
S-shaped molding = OGEE

westernmost Aleutian island = ATTU — ATTU
ancient road to Rome = ITER

muse of love poems = ERATO — ETUI
small ornamental case = ETUI

petri dish gelatin = AGAR — AGAR
British WWII gun = STEN

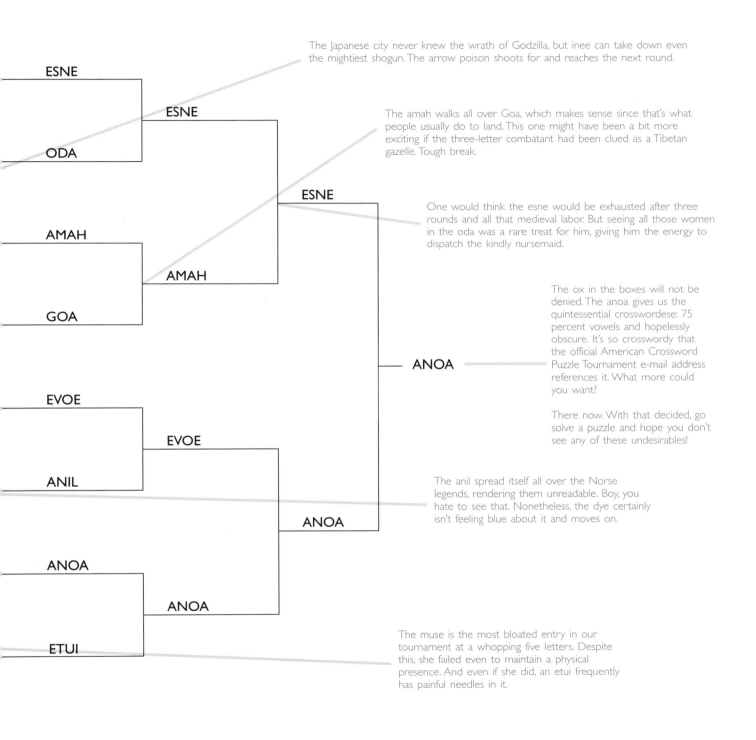

ESNE

ODA

ESNE

AMAH

GOA

AMAH

ESNE

EVOE

ANIL

EVOE

ANOA

ETUI

ANOA

ANOA

ANOA

The Japanese city never knew the wrath of Godzilla, but inee can take down even the mightiest shogun. The arrow poison shoots for and reaches the next round.

The amah walks all over Goa, which makes sense since that's what people usually do to land. This one might have been a bit more exciting if the three-letter combatant had been clued as a Tibetan gazelle. Tough break.

One would think the esne would be exhausted after three rounds and all that medieval labor. But seeing all those women in the oda was a rare treat for him, giving him the energy to dispatch the kindly nursemaid.

The ox in the boxes will not be denied. The anoa gives us the quintessential crosswordese: 75 percent vowels and hopelessly obscure. It's so crosswordy that the official American Crossword Puzzle Tournament e-mail address references it. What more could you want?

There now. With that decided, go solve a puzzle and hope you don't see any of these undesirables!

The anil spread itself all over the Norse legends, rendering them unreadable. Boy, you hate to see that. Nonetheless, the dye certainly isn't feeling blue about it and moves on.

The muse is the most bloated entry in our tournament at a whopping five letters. Despite this, she failed even to maintain a physical presence. And even if she did, an etui frequently has painful needles in it.

Dangerous Sports

by SIMON TREWIN

There is obviously something in our psyche that makes us always want to push things just a little further. Not content with sitting there dribbling as babies we decide to explore the room by crawling, we then get bored of that and start to tentatively stand up and stumble around like a drunk (a role many of us return to in later life) and then we go to school and we have to run around the playground and, in my case, across Hampstead Heath in the pouring rain. This is when things start to get truly interesting. Some people stop there but others think 'If I can run maybe I can run for miles and miles and then jump out of a perfectly good aeroplane before freefalling on to a trampoline and then off a suspension bridge attached to a piece of elastic before severing the rope and landing in a white water raft and then waterskiing over Niagara falls before going home for my tea . . . on a snowboard'. Idiots all but in the interests of research I think it is important to pronounce on which dangerous sport is most likely to make your mum wrap her head in a cold towel and scream, 'Where did it all go wrong?

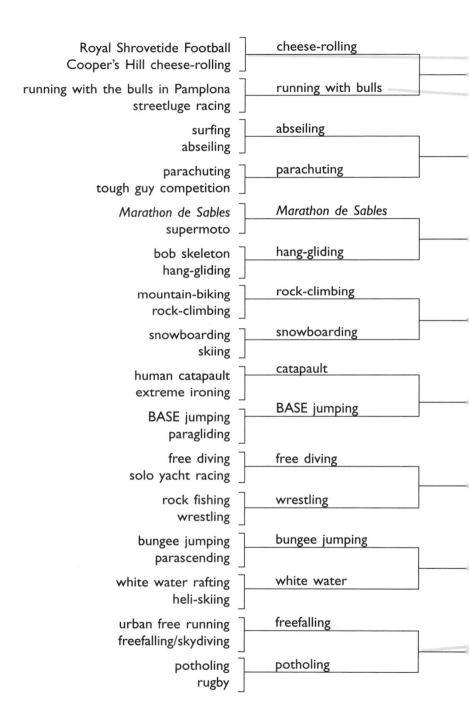

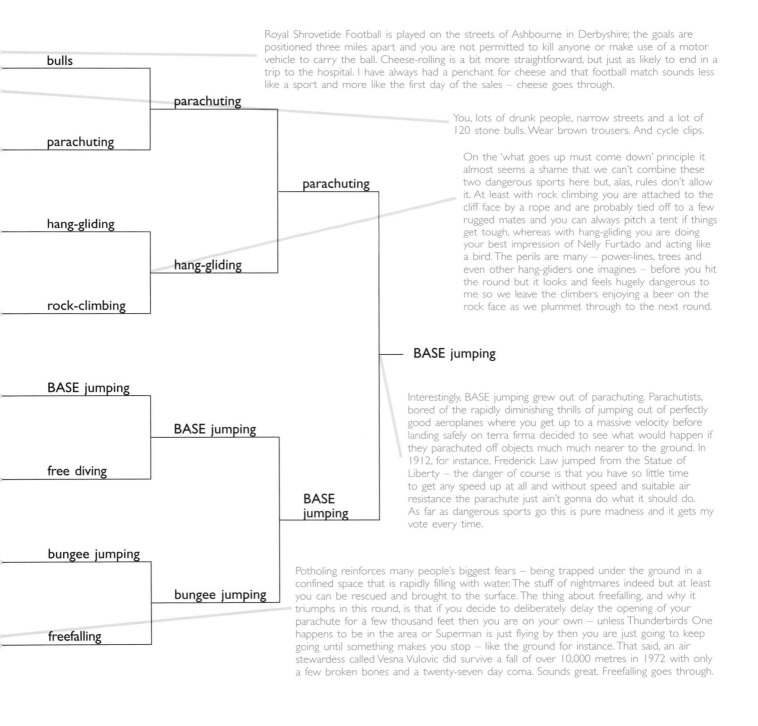

bulls

parachuting

parachuting

hang-gliding

rock-climbing

parachuting

hang-gliding

parachuting

BASE jumping

BASE jumping

free diving

BASE jumping

bungee jumping

bungee jumping

freefalling

BASE jumping

Royal Shrovetide Football is played on the streets of Ashbourne in Derbyshire; the goals are positioned three miles apart and you are not permitted to kill anyone or make use of a motor vehicle to carry the ball. Cheese-rolling is a bit more straightforward, but just as likely to end in a trip to the hospital. I have always had a penchant for cheese and that football match sounds less like a sport and more like the first day of the sales – cheese goes through.

You, lots of drunk people, narrow streets and a lot of 120 stone bulls. Wear brown trousers. And cycle clips.

On the 'what goes up must come down' principle it almost seems a shame that we can't combine these two dangerous sports here but, alas, rules don't allow it. At least with rock climbing you are attached to the cliff face by a rope and are probably tied off to a few rugged mates and you can always pitch a tent if things get tough, whereas with hang-gliding you are doing your best impression of Nelly Furtado and acting like a bird. The perils are many – power-lines, trees and even other hang-gliders one imagines – before you hit the round but it looks and feels hugely dangerous to me so we leave the climbers enjoying a beer on the rock face as we plummet through to the next round.

Interestingly, BASE jumping grew out of parachuting. Parachutists, bored of the rapidly diminishing thrills of jumping out of perfectly good aeroplanes where you get up to a massive velocity before landing safely on terra firma decided to see what would happen if they parachuted off objects much much nearer to the ground. In 1912, for instance, Frederick Law jumped from the Statue of Liberty – the danger of course is that you have so little time to get any speed up at all and without speed and suitable air resistance the parachute just ain't gonna do what it should do. As far as dangerous sports go this is pure madness and it gets my vote every time.

Potholing reinforces many people's biggest fears – being trapped under the ground in a confined space that is rapidly filling with water. The stuff of nightmares indeed but at least you can be rescued and brought to the surface. The thing about freefalling, and why it triumphs in this round, is that if you decide to deliberately delay the opening of your parachute for a few thousand feet then you are on your own – unless Thunderbirds One happens to be in the area or Superman is just flying by then you are just going to keep going until something makes you stop – like the ground for instance. That said, an air stewardess called Vesna Vulovic did survive a fall of over 10,000 metres in 1972 with only a few broken bones and a twenty-seven day coma. Sounds great. Freefalling goes through.

26

Desert Island Luxuries

by SIMON TREWIN

Desert Island Discs has been on BBC Radio 4 since 1942 and is the longest running music programme in the history of radio. We all know the formula — guests are invited to select eight pieces of music to accompany them to this mythical desert island and the presenter (Roy Plumley, Michael Parkinson, Sue Lawley and now Kirsty Young) use these choices as a springboard for discussion of the life story of the week's castaway. The music is always fairly interesting (although I am getting slightly fed up of hearing Elgar's Nimrod variations time and time and time again) but the best bit is when the celebrity is asked to choose a book and a luxury. We are not interested in the books here. People usually lie and choose something brainy just to look good. It is the luxuries we want to zoom in on. Personally my luxury would be SatNav but I suppose that wouldn't be allowed. Anyway, who gets our Robinson Crusoe award for best luxury and who remains lost forever?

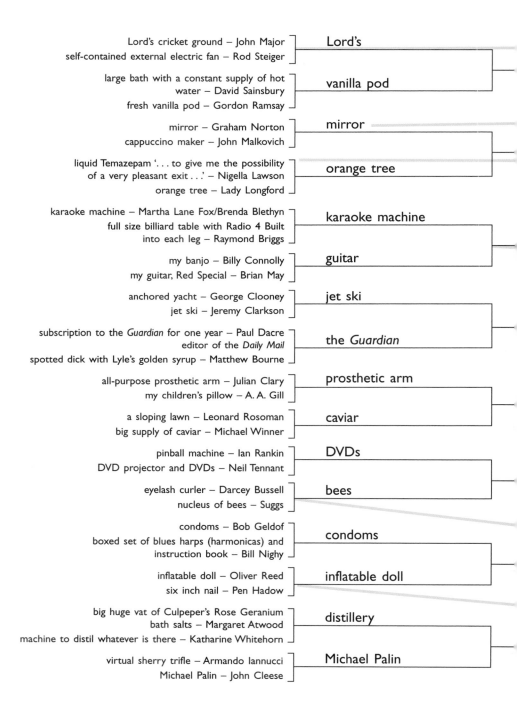

Lord's cricket ground — John Major
self-contained external electric fan — Rod Steiger
Lord's

large bath with a constant supply of hot water — David Sainsbury
fresh vanilla pod — Gordon Ramsay
vanilla pod

mirror — Graham Norton
cappuccino maker — John Malkovich
mirror

liquid Temazepam '. . . to give me the possibility of a very pleasant exit . . .' — Nigella Lawson
orange tree — Lady Longford
orange tree

karaoke machine — Martha Lane Fox/Brenda Blethyn
full size billiard table with Radio 4 Built into each leg — Raymond Briggs
karaoke machine

my banjo — Billy Connolly
my guitar, Red Special — Brian May
guitar

anchored yacht — George Clooney
jet ski — Jeremy Clarkson
jet ski

subscription to the *Guardian* for one year — Paul Dacre editor of the *Daily Mail*
spotted dick with Lyle's golden syrup — Matthew Bourne
the *Guardian*

all-purpose prosthetic arm — Julian Clary
my children's pillow — A. A. Gill
prosthetic arm

a sloping lawn — Leonard Rosoman
big supply of caviar — Michael Winner
caviar

pinball machine — Ian Rankin
DVD projector and DVDs — Neil Tennant
DVDs

eyelash curler — Darcey Bussell
nucleus of bees — Suggs
bees

condoms — Bob Geldof
boxed set of blues harps (harmonicas) and instruction book — Bill Nighy
condoms

inflatable doll — Oliver Reed
six inch nail — Pen Hadow
inflatable doll

big huge vat of Culpeper's Rose Geranium bath salts — Margaret Atwood
machine to distil whatever is there — Katharine Whitehorn
distillery

virtual sherry trifle — Armando Iannucci
Michael Palin — John Cleese
Michael Palin

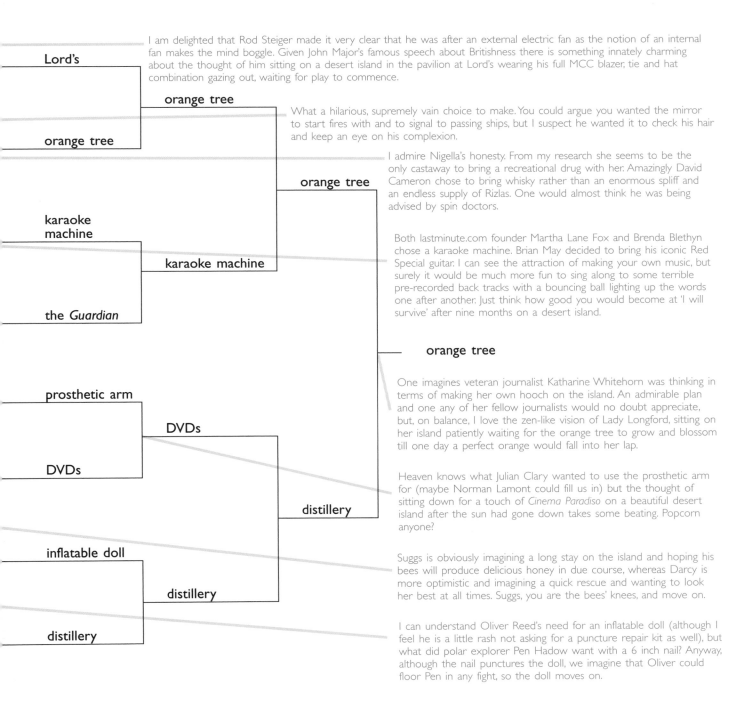

Lord's

orange tree

orange tree

I am delighted that Rod Steiger made it very clear that he was after an external electric fan as the notion of an internal fan makes the mind boggle. Given John Major's famous speech about Britishness there is something innately charming about the thought of him sitting on a desert island in the pavilion at Lord's wearing his full MCC blazer, tie and hat combination gazing out, waiting for play to commence.

What a hilarious, supremely vain choice to make. You could argue you wanted the mirror to start fires with and to signal to passing ships, but I suspect he wanted it to check his hair and keep an eye on his complexion.

orange tree

karaoke machine

karaoke machine

the *Guardian*

I admire Nigella's honesty. From my research she seems to be the only castaway to bring a recreational drug with her. Amazingly David Cameron chose to bring whisky rather than an enormous spliff and an endless supply of Rizlas. One would almost think he was being advised by spin doctors.

Both lastminute.com founder Martha Lane Fox and Brenda Blethyn chose a karaoke machine. Brian May decided to bring his iconic Red Special guitar. I can see the attraction of making your own music, but surely it would be much more fun to sing along to some terrible pre-recorded back tracks with a bouncing ball lighting up the words one after another. Just think how good you would become at 'I will survive' after nine months on a desert island.

orange tree

prosthetic arm

DVDs

DVDs

distillery

One imagines veteran journalist Katharine Whitehorn was thinking in terms of making her own hooch on the island. An admirable plan and one any of her fellow journalists would no doubt appreciate, but, on balance, I love the zen-like vision of Lady Longford, sitting on her island patiently waiting for the orange tree to grow and blossom till one day a perfect orange would fall into her lap.

Heaven knows what Julian Clary wanted to use the prosthetic arm for (maybe Norman Lamont could fill us in) but the thought of sitting down for a touch of *Cinema Paradiso* on a beautiful desert island after the sun had gone down takes some beating. Popcorn anyone?

inflatable doll

distillery

distillery

Suggs is obviously imagining a long stay on the island and hoping his bees will produce delicious honey in due course, whereas Darcy is more optimistic and imagining a quick rescue and wanting to look her best at all times. Suggs, you are the bees' knees, and move on.

I can understand Oliver Reed's need for an inflatable doll (although I feel he is a little rash not asking for a puncture repair kit as well), but what did polar explorer Pen Hadow want with a 6 inch nail? Anyway, although the nail punctures the doll, we imagine that Oliver could floor Pen in any fight, so the doll moves on.

27

Diarists
by ION TREWIN

The best, the most memorable diaries, those one turns to again and again, are – to quote Alan Clark, one of the all-time greats – 'sometimes lacking in charity; often trivial; occasionally lewd; cloyingly sentimental, repetitious, whingeing and imperfectly formed.' They are a phenomenon where the British excel. I could have included fictional diaries – Sue Townsend's Adrian Mole, Christopher Matthew's Crisp – but decided to restrict my selection to diarists recording, mostly, some aspect of work, and not just writers, but politicians, artists, actors and a theatre/film director. Why do people keep diaries? The answer to that is a book in itself. Michael Palin started his in his twenties as a replacement for smoking – and he's still writing enthrallingly every day. There are of course those who suggest that diarists are simply frustrated novelists, who wish to create an impression of verisimilitude. But Alan Clark's celebrated account of presenting a ministerial order to the House of Commons late one evening after a wine tasting when he imbibed wisely, but rather too much, improves on the Hansard official record only in the telling, not in the content. Great diaries are more often than not written by fine writers.

ION TREWIN juggles more in retirement than when he was editor-in-chief of a London publishers or when he was literary editor of The Times. He still edits, he administers the Man Booker prizes and he is writing the biography of Alan Clark, whose diaries he edited. He has never managed to keep a diary himself.

All day drawing. On the way to a quick office lunch pass a nun changing a wheel in Cromwell Road. Ashamed to say I don't stop to help. – Hugh Casson, 1980

Wrote all the morning, with infinite pleasure, which is queer . . . I know all the time there is no reason to be pleased with what I write, & that in 6 weeks or even days, I shall hate it. – Virginia Woolf, 1915

Put leeches on my throat, and whilst they were adhering read the romantic play translated by Mrs Sloman, which promises very well. – William Macready, 1838

The PM [Churchill] signed a number of books . . . and sent off presents to the King and Queen: a siren suit for the King and Fowler's English Usage for the Queen. – John Colville, 1940

I told the Queen how moved I had been by Prince Charles's Investiture, and she gaily shattered my sentimental illusions by saying that they were both struggling not to giggle because at the dress rehearsal the crown was too big and extinguished him like a candle-snuffer! – Noël Coward, 1969

Began reading Mrs Gaskell's North and South. I began with a great feeling of relief; I was reading something which had nothing to do with work. Within four chapters, I caught myself thinking of it as a film . . . – Peter Hall, 1973

Worked lazily – saw nothing distinctly. The model was exhausted and I was dull; and so, after five hours' twaddling I gave up. – B.R. Haydon, 1826

We have decided to try and invite someone every evening. We have scoured the island . . . Marty Feldman cannot be traced, though he's supposed to be here, as is Michael Caine . . . Celebrity note: the Michael Caine/Marty Feldman rumours have taken a bizarre twist. It appears that neither Marty nor Michael Caine are on the island, but Marti Caine is. – Michael Palin, 1978

Wrote six leaves today and am tired – that's all. – Walter Scott, 1827

I have discovered that I cannot burn the candle at one end and write a book with the other. – Katherine Mansfield, 1919

Children have all returned to school. The weather is delicious, the house is silent, there is no reason for me not to work. I will try one day soon. I did a little work. – Evelyn Waugh, 1956

On the hottest day of the year I saw two nuns buying a typewriter in Selfridges. Oh, what were they going to do with it? – Barbara Pym, 1939

This entry in my diary is an example of inadequate and unskilful diarizing. But, when all is said and done, leading a good life is more important than keeping a good diary. – Siegfried Sassoon, 1923

'You realize,' said Jack Bergel, 'what bringing this out now means?' This was Ego 4. 'It means that you regard your Diary as more important than the war.' I said, 'Well, isn't it? The war is vital, not important.' – James Agate, 1940

The archway exit from Speaker's Court was blocked by the PM's Jaguar. She [Margaret Thatcher] had just taken her seat, and as the detective's door slammed the interior light went out and the car slid away. I realized with a shock that this was in all probability her last night as Prime Minister. I came in with her. I go out with her. – Alan Clark, 1990

Pavlova dancing the dying swan. Feather falls off her dress. Two silent Englishmen. One says, 'Moulting'. That is all they say. – Arnold Bennett, 1911

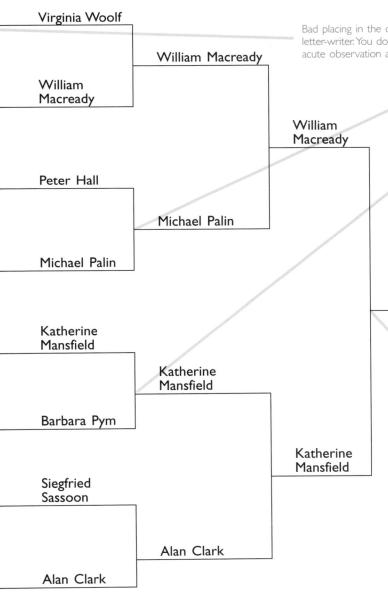

Bad placing in the draw for Casson. Woolf is a serious diarist, and letter-writer. You don't get many jokes. She goes through for her acute observation and insight into her own state of mind.

A tough call, but the Marti Caine story is not only a good gag, but it gains a point for being genuine. Palin goes into the next round ahead of Hall, who managed keeping a diary even in a busy life running the National Theatre. But he *dictated*. A point lost for not writing.

A novelist who was forgotten, but revived in her own lifetime thanks to Philip Larkin, Pym appears prim and maiden aunt-like, but inside her diaries is a woman not shy of occasionally baring her sexuality. Interesting that here, as with the artist Hugh Casson, what nuns do makes one smile. But Mansfield serves an ace to win the set.

Katherine Mansfield, 1919

No-one could have made up the leeches angle, but in the end I have to choose. Mansfield, the sole colonial, who might have gone on to be one of the all-time greats among literary diarists if she hadn't died aged thirty-five of TB. Even Macready's leeches would recoil against the Mansfield service.

28

Dickensian Names

by TIM MARTIN

Some people will tell you that the names of Charles Dickens's characters are one of English Literature's most valuable treasures, both charmingly quaint and insinuatingly suggestive, open to all kinds of intriguing onomastic scrutiny. And these people, clearly, have never worked where I used to work, in Wapping, East London, which is Dickens Country and positively determined that no one will ever forget it. You can barely cover two hundred metres without hitting a snack bar, or a pub, or, I don't know, a massage parlour named after a Dickens character. You eat lunch in Pumblechooks or Chuzzlewits; you nip in resignedly for a pint in the Dickens Inn; the Artful Dodger jealously guards the region's only pool table. So it goes on. If the names weren't already enough to make you grind your teeth, six months at Dickens Ground Zero will have you cursing the great man's name through bloody gums each lunchtime.

TIM MARTIN no longer works in Wapping. He also sincerely hopes that he isn't anyone else's Mr Slurk.

'Weevle' Jobling (*Bleak House*)
Seth Pecksniff (*Martin Chuzzlewit*) — **Pecksniff**

Luke Honeythunder (*The Mystery of Edwin Drood*)
Prince Turveydrop (*Bleak House*) — **Honeythunder**

Ebenezer Scrooge (*A Christmas Carol*)
John Peerybingle (*The Cricket on the Hearth*) — **Scrooge**

Anne Chickenstalker (*The Chimes*)
Dolge Orlick (*Great Expectations*) — **Chickenstalker**

Pleasant Riderhood (*Our Mutual Friend*)
Cleopatra Skewton (*Dombey & Son*) — **Riderhood**

Sophie Wackles (*The Old Curiosity Shop*)
Poll Sweedlepipe (*Martin Chuzzlewit*) — **Wackles**

Wackford Squeers (*Nicholas Nickleby*)
General Cyrus Choke (*Martin Chuzzlewit*) — **Squeers**

M'Choakumchild (*Hard Times*)
Newman Noggs (*Nicholas Nickleby*) — **M'Choakumchild**

Mr Slurk (*The Pickwick Papers*)
Silas Wegg (*Our Mutual Friend*) — **Slurk**

Peg Sliderskew (*Nicholas Nickleby*)
Montigue Tigg / Tigg Montigue (*Martin Chuzzlewit*) — **Sliderskew**

Ham Peggotty (*David Copperfield*)
Abel Magwitch (*Great Expectations*) — **Peggotty**

John Podsnap (*Our Mutual Friend*)
Volumnia Dedlock (*Bleak House*) — **Dedlock**

Edwin Drood (duh)
Jeremiah Flintwinch (*Little Dorrit*) — **Drood**

Sairey Gamp (*Martin Chuzzlewit*)
Miss Mowcher (*David Copperfield*) — **Gamp**

'Lord Chancellor' Krook (*Bleak House*)
Henrietta Petowker (*Nicholas Nickleby*) — **Krook**

Hiram Grewgious (*The Mystery of Edwin Drood*)
Caddy Jellyby (*Bleak House*) — **Grewgious**

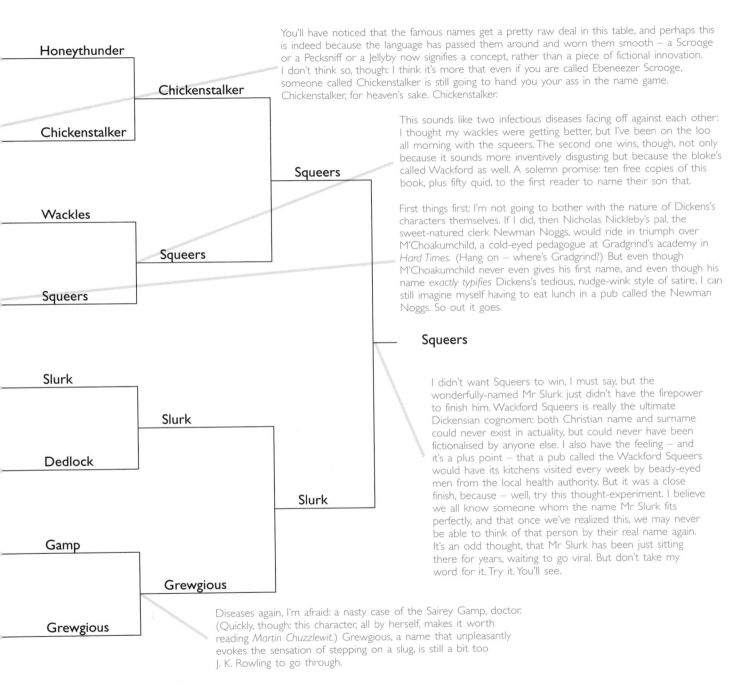

You'll have noticed that the famous names get a pretty raw deal in this table, and perhaps this is indeed because the language has passed them around and worn them smooth – a Scrooge or a Pecksniff or a Jellyby now signifies a concept, rather than a piece of fictional innovation. I don't think so, though: I think it's more that even if you are called Ebeneezer Scrooge, someone called Chickenstalker is still going to hand you your ass in the name game. Chickenstalker, for heaven's sake. Chickenstalker.

This sounds like two infectious diseases facing off against each other: I thought my wackles were getting better, but I've been on the loo all morning with the squeers. The second one wins, though, not only because it sounds more inventively disgusting but because the bloke's called Wackford as well. A solemn promise: ten free copies of this book, plus fifty quid, to the first reader to name their son that.

First things first: I'm not going to bother with the nature of Dickens's characters themselves. If I did, then Nicholas Nickleby's pal, the sweet-natured clerk Newman Noggs, would ride in triumph over M'Choakumchild, a cold-eyed pedagogue at Gradgrind's academy in *Hard Times*. (Hang on – where's Gradgrind?) But even though M'Choakumchild never even gives his first name, and even though his name *exactly typifies* Dickens's tedious, nudge-wink style of satire, I can still imagine myself having to eat lunch in a pub called the Newman Noggs. So out it goes.

I didn't want Squeers to win, I must say, but the wonderfully-named Mr Slurk just didn't have the firepower to finish him. Wackford Squeers is really the ultimate Dickensian cognomen: both Christian name and surname could never exist in actuality, but could never have been fictionalised by anyone else. I also have the feeling – and it's a plus point – that a pub called the Wackford Squeers would have its kitchens visited every week by beady-eyed men from the local health authority. But it was a close finish, because – well, try this thought-experiment. I believe we all know someone whom the name Mr Slurk fits perfectly, and that once we've realized this, we may never be able to think of that person by their real name again. It's an odd thought, that Mr Slurk has been just sitting there for years, waiting to go viral. But don't take my word for it. Try it. You'll see.

Diseases again, I'm afraid: a nasty case of the Sairey Gamp, doctor. (Quickly, though: this character, all by herself, makes it worth reading *Martin Chuzzlewit*.) Grewgious, a name that unpleasantly evokes the sensation of stepping on a slug, is still a bit too J. K. Rowling to go through.

29

Doctor Who Companions
by SIMON TREWIN

The BBC's never-ending serial *Doctor Who* about the time-travelling adventures of a mysterious problem-solving and wrong-righting man[1] known only as the Doctor may be the longest running science fiction television series in the world but for me it is really about the egg-boxes that seemed to cover the Dalek costumes, the quarries in which everything seemed to be filmed, Tom Baker's overlong scarf and, of course, Doctor Who's string of brainy companions. How deep this companionship went we were never sure but what with the conditions of that Tardis and those long journeys they were always going on we imagine things got pretty hot and steamy as they traversed the space-time continuum. They say you judge a person by his friends so, come on then, let's set the controls of the Tardis and find out who was the greatest of these fellow travellers.

Rose Tyler (Billie Piper) asst to Christopher Eccleston and David Tennant
Dr Grace Holloway (Daphne Ashbrook) asst to Paul McGann
— **Rose**

Dorothea Chaplet/Dodo (Jackie Lane) asst to William Hartnell
Captain Jack Harkness (John Barrowman) asst to Christopher Eccleston and David Tennant
— **Captain Jack**

Peri Brown (Nicola Bryant) asst to Peter Davison and Colin Baker
Adric (Matthew Waterhouse) asst to Peter Davison
— **Peri Brown**

Mel Bush (Bonnie Langford) asst to Colin Baker and Sylvester McCoy
Tegan Jovanka (Janet Fielding) asst to Peter Davison
— **Mel Bush**

Vislor Turlough (Mark Strickson) asst to Peter Davison
Adam Mitchell (Bruno Langley) asst to Christopher Eccleston
— **Vislor**

Kamelion (voiced by Gerald Flood) asst to Peter Davison
Sarah Jane Smith (Elisabeth Sladen) asst to John Pertwee and Tom Baker
— **Kamelion**

Harry Sullivan (Ian Marter) asst to Tom Baker
Leela (Louise Jameson) asst to Tom Baker
— **Leela**

K-9 Mark I (voiced by John Leeson) asst to Tom Baker
Romana (Mary Tamm then Lalla Ward) asst to Tom Baker
— **K-9 Mark I**

Nyssa (Sarah Sutton) asst to Tom Baker
Dr Elizabeth 'Liz' Shaw (Caroline John) asst to Jon Pertwee
— **Nyssa**

Josephine "Jo" Grant (Katy Manning) asst to Jon Pertwee
Ace (Sophie Aldred) asst to Sylvester McCoy
— **Josephine Grant**

Polly (Anneke Wills) asst to Patrick Troughton
Jamie McCrimmon (Frazer Hines) asst to Patrick Troughton
— **Jamie McCrimmon**

Victoria Waterfield (Deborah Watling) asst to Patrick Troughton
Zoe Heriot (Wendy Padbury) asst to Patrick Troughton
— **Victoria Waterfield**

Susan Foreman (Carole Ann Ford) asst to William Hartnell
Barbara Wright (Jacqueline Hill) asst to William Hartnell
— **Susan Foreman**

Ian Chesterton (William Russell) asst to William Hartnell
Vicki (Maureen O'Brien) asst to William Hartnell
— **Vicki**

Steven Taylor (Peter Purves) asst to William Hartnell
Sara Kingdom (Jean Marsh) asst to William Hartnell
— **Steven Taylor**

Polly (Anneke Wills) asst to William Hartnell
Ben Jackson (Michael Craze) asst to William Hartnell and Patrick Troughton
— **Ben Jackson**

To be honest, Dodo didn't get off to a great start – she stupidly entered the Tardis thinking it was a real Police Box and then managed to infect a community of space tourists with her cold which allowed their servants, the reptile-like Monoids, to plot and execute a successful rebellion. Doh! So when pitted against gorgeous pouting pansexual rogue Captain Jack Harkness she had no chance. Not only is he a total flirt but he managed to have a successful career as a soldier of fortune in more time periods than you can shake a fully loaded Tardis at. He even managed to help choose an actress to appear in *The Sound Of Music*. Move over Dodo – you're extinct.

The facts are simple – she was the posh daughter of Counsel Tremas who had been chosen to become the next Keeper but The Master regenerated and merged with Nyssa's dad leaving her orphaned. But actually why she has zoomed through so many rounds to end up here in the semi-finals is because the BBC decided to give her shorter and shorter costumes and many Dads decided this was a great time to do some father-son bonding and watch *Doctor Who* with their children. Alas though she is no match in the nation's affections when it comes to that wonderful little cuboid canine creation – the little loyal robot with a mind of his own and a rather powerful blaster. He is as iconic as the Tardis and Tom Baker's scarf so we salute you K-9 as the winner of our quest.

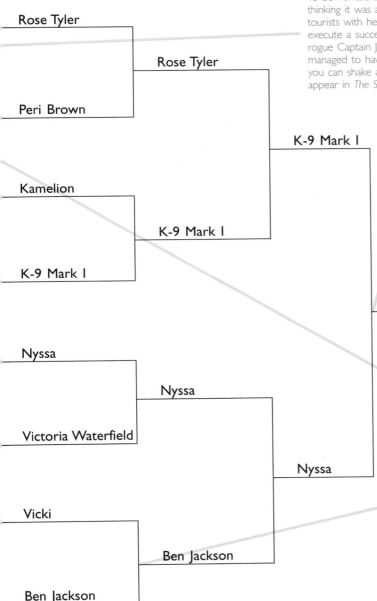

K-9 Mark I

We can make a great case for Miss Perpugilliam Brown – she was a babelicious teenage American botany student holidaying in Lanzarote, rescued when she tried to swim to shore, she helped the Doctor through a particularly nasty regeneration and was generally a great companion. That said there is the small matter of her being possessed by aliens and maybe being murdered (opinions differ). But she wins over Mel Bush for two reasons and two reasons alone – Bonnie and Langford.

Ben was a bit of a dude really – for starters he met the Doctor not in the middle of a disused quarry in Wales but in the Inferno nightclub while on shore leave from his real job as a sailor. Hello! He unwittingly ended up in the Tardis (along with Professor Brett's secretary Polly) and took part in one of the greatest episodes of *Doctor Who* ever when those gleeful villains the Cybermen appeared. He even got to see the Doctor regenerating. Vicki's discovery was more dramatic but slightly less exciting – she was one of two survivors in a crashed Earth space craft in the twenty-fifth century on the planet Dido. Dido vs Inferno – not looking good for Vicki is it? It has to be said that they both end up dumping on the poor Doctor – Vicki ran off with Troilus (in ancient Troy) and changed her name to Cressida and Ben, of course, ran off with Polly. On balance though that whole Sailor/Nightclub/Cybermen combi wins out hands down.

30

Emoticons
by J. D. BIERSDORFER

In the disembodied world of bites and bytes, hundreds of emoticons roam the Internet and have done so since computer geeks, armed with a handful of common punctuation symbols, looked for simple ways to represent mood and facial expression in basic e-mail communications. (Tilt your head to the left to get the picture.) Emoticons can be annoying, even childish, but these rudimentary graphics provide necessary nuance and meaning to words that might be misinterpreted when read and not spoken. This is a battle to be the most recognizable and creative representations of voiceless conversations. (Keep your head tilted.)

J. D. BIERSDORFER writes about art and technology for the *New York Times* and is also the author of *iPod & iTunes: The Missing Manual* and coauthor of *The Internet: The Missing Manual.*

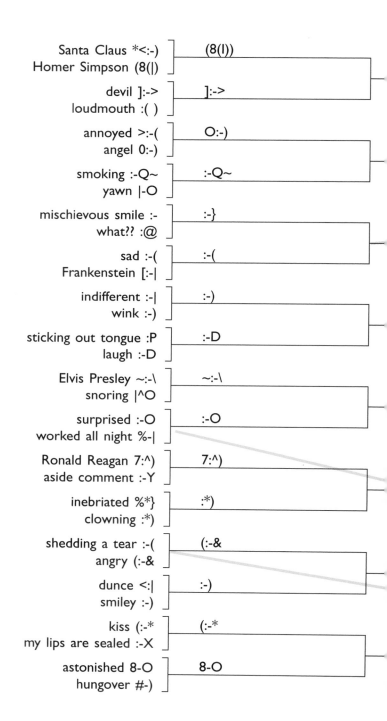

Santa Claus *<:-)
Homer Simpson (8(|)   (8(|))

devil]:->
loudmouth :( )   ]:->

annoyed >:-(
angel 0:-)   O:-)

smoking :-Q~
yawn |-O   :-Q~

mischievous smile :-
what?? :@   :-}

sad :-(
Frankenstein [:-| :-(

indifferent :-|
wink :-)   :-)

sticking out tongue :P
laugh :-D   :-D

Elvis Presley ~:-\
snoring |^O   ~:-\

surprised :-O
worked all night %-| :-O

Ronald Reagan 7:^)
aside comment :-Y   7:^)

inebriated %*}
clowning :*)   :*)

shedding a tear :-(
angry (:-&   (:-&

dunce <:|
smiley :-)   :-)

kiss (:-*
my lips are sealed :-X   (:-*

astonished 8-O
hungover #-)   8-O

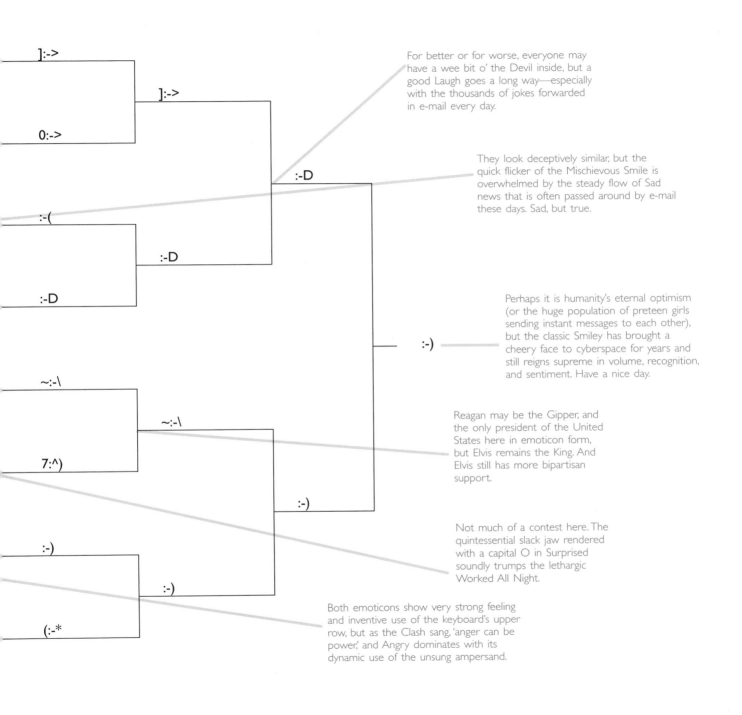

]:->

]:->

0:->

:-D

:-(

:-D

:-D

For better or for worse, everyone may have a wee bit o' the Devil inside, but a good Laugh goes a long way—especially with the thousands of jokes forwarded in e-mail every day.

They look deceptively similar, but the quick flicker of the Mischievous Smile is overwhelmed by the steady flow of Sad news that is often passed around by e-mail these days. Sad, but true.

:-)

Perhaps it is humanity's eternal optimism (or the huge population of preteen girls sending instant messages to each other), but the classic Smiley has brought a cheery face to cyberspace for years and still reigns supreme in volume, recognition, and sentiment. Have a nice day.

~:-\

~:-\

7:^)

:-)

Reagan may be the Gipper, and the only president of the United States here in emoticon form, but Elvis remains the King. And Elvis still has more bipartisan support.

:-)

:-)

Not much of a contest here. The quintessential slack jaw rendered with a capital O in Surprised soundly trumps the lethargic Worked All Night.

(:-*

Both emoticons show very strong feeling and inventive use of the keyboard's upper row, but as the Clash sang, 'anger can be power,' and Angry dominates with its dynamic use of the unsung ampersand.

31

Eskimo Words for Snow

by SIMON TREWIN

It may be that we all suffer from false-memory syndrome when it comes to snow and our childhoods but there certainly did seem to be a lot more of it around way back then. I remember waist-deep snow, tobogganing madly on Hampstead Heath, school being shut because of frozen pipes, sliding cars spinning on black ice and enormous snowmen (and snow women and even snow cats) taking up residence in our garden for what seemed like weeks on end until they eventually melted away leaving just a hat and a frozen carrot on the ground. We talked endlessly about snow, blizzards, sleet and then eventually slush from early December to late February but now snow is a rare visitor to these isles. If we get one or two days' snow in the South East we are pretty lucky and on most occasions it struggles to get to tea-time without all traces of it disappearing. So when I read in *Snow Falling On Cedars* that the Eskimo have hundreds of words for snow I was intrigued and puzzled. Then I realised that if you live in a world where snow was the norm and it lay on the ground for months on end then you would need words to differentiate every nuance.

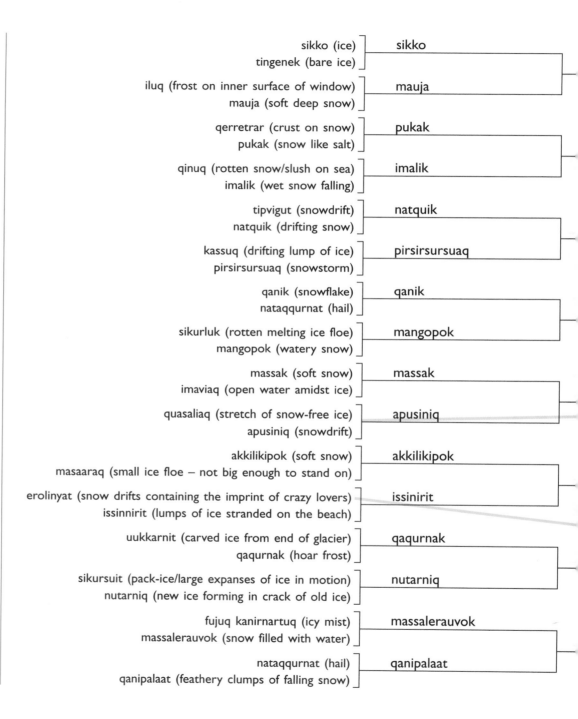

sikko (ice) — sikko
tingenek (bare ice)

iluq (frost on inner surface of window) — mauja
mauja (soft deep snow)

qerretrar (crust on snow) — pukak
pukak (snow like salt)

qinuq (rotten snow/slush on sea) — imalik
imalik (wet snow falling)

tipvigut (snowdrift) — natquik
natquik (drifting snow)

kassuq (drifting lump of ice) — pirsirsursuaq
pirsirsursuaq (snowstorm)

qanik (snowflake) — qanik
nataqqurnat (hail)

sikurluk (rotten melting ice floe) — mangopok
mangopok (watery snow)

massak (soft snow) — massak
imaviaq (open water amidst ice)

quasaliaq (stretch of snow-free ice) — apusiniq
apusiniq (snowdrift)

akkilikipok (soft snow) — akkilikipok
masaaraq (small ice floe – not big enough to stand on)

erolinyat (snow drifts containing the imprint of crazy lovers) — issinirit
issinnirit (lumps of ice stranded on the beach)

uukkarnit (carved ice from end of glacier) — qaqurnak
qaqurnak (hoar frost)

sikursuit (pack-ice/large expanses of ice in motion) — nutarniq
nutarniq (new ice forming in crack of old ice)

fujuq kanirnartuq (icy mist) — massalerauvok
massalerauvok (snow filled with water)

nataqqurnat (hail) — qanipalaat
qanipalaat (feathery clumps of falling snow)

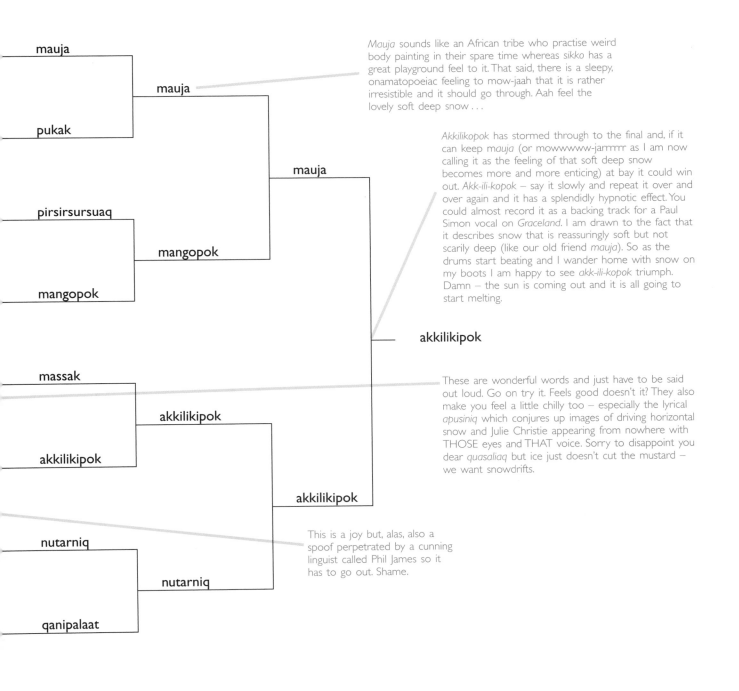

mauja

mauja

pukak

mauja

mauja

pirsirsursuaq

mangopok

mangopok

akkilikipok

massak

akkilikipok

akkilikipok

akkilikipok

akkilikipok

nutarniq

nutarniq

nutarniq

qanipalaat

Mauja sounds like an African tribe who practise weird body painting in their spare time whereas *sikko* has a great playground feel to it. That said, there is a sleepy, onamatopoeiac feeling to mow-jaah that it is rather irresistible and it should go through. Aah feel the lovely soft deep snow . . .

Akkilikopok has stormed through to the final and, if it can keep *mauja* (or mowwwww-jarrrrrr as I am now calling it as the feeling of that soft deep snow becomes more and more enticing) at bay it could win out. *Akk-ili-kopok* – say it slowly and repeat it over and over again and it has a splendidly hypnotic effect. You could almost record it as a backing track for a Paul Simon vocal on *Graceland*. I am drawn to the fact that it describes snow that is reassuringly soft but not scarily deep (like our old friend *mauja*). So as the drums start beating and I wander home with snow on my boots I am happy to see *akk-ili-kopok* triumph. Damn – the sun is coming out and it is all going to start melting.

These are wonderful words and just have to be said out loud. Go on try it. Feels good doesn't it? They also make you feel a little chilly too – especially the lyrical *apusiniq* which conjures up images of driving horizontal snow and Julie Christie appearing from nowhere with THOSE eyes and THAT voice. Sorry to disappoint you dear *quasaliaq* but ice just doesn't cut the mustard – we want snowdrifts.

This is a joy but, alas, also a spoof perpetrated by a cunning linguist called Phil James so it has to go out. Shame.

32

Estate Agent Speak

by SIMON TREWIN

There is a creative art to drafting those enticing ads that grace the pages of the Saturday property sections and the estate agent details that proliferate on the web. The art is basically one of making silk purses out of sow ears, encouraging you to schlep half way across town in rush hour traffic to view a 'must-see opportunity to be part of a compact development in urban living'. Chances are it will turn out to be a tiny one-bedroom, erm, room with en-suite kettle in a converted slaughterhouse on some wasteland overlooked by the sort of tower block that even Banksy would think twice about venturing into. We are now wising up to their evil ways but I still love being led up the garden path (sorry – that should read 'being led up the meandering hand-laid York stone patio-style approach through the country cottage garden). Step this way . . .

Good decorative order. (Recently painted white throughout.)
Original features. (Lead pipes, septic tank and a tramp living in the basement stairwell.)

Priced to sell. (PLEASE JUST BUY IT!)
Viewing recommended at earliest opportunity. (We are desperate to sell.)

Studio flat. (You can hoover the whole flat from one socket.)
An area popular with young professionals. (Families know better.)

Run-down. (Doesn't currently have a roof.)
Family bathroom. (As opposed to what, exactly?)

A wealth of exposed beams. (Would suit crouching dwarf.)
Investment opportunity. (Currently a squat.)

Character property. (Not for the faint hearted.)
Within walking distance of local shops. (Adjacent to SavaCentre carpark.)

Mainly laid to lawn. (The rest of the garden is laid to rubble.)
Period property. (Built anytime before 1976 – when the Estate Agent was born.)

Would benefit from some cosmetic updating. (A complete tip.)
Villagey atmosphere. (Surrounded by curtain-twitchers.)

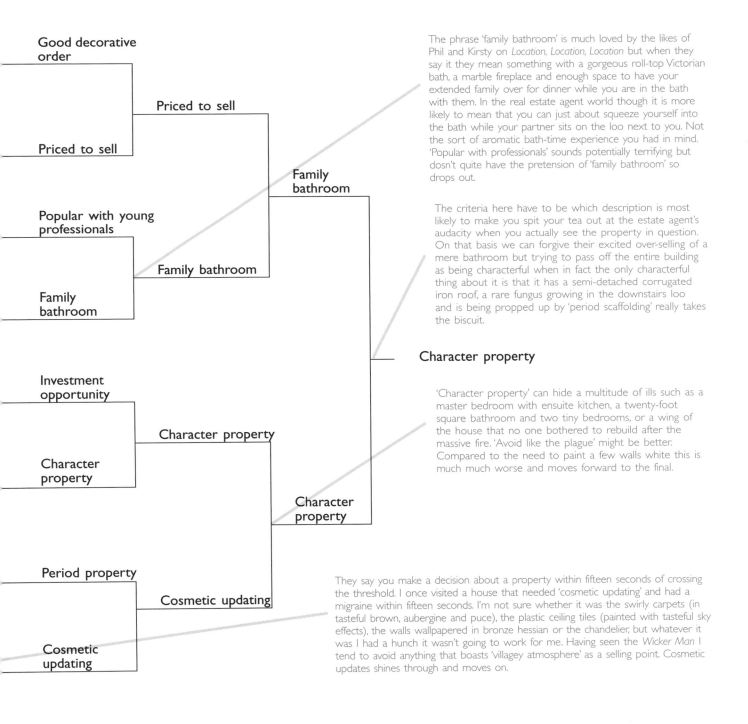

Good decorative
order

Priced to sell

Priced to sell

Popular with young
professionals

Family bathroom

Family
bathroom

Priced to sell

Family
bathroom

Investment
opportunity

Character property

Character
property

Character
property

Period property

Cosmetic updating

Cosmetic
updating

Character
property

Character property

The phrase 'family bathroom' is much loved by the likes of Phil and Kirsty on *Location, Location, Location* but when they say it they mean something with a gorgeous roll-top Victorian bath, a marble fireplace and enough space to have your extended family over for dinner while you are in the bath with them. In the real estate agent world though it is more likely to mean that you can just about squeeze yourself into the bath while your partner sits on the loo next to you. Not the sort of aromatic bath-time experience you had in mind. 'Popular with professionals' sounds potentially terrifying but doesn't quite have the pretension of 'family bathroom' so drops out.

The criteria here have to be which description is most likely to make you spit your tea out at the estate agent's audacity when you actually see the property in question. On that basis we can forgive their excited over-selling of a mere bathroom but trying to pass off the entire building as being characterful when in fact the only characterful thing about it is that it has a semi-detached corrugated iron roof, a rare fungus growing in the downstairs loo and is being propped up by 'period scaffolding' really takes the biscuit.

'Character property' can hide a multitude of ills such as a master bedroom with ensuite kitchen, a twenty-foot square bathroom and two tiny bedrooms, or a wing of the house that no one bothered to rebuild after the massive fire. 'Avoid like the plague' might be better. Compared to the need to paint a few walls white this is much much worse and moves forward to the final.

They say you make a decision about a property within fifteen seconds of crossing the threshold. I once visited a house that needed 'cosmetic updating' and had a migraine within fifteen seconds. I'm not sure whether it was the swirly carpets (in tasteful brown, aubergine and puce), the plastic ceiling tiles (painted with tasteful sky effects), the walls wallpapered in bronze hessian or the chandelier, but whatever it was I had a hunch it wasn't going to work for me. Having seen the *Wicker Man* I tend to avoid anything that boasts 'villagey atmosphere' as a selling point. Cosmetic updates shines through and moves on.

33

Everyday Complaints

by SIMON TREWIN

You can tell a lot about a nation from how people complain and what they complain about. Americans complain very loudly about things that the British are happy to put up with. The French will complain with a lot of tutting about things that no one else will see any problem with at all. Everyone else will happily complain about the French given half a chance. I rarely complain out loud, instead I mutter a lot and wish things were otherwise when it's too late. Being British I have even done that inexplicable thing of sitting with a table of other Brits complaining about the rubbish service, lukewarm food and terrible muzak only to smile sweetly and say, 'Oh, thank you. Everything's lovely!' when the waitress breezes by to check on us. So I was thrilled to see that the Finnish artists Tellervo Kalleinen and Oliver Kochta-Kalleinen have initiated a number of community-based complaints choirs worldwide who compose songs by, with, and about their local cities. Look no further than www.youtube.com or www.complaintschoir.org to see what a joy this all is. The Birmingham choir one, for instance, is totally addictive and I even found myself singing it in the bath the other night. In the interests of research I decided to look beyond just Brum and see what the inhabitants of three other fine cities – Hamburg, Helsinki and St Petersburg – wanted to complain about. Think of this as a European Complaints Contest but without the withering charm of Terry Wogan.

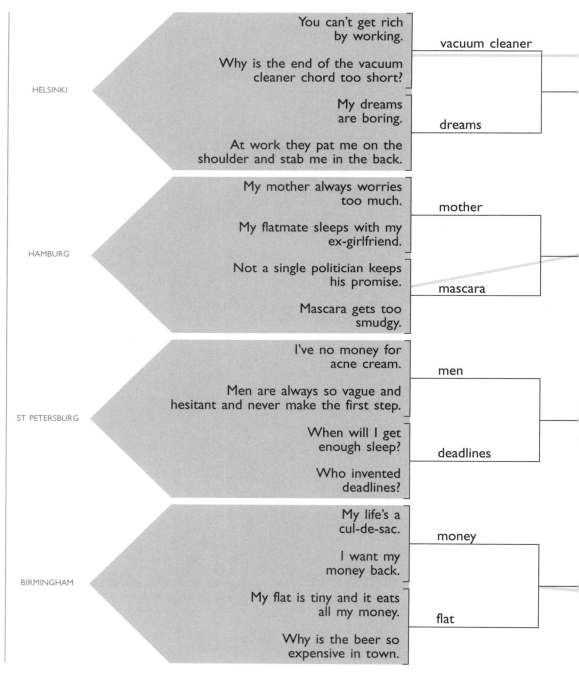

HELSINKI

You can't get rich by working.

Why is the end of the vacuum cleaner chord too short?

My dreams are boring.

At work they pat me on the shoulder and stab me in the back.

HAMBURG

My mother always worries too much.

My flatmate sleeps with my ex-girlfriend.

Not a single politician keeps his promise.

Mascara gets too smudgy.

ST PETERSBURG

I've no money for acne cream.

Men are always so vague and hesitant and never make the first step.

When will I get enough sleep?

Who invented deadlines?

BIRMINGHAM

My life's a cul-de-sac.

I want my money back.

My flat is tiny and it eats all my money.

Why is the beer so expensive in town.

vacuum cleaner

dreams

mother

mascara

men

deadlines

money

flat

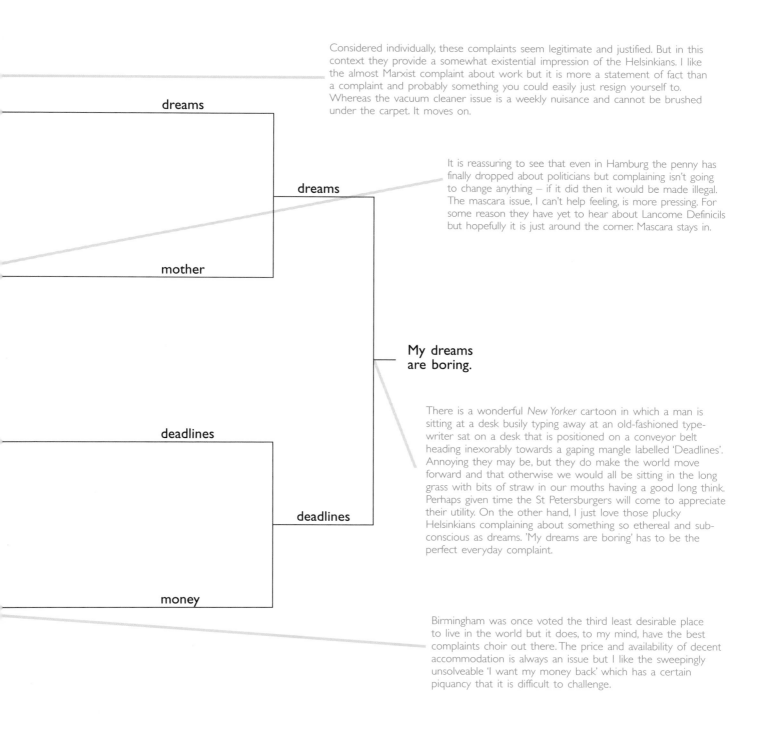

Considered individually, these complaints seem legitimate and justified. But in this context they provide a somewhat existential impression of the Helsinkians. I like the almost Marxist complaint about work but it is more a statement of fact than a complaint and probably something you could easily just resign yourself to. Whereas the vacuum cleaner issue is a weekly nuisance and cannot be brushed under the carpet. It moves on.

It is reassuring to see that even in Hamburg the penny has finally dropped about politicians but complaining isn't going to change anything — if it did then it would be made illegal. The mascara issue, I can't help feeling, is more pressing. For some reason they have yet to hear about Lancome Definicils but hopefully it is just around the corner. Mascara stays in.

dreams

dreams

mother

My dreams are boring.

deadlines

deadlines

money

There is a wonderful *New Yorker* cartoon in which a man is sitting at a desk busily typing away at an old-fashioned type-writer sat on a desk that is positioned on a conveyor belt heading inexorably towards a gaping mangle labelled 'Deadlines'. Annoying they may be, but they do make the world move forward and that otherwise we would all be sitting in the long grass with bits of straw in our mouths having a good long think. Perhaps given time the St Petersburgers will come to appreciate their utility. On the other hand, I just love those plucky Helsinkians complaining about something so ethereal and sub-conscious as dreams. 'My dreams are boring' has to be the perfect everyday complaint.

Birmingham was once voted the third least desirable place to live in the world but it does, to my mind, have the best complaints choir out there. The price and availability of decent accommodation is always an issue but I like the sweepingly unsolveable 'I want my money back' which has a certain piquancy that it is difficult to challenge.

34

Fairy Tales
by HELEN ADIE

Listen to the magical words 'Once upon a time' and you enter into an imaginary world where good and bad are sharply delineated, where things like wishes and tasks happen in threes, and where journeys and adventures will lead through danger to resolution. Who could forget the cruel temptation of the gingerbread house or the devious wolf dressed up in Granny's frilly cap? Few of our most well-known tales actually contain fairies, but they have plenty of witches, step-mothers and eccentrics instead. There are some marvellous lesser known tales to consider, but I have chosen to focus on the most widely known and even here there are bound to be omissions. Which story, I wonder, will it be? Let me see . . .

HELEN ADIE has been variously a mother, actress, teacher, poet and artist but still manages to remain young at heart.

Hansel and Gretel
Sleeping Beauty

The Emperor's New Clothes
The Princess and the Pea

Goldilocks and the Three Bears
Little Red Riding Hood

Rapunzel
Cinderella

The Ugly Duckling
Snow White and the Seven Dwarves

The Three Little Pigs
Rumpelstiltskin

Bluebeard
Beauty and the Beast

Sleeping Beauty
Jack and the Beanstalk

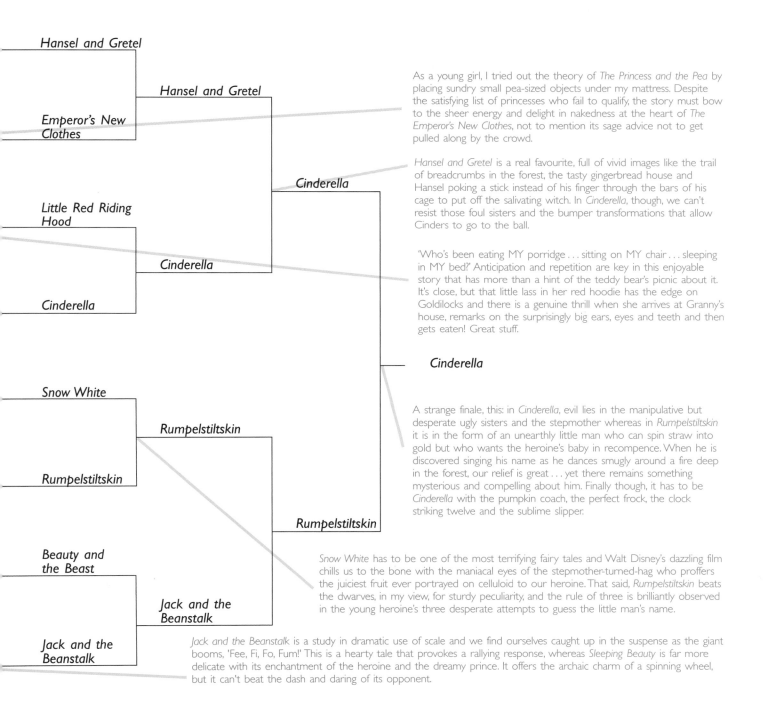

Hansel and Gretel

Emperor's New Clothes

Hansel and Gretel

Little Red Riding Hood

Cinderella

Cinderella

Cinderella

Snow White

Rumpelstiltskin

Rumpelstiltskin

Beauty and the Beast

Jack and the Beanstalk

Jack and the Beanstalk

Rumpelstiltskin

Cinderella

As a young girl, I tried out the theory of *The Princess and the Pea* by placing sundry small pea-sized objects under my mattress. Despite the satisfying list of princesses who fail to qualify, the story must bow to the sheer energy and delight in nakedness at the heart of *The Emperor's New Clothes*, not to mention its sage advice not to get pulled along by the crowd.

Hansel and Gretel is a real favourite, full of vivid images like the trail of breadcrumbs in the forest, the tasty gingerbread house and Hansel poking a stick instead of his finger through the bars of his cage to put off the salivating witch. In *Cinderella*, though, we can't resist those foul sisters and the bumper transformations that allow Cinders to go to the ball.

'Who's been eating MY porridge . . . sitting on MY chair . . . sleeping in MY bed?' Anticipation and repetition are key in this enjoyable story that has more than a hint of the teddy bear's picnic about it. It's close, but that little lass in her red hoodie has the edge on Goldilocks and there is a genuine thrill when she arrives at Granny's house, remarks on the surprisingly big ears, eyes and teeth and then gets eaten! Great stuff.

A strange finale, this: in *Cinderella*, evil lies in the manipulative but desperate ugly sisters and the stepmother whereas in *Rumpelstiltskin* it is in the form of an unearthly little man who can spin straw into gold but who wants the heroine's baby in recompense. When he is discovered singing his name as he dances smugly around a fire deep in the forest, our relief is great . . . yet there remains something mysterious and compelling about him. Finally though, it has to be *Cinderella* with the pumpkin coach, the perfect frock, the clock striking twelve and the sublime slipper.

Snow White has to be one of the most terrifying fairy tales and Walt Disney's dazzling film chills us to the bone with the maniacal eyes of the stepmother-turned-hag who proffers the juiciest fruit ever portrayed on celluloid to our heroine. That said, *Rumpelstiltskin* beats the dwarves, in my view, for sturdy peculiarity, and the rule of three is brilliantly observed in the young heroine's three desperate attempts to guess the little man's name.

Jack and the Beanstalk is a study in dramatic use of scale and we find ourselves caught up in the suspense as the giant booms, 'Fee, Fi, Fo, Fum!' This is a hearty tale that provokes a rallying response, whereas *Sleeping Beauty* is far more delicate with its enchantment of the heroine and the dreamy prince. It offers the archaic charm of a spinning wheel, but it can't beat the dash and daring of its opponent.

35

Family Games
by SIMON TREWIN

Say the word 'games' to anyone under the age of 24 and they will immediately think of the Nintendo Wii, the Playstation 2 and the latest KillFightRunBurnDie sensaround experience from those cuddly humanitarians in silicon valley. So big apologies to any of you 'kids' reading this (if indeed you can read) as you probably won't understand the antediluvian notion of a family sitting around a table talking to each other and playing proper games involving laminated cardboard, dice and Dad getting a bit cross while Mum asks for the rules to be explained again. I bought my friend Geoff a hilarious diecast metal horses/canvas/rubber-band racecourse combi racing game called *Escalado* from ebay two years ago which brought back memories from his childhood and we had a fantastic time playing it. Even game-meisters Jack B, Bobsleigh and Jack T got involved and even forgave it for not having batteries, a wireless remote or a dedicated website with 'cheats' and 'tips'. Just. Anyway — which games will stay on top of the wardrobe in the spare room and which will make it on to the kitchen table?

The Mousetrap box promises so much — a finely engineered collection of machine-tooled plastic components that get slotted together to create a hilarious chain reaction of metal balls, weird spiral staircase, diving board, swimming pool, all culminating in the descent of the huge cage on to your opponent's mouse. The reality is perhaps not quite as hilarious but still gives you a good bang for your buck. It doesn't, though, have the tantric brain-frying potential of the timeless Scrabble. See number 77 for wicked ways of sharpening your game. Scrabble has to win this round.

Monopoly
Cluedo

Mousetrap
Scrabble

Cranium
Backgammon

Battleships
Taboo

Risk
Frustration

Chess
Ludo

Drafts
Snakes and Ladders

Pictionary
Trivial Pursuit

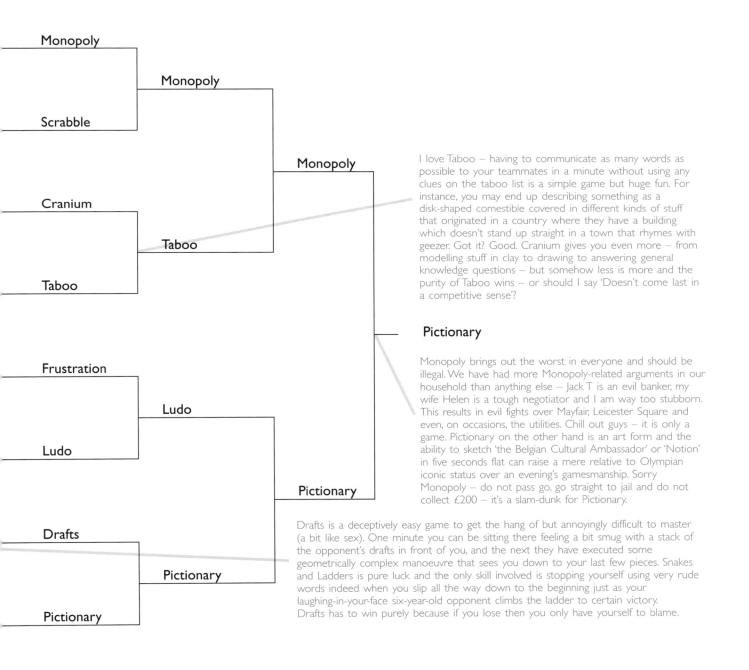

Monopoly

Monopoly
Scrabble

Monopoly

Cranium

Taboo

Taboo

Monopoly

Pictionary

I love Taboo – having to communicate as many words as possible to your teammates in a minute without using any clues on the taboo list is a simple game but huge fun. For instance, you may end up describing something as a disk-shaped comestible covered in different kinds of stuff that originated in a country where they have a building which doesn't stand up straight in a town that rhymes with geezer. Got it? Good. Cranium gives you even more – from modelling stuff in clay to drawing to answering general knowledge questions – but somehow less is more and the purity of Taboo wins – or should I say 'Doesn't come last in a competitive sense'?

Frustration

Ludo

Ludo

Pictionary

Monopoly brings out the worst in everyone and should be illegal. We have had more Monopoly-related arguments in our household than anything else – Jack T is an evil banker; my wife Helen is a tough negotiator and I am way too stubborn. This results in evil fights over Mayfair, Leicester Square and even, on occasions, the utilities. Chill out guys – it is only a game. Pictionary on the other hand is an art form and the ability to sketch 'the Belgian Cultural Ambassador' or 'Notion' in five seconds flat can raise a mere relative to Olympian iconic status over an evening's gamesmanship. Sorry Monopoly – do not pass go, go straight to jail and do not collect £200 – it's a slam-dunk for Pictionary.

Drafts

Pictionary

Pictionary

Drafts is a deceptively easy game to get the hang of but annoyingly difficult to master (a bit like sex). One minute you can be sitting there feeling a bit smug with a stack of the opponent's drafts in front of you, and the next they have executed some geometrically complex manoeuvre that sees you down to your last few pieces. Snakes and Ladders is pure luck and the only skill involved is stopping yourself using very rude words indeed when you slip all the way down to the beginning just as your laughing-in-your-face six-year-old opponent climbs the ladder to certain victory. Drafts has to win purely because if you lose then you only have yourself to blame.

36

Famous Couples
by CLARE BENNETT

It's hard to know how to judge this one – should I go for love brands Beckham or Blair? Becks could win on looks alone – Cherie can't help lovin' that man of hers, even though everyone else thinks he's a tosser, which is quite sweet. There are those who found their soul mate and a deal with *OK! Magazine* on the telly, like the Andres, who now so obligingly share their most intimate details with anyone who cares to listen, pouting in an amorous embrace under admirable headlines like 'How often we have sex and what it's like.' In stark contrast we have killjoys Jay-Z and Beyonce, who pretend they're not actually going out, annoyingly won't say a word about the other one and therefore must be penalized for being so damn private – you belong to us, not each other, what's wrong with you people?!!

The first man CLARE BENNETT ever loved was Jesus. She then started a serious relationship with Harrison Ford when she was seven that lasted several years, but dumped him when he had a mid life crisis, got his ear pierced and started taking barging holidays in North Wales. She was lost in love's Bermuda Triangle of obvious pretty boys for most of her teens, charging through Rob Lowe, River Phoenix, Mark *and* Robbie from Take That, Keanu Reeves, Johnny Depp blah blah blah. But with age and experience comes wisdom and the older man (ask Catherine Zeta-Jones) and she is now happily settled in an entirely imaginary relationship with Sir David Attenborough.

Tom and Katie

Elton and David

Kate and Pete

Charlotte and Gavin

Preston and Chantelle

Tony and Cherie

Posh and Becks

Beyonce and Jay-Z

Madonna and Guy

Chris and Gwyneth

Brad and Angelina

Cheryl and Ashley

Charles and Camilla

Elizabeth and Arun

Jordan and Peter

Catherine and Michael

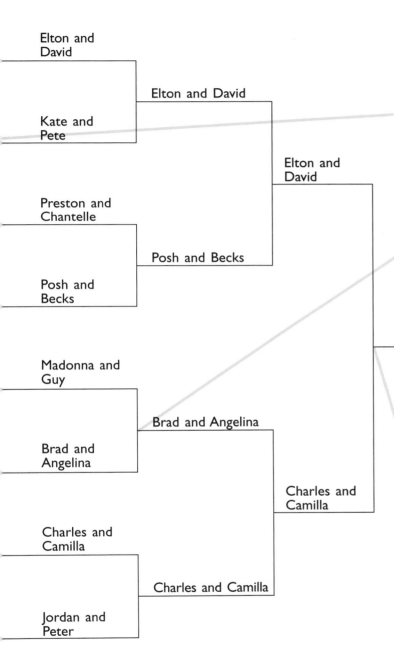

Elton and David

Kate and Pete

Elton and David

Preston and Chantelle

Posh and Becks

Posh and Becks

Elton and David

Madonna and Guy

Brad and Angelina

Brad and Angelina

Charles and Camilla

Charles and Camilla

Charles and Camilla

Jordan and Peter

A lot of people were quite down on Kate Moss, Pete Doherty and their no good smacked up ways. While *I* could never see the attraction in a bleary-eyed dragon chaser who appears to speak without the use of consonants, he did manage to bag Croydon's hottest girl in skinny jeans for a time, so he's clearly got more than a wrap of coke up his sleeve. Alternatively, we have glorious Welsh beef cakes Charlotte Church and Gavin Hewson, who I love, but are smoked out in a cloud of purple haze by *La belle et la bête*.

And so to the rainbow families. Madonna and Guy's was a pretty straightforward 'boy meets world's most massive star and then marries her with almost alarming normality' story. Brad and Ange decided to play a bit of cat and mouse, using the shoot of *Mr and Mrs Smith* as a cheeky bit of foreplay before abandoning all and running off round the world to gather babies. Jennifer Aniston's a doll, but quite frankly even I'd leave my wife for Angelina, so the Jolie-Pitts and their absurd good looks must make the next round.

Charles and Camilla

Roll up your sleeves for the Clash of the Titles. In one corner we have the mighty love story that is Sir Elton and Lady John. It was a great day for equality when, as the *Sun* so magnificently put it, 'Elton took David up the aisle.' However, I am unable to resist this other power house of love (or Windsor) – bow your head, or do a little curtsey, and show some R.E.S.P.E.C.T. for the royal love birds who, after years of dodging about fancying each other from afar at polo matches (and in close proximity at other times) finally triumphed over adversity, turning to the world and saying, 'We jolly well love each other, get over it.' That leaves one question: was the first dance at their wedding to 'Your Love is King' by Sade or 'Let Love Rule' by Lenny Kravitz?

What a happy ending. True Love, thy name is Charles and Camilla.

37

Famous Last Words

by SIMON TREWIN

When I finally shuffle off this mortal coil, I dearly hope I will say something wonderfully fitting, full of exactly the right measure of pathos and wit to ensure that my name echoes forever through cyberspace. There is, of course, the small matter of achieving enough between now and then for people to actually care, but I am ever the optimist. Compiling this list was actually a rather moving and depressing experience. There is, of course, the possibility that a number of these quotes have been 'improved' over the years by various family members and hagiographers to form the well-rounded little gems I offer up to you. They may originally have said something like: 'Did you bring the cat in?', 'I stole all my ideas from a book I bought in an Oxfam shop for 20p' or 'Don't point that thing at me — it might be loaded.' But let us take these at face value and not speak ill of the dead. Whose words deserve a state funeral and whose will be buried in a cardboard coffin on unconsecrated ground?

'Pardonnez-moi, monsieur. Je ne l'ai pas fait exprès.' Marie Antoinette
'It's all been rather lovely.' John Le Mesurier

Le Mesurier

'The bastards got me, but they won't get everybody.' Alexander Litvinenko
'Hold the cross high so I may see it through the flames!' Joan Of Arc

Joan Of Arc

'I want nothing but death.' Jane Austen
'Die, my dear? Why that's the last thing I'll do!' Henry Palmerston,

Palmerston

'I am a queen, but I have not the power to 'move my arms.' Louise, Queen of Prussia
'That was the best ice-cream soda I ever tasted.' Lou Costello

Queen Of Prussia

'Am I dying, or is this my birthday?' Nancy, Lady Astor
'Bugger Bognor.' George V

George V

'Applaud, my friends, the comedy is finished.' Ludwig van Beethoven
'How were the receipts today at Madison Square Garden?' P T Barnum

Beethoven

'I've had a hell of a lot of fun and I've enjoyed every minute of it.' Errol Flynn
'Dying is easy, comedy is hard.' George Bernard Shaw

Bernard Shaw

'I haven't had champagne for a long time.' Anton Chekhov
'I'm going away tonight.' James Brown

Brown

'Where is my clock?' Salvador Dali
'If you don't like it, you can just fuck off!' Keith Moon

Moon

'Be sure to sing 'Blessed Lord' tonight — and sing it well.' Martin Luther King Jr.
'Don't let poor Nelly starve.' Charles II

King

'Goodnight, my darlings, I'll see you tomorrow.' Noel Coward
'My wallpaper and I are fighting a duel to the death. One or the other of us has to go.' Oscar Wilde

Wilde

'I just had eighteen straight scotches. I think that's the record . . . After thirty-nine years, this is all I've done.' Dylan Thomas
'Thank God I have done my duty.' Vice Admiral Horatio Nelson

Thomas

'I'm bored with it all.' Winston Churchill
'Is it bad? Please don't. Don't lift me.' John F. Kennedy

Churchill

'I told you I was ill.' Spike Milligan
'Go on, get out! Last words are for fools who haven't said enough!' Karl Marx

Marx

'I don't have the passion anymore, and so remember, it's better to burn out than to fade away.' Peace, Love, Empathy. Kurt Cobain
'I should never have switched from scotch to Martinis.' Humphrey Bogart

Cobain

'I am just going outside. I may be some time.' Captain Lawrence Oates
'I must go in, the fog is rising.' Emily Dickinson

Oates

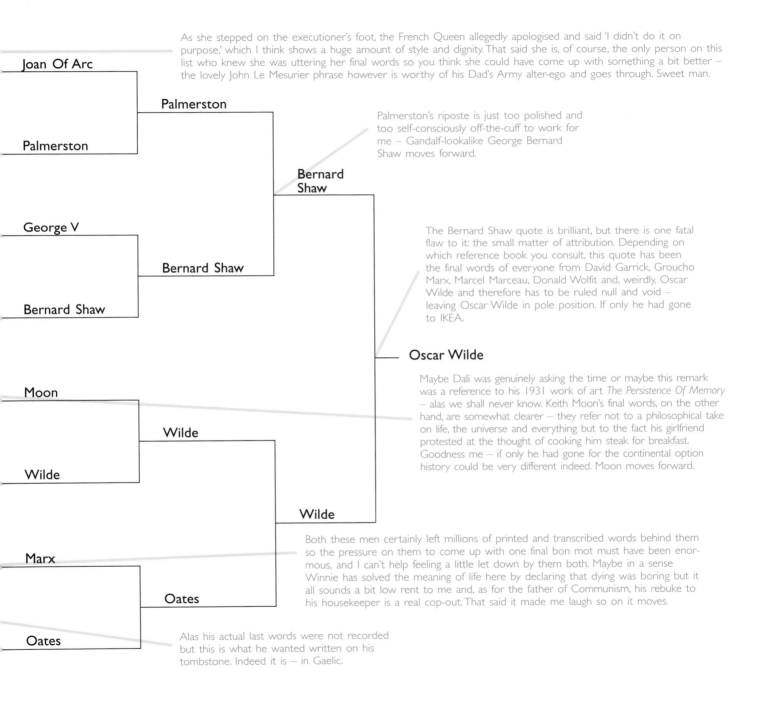

Joan Of Arc

Palmerston

Palmerston

As she stepped on the executioner's foot, the French Queen allegedly apologised and said 'I didn't do it on purpose,' which I think shows a huge amount of style and dignity. That said she is, of course, the only person on this list who knew she was uttering her final words so you think she could have come up with something a bit better – the lovely John Le Mesurier phrase however is worthy of his Dad's Army alter-ego and goes through. Sweet man.

Palmerston's riposte is just too polished and too self-consciously off-the-cuff to work for me – Gandalf-lookalike George Bernard Shaw moves forward.

Bernard Shaw

George V

Bernard Shaw

Bernard Shaw

The Bernard Shaw quote is brilliant, but there is one fatal flaw to it: the small matter of attribution. Depending on which reference book you consult, this quote has been the final words of everyone from David Garrick, Groucho Marx, Marcel Marceau, Donald Wolfit and, weirdly, Oscar Wilde and therefore has to be ruled null and void – leaving Oscar Wilde in pole position. If only he had gone to IKEA.

Oscar Wilde

Moon

Wilde

Wilde

Maybe Dali was genuinely asking the time or maybe this remark was a reference to his 1931 work of art *The Persistence Of Memory* – alas we shall never know. Keith Moon's final words, on the other hand, are somewhat clearer – they refer not to a philosophical take on life, the universe and everything but to the fact his girlfriend protested at the thought of cooking him steak for breakfast. Goodness me – if only he had gone for the continental option history could be very different indeed. Moon moves forward.

Wilde

Marx

Oates

Both these men certainly left millions of printed and transcribed words behind them so the pressure on them to come up with one final bon mot must have been enormous, and I can't help feeling a little let down by them both. Maybe in a sense Winnie has solved the meaning of life here by declaring that dying was boring but it all sounds a bit low rent to me and, as for the father of Communism, his rebuke to his housekeeper is a real cop-out. That said it made me laugh so on it moves.

Oates

Alas his actual last words were not recorded but this is what he wanted written on his tombstone. Indeed it is – in Gaelic.

38

Fictional Detectives

by SIMON TREWIN

There is something endlessly appealing about settling down in front of the telly for a whodunnit. Dress the scenario up anyway you want – whether it be medieval times (*Cadfael*), chocolate boxy villages (*Midsomer Murders, Bergerac* or *Miss Marple*), exotic locations (*Poirot* or *Miami Vice*) and it is well nigh impossible to turn off before the murderer is unmasked. Is it that strange woman at the post office who is always leaving just before the next dead body is discovered? Or maybe the mad monk from the craggy cliff-top hideaway? Or possibly even the guy who runs the surf-board concession over on Liberty beach? In a sense, none of this really matters. What I love as a viewer is settling down and playing detective myself – can I get to the solution before our man with the deerstalker/the irascible old policeman with a vintage car/the lady with the shopping basket gets there first? I have gathered thirty-two of the world's finest fictional detectives together in the oak-panelled library and I think it is time to unmask who the chosen one is. Ladies and gentlemen, thanks for coming out on such a wild and windy night.

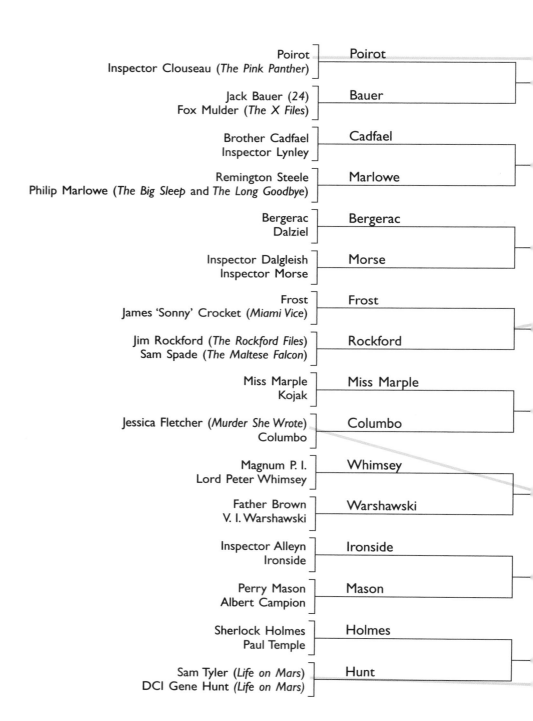

Poirot	Poirot
Inspector Clouseau (*The Pink Panther*)	
Jack Bauer (*24*)	Bauer
Fox Mulder (*The X Files*)	
Brother Cadfael	Cadfael
Inspector Lynley	
Remington Steele	Marlowe
Philip Marlowe (*The Big Sleep* and *The Long Goodbye*)	
Bergerac	Bergerac
Dalziel	
Inspector Dalgleish	Morse
Inspector Morse	
Frost	Frost
James 'Sonny' Crocket (*Miami Vice*)	
Jim Rockford (*The Rockford Files*)	Rockford
Sam Spade (*The Maltese Falcon*)	
Miss Marple	Miss Marple
Kojak	
Jessica Fletcher (*Murder She Wrote*)	Columbo
Columbo	
Magnum P. I.	Whimsey
Lord Peter Whimsey	
Father Brown	Warshawski
V. I. Warshawski	
Inspector Alleyn	Ironside
Ironside	
Perry Mason	Mason
Albert Campion	
Sherlock Holmes	Holmes
Paul Temple	
Sam Tyler (*Life on Mars*)	Hunt
DCI Gene Hunt (*Life on Mars*)	

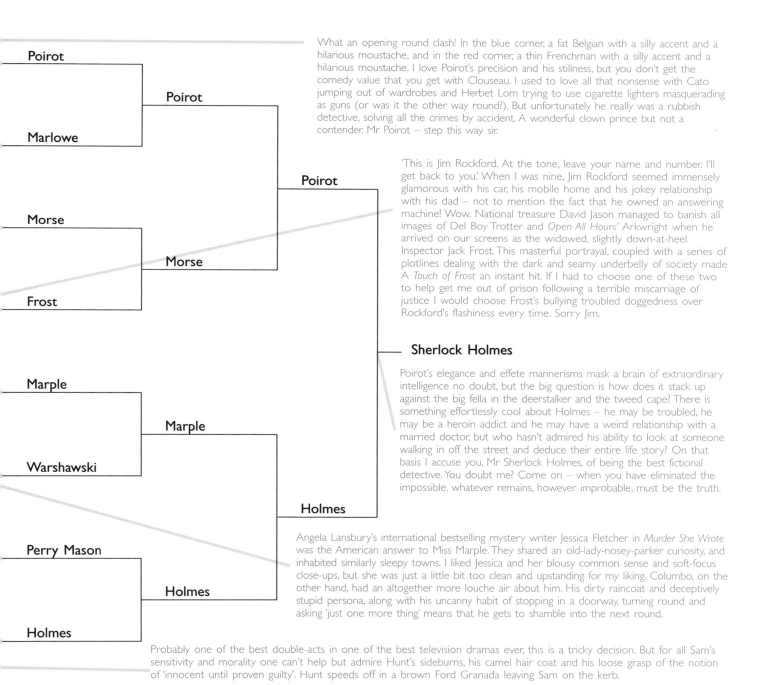

```
Poirot ─┐
        ├─ Poirot ─┐
Marlowe ─┘         │
                   ├─ Poirot ─┐
Morse ──┐          │          │
        ├─ Morse ──┘          │
Frost ──┘                     │
                              ├─ Sherlock Holmes
Marple ──────┐                │
             ├─ Marple ─┐     │
Warshawski ──┘          │     │
                        ├─ Holmes ─┘
Perry Mason ─┐          │
             ├─ Holmes ─┘
Holmes ──────┘
```

What an opening round clash! In the blue corner, a fat Belgian with a silly accent and a hilarious moustache, and in the red corner, a thin Frenchman with a silly accent and a hilarious moustache. I love Poirot's precision and his stillness, but you don't get the comedy value that you get with Clouseau. I used to love all that nonsense with Cato jumping out of wardrobes and Herbet Lom trying to use cigarette lighters masquerading as guns (or was it the other way round?). But unfortunately he really was a rubbish detective, solving all the crimes by accident. A wonderful clown prince but not a contender. Mr Poirot – step this way sir.

'This is Jim Rockford. At the tone, leave your name and number. I'll get back to you.' When I was nine, Jim Rockford seemed immensely glamorous with his car, his mobile home and his jokey relationship with his dad – not to mention the fact that he owned an answering machine! Wow. National treasure David Jason managed to banish all images of Del Boy Trotter and *Open All Hours'* Arkwright when he arrived on our screens as the widowed, slightly down-at-heel Inspector Jack Frost. This masterful portrayal, coupled with a series of plotlines dealing with the dark and seamy underbelly of society made *A Touch of Frost* an instant hit. If I had to choose one of these two to help get me out of prison following a terrible miscarriage of justice I would choose Frost's bullying troubled doggedness over Rockford's flashiness every time. Sorry Jim.

Sherlock Holmes

Poirot's elegance and effete mannerisms mask a brain of extraordinary intelligence no doubt, but the big question is how does it stack up against the big fella in the deerstalker and the tweed cape? There is something effortlessly cool about Holmes – he may be troubled, he may be a heroin addict and he may have a weird relationship with a married doctor, but who hasn't admired his ability to look at someone walking in off the street and deduce their entire life story? On that basis I accuse you, Mr Sherlock Holmes, of being the best fictional detective. You doubt me? Come on – when you have eliminated the impossible, whatever remains, however improbable, must be the truth.

Angela Lansbury's international bestselling mystery writer Jessica Fletcher in *Murder She Wrote* was the American answer to Miss Marple. They shared an old-lady-nosey-parker curiosity, and inhabited similarly sleepy towns. I liked Jessica and her blousy common sense and soft-focus close-ups, but she was just a little bit too clean and upstanding for my liking. Columbo, on the other hand, had an altogether more louche air about him. His dirty raincoat and deceptively stupid persona, along with his uncanny habit of stopping in a doorway, turning round and asking 'just one more thing' means that he gets to shamble into the next round.

Probably one of the best double-acts in one of the best television dramas ever, this is a tricky decision. But for all Sam's sensitivity and morality one can't help but admire Hunt's sideburns, his camel hair coat and his loose grasp of the notion of 'innocent until proven guilty'. Hunt speeds off in a brown Ford Granada leaving Sam on the kerb.

39

Film Deaths
by MATTHEW SHEPATIN

You don't need to be Freud to figure out why movie audiences would voluntarily watch people be shot, slashed, poisoned, eaten by a shark, disemboweled by an alien, or decapitated by plate glass. Then again, the best screen fatalities deliver an emotional wallop. They are visually compelling. They spark a visceral response: fear, disgust, laughter, sorrow, or even faith. For all those reasons, it's not surprising to find 16 Oscar nominees for Best Picture here (and 7 winners). While horror film directors make a living serving up spectacular killings, accomplished directors such as Steven Spielberg, who has 2 entries (sorry, kids, E.T. lives), know the tremendous power expelled in that final breath.

MATTHEW SHEPATIN, ace researcher on this book, is a freelance writer whose articles have appeared in the *Los Angeles Times*, *Playboy*, the *Village Voice*, and *Time Out New York*.

King Kong falls from Empire State Building
cancer-stricken Debra Winger dies in hospital

King Kong falls

Bonnie and Clyde riddled with bullets
Walken loses Russian roulette in *The Deer Hunter*

Bonnie and Clyde shot

Titanic sinks and DiCaprio drowns
Bambi's mom shot by hunters

Bambi's mom shot

Alec Guinness blows up *The Bridge Over the River Kwai*
Susan Hayward gets the chair in *I Want To Live!*

Hayward gets chair

Nazis melt in *Raiders of the Lost Ark*
dirty cop suffocates in corn silo in *Witness*

Nazis melt

Scarface goes out with a bang
Wicked Witch melts

Wicked Witch melts

Alan Rickman's skyscraper plunge in *Die Hard*
Cagney goes up in flames in *White Heat*

Rickman's fall

Wallace Shawn's wine poisoning in *The Princess Bride*
Robocop criminal gets toxic waste bath

Shawn's poisoning

David Warner's decapitation in *The Omen*
John Hurt's bursting stomach in *Alien*

Hurt's bursting stomach

telekinetic Carrie sends knives into her mom
Travolta shoots backseat passenger in *Pulp Fiction*

Travolta shoots passenger

airbag accidentally deploys, killing *Final Destination* girl
Mr. Big expands and pops in *Live and Let Die*

airbag in *Final Destination*

Psycho shower scene
shark attack on female swimmer in *Jaws* opener

***Psycho* shower scene**

Sonny Corleone gunned down at tollbooth
Darth Vader strikes down Obi-Wan Kenobi

Vader kills Obi-Wan

Dr. Strangelove's Slim Pickens rides nuclear bomb
babes chase sexist off cliff in Python's *Meaning of Life*

Pickens rides bomb

Willem Dafoe's fatal battlefield collapse in *Platoon*
Tom Hanks shot on bridge in *Saving Private Ryan*

Dafoe dies in battle

Thelma and Louise drive car off edge of Grand Canyon
Russell Crowe's death match in Roman coliseum

Crowe stabbed

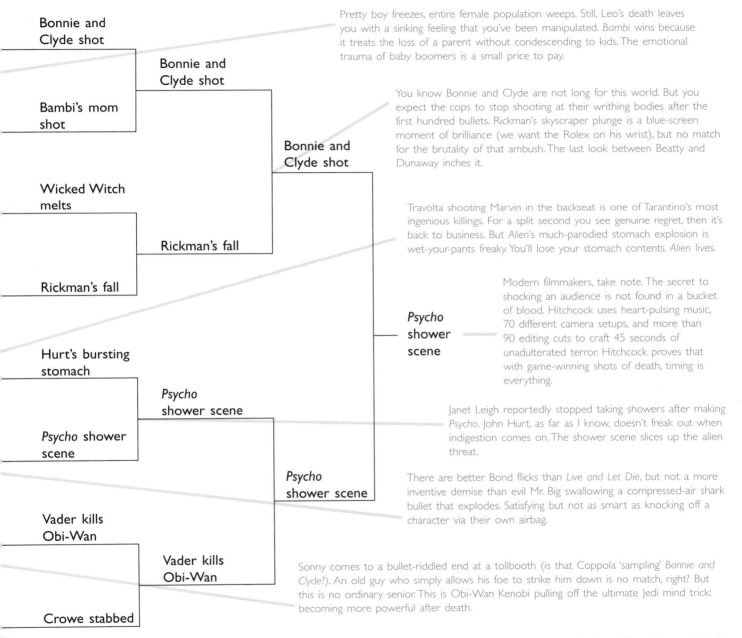

Bonnie and Clyde shot

Bambi's mom shot

Bonnie and Clyde shot

Wicked Witch melts

Rickman's fall

Rickman's fall

Bonnie and Clyde shot

Pretty boy freezes, entire female population weeps. Still, Leo's death leaves you with a sinking feeling that you've been manipulated. *Bambi* wins because it treats the loss of a parent without condescending to kids. The emotional trauma of baby boomers is a small price to pay.

You know Bonnie and Clyde are not long for this world. But you expect the cops to stop shooting at their writhing bodies after the first hundred bullets. Rickman's skyscraper plunge is a blue-screen moment of brilliance (we want the Rolex on his wrist), but no match for the brutality of that ambush. The last look between Beatty and Dunaway inches it.

Travolta shooting Marvin in the backseat is one of Tarantino's most ingenious killings. For a split second you see genuine regret, then it's back to business. But *Alien*'s much-parodied stomach explosion is wet-your-pants freaky. You'll lose your stomach contents. *Alien* lives.

Hurt's bursting stomach

Psycho shower scene

Psycho shower scene

Psycho shower scene

Psycho shower scene

Modern filmmakers, take note. The secret to shocking an audience is not found in a bucket of blood. Hitchcock uses heart-pulsing music, 70 different camera setups, and more than 90 editing cuts to craft 45 seconds of unadulterated terror. Hitchcock proves that with game-winning shots of death, timing is everything.

Janet Leigh reportedly stopped taking showers after making *Psycho*. John Hurt, as far as I know, doesn't freak out when indigestion comes on. The shower scene slices up the alien threat.

There are better Bond flicks than *Live and Let Die*, but not a more inventive demise than evil Mr. Big swallowing a compressed-air shark bullet that explodes. Satisfying but not as smart as knocking off a character via their own airbag.

Vader kills Obi-Wan

Vader kills Obi-Wan

Crowe stabbed

Sonny comes to a bullet-riddled end at a tollbooth (is that Coppola 'sampling' *Bonnie and Clyde*?). An old guy who simply allows his foe to strike him down is no match, right? But this is no ordinary senior. This is Obi-Wan Kenobi pulling off the ultimate Jedi mind trick: becoming more powerful after death.

A pair of Academy Award winners take aim at each other: Dafoe's elegiac Christ-like collapse in Nam affirms that war is hell, but Crowe's final victory after his fatal stabbing argues more forcefully that payback's a bitch. Maximus moves on. Toga party!

40

Film Quotations
by SIMON TREWIN

It is interesting how few of these quotations come from the recent past – it may be that film scripts are becoming more and more economical and the emphasis is much less on dialogue and much more on action. Or it may just be that we live in such a multi-channel environment that few films ever gain that 'must see this week' status that films attained in the past, when Odeon 'picture palaces' had one huge screen where up to two thousand people at a time could share the experience of seeing *Casablanca, Some Like It Hot* or *The Wizard Of Oz* for the first time. Perhaps films have to work that little extra these days to permeate to the same degree but, happily, a few have broken through and feature here. The joy of these quotations comes not only from the memories they bring back but also from the opportunity it gives us to stand in front of the mirror and do bad imitations of the actors who first uttered them. I defy you to read the *Dirty Harry* quote without adopting a steely-eyed steady gaze and speaking very deliberately with sinister undertones. Try it on your cat next time he asks for food at a non-designated dinner time, I guarantee the furry beast will turn on his heels and dash for the cat flap. Just in time for you to say 'Frankly my dear – I don't give a damn.'

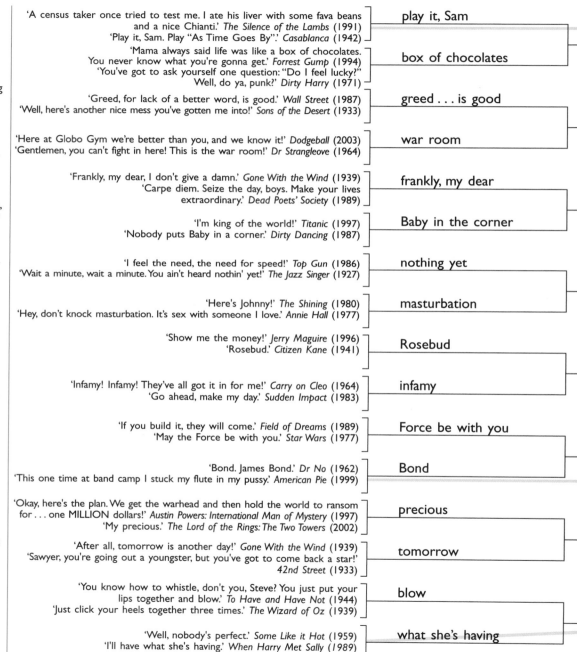

'A census taker once tried to test me. I ate his liver with some fava beans and a nice Chianti.' *The Silence of the Lambs* (1991)
'Play it, Sam. Play "As Time Goes By".' *Casablanca* (1942)

play it, Sam

'Mama always said life was like a box of chocolates. You never know what you're gonna get.' *Forrest Gump* (1994)
'You've got to ask yourself one question: "Do I feel lucky?" Well, do ya, punk?' *Dirty Harry* (1971)

box of chocolates

'Greed, for lack of a better word, is good.' *Wall Street* (1987)
'Well, here's another nice mess you've gotten me into!' *Sons of the Desert* (1933)

greed . . . is good

'Here at Globo Gym we're better than you, and we know it!' *Dodgeball* (2003)
'Gentlemen, you can't fight in here! This is the war room!' *Dr Strangelove* (1964)

war room

'Frankly, my dear, I don't give a damn.' *Gone With the Wind* (1939)
'Carpe diem. Seize the day, boys. Make your lives extraordinary.' *Dead Poets' Society* (1989)

frankly, my dear

'I'm king of the world!' *Titanic* (1997)
'Nobody puts Baby in a corner.' *Dirty Dancing* (1987)

Baby in the corner

'I feel the need, the need for speed!' *Top Gun* (1986)
'Wait a minute, wait a minute. You ain't heard nothin' yet!' *The Jazz Singer* (1927)

nothing yet

'Here's Johnny!' *The Shining* (1980)
'Hey, don't knock masturbation. It's sex with someone I love.' *Annie Hall* (1977)

masturbation

'Show me the money!' *Jerry Maguire* (1996)
'Rosebud.' *Citizen Kane* (1941)

Rosebud

'Infamy! Infamy! They've all got it in for me!' *Carry on Cleo* (1964)
'Go ahead, make my day.' *Sudden Impact* (1983)

infamy

'If you build it, they will come.' *Field of Dreams* (1989)
'May the Force be with you.' *Star Wars* (1977)

Force be with you

'Bond. James Bond.' *Dr No* (1962)
'This one time at band camp I stuck my flute in my pussy.' *American Pie* (1999)

Bond

'Okay, here's the plan. We get the warhead and then hold the world to ransom for . . . one MILLION dollars!' *Austin Powers: International Man of Mystery* (1997)
'My precious.' *The Lord of the Rings: The Two Towers* (2002)

precious

'After all, tomorrow is another day!' *Gone With the Wind* (1939)
'Sawyer, you're going out a youngster, but you've got to come back a star!' *42nd Street* (1933)

tomorrow

'You know how to whistle, don't you, Steve? You just put your lips together and blow.' *To Have and Have Not* (1944)
'Just click your heels together three times.' *The Wizard of Oz* (1939)

blow

'Well, nobody's perfect.' *Some Like it Hot* (1959)
'I'll have what she's having.' *When Harry Met Sally* (1989)

what she's having

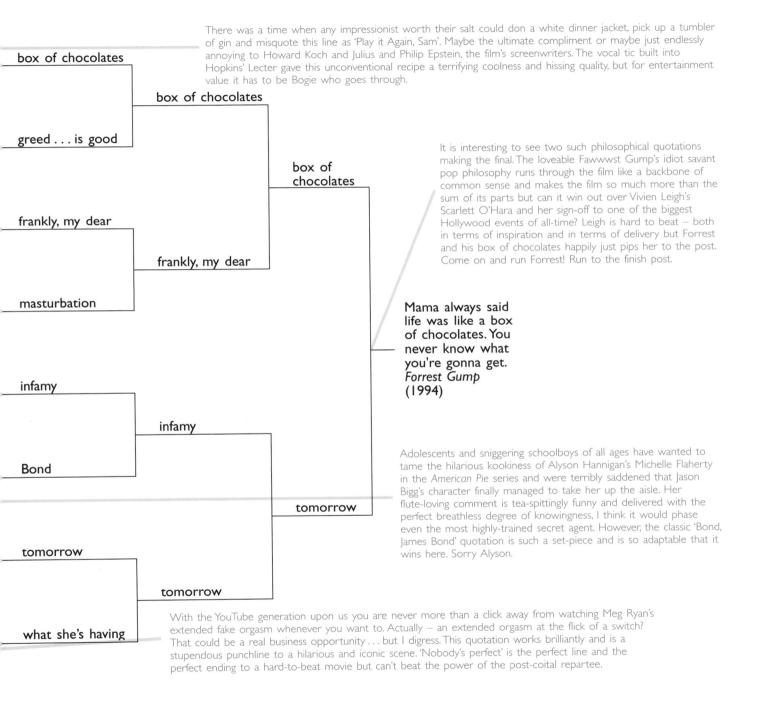

box of chocolates

greed . . . is good

box of chocolates

frankly, my dear

box of
chocolates

masturbation

frankly, my dear

infamy

infamy

Bond

tomorrow

tomorrow

tomorrow

what she's having

There was a time when any impressionist worth their salt could don a white dinner jacket, pick up a tumbler of gin and misquote this line as 'Play it Again, Sam'. Maybe the ultimate compliment or maybe just endlessly annoying to Howard Koch and Julius and Philip Epstein, the film's screenwriters. The vocal tic built into Hopkins' Lecter gave this unconventional recipe a terrifying coolness and hissing quality, but for entertainment value it has to be Bogie who goes through.

It is interesting to see two such philosophical quotations making the final. The loveable Fawwwst Gump's idiot savant pop philosophy runs through the film like a backbone of common sense and makes the film so much more than the sum of its parts but can it win out over Vivien Leigh's Scarlett O'Hara and her sign-off to one of the biggest Hollywood events of all-time? Leigh is hard to beat – both in terms of inspiration and in terms of delivery but Forrest and his box of chocolates happily just pips her to the post. Come on and run Forrest! Run to the finish post.

Mama always said life was like a box of chocolates. You never know what you're gonna get.
Forrest Gump
(1994)

Adolescents and sniggering schoolboys of all ages have wanted to tame the hilarious kookiness of Alyson Hannigan's Michelle Flaherty in the *American Pie* series and were terribly saddened that Jason Bigg's character finally managed to take her up the aisle. Her flute-loving comment is tea-spittingly funny and delivered with the perfect breathless degree of knowingness, I think it would phase even the most highly-trained secret agent. However, the classic 'Bond, James Bond' quotation is such a set-piece and is so adaptable that it wins here. Sorry Alyson.

With the YouTube generation upon us you are never more than a click away from watching Meg Ryan's extended fake orgasm whenever you want to. Actually – an extended orgasm at the flick of a switch? That could be a real business opportunity . . . but I digress. This quotation works brilliantly and is a stupendous punchline to a hilarious and iconic scene. 'Nobody's perfect' is the perfect line and the perfect ending to a hard-to-beat movie but can't beat the power of the post-coital repartee.

41

First Lines

by SIMON TREWIN

In the beginning was the Word.

I thought many times how to start this introduction. I thought about describing the weather, the chair in which I'm sitting while I write this and finally I thought about describing the thought processes behind starting this category altogether. Making a good start with any piece of writing is vital. In my day job I read up to six thousand manuscripts a year, so I am exposed to the very worst and occasionally the very mediocre and even more occasionally the very best in opening lines. Weather, to my mind, is never a good way to start. I have made one exception to my weather rule below. Are you sitting comfortably? Then we will begin.

After killing the red-haired man, I took myself off to Quinn's for an oyster supper. *The Meaning Of Night* Michael Cox (2006)

It is a truth universally acknowledged, That a single man in possession of a good fortune, must be in want of a wife. *Pride and Prejudice* Jane Austen (1813)

Happy families are all alike; every unhappy family is unhappy in its own way. *Anna Karenina* Leo Tolstoy (trans. Constance Garnett, 1877)

It was the best of times, it was the worst of times. *A Tale of Two Cities* Charles Dickens (1859)

If you really want to hear about it, the first thing you'll probably want to know is where I was born, and what my lousy childhood was like, and how my parents were occupied and all before they had me, and all that David Copperfield kind of crap, but I don't feel like going into it, if you want to know the truth. *The Catcher in the Rye* J. D. Salinger (1951)

Once upon a time and a very good time it was there was a moocow coming down along the road and this moocow that was coming down along the road met a nicens little boy named baby tuckoo. *A Portrait of the Artist as a Young Man* James Joyce (1916)

He – for there could be no doubt of his sex, though the fashion of the time did something to disguise it – was in the act of slicing at the head of a Moor which swung from the rafters. *Orlando* Virginia Woolf (1928)

Whether I shall turn out to be the hero of my own life, or whether that station will be held by anybody else, these pages must show. *David Copperfield* Charles Dickens (1850)

Mrs Dalloway said she would buy the flowers herself. *Mrs Dalloway* Virginia Woolf (1925)

There was a boy called Eustace Clarence Scrubb, and he almost deserved it. *The Voyage of the Dawn Treader* C. S. Lewis (1952)

It was a queer, sultry summer, the summer they electrocuted the Rosenbergs, and I didn't know what I was doing in New York. *The Bell Jar* Sylvia Plath (1963)

I was born twice: first, as a baby girl, on a remarkably smogless Detroit day in January of 1960; and then again, as a teenage boy, in an emergency room near Petoskey, Michigan, in August of 1974. *Middlesex* Jeffrey Eugenides (2002)

Miss Brooke had that kind of beauty which seems to be thrown into relief by poor dress. *Middlemarch* George Eliot (1872)

In my younger and more vulnerable years my father gave me some advice that I've been turning over in my mind ever since. *The Great Gatsby* F. Scott Fitzgerald (1925)

The past is a foreign country; they do things differently there. *The Go-Between* L. P. Hartley (1953)

They say when trouble comes close ranks, and so the white people did. *Wide Sargasso Sea* Jean Rhys (1966)

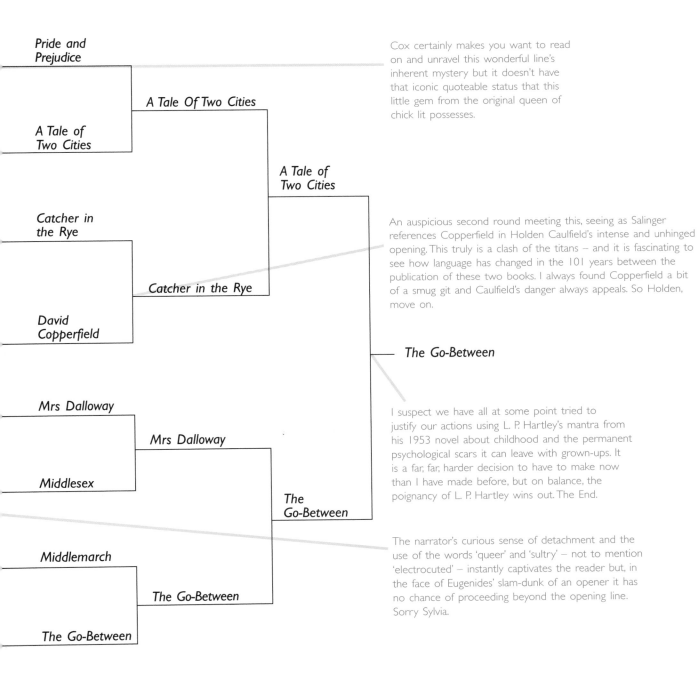

Pride and
Prejudice

A Tale of
Two Cities

A Tale Of Two Cities

A Tale of
Two Cities

Catcher in
the Rye

David
Copperfield

Catcher in the Rye

Mrs Dalloway

Middlesex

Mrs Dalloway

Middlemarch

The Go-Between

The Go-Between

The
Go-Between

The Go-Between

Cox certainly makes you want to read on and unravel this wonderful line's inherent mystery but it doesn't have that iconic quoteable status that this little gem from the original queen of chick lit possesses.

An auspicious second round meeting this, seeing as Salinger references Copperfield in Holden Caulfield's intense and unhinged opening. This truly is a clash of the titans – and it is fascinating to see how language has changed in the 101 years between the publication of these two books. I always found Copperfield a bit of a smug git and Caulfield's danger always appeals. So Holden, move on.

I suspect we have all at some point tried to justify our actions using L. P. Hartley's mantra from his 1953 novel about childhood and the permanent psychological scars it can leave with grown-ups. It is a far, far, harder decision to have to make now than I have made before, but on balance, the poignancy of L. P. Hartley wins out. The End.

The narrator's curious sense of detachment and the use of the words 'queer' and 'sultry' – not to mention 'electrocuted' – instantly captivates the reader but, in the face of Eugenides' slam-dunk of an opener it has no chance of proceeding beyond the opening line. Sorry Sylvia.

42

Fruit
by NEIL AMDUR

Fruit is in our cereal, our yogurt, our drinks, our salads, even our Coronas. We pour it into our blenders, buy it in bulk at Costco, and enrich Jamba Juice with our smoothie orders. But when was the last time you appreciated a piece of fruit as you would a slice of Godiva cheesecake or an exotic appetizer? Each fruit has its own texture and sweetness, taste and lusciousness, health benefits and dependability. Indeed, the personality of your preferred fruit can define who you are.

NEIL AMDUR has spent a lifetime covering tournaments of all kinds – from tennis to the Olympics – as a reporter and then as sports editor of the *New York Times* for 12 years. One of the last questions he would routinely ask a recruit applying for a job was "If you were a fruit, what would you be?" Amdur is an apricot. More important, he has a doctorate in fruitology, whatever that means.

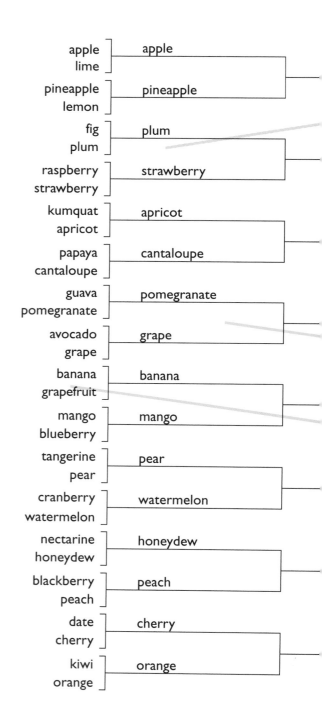

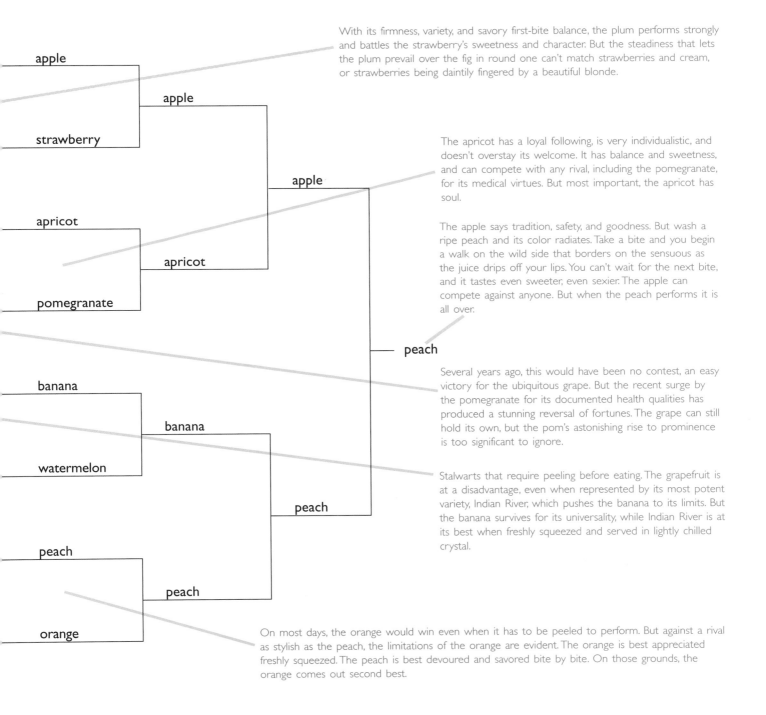

apple

apple

strawberry

apple

apricot

apricot

apple

pomegranate

peach

banana

banana

watermelon

peach

peach

peach

orange

With its firmness, variety, and savory first-bite balance, the plum performs strongly and battles the strawberry's sweetness and character. But the steadiness that lets the plum prevail over the fig in round one can't match strawberries and cream, or strawberries being daintily fingered by a beautiful blonde.

The apricot has a loyal following, is very individualistic, and doesn't overstay its welcome. It has balance and sweetness, and can compete with any rival, including the pomegranate, for its medical virtues. But most important, the apricot has soul.

The apple says tradition, safety, and goodness. But wash a ripe peach and its color radiates. Take a bite and you begin a walk on the wild side that borders on the sensuous as the juice drips off your lips. You can't wait for the next bite, and it tastes even sweeter, even sexier. The apple can compete against anyone. But when the peach performs it is all over.

Several years ago, this would have been no contest, an easy victory for the ubiquitous grape. But the recent surge by the pomegranate for its documented health qualities has produced a stunning reversal of fortunes. The grape can still hold its own, but the pom's astonishing rise to prominence is too significant to ignore.

Stalwarts that require peeling before eating. The grapefruit is at a disadvantage, even when represented by its most potent variety, Indian River, which pushes the banana to its limits. But the banana survives for its universality, while Indian River is at its best when freshly squeezed and served in lightly chilled crystal.

On most days, the orange would win even when it has to be peeled to perform. But against a rival as stylish as the peach, the limitations of the orange are evident. The orange is best appreciated freshly squeezed. The peach is best devoured and savored bite by bite. On those grounds, the orange comes out second best.

43

Gameshow Hosts
by SIMON TREWIN

We are a nation obsessed with gameshows – turn on the television any hour of any day of any week, flick across the full spectrum of satellite channels and you will have at least five different gameshows to choose from at any moment. Trust me, I've tried. There is even a website www.ukgameshows.com which contains more information than anyone would ever admit to needing to know about everything from such obscure gameshows such as *A Kick in the Ballots* (which was presented by Charles Kennedy MP on Carlton in 1993 for a grand total of two episodes) to the world famous (not), *That's My Dog* (the Westwood ITV classic from the early 80s presented by the inimitable Derek Hobson, (that's right I haven't heard of him either)). The idea behind *That's My Dog* was, wait for it, that a gameshow that tried to determine whose dog is best. There was a dog assault course, a maze, and probably an IQ test as well. Surprisingly, it hasn't been reinvented as *Celebrity That's My Dog* but by the time this book is published I suspect that this massive oversight will have been remedied. Where does this obsession with gameshows come from? Is it the inherently competitive culture we all live and work in, or is it the fact that, with get rich quick programmes such as *Who Wants to be a Millionaire*, we like the idea of somebody working hard at school, assimilating vast amounts of knowledge and then using that knowledge to change their lives through becoming a winner? I suspect it is none of these, we just enjoy watching people making complete tits of themselves by getting obvious questions wrong. Anne Robinson, after all, has made a whole career out of this with her withering looks and flirtatious teasing of those people who dare to give a stupid answer on *The Weakest Link*. Anyway, from the thirty-two listed here, which are going to do the walk of shame and which one will emerge as the champion clutching a four foot long cheque and a perspex trophy? Fingers on buzzers, please.

When I heard that Paxo was going to take over from Bamber Gascoigne on *University Challenge* I had visions of crying undergraduates slitting their wrists live on air after being asked the same question seventeen times in a row until they got it right. I was only partially wrong but his appearances on this show are very clever – his hyper-intelligence and self-awareness means that he has created an alter-ego, a sort of Jeremy Paxman tribute act that works incredibly well.

Noel Edmonds on *Deal Or No Deal*
Robert Robinson on *Ask The Family* — **Robert Robinson**

Stephen Fry on *QI*
Bob Holness on *Blockbusters* — **Bob Holness**

Bruce Forsyth on *Play Your Cards Right*
Bruce Forsyth on *The Generation Game* — **Bruce/*Generation***

Nicholas Parsons on *Sale Of the Century*
Cilla Black on *Blind Date* — **Nicholas Parsons**

Ted Rogers on *3-2-1*
Jim Bowen on *Bullseye* — **Ted Rogers**

Terry Wogan on *Blankety Blank*
Anneka Rice on *Treasure Hunt* — **Terry Wogan**

Richard Whiteley on *Countdown*
Derek Batey on *Mr and Mrs* — **Richard Whiteley**

Peter Simon on *Double Dare*
William G. Stewart on *Fifteen-to-One* — **William G. Stewart**

Les Dennis on *Family Fortunes*
Michael Aspel on *Give Us A Clue* — **Les Dennis**

Eammon Andrews on *What's My Line?*
John Leslie on *Wheel Of Fortune* — **John Leslie**

Ant and Dec on *I'm A Celebrity Get Me Out Of Here*
Magnus Magnusson on *Mastermind* — **Magnus Magnusson**

Bamber Gascoigne on *University Challenge*
Jeremy Paxman on *University Challenge* — **Jeremy Paxman**

Gordon Burns on *The Krypton Factor*
Michael Rodd on *Screen Test* — **Gordon Burns**

William Franklyn on *The Masterspy*
Hughie Green on *Opportunity Knocks* — **Hughie Green**

Mike Read on *Pop Quiz*
Leslie Crowther on *The Price Is Right* — **Leslie Crowther**

Bob Monkhouse on *Family Fortunes*
Michael Barrymore on *Strike It Lucky* — **Michael Barrymore**

Noel has really come into his own (which is a clever trick if you can do it) with the no-brainer format of *Deal or No Deal* which is not a million miles away from the 'open the box or take the money' format of days gone by. This is Noel at his best – he winds the tension up like an absolute master and it is truly impossible to turn the show off once it is on. Let's leave Noel to one side for the moment, probably on the phone to the banker, or staring in a Very Serious Way at the poor flustered contestant, and turn our attentions to everybody's favourite 1970s uncle Robert Robinson on the programme that in many ways encapsulates middle England, *Ask The Family*. All the families seemed to wear glasses, there was a proliferation of knitted tank tops and even the children wore ties, and no family had more than two children. I used to particularly enjoy the close-up photo round as the answer always seemed to be a colander or a piece of broccoli. Robert Robinson had the persona of a seemingly straight-laced uncle who after a glass of dry sherry at Christmas would suddenly display propensity for conjuring tricks that would delight the whole family for hours. He also had great Arthur Scargill comb-over hair and for that reason and because he quite clearly isn't the smug git that Edmonds appears to be, Mr Robinson goes through to the next round.

Goodness me where do we start? Nice to see you, to see you, nice. But, now that we've started am I allowed to finish? Of course. Magnus Magnusson (so good, they named him twice) is a national treasure and a man who brought great dignity and learning to what was essentially a very straightforward quizshow. I once went to a recording of Mastermind, and the reverence with which the black chair was treated by the stage crew and floor manager far exceeded the reverence they afforded to Magnus himself. That said, he brought a solemn seriousness to the format, and always seemed to be silently rooting for the contestants. Bruce Forsyth, on the hand, is a man who even now deserves the title 'Mr Showbiz'. That chin, those catchphrases and an ability to reinvent himself for every generation makes him our winner tonight.

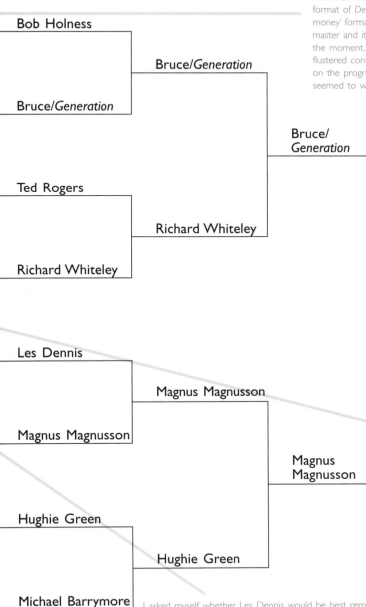

Bob Holness

Bruce/*Generation*

Bruce/*Generation*

Ted Rogers

Richard Whiteley

Richard Whiteley

Les Dennis

Magnus Magnusson

Magnus Magnusson

Hughie Green

Hughie Green

Michael Barrymore

Bruce/*Generation*

Magnus Magnusson

Bruce Forsyth on
The Generation Game

In *Mr and Mrs*, two couples 'from all over the British Isles' were asked a bunch of questions separately about their other halves while their partner sat in a soundproof booth with enormous and hilarious 1970s headphones on listening to muzak. They then swapped positions and it was usually revealed that the men knew nothing about their wives and the women knew everything about their husbands. Derek Batey had the teeth and tan, constant smile (and dress sense) of a Butlins Yellow Coat and seemed to enjoy the whole experience effortlessly – even handing over the crisp tenners and the carriage clock but to be honest there is no way Derek Batey was ever going to win out over the dear departed Richard Whiteley. The first man to appear on Channel 4, the owner of a thousand ties, the endlessly twinkling on-screen companion of Carol Vorderman, he fronted the quizshow that the Queen always made a point of watching. We only really appreciated his genius (and genius it was) when he had gone. Des Lynam just didn't seem the same. As the second hand swirls towards the top and we hear that distinctive sound . . . Richard Whiteley sweeps through to the next round.

I asked myself whether Les Dennis would be best remembered for *Family Fortunes* or for parodying his own appearance on *Family Fortunes* on Ricky Gervais's *Extras*. I decided he hopes he would be remembered as being an all-round family entertainer, great humanitarian, popular philosopher, and one half of one of the all-time great comedy double acts. Unfortunately our survey said he would be remembered as the man who almost had a nervous breakdown live on *Celebrity Big Brother* discussing his break-up from Amanda Holden.

44

Guilty Pleasures

by SIMON TREWIN,
TOM BROMLEY and
MICHAEL MORAN

Guilty pleasures are those indulgences that you confess only to your closest friends (if at all). They fill us with shame and pleasure in equal measure. We prefer to celebrate them. Using a geek logic equation – the Employment Frequency Algorithm (how often do you do this?) times Social Scorn Ratio (how many peers do it too?) plus Ironic Boastfulness Factor (would you actually brag about it after four beers!) divided by Happiness Quota (do you smile during the deed?), we came up with these 32. Think of the process as the first step down the rocky road toward cultural rehabilitation. You'll find comfort knowing you are not alone in your appalling lapses in taste and judgment.

SIMON. TOM, and MICHAEL are the coauthors collectively of the UK bestseller *The Encyclopaedia of Guilty Pleasures. 1001 Things You Hate to Love* and the forthcoming philosophical tract (with Amanda Astil) *Shopping While Drunk.* www.myspace.com/shoppingwhiledrunk.

looking in people's bathroom cabinets
not waking people up on last train home
→ **bathroom cabinets**

able-bodied use of disabled bathrooms
getting an upgrade to first class
→ **first-class upgrade**

faking out dogs with pretend ball throws
having a fat pet
→ **faking out dogs**

DVD extras (wasting time watching)
dirty images on Google (wasting time searching for)
→ **DVD extras**

e-mail offering free money from Nigeria
e-mail (pretending to be someone else when sending)
→ **Nigerian e-mail**

insisting on English wherever you are
misdirecting tourists
→ **misdirecting tourists**

finding and taking last seat on bus or train
farting in the elevator (just before getting out)
→ **farting in elevator**

telling truth about a girlfriend's appearance
peeing in the shower
→ **peeing in shower**

gym (not going to the)
gym (going to the)
→ **gym (not going)**

hair straighteners
nostril hair trimmers
→ **nostril hair trimmers**

lying about having met heroes
kissing and telling
→ **heroes**

Paris Hilton
Donald Trump
→ **Paris Hilton**

faking it
masturbation
→ **masturbation**

stealing from hotel rooms
cheating on expenses (petty or not)
→ **cheating on expenses**

Molly Ringwald in *The Breakfast Club*
Romy and Michele's High School Reunion
→ **Molly Ringwald**

diet fads (believing in)
Krispy Kreme donuts (consumption of)
→ **Krispy Kreme donuts**

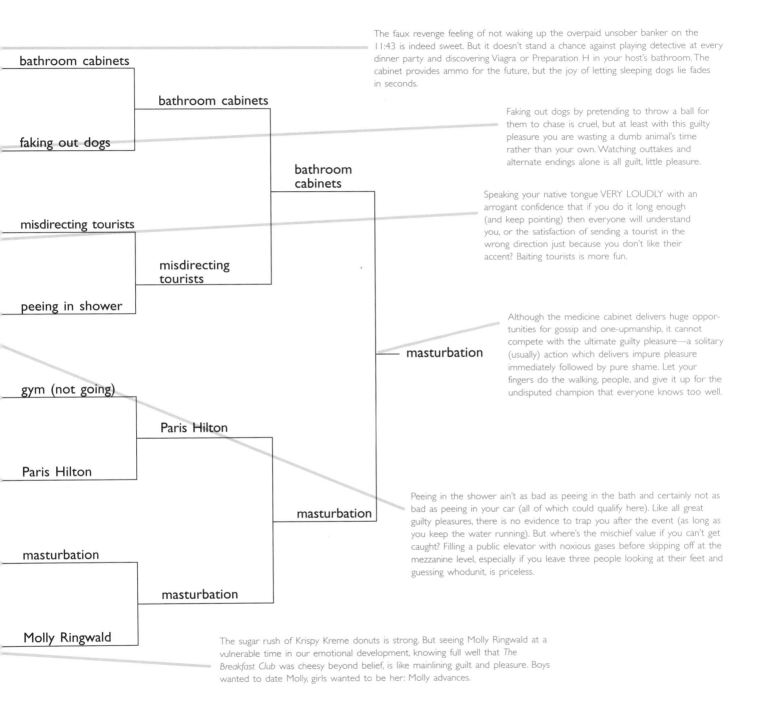

bathroom cabinets

faking out dogs

bathroom cabinets

misdirecting tourists

peeing in shower

bathroom cabinets

misdirecting tourists

gym (not going)

Paris Hilton

Paris Hilton

masturbation

masturbation

Molly Ringwald

masturbation

The faux revenge feeling of not waking up the overpaid unsober banker on the 11:43 is indeed sweet. But it doesn't stand a chance against playing detective at every dinner party and discovering Viagra or Preparation H in your host's bathroom. The cabinet provides ammo for the future, but the joy of letting sleeping dogs lie fades in seconds.

Faking out dogs by pretending to throw a ball for them to chase is cruel, but at least with this guilty pleasure you are wasting a dumb animal's time rather than your own. Watching outtakes and alternate endings alone is all guilt, little pleasure.

Speaking your native tongue VERY LOUDLY with an arrogant confidence that if you do it long enough (and keep pointing) then everyone will understand you, or the satisfaction of sending a tourist in the wrong direction just because you don't like their accent? Baiting tourists is more fun.

Although the medicine cabinet delivers huge opportunities for gossip and one-upmanship, it cannot compete with the ultimate guilty pleasure—a solitary (usually) action which delivers impure pleasure immediately followed by pure shame. Let your fingers do the walking, people, and give it up for the undisputed champion that everyone knows too well.

Peeing in the shower ain't as bad as peeing in the bath and certainly not as bad as peeing in your car (all of which could qualify here). Like all great guilty pleasures, there is no evidence to trap you after the event (as long as you keep the water running). But where's the mischief value if you can't get caught? Filling a public elevator with noxious gases before skipping off at the mezzanine level, especially if you leave three people looking at their feet and guessing whodunit, is priceless.

The sugar rush of Krispy Kreme donuts is strong. But seeing Molly Ringwald at a vulnerable time in our emotional development, knowing full well that *The Breakfast Club* was cheesy beyond belief, is like mainlining guilt and pleasure. Boys wanted to date Molly, girls wanted to be her: Molly advances.

45

Hangover Cures
by SIMON TREWIN

We've all done it – drunk a little bit too much the night before and then crashed out wearing one sock, half a pair of pyjamas, some deeley boppers and a Bluetooth earpiece with the room spinning round and round (like a record baby right round right round). The next morning, you know that there is going to be a hangover devil using a pneumatic drill on your skull and shouting rude things in your ears. Short of drinking your entire body weight in water the night before there is little you can do to avoid this, but when you are struggling into consciousness ahead of a busy day at the office what is the cure to beat all cures?

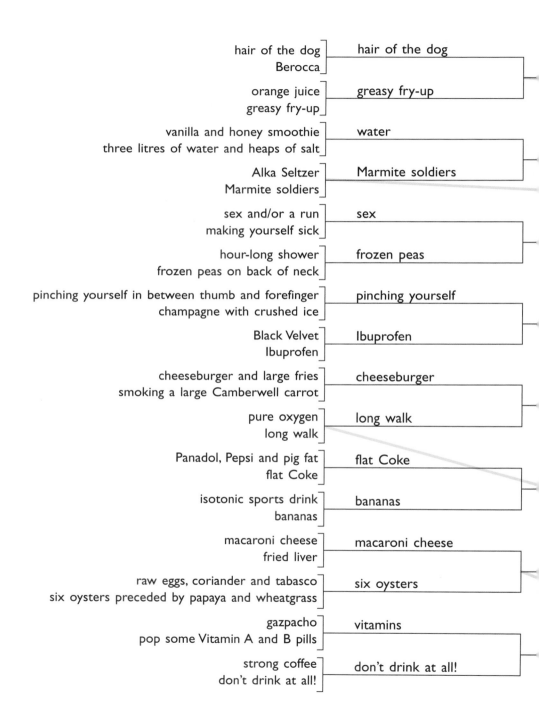

hair of the dog
Berocca
→ hair of the dog

orange juice
greasy fry-up
→ greasy fry-up

vanilla and honey smoothie
three litres of water and heaps of salt
→ water

Alka Seltzer
Marmite soldiers
→ Marmite soldiers

sex and/or a run
making yourself sick
→ sex

hour-long shower
frozen peas on back of neck
→ frozen peas

pinching yourself in between thumb and forefinger
champagne with crushed ice
→ pinching yourself

Black Velvet
Ibuprofen
→ Ibuprofen

cheeseburger and large fries
smoking a large Camberwell carrot
→ cheeseburger

pure oxygen
long walk
→ long walk

Panadol, Pepsi and pig fat
flat Coke
→ flat Coke

isotonic sports drink
bananas
→ bananas

macaroni cheese
fried liver
→ macaroni cheese

raw eggs, coriander and tabasco
six oysters preceded by papaya and wheatgrass
→ six oysters

gazpacho
pop some Vitamin A and B pills
→ vitamins

strong coffee
don't drink at all!
→ don't drink at all!

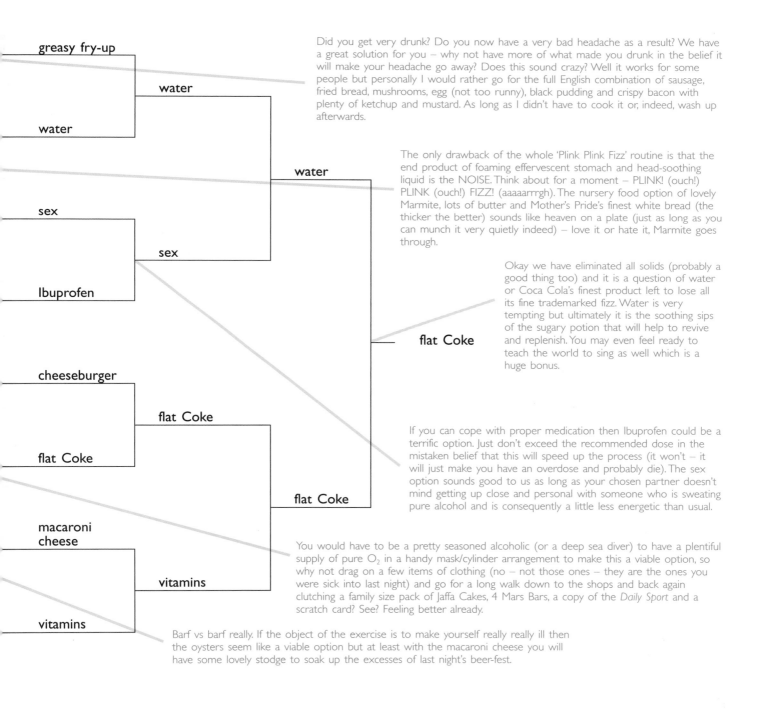

greasy fry-up

water

water

water

sex

sex

Ibuprofen

water

cheeseburger

flat Coke

flat Coke

flat Coke

flat Coke

macaroni cheese

vitamins

vitamins

Did you get very drunk? Do you now have a very bad headache as a result? We have a great solution for you – why not have more of what made you drunk in the belief it will make your headache go away? Does this sound crazy? Well it works for some people but personally I would rather go for the full English combination of sausage, fried bread, mushrooms, egg (not too runny), black pudding and crispy bacon with plenty of ketchup and mustard. As long as I didn't have to cook it or, indeed, wash up afterwards.

The only drawback of the whole 'Plink Plink Fizz' routine is that the end product of foaming effervescent stomach and head-soothing liquid is the NOISE. Think about for a moment – PLINK! (ouch!) PLINK (ouch!) FIZZ! (aaaaarrrgh). The nursery food option of lovely Marmite, lots of butter and Mother's Pride's finest white bread (the thicker the better) sounds like heaven on a plate (just as long as you can munch it very quietly indeed) – love it or hate it, Marmite goes through.

Okay we have eliminated all solids (probably a good thing too) and it is a question of water or Coca Cola's finest product left to lose all its fine trademarked fizz. Water is very tempting but ultimately it is the soothing sips of the sugary potion that will help to revive and replenish. You may even feel ready to teach the world to sing as well which is a huge bonus.

If you can cope with proper medication then Ibuprofen could be a terrific option. Just don't exceed the recommended dose in the mistaken belief that this will speed up the process (it won't – it will just make you have an overdose and probably die). The sex option sounds good to us as long as your chosen partner doesn't mind getting up close and personal with someone who is sweating pure alcohol and is consequently a little less energetic than usual.

You would have to be a pretty seasoned alcoholic (or a deep sea diver) to have a plentiful supply of pure O_2 in a handy mask/cylinder arrangement to make this a viable option, so why not drag on a few items of clothing (no – not those ones – they are the ones you were sick into last night) and go for a long walk down to the shops and back again clutching a family size pack of Jaffa Cakes, 4 Mars Bars, a copy of the *Daily Sport* and a scratch card? See? Feeling better already.

Barf vs barf really. If the object of the exercise is to make yourself really really ill then the oysters seem like a viable option but at least with the macaroni cheese you will have some lovely stodge to soak up the excesses of last night's beer-fest.

46

Horrible Smells
by SIMON TREWIN

Yuk, yuk, yuk, yuk. Just thinking about this bracket makes me want to wash my hands, have a bath and put on a clean shirt. However rich or poor we are, however much we may have dressed up to the nines, we are, underneath it all, just bodies, and bodies have an ability to smell really bad. Anyone who has ever walked into a room of teenagers with their shoes off and their feet up on the coffee table watching a football match can attest to that – a heady mix of sweat, cheesy feet and halitosis reminds you that teenagers' fear of water is second only to cats'. Estate agents still reckon that the smell of baking bread will entice potential buyers across the threshold in a positive frame of mind and personally I am unable to pass a branch of the shop Lush without finding myself drawn in to have a good sniff at the lemon soap. Pure heaven. That said, there are some smells that I simply cannot bear. Here are thirty-two of them, but which one will be awarded the golden clothes peg?

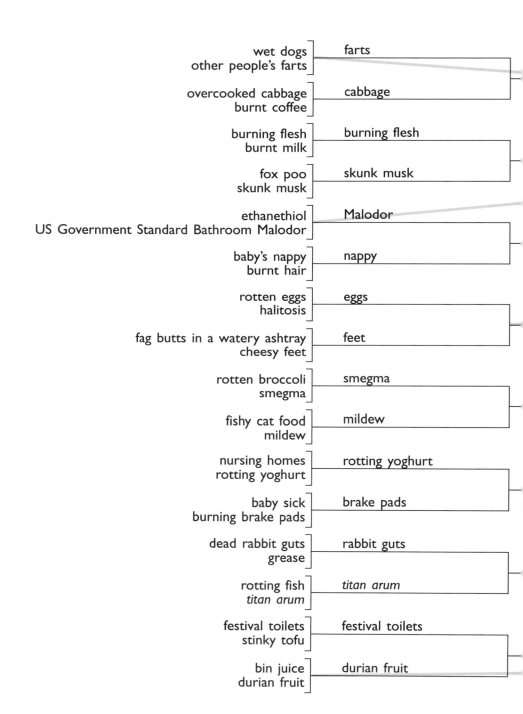

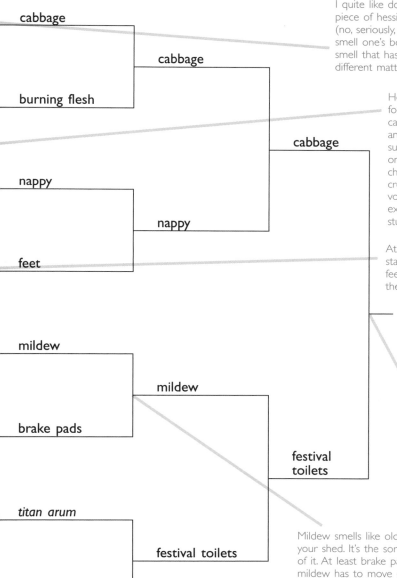

I quite like dogs. When they are dry. When they are wet they smell like a rotting piece of hessian carpet that you have left out on the back step. Yuk. We all fart (no, seriously, even the Queen) and it is always interesting to see what kind of smell one's body comes up with. I don't think I have ever been grossed out by the smell that has come out of my own bottom, but other peoples' farts are a different matter altogether, particularly in lifts. Farts move on. Sorry, was that me?

Here is the science bit. Ethanethiol is an organic compound with the formula CH_3CH_2SH. It has a hugely disgusting odour that we humans can detect in minute concentrations. It smells like disgusting smelly leeks and the *Guinness Book of World Records* has ranked this as the smelliest substance in existence. The US government, however, have taken things one step further by creating their 'Malodor'. It is a mix of eight chemicals with smells resembling human faeces and rotten eggs that was created to test the effectiveness of air-fresheners. In a test, volunteers began to scream and curse after just a few seconds' exposure. Forget the *Guinness Book of Records*, this sounds like serious stuff and moves on.

At least you can throw rotten eggs away. Really cheesy feet seem to stay cheesy even after they have been washed several times. Cheesy feet in a hot car on a warm day are enough to make you gag and so they move on to the next round.

festival toilets

I associate overcooked cabbage with the culinary delights of my primary school – you could tell all morning if cabbage was being cooked for lunch. And by the time you queued up to go into the dining hall the stench was almost overpowering. No one seemed to eat it and I could never work out why they bothered to cook it. The smell of festival loos are so bad it is enough to turn anyone blessed with regular bowel movements into the most constipated person around. But it's not just the nose-burning smell that gets to you, it's also the visual accompaniments of filthy floors and poo-encrusted seats. Even if you pick your cubicle with care there is usually a small slick of vomit to step over before you can lower yourself on to the filthy stainless steel loo seat. The whole experience is so gut-wrenching that festival loos are awarded the golden clothes' peg.

Mildew smells like old people, neglected houses and that old pair of gardening gloves in your shed. It's the sort of smell that lingers and I've never managed to completely get rid of it. At least brake pads (after a long uphill stop/start climb) calm down after a while, so mildew has to move on. (Incidentally, if anyone knows of how to get rid of the smell, please do let me know.)

Bin juice is that disgusting gloopy syrupy gunk left inside the bin when you have removed the black sack. Orang-utans love durian fruit. Travel writer Richard Stirling describes it as 'smelling like pig shit, turpentine and onions garnished with a gym sock'. That's good enough for me; it moves on.

47

Hot Fictional Men
by CLARE BENNETT

I heard a best man once advise women to treat men like grapes: 'First, you've got to crush them,' he said, 'and then let them mature into something you'd like to have dinner with.' One could draw a similar analogy with men and shoes: with some you have to suffer enormous discomfort to break them in until they become comfortable enough for you to walk all over. With others, you look at them and think 'You don't go with anything, what possessed me to buy you?' and you have to get rid of them. Not so with the glorious leading men of literature – the beauty of them is they are exactly what you want them to be. They don't watch sport all summer on the telly, they don't not call when they said they would, they don't come back from the hairdresser with terrible haircuts and expect you to still fancy them. And there are so many to choose from! Captain Corelli is just heaven, and bucks the trend with most Italians, who are notorious for their grand exclamations to get what they want and total abandonment when they get it (ask my friends Hen and Sophie). I have only included one Jane Austen hero, although I could easily have included Captain Wentworth and Mr Knightley – for a girl who never married, she just goes to show, you don't need to have experienced it in real life to know exactly how it should be. My disbelief is so willingly suspended, it's ridiculous.

CLARE BENNETT reads a lot. But for all the wrong reasons.

Atticus Finch
Julian Sorel

Heathcliff
James Bond

Odysseus
Stanley Kowalski

Maxim de Winter
Romeo

Mr Rochester
Captain Corelli

Gabriel Oak
Will Ladislaw

King Arthur
Rhett Butler

Sebastian Flyte
Mr Darcy

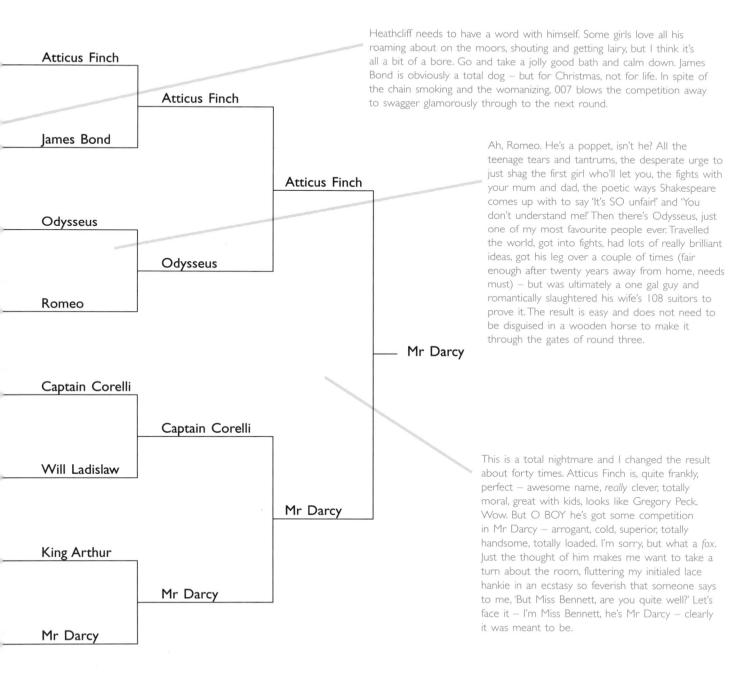

Atticus Finch

Atticus Finch

James Bond

Atticus Finch

Odysseus

Odysseus

Romeo

Atticus Finch

Mr Darcy

Captain Corelli

Captain Corelli

Will Ladislaw

Mr Darcy

King Arthur

Mr Darcy

Mr Darcy

Heathcliff needs to have a word with himself. Some girls love all his roaming about on the moors, shouting and getting lairy, but I think it's all a bit of a bore. Go and take a jolly good bath and calm down. James Bond is obviously a total dog – but for Christmas, not for life. In spite of the chain smoking and the womanizing, 007 blows the competition away to swagger glamorously through to the next round.

Ah, Romeo. He's a poppet, isn't he? All the teenage tears and tantrums, the desperate urge to just shag the first girl who'll let you, the fights with your mum and dad, the poetic ways Shakespeare comes up with to say 'It's SO unfair!' and 'You don't understand me!' Then there's Odysseus, just one of my most favourite people ever. Travelled the world, got into fights, had lots of really brilliant ideas, got his leg over a couple of times (fair enough after twenty years away from home, needs must) – but was ultimately a one gal guy and romantically slaughtered his wife's 108 suitors to prove it. The result is easy and does not need to be disguised in a wooden horse to make it through the gates of round three.

This is a total nightmare and I changed the result about forty times. Atticus Finch is, quite frankly, perfect – awesome name, *really* clever, totally moral, great with kids, looks like Gregory Peck. Wow. But O BOY he's got some competition in Mr Darcy – arrogant, cold, superior, totally handsome, totally loaded. I'm sorry, but what a *fox*. Just the thought of him makes me want to take a turn about the room, fluttering my initialed lace hankie in an ecstasy so feverish that someone says to me, 'But Miss Bennett, are you quite well?' Let's face it – I'm Miss Bennett, he's Mr Darcy – clearly it was meant to be.

48

Iconic Rock Fashion Items

by PAUL GORMAN

These are the iconic items of rock & roll fashion I would like to own, even if some of them would neither suit nor fit me. I'm not sure I have the hips for the ball gown with sequined face mask designed for Bjork in 2005 by Alexander McQueen, nor the thighs for the tiny gold hot pants sported by Kylie Minogue in the video for her hit song 'Can't Get You Out Of My Mind'. I'm not the biggest fan of some of the artists, but all of the designers would get my vote. Having spent decades submerging myself in this subject, I have created this series of play-offs on the basis of iconic value, mould-breaking design value and pure personal prejudice.

PAUL GORMAN, 47, is a London-based writer. He has contributed to a wide variety of publications from the *Evening Standard, Screen International,* the *Daily Telegraph* and *Radio Times* to *Word, Heat, Mojo, Garageland* and *Music Week.* His style bible, *The Look: Adventures in Rock and Pop Fashion.*

Iggy Pop's tiger-backed jacket, Raw Power sleeve (Wonder Workshop, 1972)
Andy Warhol's BOY cap (Boy, 1988) — **Iggy's jacket**

Keith Richard's velvet 'bolero' suit (Granny Takes A Trip, 1970)
Andy MacKay's gold brothel creepers, For Your Pleasure (City Lights Studio, 1973) — **Andy's brothel creepers**

Frank Sinatra's sharkskin suit (Sy Devore, 1962)
Bob Dylan's polka-dot tab-collared shirt (DeVoss, 1966) — **Frank's suit**

David Bowie's blue box-jacketed suit (City Lights Studio, 1973)
Kevin Rowland's Ivy league wingtips (Florsheim's, 1985) — **David's suit**

Geri Halliwell's platform-soled trainers (1996)
Madonna's conical bra (Jean Paul Gaultier, 1989) — **Madge's bra**

Liam Gallagher's parka (Fake of London, 2002)
Gram Parson's marijuana leaf-embroidered suit (Nudie Cohn, 1968) — **Gram's suit**

Kylie Minogue's gold hot pants (Charity shop, 2002)
Pete Townshend's Union Jack jacket (Carnaby Street ,1965) — **Kylie's pants**

Elvis's black and pink peg slacks (Lanskys, 1954)
Johnny Rotten's bondage suit (Seditionaries, 1976) — **Bondage suit**

Ian Brown's dollar bill top (1988)
Rod Stewart's pink satin suit (Granny Takes A Trip, 1970) — **Rod's suit**

Mick Jagger's white man dress and trousers (Mr Fish, 1970)
The Beatles round/velvet collared jackets (Dougie Millings, 1963) — **Jagger's dress**

Jimi Hendrix Hussar's waistcoat (I Was Lord Kitchener's Valet, 1967)
Boy George's Hassidic smock (The Foundry, 1982) — **Jimi's waistcoat**

Pete Doherty's porkpie hat (Hedi Slimane, 2005)
Nancy Sinatra's go-go boots (Jax Of Hollywood, 1966) — **Pete's porkpie**

Joe Strummer's zippered jacket (Michon Kolowska, 1977)
James Brown's tight three-piece suit (1964) — **Strummer's Clash jacket**

George Michael's 45-backed studded leather biker's jacket and steel-tipped boots as worn
Prince's purple satin pantsuit (Johnson's, 1987) — **George's jacket/boots**

Mick Jagger's satin jumpsuit (Ossie Clark ,1972)
Andre 3000's tweed plus fours and matching cap (AndreBenjamin, 2005) — **Jagger's jumpsuit**

Bjork's sequin-masked Fashion Rocks outfit (Alexander McQueen, 2005)
Bryan Ferry's white tuxedo (Antony Price, 1972) — **Ferry's tux**

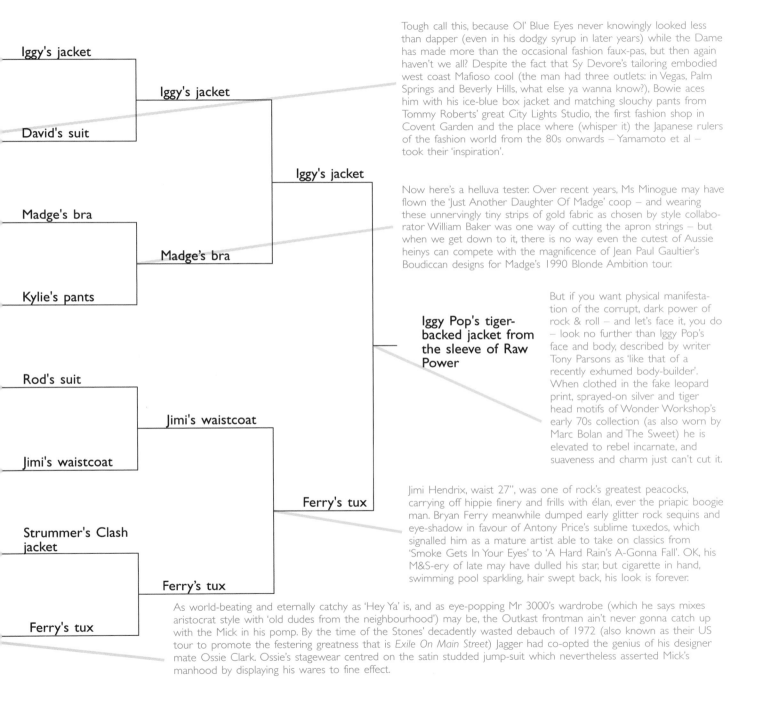

Iggy's jacket

Iggy's jacket

David's suit

Iggy's jacket

Iggy's jacket

Madge's bra

Madge's bra

Kylie's pants

Iggy Pop's tiger-backed jacket from the sleeve of Raw Power

Rod's suit

Jimi's waistcoat

Jimi's waistcoat

Ferry's tux

Strummer's Clash jacket

Ferry's tux

Ferry's tux

Tough call this, because Ol' Blue Eyes never knowingly looked less than dapper (even in his dodgy syrup in later years) while the Dame has made more than the occasional fashion faux-pas, but then again haven't we all? Despite the fact that Sy Devore's tailoring embodied west coast Mafioso cool (the man had three outlets: in Vegas, Palm Springs and Beverly Hills, what else ya wanna know?), Bowie aces him with his ice-blue box jacket and matching slouchy pants from Tommy Roberts' great City Lights Studio, the first fashion shop in Covent Garden and the place where (whisper it) the Japanese rulers of the fashion world from the 80s onwards – Yamamoto et al – took their 'inspiration'.

Now here's a helluva tester. Over recent years, Ms Minogue may have flown the 'Just Another Daughter Of Madge' coop – and wearing these unnervingly tiny strips of gold fabric as chosen by style collaborator William Baker was one way of cutting the apron strings – but when we get down to it, there is no way even the cutest of Aussie heinys can compete with the magnificence of Jean Paul Gaultier's Boudiccan designs for Madge's 1990 Blonde Ambition tour.

But if you want physical manifestation of the corrupt, dark power of rock & roll – and let's face it, you do – look no further than Iggy Pop's face and body, described by writer Tony Parsons as 'like that of a recently exhumed body-builder'. When clothed in the fake leopard print, sprayed-on silver and tiger head motifs of Wonder Workshop's early 70s collection (as also worn by Marc Bolan and The Sweet) he is elevated to rebel incarnate, and suaveness and charm just can't cut it.

Jimi Hendrix, waist 27", was one of rock's greatest peacocks, carrying off hippie finery and frills with élan, ever the priapic boogie man. Bryan Ferry meanwhile dumped early glitter rock sequins and eye-shadow in favour of Antony Price's sublime tuxedos, which signalled him as a mature artist able to take on classics from 'Smoke Gets In Your Eyes' to 'A Hard Rain's A-Gonna Fall'. OK, his M&S-ery of late may have dulled his star, but cigarette in hand, swimming pool sparkling, hair swept back, his look is forever.

As world-beating and eternally catchy as 'Hey Ya' is, and as eye-popping Mr 3000's wardrobe (which he says mixes aristocrat style with 'old dudes from the neighbourhood') may be, the Outkast frontman ain't never gonna catch up with the Mick in his pomp. By the time of the Stones' decadently wasted debauch of 1972 (also known as their US tour to promote the festering greatness that is *Exile On Main Street*) Jagger had co-opted the genius of his designer mate Ossie Clark. Ossie's stagewear centred on the satin studded jump-suit which nevertheless asserted Mick's manhood by displaying his wares to fine effect.

49

Internet Innovations

by ROBIN VINCENT

Few things, except for perhaps natural disasters, have had such a transformational effect on the world in such an alarmingly short space of time as the Internet. When Tim Berners-Lee slapped up the first web page in 1991 I wonder if he had any idea what the World Wide Web and the surrounding Internet infrastructure would lead to ten or twenty years down the line. It has become so baked into our lives that we rarely take any notice of it anymore; like central heating, or refrigerators. But which technology, spawned from this notion of connectivity, has had the largest impact on our lives? Is its influence all about new devices or is it the evolution of ways and methods into electronic, digital versions of what we used to labour over? Maybe all the good ideas have come along already, or maybe this suggests an inkling of what the future may hold.

ROBIN VINCENT is a technology writer, musician and director of specialist computer company Rain Recording Ltd. Robin splits his time between building computers for audio/media production (www.rainrecording.co.uk), creating meditative soundscapes (www.moltenmeditation.com), advising musicians on the latest in computer music technology (www.pc-music.com) and playing with his baby son Alfie (www.alfredray.com).

Predating Berners-Lee and the World Wide Web this was how the Internet was first used for mass public networking. Bulletin Board Systems were simply electronic versions of a sheet of cork pinned to a wall. Users would dial in (old phone handset jammed into a rubber holder à la *War Games*) and read and post messages, as well as download data and other information. Internet Relay Chat invented the concept of being online in 'real-time' as your comments were displayed instantly to anyone logged into your server. The 'chat room' was born and now previously inept social misfits could converse with similarly minded technology junkies all over the known world (well, the US and Europe anyway). It was the father of Microsoft Messenger and was the first technology to create a genuine sense of virtual community.

The original dotcom: a seller of books, online, light years before anyone else had thought of selling through the Internet, Amazon began its slow drift into profitability. But then why buy books from a shop when you can buy them second hand just as easily on eBay while, at the same time, selling an old wardrobe, worn out socks and that jumper you got for Christmas? eBay puts the commercial power of the Internet into the hands of anyone who gets excited by a car boot sale (let's face it, who doesn't?). It's created its own form of broker – people who make a living buying low, selling high and moving someone's unwanted crap from one place to another. Truly useful and probably the saviour of the Post Office.

HTML– Hypertext Markup Language	**HTML**
FTP – File Transfer Protocol	
Java – object orientated programming	**Java**
Flash – web-based media presentation	
BBS – Bulletin Boards	**mIRC**
mIRC – Internet Relay Chat	
Email – electronic mail	**Email**
MSM – Microsoft Messenger	
RSS – Really Simple Syndication	**Blog**
Blog – web-logging or journalling	
MP3 – audio streaming/download format	**Podcast**
Podcast – subscribable audio/video broadcast	
eBay – online auction house	**eBay**
Amazon – online shop	
iTunes – music download application	**MySpace**
MySpace – network based online residence	
Google – search engine	**Google**
Yahoo – search engine	
Netscape – browser	**Explorer**
Explorer – browser	
Paypal – banking/merchant services	**Paypal**
WorldPay – banking/merchant services	
DotCom – company web domain designation	**DotOrg**
DotOrg – charity web domain designation	
Gambling – online casinos	**Gambling**
Pornography – 'nuff said	
Virus – computer infection	**Spam**
Spam – unsolicited advertising, junk email	
Second Life – Linden Labs' virtual world	**Second Life**
Multiplayer online gaming	
VOIP – Voice Over IP Internet telephony	**VOIP**
Video Conferencing – seeing who you talk to	

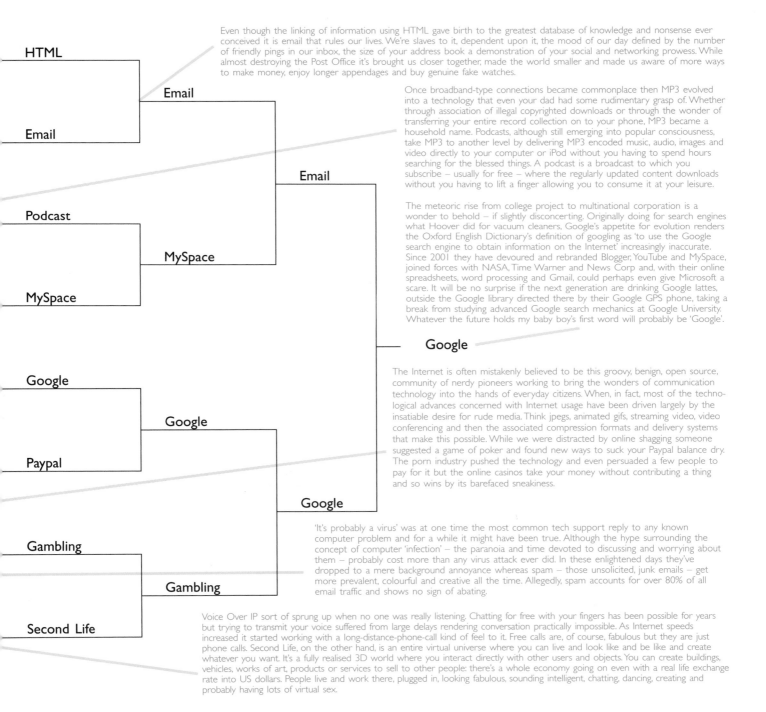

HTML

Email

Email

Email

Podcast

MySpace

MySpace

Email

Google

Google

Paypal

Google

Google

Gambling

Google

Second Life

Gambling

Even though the linking of information using HTML gave birth to the greatest database of knowledge and nonsense ever conceived it is email that rules our lives. We're slaves to it, dependent upon it, the mood of our day defined by the number of friendly pings in our inbox, the size of your address book a demonstration of your social and networking prowess. While almost destroying the Post Office it's brought us closer together, made the world smaller and made us aware of more ways to make money, enjoy longer appendages and buy genuine fake watches.

Once broadband-type connections became commonplace then MP3 evolved into a technology that even your dad had some rudimentary grasp of. Whether through association of illegal copyrighted downloads or through the wonder of transferring your entire record collection on to your phone, MP3 became a household name. Podcasts, although still emerging into popular consciousness, take MP3 to another level by delivering MP3 encoded music, audio, images and video directly to your computer or iPod without you having to spend hours searching for the blessed things. A podcast is a broadcast to which you subscribe – usually for free – where the regularly updated content downloads without you having to lift a finger allowing you to consume it at your leisure.

The meteoric rise from college project to multinational corporation is a wonder to behold – if slightly disconcerting. Originally doing for search engines what Hoover did for vacuum cleaners, Google's appetite for evolution renders the Oxford English Dictionary's definition of googling as 'to use the Google search engine to obtain information on the Internet' increasingly inaccurate. Since 2001 they have devoured and rebranded Blogger, YouTube and MySpace, joined forces with NASA, Time Warner and News Corp and, with their online spreadsheets, word processing and Gmail, could perhaps even give Microsoft a scare. It will be no surprise if the next generation are drinking Google lattes, outside the Google library directed there by their Google GPS phone, taking a break from studying advanced Google search mechanics at Google University. Whatever the future holds my baby boy's first word will probably be 'Google'.

The Internet is often mistakenly believed to be this groovy, benign, open source, community of nerdy pioneers working to bring the wonders of communication technology into the hands of everyday citizens. When, in fact, most of the technological advances concerned with Internet usage have been driven largely by the insatiable desire for rude media. Think jpegs, animated gifs, streaming video, video conferencing and then the associated compression formats and delivery systems that make this possible. While we were distracted by online shagging someone suggested a game of poker and found new ways to suck your Paypal balance dry. The porn industry pushed the technology and even persuaded a few people to pay for it but the online casinos take your money without contributing a thing and so wins by its barefaced sneakiness.

'It's probably a virus' was at one time the most common tech support reply to any known computer problem and for a while it might have been true. Although the hype surrounding the concept of computer 'infection' – the paranoia and time devoted to discussing and worrying about them – probably cost more than any virus attack ever did. In these enlightened days they've dropped to a mere background annoyance whereas spam – those unsolicited, junk emails – get more prevalent, colourful and creative all the time. Allegedly, spam accounts for over 80% of all email traffic and shows no sign of abating.

Voice Over IP sort of sprung up when no one was really listening. Chatting for free with your fingers has been possible for years but trying to transmit your voice suffered from large delays rendering conversation practically impossible. As Internet speeds increased it started working with a long-distance-phone-call kind of feel to it. Free calls are, of course, fabulous but they are just phone calls. Second Life, on the other hand, is an entire virtual universe where you can live and look like and be like and create whatever you want. It's a fully realised 3D world where you interact directly with other users and objects. You can create buildings, vehicles, works of art, products or services to sell to other people: there's a whole economy going on even with a real life exchange rate into US dollars. People live and work there, plugged in, looking fabulous, sounding intelligent, chatting, dancing, creating and probably having lots of virtual sex.

50

Inventions
by ADI IGNATIUS

How do you rank innovation? How do you compare one invention's contribution to society against another's? What's more worthy, birth control or Viagra? The guillotine or Prozac? Paper or plastic? The fact is, a great invention doesn't have to be a great leap forward technologically. It has to improve our lives and help us in that most meaningful activity: the pursuit of happiness. Marvelous as some of these innovations are, it's hard to see how airplanes — or even TVs and PCs — truly make us happier. The former is as much an agent of destruction as a means of transportation, the latter two perhaps the biggest time wasters in history.

ADI IGNATIUS is an executive editor of *Time* magazine, and a former *Wall Street Journal* bureau chief in Beijing and Moscow. His favourite childhood innovations involved adapting baseball for the backyard. None of his friends or siblings could keep these straight, particularly the one where you hit the ball with a tennis racket off the roof.

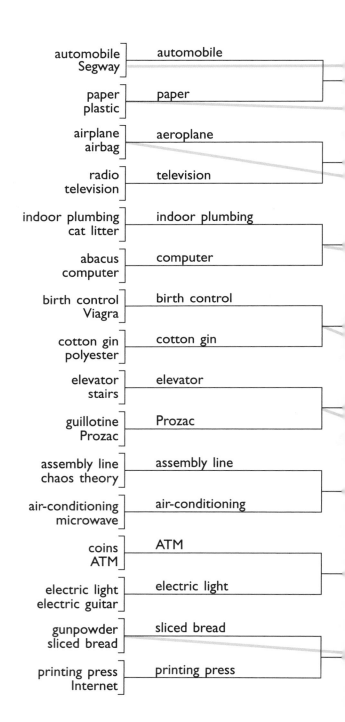

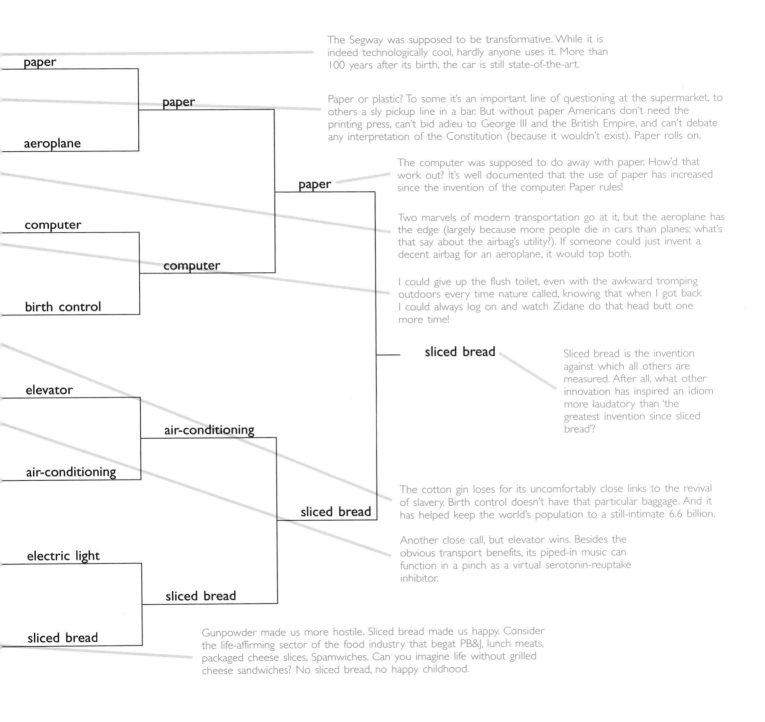

paper

paper

aeroplane

The Segway was supposed to be transformative. While it is indeed technologically cool, hardly anyone uses it. More than 100 years after its birth, the car is still state-of-the-art.

Paper or plastic? To some it's an important line of questioning at the supermarket, to others a sly pickup line in a bar. But without paper Americans don't need the printing press, can't bid adieu to George III and the British Empire, and can't debate any interpretation of the Constitution (because it wouldn't exist). Paper rolls on.

paper

computer

computer

birth control

The computer was supposed to do away with paper. How'd that work out? It's well documented that the use of paper has increased since the invention of the computer. Paper rules!

Two marvels of modern transportation go at it, but the aeroplane has the edge (largely because more people die in cars than planes; what's that say about the airbag's utility?). If someone could just invent a decent airbag for an aeroplane, it would top both.

I could give up the flush toilet, even with the awkward tromping outdoors every time nature called, knowing that when I got back I could always log on and watch Zidane do that head butt one more time!

sliced bread

Sliced bread is the invention against which all others are measured. After all, what other innovation has inspired an idiom more laudatory than 'the greatest invention since sliced bread'?

elevator

air-conditioning

air-conditioning

sliced bread

The cotton gin loses for its uncomfortably close links to the revival of slavery. Birth control doesn't have that particular baggage. And it has helped keep the world's population to a still-intimate 6.6 billion.

Another close call, but elevator wins. Besides the obvious transport benefits, its piped-in music can function in a pinch as a virtual serotonin-reuptake inhibitor.

electric light

sliced bread

sliced bread

Gunpowder made us more hostile. Sliced bread made us happy. Consider the life-affirming sector of the food industry that begat PB&J, lunch meats, packaged cheese slices, Spamwiches. Can you imagine life without grilled cheese sandwiches? No sliced bread, no happy childhood.

51

James Bond Gadgets

by LOIS H. GRESH and ROBERT WEINBERG

James Bond is defined by girls, martinis, guns, cars, and toys that are outlandish and, therefore, Bondish. Some are more Bondish than others, meaning they are more clever, high-tech, outrageous, yet still realistic. In making our choices, coolness was a factor too. Of course, if coolness was the sole criterion and we didn't have to concern ourselves with gadgets not being people and people not being gadgets, then Sean Connery would be the ultimate Bond gadget of all.

LOIS H. GRESH is the author of 17 books and serves as technical communications director of science, technology, engineering, and math at the University of Rochester. ROBERT WEINBERG is the author of 34 books and a two-time winner of the World Fantasy Award. Together, they are coauthors of *The Science of James Bond* (Wiley, 2006), which explains everything from dirty bombs to space lasers to the medicinal merits of the martini.

Matchup	Winner
Walther PPK 7.65 mm firearm (*Dr. No*, 1962) / dirty bomb (*Goldfinger*, 1964)	Walther PPK 7.65 mm
nuclear weapon (*Thunderball*, 1965) / Solex agitator (*The Man with the Golden Gun*, 1974)	Solex agitator
artificial fingerprints (*Diamonds are Forever*, 1971) / Lektor message decoder (*From Russia with Love*, 1963)	Lektor message decoder
voice duplicator (*Diamonds Are Forever*, 1971) / U.S. Clipper Chip (*GoldenEye*, 1995)	U.S. Clipper Chip
video camera ring (*A View to a Kill*, 1985) / camera rocket launcher (*The Man with the Golden Gun*, 1974)	video camera ring
1961 Sunbeam Alpine light blue convertible (*Dr No*, 1962) / martini (nearly all Bond movies)	martini
BMW Z8 car (*The World Is Not Enough*, 1999) / Aston Martin DB5 car (*Goldfinger*, 1964)	Aston Martin DB5
Bentley Mark IV convertible (*From Russia with Love*, 1963) / invisible Aston Martin VI2 Vanquish (*Die Another Day*, 2002)	Aston Martin VI2
AMC Matador flying car (*The Man with the Golden Gun*, 1974) / Lotus Esprit car-submarine (*The Spy Who Loved Me*, 1977)	Lotus car-sub
Geiger counter wristwatch (*Thunderball*, 1965) / Omega wristwatch bomb detonator (*Tomorrow Never Dies*, 1997)	Geiger counter watch
Omega bomb-arming wristwatch with laser cutter (*GoldenEye*, 1995) / circular saw wristwatch (*Live and Let Die*, 1973)	bomb-arming watch
hydrofoil boat (*Thunderball*, 1965) / gondola hovercraft (*Moonraker*, 1979)	hydrofoil boat
invisible stealth ship (*Tomorrow Never Dies*, 1997) / gobbling spaceship (*You Only Live Twice*, 1967)	gobbling spaceship
Moonraker space station (*Moonraker*, 1979) / autogyro (*You Only Live Twice*, 1967)	Moonraker space station
Gustav Graves DNA plastic surgery (*Die Another Day*, 2002) / Jaws (*The Spy Who Loved Me*, 1977, and *Moonraker*, 1979)	Jaws
Max Zorin Nazi genetics research (*A View to a Kill*, 1985) / Jill Masterson golden girl (*Goldfinger*, 1964)	Jill Masterson golden girl

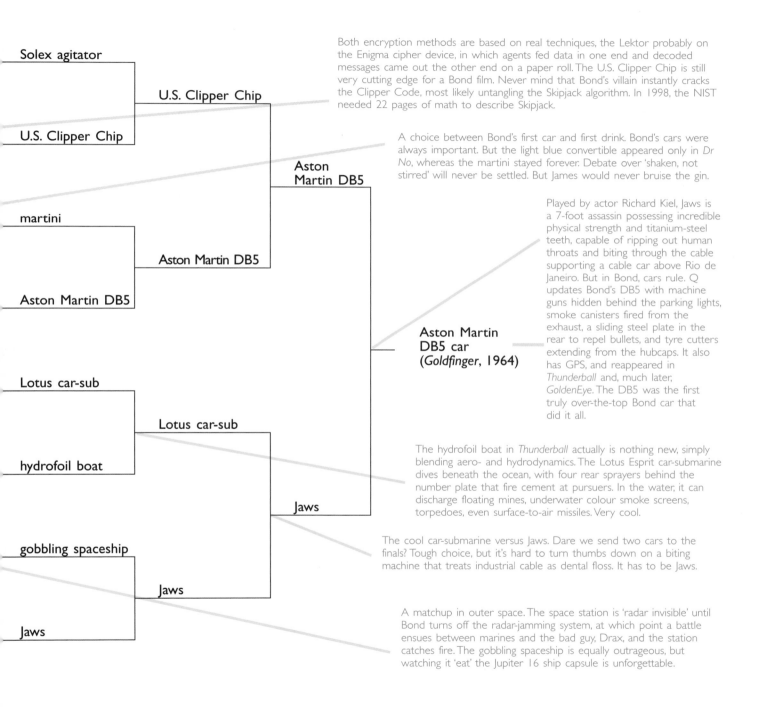

Solex agitator

U.S. Clipper Chip

U.S. Clipper Chip

martini

Aston Martin DB5

Aston Martin DB5

Aston Martin DB5

Lotus car-sub

Lotus car-sub

hydrofoil boat

Jaws

gobbling spaceship

Jaws

Jaws

Aston Martin DB5 car (*Goldfinger*, 1964)

Both encryption methods are based on real techniques, the Lektor probably on the Enigma cipher device, in which agents fed data in one end and decoded messages came out the other end on a paper roll. The U.S. Clipper Chip is still very cutting edge for a Bond film. Never mind that Bond's villain instantly cracks the Clipper Code, most likely untangling the Skipjack algorithm. In 1998, the NIST needed 22 pages of math to describe Skipjack.

A choice between Bond's first car and first drink. Bond's cars were always important. But the light blue convertible appeared only in *Dr No*, whereas the martini stayed forever. Debate over 'shaken, not stirred' will never be settled. But James would never bruise the gin.

Played by actor Richard Kiel, Jaws is a 7-foot assassin possessing incredible physical strength and titanium-steel teeth, capable of ripping out human throats and biting through the cable supporting a cable car above Rio de Janeiro. But in Bond, cars rule. Q updates Bond's DB5 with machine guns hidden behind the parking lights, smoke canisters fired from the exhaust, a sliding steel plate in the rear to repel bullets, and tyre cutters extending from the hubcaps. It also has GPS, and reappeared in *Thunderball* and, much later, *GoldenEye*. The DB5 was the first truly over-the-top Bond car that did it all.

The hydrofoil boat in *Thunderball* actually is nothing new, simply blending aero- and hydrodynamics. The Lotus Esprit car-submarine dives beneath the ocean, with four rear sprayers behind the number plate that fire cement at pursuers. In the water, it can discharge floating mines, underwater colour smoke screens, torpedoes, even surface-to-air missiles. Very cool.

The cool car-submarine versus Jaws. Dare we send two cars to the finals? Tough choice, but it's hard to turn thumbs down on a biting machine that treats industrial cable as dental floss. It has to be Jaws.

A matchup in outer space. The space station is 'radar invisible' until Bond turns off the radar-jamming system, at which point a battle ensues between marines and the bad guy, Drax, and the station catches fire. The gobbling spaceship is equally outrageous, but watching it 'eat' the Jupiter 16 ship capsule is unforgettable.

52

Kevin Keeganisms

by SUE MONGREDIEN

I've always loved Kevin Keegan, right from his days of tight little shorts and crazy hair back in the 70s, all the way through to his pearls of wisdom as a TV commentator in more recent years. My brother has a list of his finest alleged quotes pinned up on his kitchen wall, and every time I go there, I read them and laugh. But which is the funniest, the greatest of all?

At the age of six, SUE MONGREDIEN was one of the winners in a Notts County Council poetry competition with her poem entitled 'Aston Villa We Love You'. These days, she writes a wide variety of children's books, as well as adult fiction under the pen name Lucy Diamond. www.lucydiamond.co.uk

The tide is very much in our court now.
Chile have three options – they could win or they could lose.

tide

Gary always weighed up his options, especially when he had no choice.
I came to Nantes two years ago and it's much the same today, except that it's totally different.

Gary

That would have been a goal if it hadn't been saved.
There'll be no siestas in Madrid tonight.

Madrid

A tremendous strike which hit the defender full on the arm – and it nearly came off.
The good news for Nigeria is that they're 2-0 down very early in the game.

Nigeria

I'm not disappointed – just disappointed.
I don't think there's anyone bigger or smaller than Maradona.

Maradona

We deserved to win this game after hammering them 0-0 in the first half.
. . . using his strength. And that is his strength, his strength.

strength

Argentina won't be at Euro 2000 because they're from South America.
In some ways, cramp is worse than having a broken leg.

Argentina

I know what is around the corner – I just don't know where the corner is.
The onus is on us to perform and we must control the bandwagon.

corner

Young Gareth Barry – he's young.
The Germans only have one player under 22, and he's 23.

Germans

Hungary is very similar to Bulgaria – I know they're different countries.
England have the best fans in the world – and Scotland's fans are second to none.

fans

I've had an interest in racing all my life, or longer really.
He can't speak Turkey, but you can tell he's delighted.

racing

It could be far worse for me if it was easy for me.
You're not just getting international football – you're getting world football.

world

They're the second-best team in the world, and there's no higher praise than that.
I'd love to be a mole on the wall in the Liverpool dressing room at half-time.

mole

You can't do better than go away from home and get a draw.
Kanu – a guy with a heart as big as he is.

draw

It's understandable that people are keeping one eye on the pot and another up the chimney.
Goalkeepers aren't born today until they're in their late twenties or thirties.

chimney

The game has gone rather scrappy as both sides realize they could win this match or lose it.
This could be a repeat of the final.

final

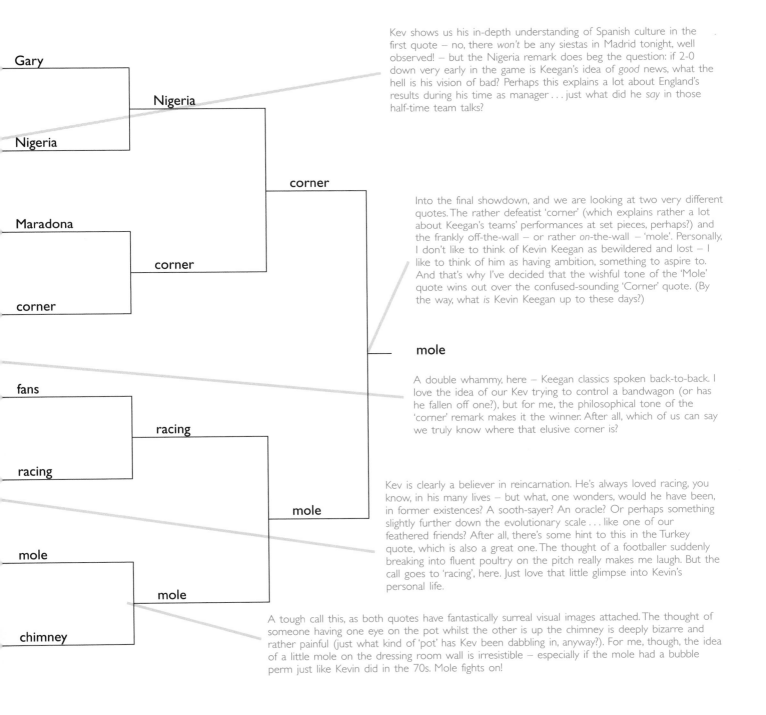

Gary

Nigeria

Nigeria

Maradona

corner

corner

corner

Nigeria

corner

mole

fans

racing

racing

mole

mole

chimney

mole

racing

mole

Kev shows us his in-depth understanding of Spanish culture in the first quote – no, there *won't* be any siestas in Madrid tonight, well observed! – but the Nigeria remark does beg the question: if 2-0 down very early in the game is Keegan's idea of *good* news, what the hell is his vision of bad? Perhaps this explains a lot about England's results during his time as manager . . . just what did he *say* in those half-time team talks?

Into the final showdown, and we are looking at two very different quotes. The rather defeatist 'corner' (which explains rather a lot about Keegan's teams' performances at set pieces, perhaps?) and the frankly off-the-wall – or rather *on*-the-wall – 'mole'. Personally, I don't like to think of Kevin Keegan as bewildered and lost – I like to think of him as having ambition, something to aspire to. And that's why I've decided that the wishful tone of the 'Mole' quote wins out over the confused-sounding 'Corner' quote. (By the way, what *is* Kevin Keegan up to these days?)

A double whammy, here – Keegan classics spoken back-to-back. I love the idea of our Kev trying to control a bandwagon (or has he fallen off one?), but for me, the philosophical tone of the 'corner' remark makes it the winner. After all, which of us can say we truly know where that elusive corner is?

Kev is clearly a believer in reincarnation. He's always loved racing, you know, in his many lives – but what, one wonders, would he have been, in former existences? A sooth-sayer? An oracle? Or perhaps something slightly further down the evolutionary scale . . . like one of our feathered friends? After all, there's some hint to this in the Turkey quote, which is also a great one. The thought of a footballer suddenly breaking into fluent poultry on the pitch really makes me laugh. But the call goes to 'racing', here. Just love that little glimpse into Kevin's personal life.

A tough call this, as both quotes have fantastically surreal visual images attached. The thought of someone having one eye on the pot whilst the other is up the chimney is deeply bizarre and rather painful (just what kind of 'pot' has Kev been dabbling in, anyway?). For me, though, the idea of a little mole on the dressing room wall is irresistible – especially if the mole had a bubble perm just like Kevin did in the 70s. Mole fights on!

53

Kings and Queens

by CLIVE ASLET

My apologies, as a loyal subject, to Henry I, Richard the Lionheart, Edward VI, and George II, who did not reach the short list. That's the cruelty of life at the top. No kings of Scotland either (before James I of England, who was also James VI of Scotland and united the thrones). A great monarch must be the dominant figure of the age, a feat more difficult the nearer we get to our own time because kings and queens have inexorably lost power to their prime ministers. He or she must be a national figurehead, leaving a permanent stamp on Britain's character. He or she must preside over, or lay the foundations for, a period of peace and prosperity. He or she must repel invasion (no King Harold, then) and successfully prosecute any foreign wars. Extra points for encouragement of the arts, music, literature, education, and connoisseurship. Most choices made themselves.

From 1993 till 2006 CLIVE ASLET was the award-winning editor of *Country Life* magazine, where he is now editor at large. He is the author of many books; his most recent. *The Landmarks of Britain*, examines 500 places where history was made. He is married with three children, and lives in London and Kent.

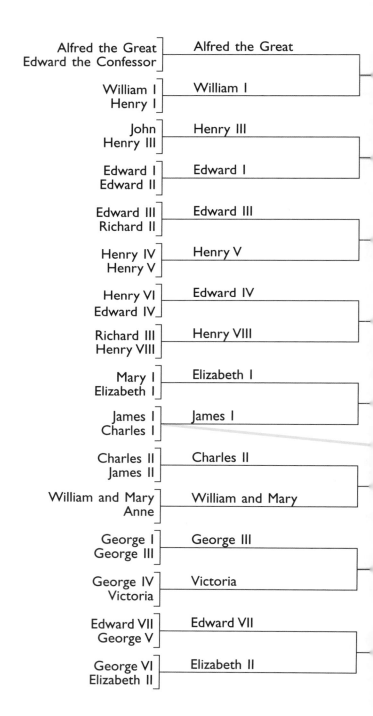

Matchup	Winner
Alfred the Great / Edward the Confessor	Alfred the Great
William I / Henry I	William I
John / Henry III	Henry III
Edward I / Edward II	Edward I
Edward III / Richard II	Edward III
Henry IV / Henry V	Henry V
Henry VI / Edward IV	Edward IV
Richard III / Henry VIII	Henry VIII
Mary I / Elizabeth I	Elizabeth I
James I / Charles I	James I
Charles II / James II	Charles II
William and Mary / Anne	William and Mary
George I / George III	George III
George IV / Victoria	Victoria
Edward VII / George V	Edward VII
George VI / Elizabeth II	Elizabeth II

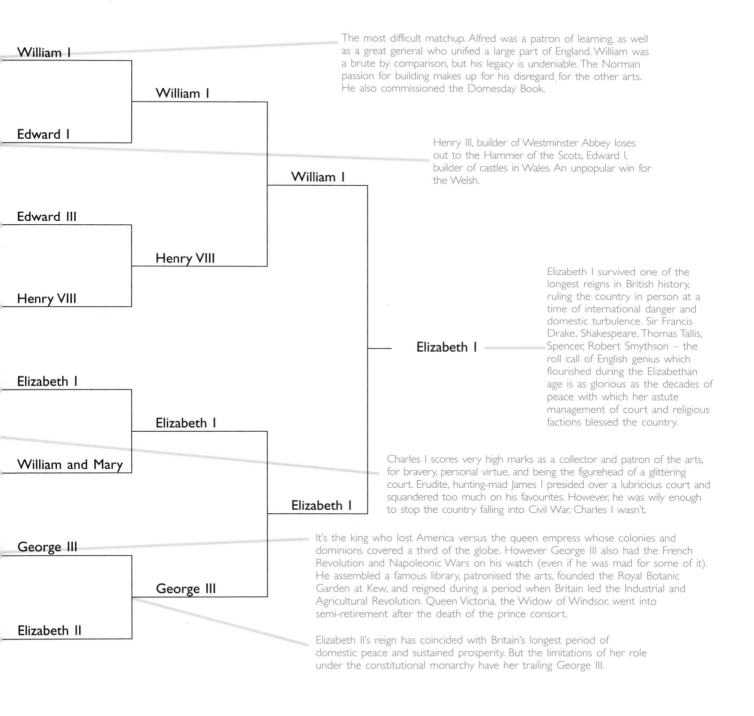

William I

William I

Edward I

William I

Edward III

Henry VIII

Henry VIII

Elizabeth I

Elizabeth I

Elizabeth I

William and Mary

Elizabeth I

George III

George III

Elizabeth II

Elizabeth I

The most difficult matchup. Alfred was a patron of learning, as well as a great general who unified a large part of England. William was a brute by comparison, but his legacy is undeniable. The Norman passion for building makes up for his disregard for the other arts. He also commissioned the Domesday Book.

Henry III, builder of Westminster Abbey loses out to the Hammer of the Scots, Edward I, builder of castles in Wales. An unpopular win for the Welsh.

Elizabeth I survived one of the longest reigns in British history, ruling the country in person at a time of international danger and domestic turbulence. Sir Francis Drake, Shakespeare, Thomas Tallis, Spencer, Robert Smythson – the roll call of English genius which flourished during the Elizabethan age is as glorious as the decades of peace with which her astute management of court and religious factions blessed the country.

Charles I scores very high marks as a collector and patron of the arts, for bravery, personal virtue, and being the figurehead of a glittering court. Erudite, hunting-mad James I presided over a lubricious court and squandered too much on his favourites. However, he was wily enough to stop the country falling into Civil War. Charles I wasn't.

It's the king who lost America versus the queen empress whose colonies and dominions covered a third of the globe. However George III also had the French Revolution and Napoleonic Wars on his watch (even if he was mad for some of it). He assembled a famous library, patronised the arts, founded the Royal Botanic Garden at Kew, and reigned during a period when Britain led the Industrial and Agricultural Revolution. Queen Victoria, the Widow of Windsor, went into semi-retirement after the death of the prince consort.

Elizabeth II's reign has coincided with Britain's longest period of domestic peace and sustained prosperity. But the limitations of her role under the constitutional monarchy have her trailing George III.

Lightbulb Jokes
by SIMON TREWIN

When I was little I used to have a joke book that was called something imaginative like 'The Funniest Joke Book Ever'. If I had understood the fundamental principles underlying the Trade Descriptions Act at the tender age of six I suspect I would have written them a stiff letter. Actually, had I been brought up in America rather than in a North London suburb, I would probably have slapped a law suit for $10,000,000 on the publishers to compensate me for the terrible psychological damage inflicted by the truly, truly rubbish jokes contained within. That said, it had the desired effect in one way and I still have a puerile sense of humour and, big confession here, find lightbulb jokes rather funny. Ish. So, how many _____ does it take to change a lightbulb? Let's find out.

Blue Peter presenters Two. One to change the light bulb and the other to say 'Here's one we changed earlier.'

Marxists None, the seeds of revolution and change are within the lightbulb itself.

Jugglers Only one, but it takes at least three lightbulbs.

Christian scientists None. But it takes at least three to sit and pray for the old one to come back on.

Psychologists Just one. But the bulb has to really WANT to change

Christians Three, but they're really one.

Feminists One and that's not funny!

Zen Masters A tree in a golden forest.

Surrealists A fish on a bicycle.

Pessimists None. Why bother? It's just going to burn out anyway.

Lawyers How many can you afford?

Necrophiliacs None, necrophiliacs prefer dead bulbs.

Amoeba One. No, 2. No, 4. No, 8. No, 16. No, 32 . . .

Jewish Mommas None. ('That's all right . . . I'll just sit here alone in the dark.')

Thought police None. There never was a light bulb.

Dadaists To get to the other side.

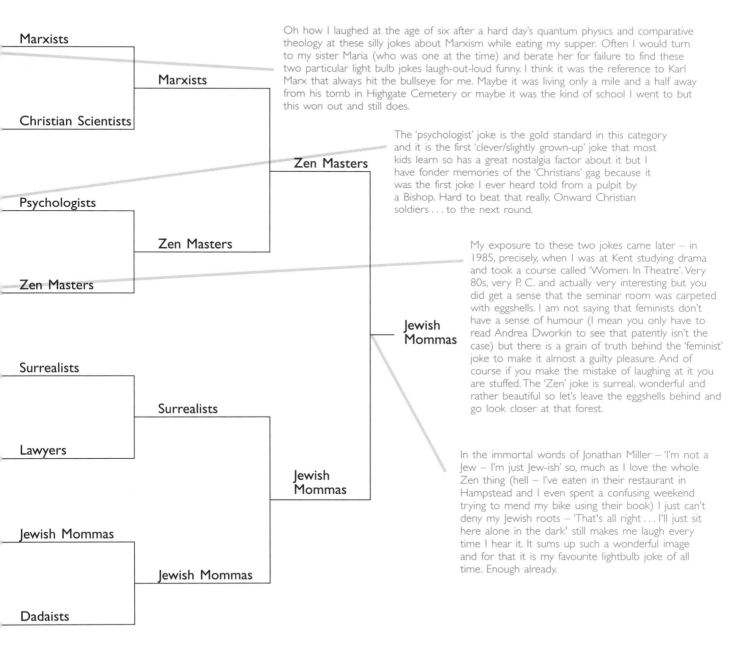

Marxists

Christian Scientists

Marxists

Psychologists

Zen Masters

Zen Masters

Zen Masters

Surrealists

Lawyers

Surrealists

Jewish Mommas

Dadaists

Jewish Mommas

Jewish Mommas

Jewish Mommas

Oh how I laughed at the age of six after a hard day's quantum physics and comparative theology at these silly jokes about Marxism while eating my supper. Often I would turn to my sister Maria (who was one at the time) and berate her for failure to find these two particular light bulb jokes laugh-out-loud funny. I think it was the reference to Karl Marx that always hit the bullseye for me. Maybe it was living only a mile and a half away from his tomb in Highgate Cemetery or maybe it was the kind of school I went to but this won out and still does.

The 'psychologist' joke is the gold standard in this category and it is the first 'clever/slightly grown-up' joke that most kids learn so has a great nostalgia factor about it but I have fonder memories of the 'Christians' gag because it was the first joke I ever heard told from a pulpit by a Bishop. Hard to beat that really. Onward Christian soldiers . . . to the next round.

My exposure to these two jokes came later – in 1985, precisely, when I was at Kent studying drama and took a course called 'Women In Theatre'. Very 80s, very P. C. and actually very interesting but you did get a sense that the seminar room was carpeted with eggshells. I am not saying that feminists don't have a sense of humour (I mean you only have to read Andrea Dworkin to see that patently isn't the case) but there is a grain of truth behind the 'feminist' joke to make it almost a guilty pleasure. And of course if you make the mistake of laughing at it you are stuffed. The 'Zen' joke is surreal, wonderful and rather beautiful so let's leave the eggshells behind and go look closer at that forest.

In the immortal words of Jonathan Miller – 'I'm not a Jew – I'm just Jew-ish' so, much as I love the whole Zen thing (hell – I've eaten in their restaurant in Hampstead and I even spent a confusing weekend trying to mend my bike using their book) I just can't deny my Jewish roots – 'That's all right . . . I'll just sit here alone in the dark' still makes me laugh every time I hear it. It sums up such a wonderful image and for that it is my favourite lightbulb joke of all time. Enough already.

Lost Property
by SIMON TREWIN

We all lose things from time to time. Our virginity, car keys, maybe a credit card or even the cat but (with the exception of the virginity) they usually turn up. Life is like that – things rarely vanish into thin air in your own home but if you lose something out there in the big scary world you may as well write it off. So thank goodness for the boys and girls of the London Transport Lost Property Office at Baker Street who devote their lives to reuniting people with their belongings. But how on earth do people get on a bus with a **BAG CONTAINING TEN THOUSAND POUNDS** or on a train with a **FOURTEEN FOOT ROWING BOAT** and then **FORGET TO TAKE THEM WITH THEM** when they get off? Keys maybe, a laptop but **A FOURTEEN FOOT ROWING BOAT?** What happens later? 'Oh great here's the River Thames and here are my lovely oars now let me get into my . . . oh . . . now . . . I'm sure I had it when I left the house . . .'. All of these are genuine items of lost property but which is the most bizarre?

dining-room chair suit of chain mail	chain mail
flat-pack coffee table TV remote	coffee table
false leg bustier	false leg
wedding dress lawyer's robes	wedding dress
sack of sultanas rowing machine	sultanas
14ft boat urn with cremation ashes	urn
briefcase containing £10,000 park bench	£10,000
grandfather clock stuffed eagle	grandfather clock
kitchen sink rocking chair	kitchen sink
train set *Titanic* buoyancy aid	*Titanic*
seven copies of *Mein Kampf* budgerigar called Aston	*Mein Kampf*
bag of glass eyes Nazi uniform	glass eyes
gorilla costume live rabbit	gorilla costume
three dead snakes jar of bull's sperm	bull's sperm
vibrator brace of pheasants	vibrator
379 used scratch cards in a mahogany box two Saddam Hussein masks	Saddam

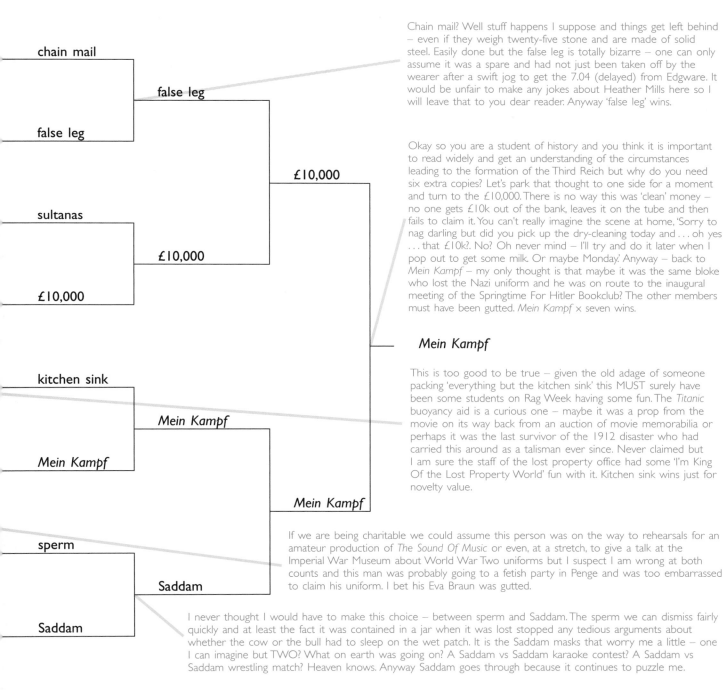

chain mail

false leg

false leg

false leg

£10,000

sultanas

£10,000

£10,000

Mein Kampf

kitchen sink

Mein Kampf

Mein Kampf

Mein Kampf

Mein Kampf

sperm

Saddam

Saddam

Saddam

Chain mail? Well stuff happens I suppose and things get left behind – even if they weigh twenty-five stone and are made of solid steel. Easily done but the false leg is totally bizarre – one can only assume it was a spare and had not just been taken off by the wearer after a swift jog to get the 7.04 (delayed) from Edgware. It would be unfair to make any jokes about Heather Mills here so I will leave that to you dear reader. Anyway 'false leg' wins.

Okay so you are a student of history and you think it is important to read widely and get an understanding of the circumstances leading to the formation of the Third Reich but why do you need six extra copies? Let's park that thought to one side for a moment and turn to the £10,000. There is no way this was 'clean' money – no one gets £10k out of the bank, leaves it on the tube and then fails to claim it. You can't really imagine the scene at home, 'Sorry to nag darling but did you pick up the dry-cleaning today and . . . oh yes . . . that £10k?. No? Oh never mind – I'll try and do it later when I pop out to get some milk. Or maybe Monday.' Anyway – back to *Mein Kampf* – my only thought is that maybe it was the same bloke who lost the Nazi uniform and he was on route to the inaugural meeting of the Springtime For Hitler Bookclub? The other members must have been gutted. *Mein Kampf* x seven wins.

This is too good to be true – given the old adage of someone packing 'everything but the kitchen sink' this MUST surely have been some students on Rag Week having some fun. The *Titanic* buoyancy aid is a curious one – maybe it was a prop from the movie on its way back from an auction of movie memorabilia or perhaps it was the last survivor of the 1912 disaster who had carried this around as a talisman ever since. Never claimed but I am sure the staff of the lost property office had some 'I'm King Of the Lost Property World' fun with it. Kitchen sink wins just for novelty value.

If we are being charitable we could assume this person was on the way to rehearsals for an amateur production of *The Sound Of Music* or even, at a stretch, to give a talk at the Imperial War Museum about World War Two uniforms but I suspect I am wrong at both counts and this man was probably going to a fetish party in Penge and was too embarrassed to claim his uniform. I bet his Eva Braun was gutted.

I never thought I would have to make this choice – between sperm and Saddam. The sperm we can dismiss fairly quickly and at least the fact it was contained in a jar when it was lost stopped any tedious arguments about whether the cow or the bull had to sleep on the wet patch. It is the Saddam masks that worry me a little – one I can imagine but TWO? What on earth was going on? A Saddam vs Saddam karaoke contest? A Saddam vs Saddam wrestling match? Heaven knows. Anyway Saddam goes through because it continues to puzzle me.

56

Madonna Songs
by CLARE BENNETT

Some people might think that by the time you are thirty-two, it's quite lame to be as obsessed with a pop star as you were when you were ten. I could probably get away with the fact that 'Like A Virgin' is my ring tone by saying it's meant to be ironic and that the tiny plastic key-ring I have for my house key of her biting on a horse whip was worth the £5 it cost me because it's got an 'M' on the other side and, er, my nickname begins with an M. However, not even I can explain or justify the alarming frequency with which I have dreams that she wants to be my best friend. I can only take solace in the fact that when my sister and I practically had to sell our internal organs in order to afford to go to her last show, the additional £150 we each spent on merchandise was, after all 'mainly to show the kids'.

CLARE BENNETT is hoping to never meet Madonna in case she turns out not to be that nice, thus rendering her entire belief system completely redundant.

Flouncy Spanish dress and maracas or telling your dad you're knocked up by your teenage boyfriend and you're making the serious mistake of thinking it's all going to work out brilliantly? My best friend when I was ten was almost in tears when Madonna appeared in the 'Papa Don't Preach' video with very cropped hair – every little girl's worst nightmare. All these years later, in an attempt to right this wrong, I'm going to have to choose 'La Isla Bonita'.

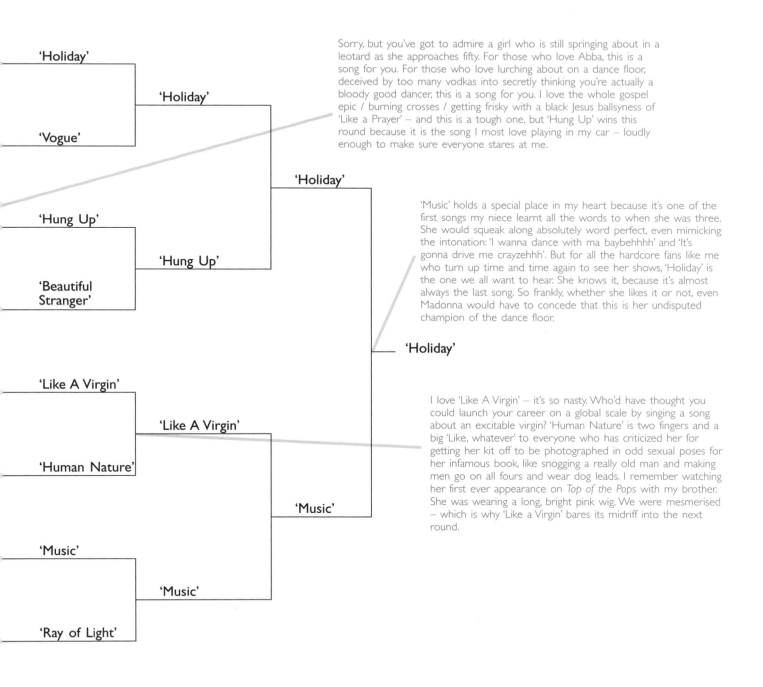

'Holiday'

'Holiday'

'Vogue'

'Holiday'

'Hung Up'

'Hung Up'

'Beautiful Stranger'

'Holiday'

Sorry, but you've got to admire a girl who is still springing about in a leotard as she approaches fifty. For those who love Abba, this is a song for you. For those who love lurching about on a dance floor, deceived by too many vodkas into secretly thinking you're actually a bloody good dancer, this is a song for you. I love the whole gospel epic / burning crosses / getting frisky with a black Jesus ballsyness of 'Like a Prayer' — and this is a tough one, but 'Hung Up' wins this round because it is the song I most love playing in my car — loudly enough to make sure everyone stares at me.

'Music' holds a special place in my heart because it's one of the first songs my niece learnt all the words to when she was three. She would squeak along absolutely word perfect, even mimicking the intonation: 'I wanna dance with ma baybehhhh' and 'It's gonna drive me crayzehhh'. But for all the hardcore fans like me who turn up time and time again to see her shows, 'Holiday' is the one we all want to hear. She knows it, because it's almost always the last song. So frankly, whether she likes it or not, even Madonna would have to concede that this is her undisputed champion of the dance floor.

'Holiday'

'Like A Virgin'

'Like A Virgin'

'Human Nature'

'Music'

'Music'

'Music'

'Ray of Light'

I love 'Like A Virgin' — it's so nasty. Who'd have thought you could launch your career on a global scale by singing a song about an excitable virgin? 'Human Nature' is two fingers and a big 'Like, whatever' to everyone who has criticized her for getting her kit off to be photographed in odd sexual poses for her infamous book, like snogging a really old man and making men go on all fours and wear dog leads. I remember watching her first ever appearance on *Top of the Pops* with my brother. She was wearing a long, bright pink wig. We were mesmerised — which is why 'Like a Virgin' bares its midriff into the next round.

57

Male Movie Actors

by ZOE MARGOLIS

Sexual objectification in the movies has long been a gentleman-only club. To the enjoyment of many a heterosexual male audience member, there's plenty of half-naked female bodies on screen to choose from. But what about female viewers? We like looking at men's bodies; in fact, we now demand to. In the last fifteen years, the on-screen sexual objectification of men has become more frequent, offering women a similar opportunity to gawp and admire the male torso as their male counterparts can with women. While this doesn't challenge sexism outright, it does offer some sexual equality, so that should be applauded. Let's find out which movies make men stand out on screen.

ZOE MARGOLIS is the author of the best-selling book *Girl With a One-track Mind*, written under the psendonym Abby Lee. When she is not busy writing, Zoe spends much of her time at the cinema, drooling.

Hmm. Men, half-dressed, struggling in a dystopian future: which film to choose? You've got Tom Cruise, a natural action hero say some; a short-arse say others, up against a taller, younger model: Will Smith. Watching them fist-fight – now *there* would be a battle worth buying popcorn for . . . It's a hard call with such buffed-up bodies, but Will Smith wins this round, if only for the long, lingering camera tilts up and down his oiled-up torso.

Historical battle films are fine with me, as long as there is sufficient eye candy on display to maintain my interest. *300* has so much it's like being in a sweet-shop, eyeing up all the confectionery, stuffing handfuls in your mouth, and then feeling violently sick afterwards. *XXX*, on the other hand, has only one man to gawp at: Vin Diesel. And very nice he is too: well-toned, well-oiled, and, well, ever-jumping into cars. He is fit, but not *that* captivating, and if I had a car fetish, I'd watch *Top Gear*, thank you very much. So it's got to be *300* then – if only for the fact that you get to laugh/drool over Gerard Butler prancing around in his underpants for two hours.

Casino Royale (2006) – Daniel Craig		Casino Royale
Speed (1994) – Keanu Reeves		
I, Robot (2004) – Will Smith		I, Robot
Minority Report (2002) – Tom Cruise		
Fight Club (1999) – Brad Pitt		Fight Club
American History X (1998) – Edward Norton		
Troy (2004) – Brad Pitt		Troy
Gladiator (2000) – Russell Crowe		
300 (2006) – Gerard Butler		300
XXX (2002) – Vin Diesel		
Spiderman (2002) – Tobey Maguire		Spiderman
Batman Begins (2005) – Christian Bale		
The Matrix (1999) – Keanu Reeves		Blade
Blade (1998) – Wesley Snipes		
Natural Born Killers (1994) – Woody Harrelson		American Psycho
American Psycho (2000) – Christian Bale		

Casino Royale

Fight Club

Casino Royale

Brad Pitt's a regular favourite for women's onscreen fantasies and directors know it. The usual approach to filming him is simple: oil up his muscles and point a camera at his torso. That's it really: why break a proven formula? Women will gawp and drool, and not care what Pitt's onscreen character says, just as long as the camera stays focused on his abs, Godamnit. This round is a tough call because both movies treat Pitt with the same level of adoration: the camera lingers lovingly over his body; he is semi-naked with regularity; he gets dirty fighting with other men. Which to choose? Knuckling down to the nitty-gritty, I think it has to be *Fight Club*: what woman doesn't want to watch half-dressed, sexy men fist-fight each other, I ask you?

In *Casino Royale* starring Daniel Craig, we get a new James Bond. A caring, sharing, empathetic James Bond: surely a first for this franchise. More importantly though, we get to see James Bond in a way all women have been waiting for since the early days of Sean Connery: slow, lingering shots of a semi-naked, sexy man on screen. *Casino Royale* positively *revels* in making Daniel Craig look delightful. Even up against Christian Bale's rippled torso, the adoring close-ups of Daniel Craig's body impress. This gives the film an advantage, but *Casino Royale*'s winning point is due to one shot: Daniel Craig in shorts, muscles rippling, exiting the ocean. This is the stuff of women's fantasy: the best sexual objectification of a male actor yet.

Casino Royale

Spiderman

American Psycho

Both of these films are adaptations: *Spiderman* from the comic book; *American Psycho* from the novel. Let's weigh up the pros and cons. *Spiderman*: Tobey Maguire as a lycra-clad superhero who saves lives and occasionally removes his tight costume to reveal his manly body. *American Psycho*: Christian Bale as a sociopathic killer who is often naked and, after murdering innocent people, narcissistically admires his own immaculately toned torso. Superhero, or antihero? It's got to be *American Psycho*, purely because you get to see Christian Bale's arse – a relevant factor I think.

American Psycho

Two comic book heroes, two well-sculpted men fighting the forces of evil – and they're dressed up in fetish wear, sorry, 'costumes'. What more could a woman want? In both films we get to see a transformation: humble, everyday bloke has a life-altering experience which catapults him into waging a war against baddies. More importantly though, we get the opportunity to watch a fit bloke prancing about, dressed up in revealing clothes. Though we are given plenty of close-up shots of his torso, Christian Bale's Batman loses out to Tobey Maguire's Spiderman for one reason: rubber may be superhero-sexy, but we see more of a man when he's dressed in lycra, so Spiderman it has to be.

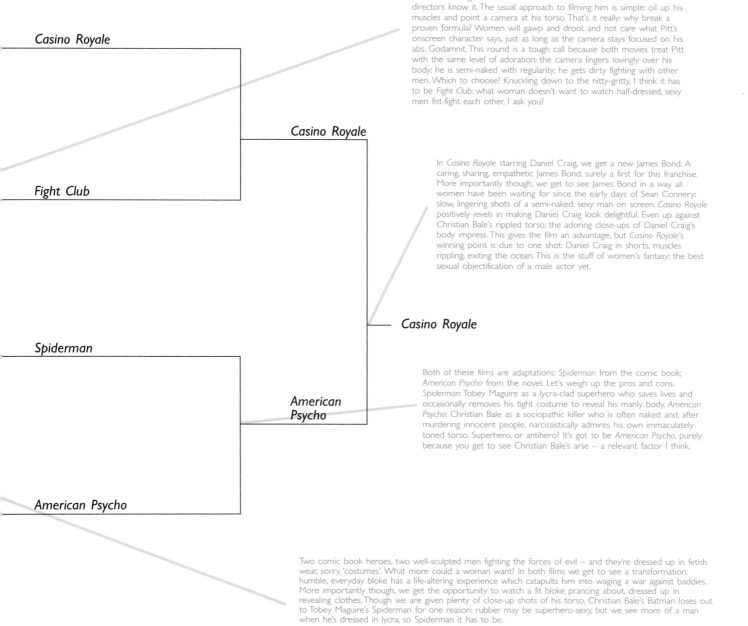

58

Misheard Lyrics
by PIEMAN BREWIN

When I was a teenager the magazine *Smash Hits* was launched. In addition to a cover shot of Jason and Kylie or Carol Decker from T'Pau its real stock-in-trade was the reproduction of lyrics from the Top 40. Great for singing along to your little battery radio in front of a mirror with a hairbrush microphone and a bit of attitude but it also had a much more important use. In those pre-Internet days, *Smash Hits* was a lifeline, because it helped settle endless playground arguments about deciphering certain lyrics. The chill that ran down your spine when you realized that you had been getting it very stupidly wrong for the last three-weeks' worth of breaks was bad enough but the fact that your friends were no doubt sniggering about it behind your back was even worse. Even researching this chart I could be found, occasionally, with my head in my hands saying 'Oh my God – babies don't come in bags – Annie Lennox was in fact singing "baby's coming back".' Doh!

PIEMAN BREWIN is a writer living in London.

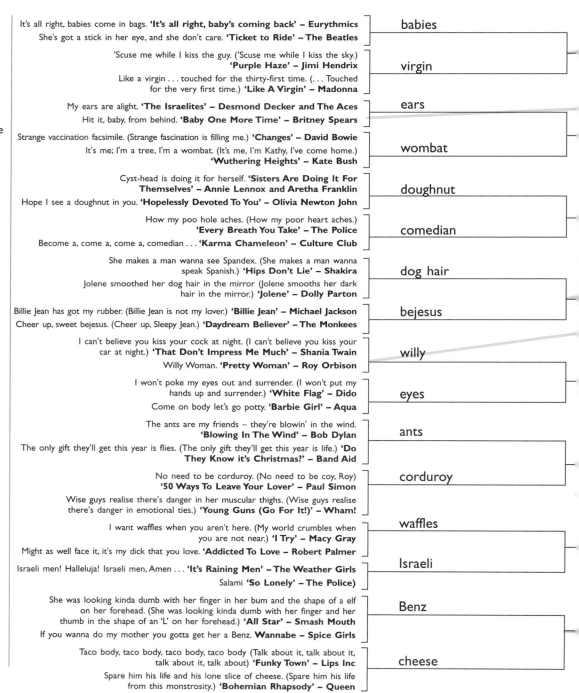

It's all right, babies come in bags. **'It's all right, baby's coming back' – Eurythmics**

She's got a stick in her eye, and she don't care. **'Ticket to Ride' – The Beatles**

'Scuse me while I kiss the guy. ('Scuse me while I kiss the sky.) **'Purple Haze' – Jimi Hendrix**

Like a virgin . . . touched for the thirty-first time. (. . . Touched for the very first time.) **'Like A Virgin' – Madonna**

My ears are alight. **'The Israelites' – Desmond Decker and The Aces**

Hit it, baby, from behind. **'Baby One More Time' – Britney Spears**

Strange vaccination facsimile. (Strange fascination is filling me.) **'Changes' – David Bowie**

It's me; I'm a tree, I'm a wombat. (It's me, I'm Kathy, I've come home.) **'Wuthering Heights' – Kate Bush**

Cyst-head is doing it for herself. **'Sisters Are Doing It For Themselves' – Annie Lennox and Aretha Franklin**

Hope I see a doughnut in you. **'Hopelessly Devoted To You' – Olivia Newton John**

How my poo hole aches. (How my poor heart aches.) **'Every Breath You Take' – The Police**

Become a, come a, come a, comedian . . . **'Karma Chameleon' – Culture Club**

She makes a man wanna see Spandex. (She makes a man wanna speak Spanish.) **'Hips Don't Lie' – Shakira**

Jolene smoothed her dog hair in the mirror (Jolene smooths her dark hair in the mirror.) **'Jolene' – Dolly Parton**

Billie Jean has got my rubber. (Billie Jean is not my lover.) **'Billie Jean' – Michael Jackson**

Cheer up, sweet bejesus. (Cheer up, Sleepy Jean.) **'Daydream Believer' – The Monkees**

I can't believe you kiss your cock at night. (I can't believe you kiss your car at night.) **'That Don't Impress Me Much' – Shania Twain**

Willy Woman. **'Pretty Woman' – Roy Orbison**

I won't poke my eyes out and surrender. (I won't put my hands up and surrender.) **'White Flag' – Dido**

Come on body let's go potty. **'Barbie Girl' – Aqua**

The ants are my friends – they're blowin' in the wind. **'Blowing In The Wind' – Bob Dylan**

The only gift they'll get this year is flies. (The only gift they'll get this year is life.) **'Do They Know it's Christmas?' – Band Aid**

No need to be corduroy. (No need to be coy, Roy) **'50 Ways To Leave Your Lover' – Paul Simon**

Wise guys realise there's danger in her muscular thighs. (Wise guys realise there's danger in emotional ties.) **'Young Guns (Go For It!)' – Wham!**

I want waffles when you aren't here. (My world crumbles when you are not near.) **'I Try' – Macy Gray**

Might as well face it, it's my dick that you love. **'Addicted To Love' – Robert Palmer**

Israeli men! Halleluja! Israeli men, Amen . . . **'It's Raining Men' – The Weather Girls**

Salami **'So Lonely' – The Police)**

She was looking kinda dumb with her finger in her bum and the shape of a elf on her forehead. (She was looking kinda dumb with her finger and her thumb in the shape of an 'L' on her forehead.) **'All Star' – Smash Mouth**

If you wanna do my mother you gotta get her a Benz. **Wannabe – Spice Girls**

Taco body, taco body, taco body, taco body (Talk about it, talk about it, talk about it, talk about) **'Funky Town' – Lips Inc**

Spare him his life and his lone slice of cheese. (Spare him his life from this monstrosity.) **'Bohemian Rhapsody' – Queen**

babies

virgin

ears

wombat

doughnut

comedian

dog hair

bejesus

willy

eyes

ants

corduroy

waffles

Israeli

Benz

cheese

This Eurythmics song delayed my understanding of childbirth for many years and, when coupled with Madonna's assertion that you could still be a virgin after thirty-one times, almost derailed my sex-life entirely. Babies go through.

The weirder Britney's life gets the less funny this misheard lyric becomes, but even she would draw the line at setting her ears alight wouldn't she? Ears goes through – just in case.

The more you think about Jolene and her canine stroking the sillier it gets, but those cheeky Monkees have to go through – we knew they were believers but it is good to see them using their songs to motivate the son of God in this helpful fashion.

History doesn't tell us whether the 'willy woman' is unimpressed or not, but the contorted image conjured up by Shania's lyric leaves an unpleasant taste in the mouth so the lady boy goes through.

In recent years Bob has become so mumbling in his delivery and so endless in his reinvention of his songs that he probably IS singing about ants for all I would know. ONJ has obviously been spending far too long carrying out colonic irrigation on people that we would think long and hard about shaking her hand. So, on balance, Robert Zimmerman triumphs.

If I were ever on trial for murder I hope Freddie's words would help my acquittal so I could spend the rest of my days quietly with a small piece of Edam. I have never met any of the Spice Girls' mothers but think it is unlikely I would want to buy any of them a car. Sorry, but that's life – the cheese goes through.

babies

ears

ears

doughnut

doughnut

doughnut

bejesus

doughnut

ants

willy

ants

ants

ants

Israeli

Israeli

cheese

59

Modern Sci-Fi Films

by ROBIN VINCENT

Definitions of what constitutes Science Fiction are as diverse as the subject matter. The only thing serious Science Fiction writers seem to agree on is their distaste for the abbreviation 'Sci-Fi', which is normally associated with low budget, 60s cinema or comic books. So, to simplify things a bit I've based this selection upon Hollywood movies within my own lifetime and by a definition of being futuristic, spacey or at least involving some kind of alien from another world. The criteria here being how well the vision was achieved on screen, combined with a simple gut-based cool factor.

ROBIN VINCENT is a technology writer, musician and director of specialist computer company Rain Recording Ltd. Robin splits his time between building computers for audio/media production (www.rainrecording.co.uk), creating meditative soundscapes (www.moltenmeditation.com), advising musicians on the latest in computer music technology (www.pc-music.com) and playing with his baby son Alfie (www.alfredray.com).

Matchup	Winner
Star Wars – George Lucas / Star Trek – Gene Roddenberry	Star Wars
ET – Steven Spielberg / AI – Steven Spielberg/Stanley Kubrick	ET
2001 a Space Odyssey – Stanley Kubrick/Arthur C. Clarke / Close Encounters of the Third Kind – Steven Spielberg	2001
Contact – Robert Zemeckis/Carl Sagan / The Abyss – James Cameron	Contact
Solaris – Steven Soderbergh/Stanislaw Lem / Silent Running – Douglas Trumbull/Deric Washburn/Michael Cimino/Steven Bochco	Solaris
Hitchhiker's Guide to the Galaxy – Garth Jennings/Douglas Adams / Dark Star – John Carpenter/Dan O'Bannon	Hitchhiker's
Total Recall – Paul Verhoeven/Philip K. Dick / The Red Planet – Antony Hoffman/Chuck Pfarrer	Total Recall
I Robot – Alex Proyas/Issac Asimov / Blade Runner – Ridley Scott/Philip K. Dick	Blade Runner
Tron – Steven Lisberger / The Black Hole – Gary Nelson/Jeb Rosebrook/Bob Barbash/Richard Landau	Tron
Rollerball – Norman Jewison/William Harrison / The Running Man – Paul Michael Glaser/Stephen King	Rollerball
Alien – Ridley Scott/Dan O'Bannon/Ronald Shusett / Terminator – James Cameron	Alien
Deep Impact – Mimi Leder/Michael Tolkin/Bruce Joel Rubin / Armageddon – Michael Bay/Robert Roy Pool	Armageddon
Minority Report – Steven Spielberg/Philip K. Dick / War of the Worlds – Steven Spielberg/H. G. Wells	Minority Report
Cube – Vincenzo Natali / Pitch Black – David Twohy/Jim Wheat/Ken Wheat	Cube
Starship Troopers – Paul Verhoeven / Robocop – Paul Verhoeven	Starship Troopers
The Matrix – Andy Wachowski/Larry Wachowski / Equilibrium – Kurt Wimmer	The Matrix

Oh, the controversy surrounding the ending of the wonderfully crafted *AI*, a collaboration between Spielberg and Kubrick which Spielberg completed after Kubrick's death in 1999. Horrified Kubrick fans blamed Spielberg for the overly schmaltzy ending, but it turned out to be the one part of the film drawn directly from Kubrick's script and design. Both *ET* and *AI* benefitted from extraordinary child performances but in the end it's *ET* that's burned itself into our consciousnesses. Maybe it's something to do with the edgy and realistic feel of small town America or the fact that it came at a time when we all longed for our own alien friend.

These two are as much alike as they are starkly in contrast to each other. *Star Wars* is responsible for so much and its effect on cinema and society is unparalleled. Just think, Yoda's words of wisdom are more familiar to some than those of Gandhi, Dr King, Plato or Jesus. But would it have been made without Kubrick's *2001, a Space Odyssey*? An altogether different film of thought, vision and poetry that can only hope to provide a glimpse of the contents of Arthur C. Clarke's mind. Although by any commercial measurement *Star Wars* would win every time the weight of influence of *2001* amongst writers, film makers and directors is so heavy that it tips the balance.

A pair of intoxicatingly slow-moving films, meandering their way across the screen. *Silent Running* is a hippy film about saving trees, the last of which are held in Eden Project-style domes attached to huge space ships (which later turn up in an episode of *Battlestar Galactica*), complete with a Joan Baez soundtrack. *Solaris*, on the other hand, flows like poetry with the magnetic Clooney maintaining a slightly sad and slightly concerned expression for the entirety of this mysterious and thoughtful drama. *Silent Running* may have pre-empted *Star Wars* with its lovable little robots but *Solaris* deals with deep emotions of love and loss. These far outstrip any cosy feelings you may have developed for the last little orange robot that blasts off in the last dome with its little watering can (sniff sniff).

Not a runaway winner by any means, the semi-finals being almost too close to call, but in the end the style, substance, vision, and performances of Ridley Scott's *Blade Runner* make it the best piece of modern sci-fi to be put on screen. The look of the film, the dirt, the dysfunction, the rain, the way Deckard needs to nudge the fluorescent light into life, the blood left in the glass as he tries to wash his wounds, the complexity and the detail sets it above your average future flick. Few words are spoken but Roy (played by the awesome Rutger Hauer) gets all the best ones, like when he remarks to the eye maker, 'If only you could see what I've seen with your eyes.' It spawned whole lifestyles of cyberpunk and neo-noir film-making and is a hugely influential cult classic.

From the moment that Trinity runs up the wall to avoid gunfire and leaps into the air as the camera revolves around in 'time-slip' slow motion your jaw drops open in amazement and stays that way until the Rage Against Machine-fuelled credits roll. In terms of cinematography it was like nothing you had ever seen before which meant that any silliness in the plot was easily forgiven. *The Matrix* seemed to give birth to a whole new sub-genre of cyber action, martial arts sci-fi and defined a style of soundtrack that Rob Zombie has never bettered.

Philip K. Dick has produced some of the most interesting, if slightly mad, sci-fi of his generation and much of it has made it to the big screen, albeit often by loose association. *Minority Report* bears a small resemblance to the original short story, but it's more the futuristic realisations of technology, media, transportation, weaponry and society that really stand out in this film, which is probably down to Spielberg consulting with a huge pool of experts when designing the production. *War of the Worlds*, a welcome update of H. G. Well's vision of an invaded Earth, seems to run out of ideas quite quickly. Beautifully made and quite chilling, it doesn't seem to take the time to really deliver on the nightmare. Perhaps familiarity with the evocative Jeff Wayne musical version will forever spoil any attempts at outdoing your own imagination.

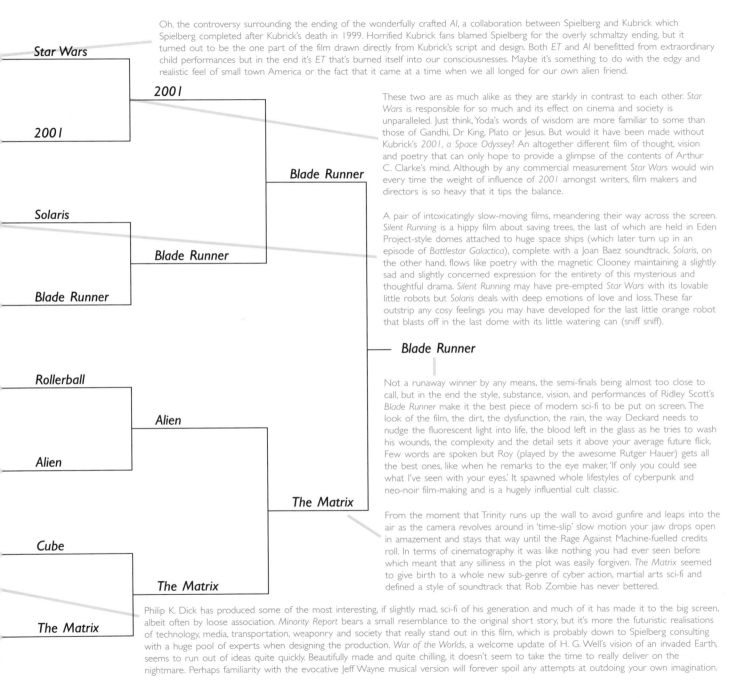

Star Wars

2001

2001

2001

Solaris

Blade Runner

Blade Runner

Blade Runner

Blade Runner

Rollerball

Alien

Alien

Alien

Cube

The Matrix

The Matrix

The Matrix

60

Most Likely to Survive the 21st Century

by MICHAEL ROGERS

When you're considering what single artefact is likely to survive until 1 January, 2100, remember what has disappeared in the past century: the passenger pigeon, celluloid, radium health tonics, singing telegrams, smallpox. Now, try to imagine what elements of today are sturdy enough to persist another 93 years — keeping in mind that the pace of change has accelerated a hundred-fold since the calendar read 1900. That's the sole criterion here: which extant thing today is most likely to be extant in 2100. An impossible task? Of course. That's why we have so many futurists: if enough of us keep guessing, somebody is bound to get it right. And yet, if you're so confounded by the challenge that you end up looking down at your feet, you're probably staring at the winner.

MICHAEL ROGERS is a novelist, journalist, and interactive media pioneer: He is futurist-in-residence for the New York Times Company and writes the Practical Futurist column for MSNBC.com.

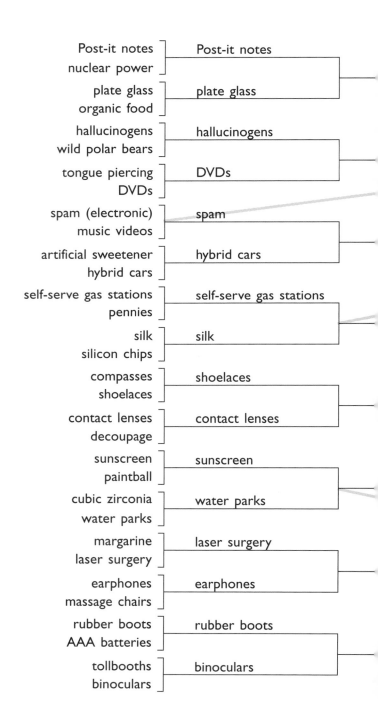

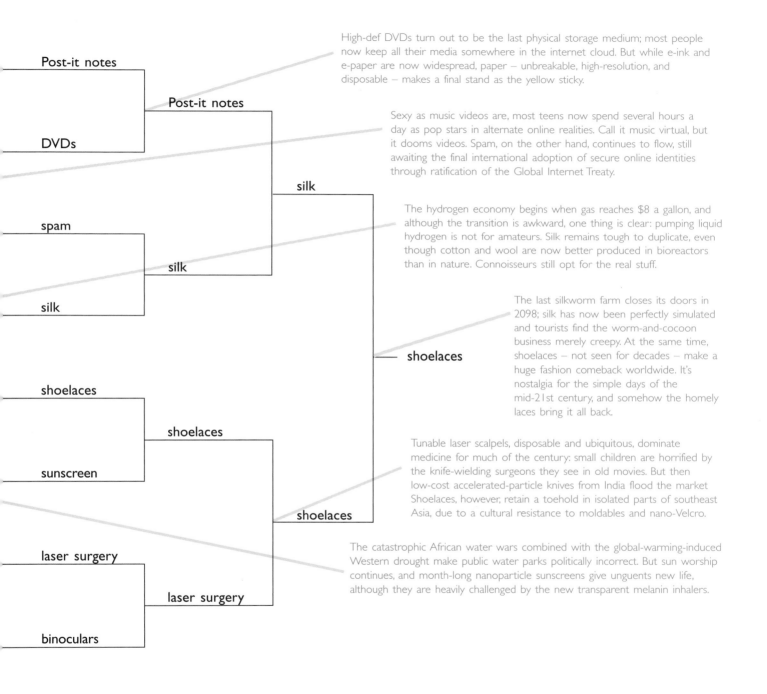

Post-it notes

DVDs

Post-it notes

spam

silk

silk

silk

shoelaces

shoelaces

sunscreen

shoelaces

shoelaces

laser surgery

laser surgery

binoculars

High-def DVDs turn out to be the last physical storage medium; most people now keep all their media somewhere in the internet cloud. But while e-ink and e-paper are now widespread, paper – unbreakable, high-resolution, and disposable – makes a final stand as the yellow sticky.

Sexy as music videos are, most teens now spend several hours a day as pop stars in alternate online realities. Call it music virtual, but it dooms videos. Spam, on the other hand, continues to flow, still awaiting the final international adoption of secure online identities through ratification of the Global Internet Treaty.

The hydrogen economy begins when gas reaches $8 a gallon, and although the transition is awkward, one thing is clear: pumping liquid hydrogen is not for amateurs. Silk remains tough to duplicate, even though cotton and wool are now better produced in bioreactors than in nature. Connoisseurs still opt for the real stuff.

The last silkworm farm closes its doors in 2098; silk has now been perfectly simulated and tourists find the worm-and-cocoon business merely creepy. At the same time, shoelaces – not seen for decades – make a huge fashion comeback worldwide. It's nostalgia for the simple days of the mid-21st century, and somehow the homely laces bring it all back.

Tunable laser scalpels, disposable and ubiquitous, dominate medicine for much of the century: small children are horrified by the knife-wielding surgeons they see in old movies. But then low-cost accelerated-particle knives from India flood the market. Shoelaces, however, retain a toehold in isolated parts of southeast Asia, due to a cultural resistance to moldables and nano-Velcro.

The catastrophic African water wars combined with the global-warming-induced Western drought make public water parks politically incorrect. But sun worship continues, and month-long nanoparticle sunscreens give unguents new life, although they are heavily challenged by the new transparent melanin inhalers.

61

Mythological Figures

by JAMES C. HOGAN

Connoisseurs of myth may question the absence of some divinities here. Zeus, ever prudent, sends his boys along to do his bidding, watching the combat from above. Poseidon feels out of his element. Ladies like Demeter and Artemis find the rowdy jostling of this knockout format repugnant, preferring to worry over their favourites from the sidelines. Keen-eyed readers will notice that rematches such as Athena vs. Ajax and Achilles vs. Hector have outcomes that are, shall we say, foreordained. More down-to-earth observers may wonder how the gods ever lose to mere heroes. Happily, I am not obliged to moralise or offer allegory. Next time Clytemnestra may not forget her ax, Hector may use more cunning, Orestes may not fall into a raving fit. In the meantime, let us admire the champion's journey to his rightful home.

JAMES C. HOGAN retired as the Frank T. McClure professor of classics at Allegheny College in 1999. He is the author of the commentaries *The Plays of Sophocles* and *The Plays of Aeschylus*.

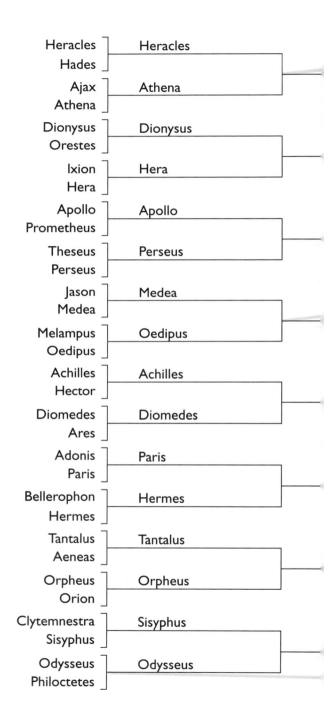

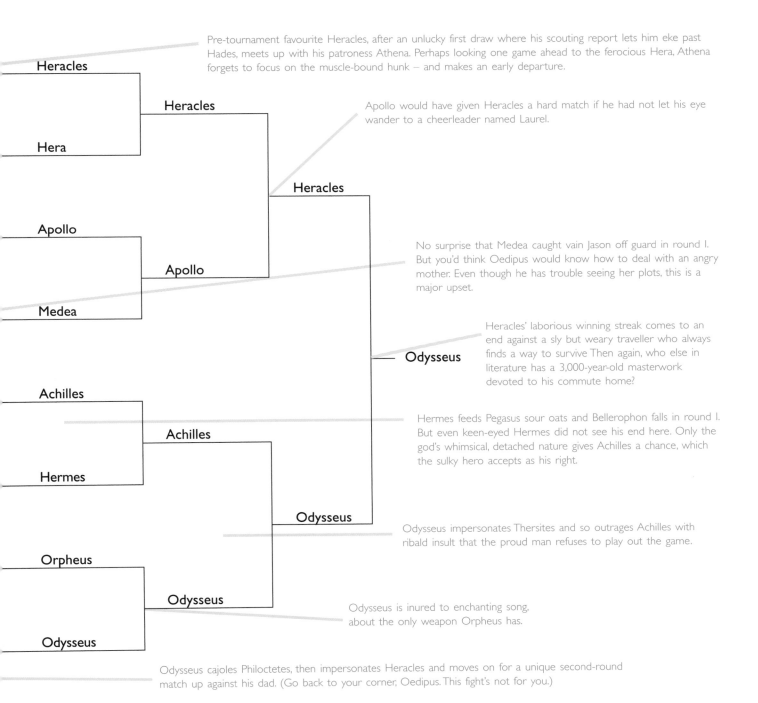

Heracles

Heracles

Hera

Heracles

Apollo

Apollo

Medea

Heracles

Odysseus

Achilles

Achilles

Hermes

Odysseus

Orpheus

Odysseus

Odysseus

Pre-tournament favourite Heracles, after an unlucky first draw where his scouting report lets him eke past Hades, meets up with his patroness Athena. Perhaps looking one game ahead to the ferocious Hera, Athena forgets to focus on the muscle-bound hunk — and makes an early departure.

Apollo would have given Heracles a hard match if he had not let his eye wander to a cheerleader named Laurel.

No surprise that Medea caught vain Jason off guard in round I. But you'd think Oedipus would know how to deal with an angry mother. Even though he has trouble seeing her plots, this is a major upset.

Heracles' laborious winning streak comes to an end against a sly but weary traveller who always finds a way to survive Then again, who else in literature has a 3,000-year-old masterwork devoted to his commute home?

Hermes feeds Pegasus sour oats and Bellerophon falls in round I. But even keen-eyed Hermes did not see his end here. Only the god's whimsical, detached nature gives Achilles a chance, which the sulky hero accepts as his right.

Odysseus impersonates Thersites and so outrages Achilles with ribald insult that the proud man refuses to play out the game.

Odysseus is inured to enchanting song, about the only weapon Orpheus has.

Odysseus cajoles Philoctetes, then impersonates Heracles and moves on for a unique second-round match up against his dad. (Go back to your corner, Oedipus. This fight's not for you.)

62

Nursery Rhymes
by SIMON TREWIN

One of the many joys of becoming a parent is the fact it gives you an opportunity to rediscover the rich and wonderfully inventive landscape of nursery rhymes. It is also a great opportunity to do some research and discover the true stories behind each song and the traditions they underpin. Not only that, they are often extremely politically incorrect, which gives them an additional frisson all of their own. But anyway, which of the next thirty-two are going to twinkle like a little star, and which is going to fall down just like London Bridge?

Polly seemed like a really nice girl. She was always ready to put the kettle on and make us all a cup of tea. I can't say I felt as positive about her sister, Sukey, who, as soon as Polly had put the kettle on, rushed in and took it off, the net result was no tea. Even with Sukey's antisocial behaviour there is a charm about Polly Put the Kettle On that makes me want it to hang around for just a little bit longer. Beats the old man any day.

Humpty Dumpty
This Little Piggy — This Little Piggy

Baa, Baa, Black Sheep
One, Two, Three, Four, Five — Black Sheep

Little Bo Peep
Hickory Dickory Dock — Dickory Dock

Mary, Mary, Quite Contrary
Miss Polly Had a Dolly — Miss Polly

Ten Green Bottles
Three Blind Mice — Ten Green Bottles

The Wheels on the Bus
Twinkle Twinkle Little Star — Wheels On the Bus

Polly Put the Kettle On
This Old Man — Polly Put The Kettle

Ladybird, Ladybird
Rain, Rain Go Away — Ladybird

Sing a Song of Sixpence
Pease Pudding Hot — Pease Pudding

London Bridge Is Falling Down
Jack and Jill — Jack and Jill

Round and Round the Garden
Little Jack Horner — Jack Horner

Little Miss Muffet
There Was An Old Lady Who Swallowed A Fly — Miss Muffet

Tom Tom the Piper's Son
There Was An Old Woman Who Lived In A Shoe — Shoe

Incy Wincey Spider
The Grand Old Duke Of York — Incy Wincey

Old King Cole
The Muffin Man — Muffin Man

Bobby Shafto
Two Little Dicky Birds — Bobby Shafto

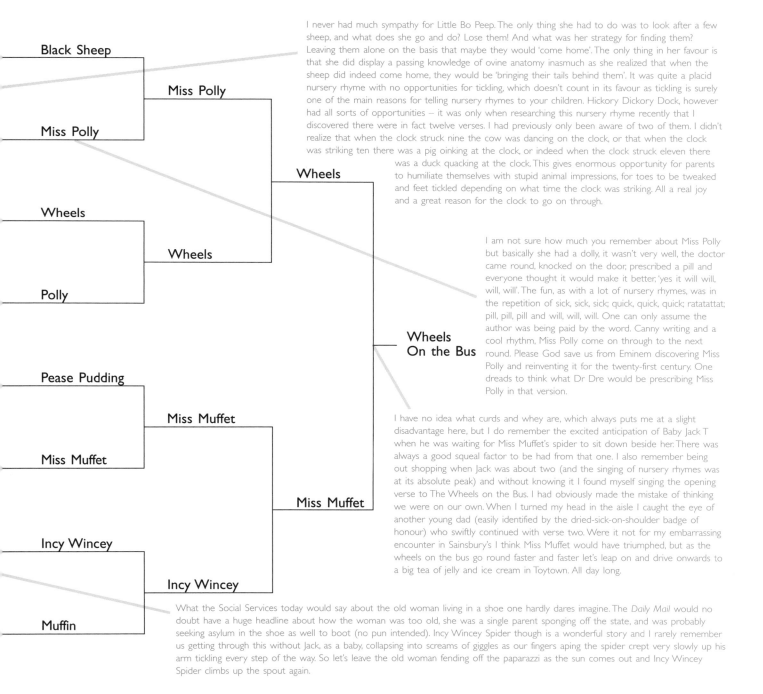

Black Sheep

Miss Polly

Miss Polly

Miss Polly

Wheels

Wheels

Wheels

Polly

Wheels

Wheels
On the Bus

Pease Pudding

Miss Muffet

Miss Muffet

Miss Muffet

Miss Muffet

Incy Wincey

Incy Wincey

Muffin

I never had much sympathy for Little Bo Peep. The only thing she had to do was to look after a few sheep, and what does she go and do? Lose them! And what was her strategy for finding them? Leaving them alone on the basis that maybe they would 'come home'. The only thing in her favour is that she did display a passing knowledge of ovine anatomy inasmuch as she realized that when the sheep did indeed come home, they would be 'bringing their tails behind them'. It was quite a placid nursery rhyme with no opportunities for tickling, which doesn't count in its favour as tickling is surely one of the main reasons for telling nursery rhymes to your children. Hickory Dickory Dock, however had all sorts of opportunities – it was only when researching this nursery rhyme recently that I discovered there were in fact twelve verses. I had previously only been aware of two of them. I didn't realize that when the clock struck nine the cow was dancing on the clock, or that when the clock was striking ten there was a pig oinking at the clock, or indeed when the clock struck eleven there was a duck quacking at the clock. This gives enormous opportunity for parents to humiliate themselves with stupid animal impressions, for toes to be tweaked and feet tickled depending on what time the clock was striking. All a real joy and a great reason for the clock to go on through.

I am not sure how much you remember about Miss Polly but basically she had a dolly, it wasn't very well, the doctor came round, knocked on the door, prescribed a pill and everyone thought it would make it better, 'yes it will will, will, will'. The fun, as with a lot of nursery rhymes, was in the repetition of sick, sick, sick; quick, quick, quick; ratatattat; pill, pill, pill and will, will, will. One can only assume the author was being paid by the word. Canny writing and a cool rhythm, Miss Polly come on through to the next round. Please God save us from Eminem discovering Miss Polly and reinventing it for the twenty-first century. One dreads to think what Dr Dre would be prescribing Miss Polly in that version.

I have no idea what curds and whey are, which always puts me at a slight disadvantage here, but I do remember the excited anticipation of Baby Jack T when he was waiting for Miss Muffet's spider to sit down beside her. There was always a good squeal factor to be had from that one. I also remember being out shopping when Jack was about two (and the singing of nursery rhymes was at its absolute peak) and without knowing it I found myself singing the opening verse to The Wheels on the Bus. I had obviously made the mistake of thinking we were on our own. When I turned my head in the aisle I caught the eye of another young dad (easily identified by the dried-sick-on-shoulder badge of honour) who swiftly continued with verse two. Were it not for my embarrassing encounter in Sainsbury's I think Miss Muffet would have triumphed, but as the wheels on the bus go round faster and faster let's leap on and drive onwards to a big tea of jelly and ice cream in Toytown. All day long.

What the Social Services today would say about the old woman living in a shoe one hardly dares imagine. The *Daily Mail* would no doubt have a huge headline about how the woman was too old, she was a single parent sponging off the state, and was probably seeking asylum in the shoe as well to boot (no pun intended). Incy Wincey Spider though is a wonderful story and I rarely remember us getting through this without Jack, as a baby, collapsing into screams of giggles as our fingers aping the spider crept very slowly up his arm tickling every step of the way. So let's leave the old woman fending off the paparazzi as the sun comes out and Incy Wincey Spider climbs up the spout again.

63

Office Revenge Strategies
by ANONYMOUS

You wouldn't like me when I am angry – I once worked for a boss who was so unpleasant and so lacking in any of the milk of human kindness that I wrote his wife an anonymous letter pretending that I had slept with him and was pregnant. Having access to his diary and knowing more than I wanted to know about all aspects of his life it was very easy to concoct a letter that contained enough detail about hotels he had stayed in and restaurants he had eaten at to make it all look worryingly credible. By the look on his face two days later he had obviously been taken to hell and back by his wife's endless questions and accusations and I had to stifle my giggles. The bastard. Luckily for him I got a new job soon afterwards but I did leave him a hidden present.

Anyway here are my top thirty-two revenge tactics against an evil boss but which one wins out?

ANONYMOUS is a P.A. working in the media sector in London. In fact she might work for you.

Leave sexy lingerie on his desk and in his briefcase.

Put a dead fish right at the bottom of his (seldomly used) gym kit bag. Put bag by radiator.

Send an email to 'All' from his computer headed 'Urgent – anyone borrowed my Anusol?'

Surf for hardcore porn on his computer, and set something filthy as his screensaver.

Put his details on every dating site you can find with his home number as a contact point.

Order a complete Indian banquet in his name to be delivered during the next board meeting.

Set autocorrect so that every time he types 'e' it defaults to 'you stupid cock'.

Fill his waste-paper basket with ripe cat food on your way home.

Add laxative to his tea and put an 'Out Of Order' sign on the loo door.

Set up an email auto-reply saying 'I am currently out of the office carrying out community service in accordance with my parole conditions. Please do not reply to this message'.

Swap the keys around on his keyboard and set the default language to Chinese.

Misfile all his confidential papers randomly throughout the office.

Fake his resignation letter and post it while he is away on holiday.

Ring his home number at night and when his wife answers giggle and then hang-up. Repeatedly. Alternate giggling with crying.

Organise a strippergram to interrupt an important client lunch.

Loosen the nuts on his swivel chair – it is only a matter of time.

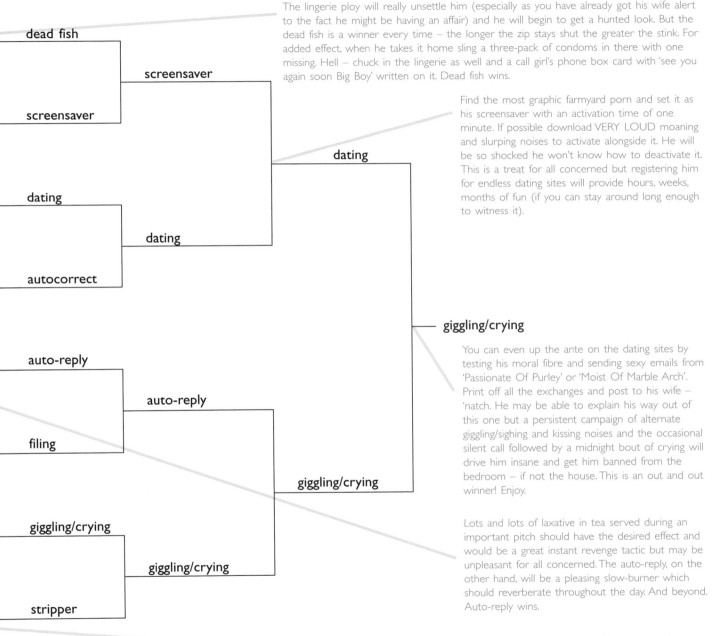

dead fish

screensaver

screensaver

dating

dating

dating

autocorrect

auto-reply

auto-reply

filing

giggling/crying

giggling/crying

giggling/crying

giggling/crying

stripper

dating

giggling/crying

The lingerie ploy will really unsettle him (especially as you have already got his wife alert to the fact he might be having an affair) and he will begin to get a hunted look. But the dead fish is a winner every time – the longer the zip stays shut the greater the stink. For added effect, when he takes it home sling a three-pack of condoms in there with one missing. Hell – chuck in the lingerie as well and a call girl's phone box card with 'see you again soon Big Boy' written on it. Dead fish wins.

Find the most graphic farmyard porn and set it as his screensaver with an activation time of one minute. If possible download VERY LOUD moaning and slurping noises to activate alongside it. He will be so shocked he won't know how to deactivate it. This is a treat for all concerned but registering him for endless dating sites will provide hours, weeks, months of fun (if you can stay around long enough to witness it).

You can even up the ante on the dating sites by testing his moral fibre and sending sexy emails from 'Passionate Of Purley' or 'Moist Of Marble Arch'. Print off all the exchanges and post to his wife – 'natch. He may be able to explain his way out of this one but a persistent campaign of alternate giggling/sighing and kissing noises and the occasional silent call followed by a midnight bout of crying will drive him insane and get him banned from the bedroom – if not the house. This is an out and out winner! Enjoy.

Lots and lots of laxative in tea served during an important pitch should have the desired effect and would be a great instant revenge tactic but may be unpleasant for all concerned. The auto-reply, on the other hand, will be a pleasing slow-burner which should reverberate throughout the day. And beyond. Auto-reply wins.

Preferably a female police officer. With handcuffs. And a truncheon. Wins out over his nuts any time.

64

Older Actresses
by REX OEDIPUS

The silent lusting after a bunch of actresses old enough to be your mother just about gets easier to talk about as you hit middle age. Just about. When you hit forty it begins to look dodgy if you're still drooling over the Keiras, Lindsays or Scarletts of this world. Far better to transfer your affection to one of these elegant women. What do all these lovely ladies have in common? Well – they are all stylish, consummate performers and embody in some way or other that difficult-to-define notion of 'Star Quality'. With that quality comes an inherent power and a fairly impressive pedestal to perch on. This unapproachability makes them all the more desirable and appealing and I am sure I am not alone in being totally smitten. I am sure there are many women out there who rejoice that even in this youth = beauty, size zero landscape some of our leading sex symbols are well into their fifties, and beyond.

REX OEDIPUS is an actor who splits his time between London and Los Angeles.

Helen Mirren
Liza Minnelli

Lauren Bacall
Raquel Welch

Meryl Streep
Greta Garbo

Charlotte Rampling
Diane Keaton

Julie Christie
Diana Rigg

Susan Sarandon
Maggie Smith

Julie Andrews
Joanna Lumley

Jane Fonda
Judi Dench

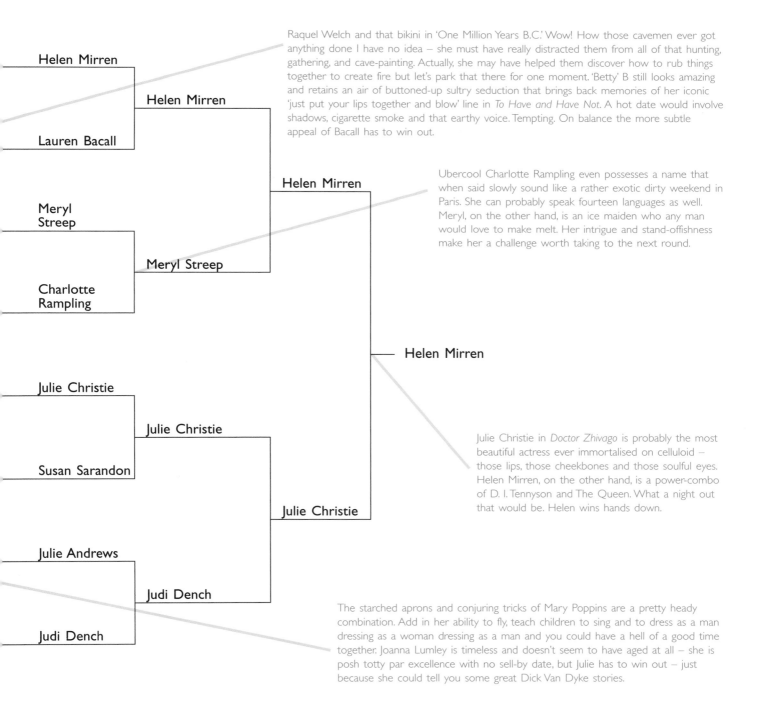

Helen Mirren

Lauren Bacall

Helen Mirren

Meryl Streep

Charlotte Rampling

Meryl Streep

Helen Mirren

Raquel Welch and that bikini in 'One Million Years B.C.' Wow! How those cavemen ever got anything done I have no idea – she must have really distracted them from all of that hunting, gathering, and cave-painting. Actually, she may have helped them discover how to rub things together to create fire but let's park that there for one moment. 'Betty' B still looks amazing and retains an air of buttoned-up sultry seduction that brings back memories of her iconic 'just put your lips together and blow' line in *To Have and Have Not*. A hot date would involve shadows, cigarette smoke and that earthy voice. Tempting. On balance the more subtle appeal of Bacall has to win out.

Ubercool Charlotte Rampling even possesses a name that when said slowly sound like a rather exotic dirty weekend in Paris. She can probably speak fourteen languages as well. Meryl, on the other hand, is an ice maiden who any man would love to make melt. Her intrigue and stand-offishness make her a challenge worth taking to the next round.

Helen Mirren

Julie Christie

Susan Sarandon

Julie Christie

Julie Andrews

Judi Dench

Julie Christie

Julie Christie in *Doctor Zhivago* is probably the most beautiful actress ever immortalised on celluloid – those lips, those cheekbones and those soulful eyes. Helen Mirren, on the other hand, is a power-combo of D. I. Tennyson and The Queen. What a night out that would be. Helen wins hands down.

The starched aprons and conjuring tricks of Mary Poppins are a pretty heady combination. Add in her ability to fly, teach children to sing and to dress as a man dressing as a woman dressing as a man and you could have a hell of a good time together. Joanna Lumley is timeless and doesn't seem to have aged at all – she is posh totty par excellence with no sell-by date, but Julie has to win out – just because she could tell you some great Dick Van Dyke stories.

Oxymorons
by SIMON TREWIN

It was a bitter sweet experience writing this section – I was sitting in a café using their wireless cable connection while sipping a medium large tea made with non-dairy creamer, reading a press release and listening to a talk show on my headphones when I had occasion to summon over the assistant supervisor who as usual looked highly depressed – it was of course an open secret that we had agreed to a partial ceasefire to settle our mutual differences about their business ethics but the look she gave me that morning was pure evil and left me with a pretty ugly taste in my mouth. It was then I noticed an uninvited guest on my plate... Enough oxymorons already - which one wins out?

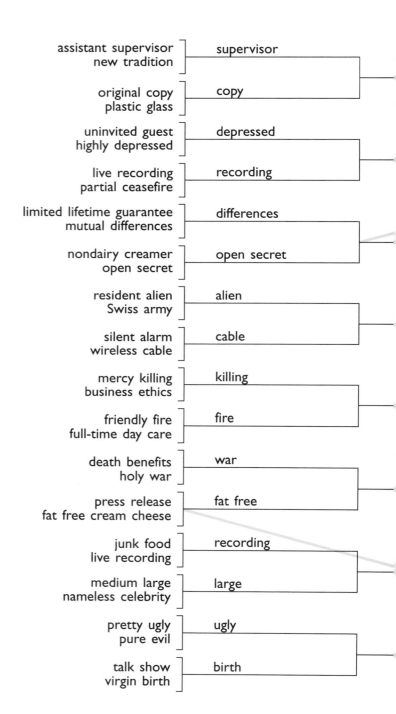

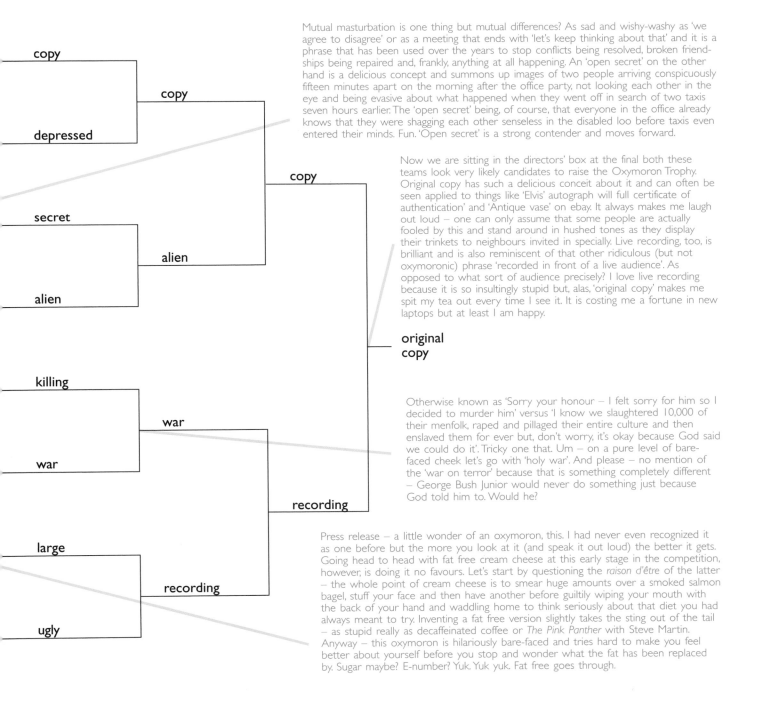

copy

depressed

copy

secret

alien

alien

copy

killing

war

war

war

recording

large

recording

ugly

copy

original
copy

recording

Mutual masturbation is one thing but mutual differences? As sad and wishy-washy as 'we agree to disagree' or as a meeting that ends with 'let's keep thinking about that' and it is a phrase that has been used over the years to stop conflicts being resolved, broken friendships being repaired and, frankly, anything at all happening. An 'open secret' on the other hand is a delicious concept and summons up images of two people arriving conspicuously fifteen minutes apart on the morning after the office party, not looking each other in the eye and being evasive about what happened when they went off in search of two taxis seven hours earlier. The 'open secret' being, of course, that everyone in the office already knows that they were shagging each other senseless in the disabled loo before taxis even entered their minds. Fun. 'Open secret' is a strong contender and moves forward.

Now we are sitting in the directors' box at the final both these teams look very likely candidates to raise the Oxymoron Trophy. Original copy has such a delicious conceit about it and can often be seen applied to things like 'Elvis' autograph will full certificate of authentication' and 'Antique vase' on ebay. It always makes me laugh out loud – one can only assume that some people are actually fooled by this and stand around in hushed tones as they display their trinkets to neighbours invited in specially. Live recording, too, is brilliant and is also reminiscent of that other ridiculous (but not oxymoronic) phrase 'recorded in front of a live audience'. As opposed to what sort of audience precisely? I love live recording because it is so insultingly stupid but, alas, 'original copy' makes me spit my tea out every time I see it. It is costing me a fortune in new laptops but at least I am happy.

Otherwise known as 'Sorry your honour – I felt sorry for him so I decided to murder him' versus 'I know we slaughtered 10,000 of their menfolk, raped and pillaged their entire culture and then enslaved them for ever but, don't worry, it's okay because God said we could do it'. Tricky one that. Um – on a pure level of bare-faced cheek let's go with 'holy war'. And please – no mention of the 'war on terror' because that is something completely different – George Bush Junior would never do something just because God told him to. Would he?

Press release – a little wonder of an oxymoron, this. I had never even recognized it as one before but the more you look at it (and speak it out loud) the better it gets. Going head to head with fat free cream cheese at this early stage in the competition, however, is doing it no favours. Let's start by questioning the *raison d'être* of the latter – the whole point of cream cheese is to smear huge amounts over a smoked salmon bagel, stuff your face and then have another before guiltily wiping your mouth with the back of your hand and waddling home to think seriously about that diet you had always meant to try. Inventing a fat free version slightly takes the sting out of the tail – as stupid really as decaffeinated coffee or *The Pink Panther* with Steve Martin. Anyway – this oxymoron is hilariously bare-faced and tries hard to make you feel better about yourself before you stop and wonder what the fat has been replaced by. Sugar maybe? E-number? Yuk. Yuk yuk. Fat free goes through.

66

Palindromes

by AMY KROUSE ROSENTHAL

I love anagrams. (Amy Rosenthal = Nasty Armhole.) I love word trivia. (The longest word you can type using only your left hand? Stewardesses. A word that has all the vowels in alphabetical order? Facetious.) I love playing with letters and words. (Turn the word OK on its side. Doesn't it look like a person?) And, as evidenced here, I really love palindromes. My ultimate palindrome fantasy is as follows: I'm hanging out at the bar *Evil Olive* (real place in Chicago) listening to Andrew Bird's song *Fake Palindromes* (real song) and in walks the actor Robert Trebor (real person.) Oh, and all this happens at 20:02 on 02/20.

AMY KROUSE ROSENTHAL is the author of the alphabetized memoir *Encyclopedia of an Ordinary Life* (Atlantic Books, 2008), as well as several books for children including *Little Pea, Cookies: Bite-Size Life Lessons* and *The OK Book*. She lives in Chicago.

Semordnilap A word, phrase or sentence that makes sense when reversed, but is not the same as the original. Like 'diaper' spelled backwards is 'repaid.' 'Desserts' spelled backwards is 'stressed.' 'Semordnilap' is 'palindromes.'

TOO BAD I HID A BOOT.

Mum	Mum
Dad	
race car	llama
a mall llama	
Dennis sinned	Rose
Stop, Rose, I prefer pies or pots	
Lisa Bonet ate no basil.	Oprah
Man, Oprah's sharp on a.m.!	
Too bad I hid a boot.	geese
Do geese see God?	
Kay, a red nude, peeped under a yak	Niagara
Niagara, O roar again!	
A man, a plan, a cat, a ham, a yak, a yam, a hat, a canal – Panama!	Panama (short)
A man, a plan, a canal, Panama!	
Go hang a salami; I'm a lasagna hog.	salami
Doc note: I dissent. A fast never prevents a fatness. I diet on cod.	
Subi dura a rudibus.	latin
Ni talar bra latin.	
Won ton? Not now.	Won ton?
Was it Eliot's toilet I saw?	
Enid and Edna dine.	Enid
If I had a Hi-Fi . . .	
Damn! I, Agassi, miss again! Mad!	Agassi
No trace, not one carton.	
Are we not drawn onward, we few, drawn onward to new era?	new era
Campus motto: Bottoms up Mac!	
saippuakauppias	saippuakauppias
Sex at noon taxes	
E. E. Borgnine drags Dad's gardening robe.	Borgnine
Isa, ala myy myymalaasi.	
never odd or even	My girlfriend
My girlfriend has a freaking weird name: Eman Driewgnikaerfasahdneirflrigym	

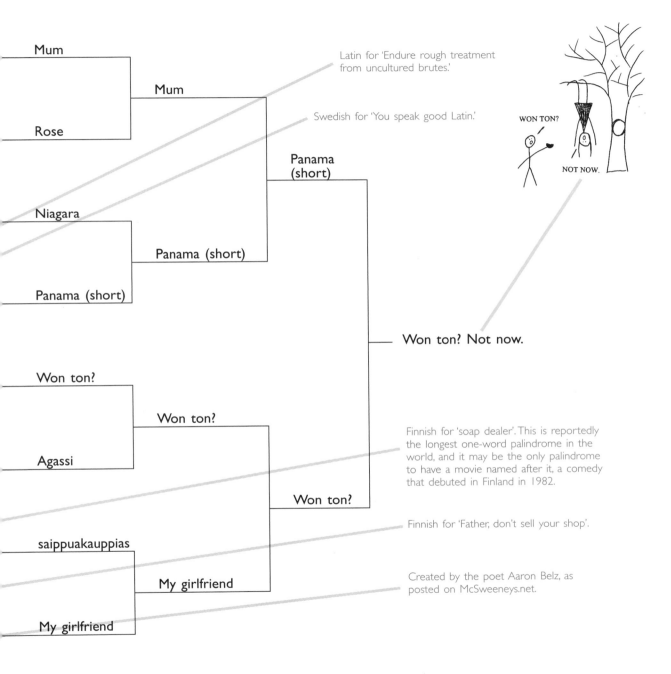

Mum

Mum

Rose

Latin for 'Endure rough treatment from uncultured brutes.'

Swedish for 'You speak good Latin.'

Panama (short)

Niagara

Panama (short)

Panama (short)

WON TON?

NOT NOW.

Won ton? Not now.

Won ton?

Won ton?

Agassi

Finnish for 'soap dealer'. This is reportedly the longest one-word palindrome in the world, and it may be the only palindrome to have a movie named after it, a comedy that debuted in Finland in 1982.

Won ton?

saippuakauppias

Finnish for 'Father, don't sell your shop'.

My girlfriend

Created by the poet Aaron Belz, as posted on McSweeneys.net.

My girlfriend

67

Phobias

by SIMON TREWIN

I am only afraid of a few things: birds flapping in a confined space (like my cat's mouth), mice that run across the carpet, getting rid of dead things (in case they might be still alive but just pretending), people creeping up on me and going '**BOO**', being on stage in a Chinese language production of *Hamlet – the Musical* in which I am playing the eponymous hero and don't know the words/music or dance steps and, finally, of just being generally 'found out' in life. Oh yes – and a large imaginary menagerie manager called Noah who I imagine is managing an imaginary menagerie called The Ark and who has a penchant for flicking imaginary thoughts in my direction with a very real catapult. And honey. And books. Apart from that I am well-adjusted and normal. Unlike the people who suffer from these freaking phobias. Weirdos.

aerophobia – fear of swallowing air
arachibutyrophobia – fear of peanut butter sticking to the roof of the mouth.

peanut butter

aulophobia – fear of flutes
clinophobia – fear of going to bed

flutes

cnidophobia – fear of string
deciophobia – fear of making decisions

decisions

didaskaleinophobia – fear of school
ergophobia – fear of work

work

geliophobia – fear of laughter
geniophobia – fear of chins

chins

hippopotomonstrosesquippedaliophobia – fear of long words
kathisophobia – fear of sitting down

long words

metrophobia – fear of poetry
nomatophobia – fear of names

names

octophobia – fear of the number eight
panophobia – fear of everything

everything

paraskavedekatriaphobia – fear of Friday 13th
peladophobia – fear of bald people

bald people

phobophobia – fear of fear
photophobia – fear of light

fear

phronemophobia – fear of thinking
pogonophobia – fear of beards

beards

verbophobia – fear of words
athazagoraphobia – fear of being ignored

ignored

anatidaephobia – fear that somewhere a duck is watching you
epistemophobia – fear of knowledge

duck

dutchphobia – fear of the Dutch
papaphobia – fear of the Pope

pope

pteronophobia – fear of being tickled by feathers
hobophobia – fear of beggars

feathers

ithyphallophobia – fear of seeing, thinking about, or having an erect penis
taphephobia – fear of being buried alive or of cemeteries

erect penis

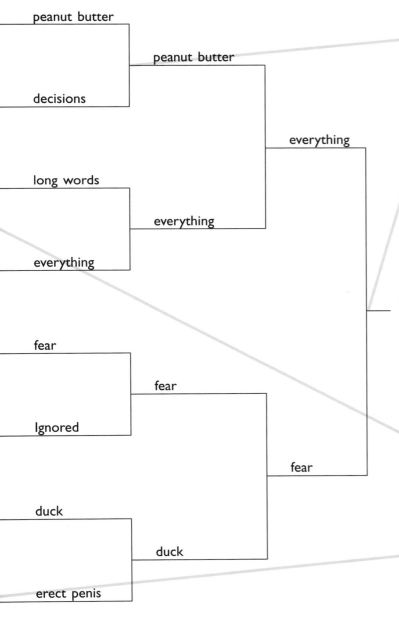

peanut butter

decisions

peanut butter

long words

everything

everything

everything

fear

Ignored

fear

duck

fear

duck

erect penis

panophobia — fear of everything

I have researched this potential peanut butter disaster in depth and found that it is quite scary with smooth and absolutely terrifying with crunchy. I hope we can just move on but, alas, I just can't make my mind up about this round. To be honest I am quite scared of making the wrong decision. Or the right one – oh I don't know – maybe I will just vote Liberal Democrat instead. Peanut butter moves on.

This is getting fairly existential now. Surely if you fear 'everything' then that 'everything' includes 'fear' so surely 'everything' wins. However if you have nothing to fear but fear itself then not only would you be afraid of fear but any other phobias you had would be exacerbated. If you were scared of, say, ducks or chins, then that fear would be double-edged: you would be afraid of the fear itself but also afraid of what you were afraid of. Gosh – this is getting quite scary now and I can sense an attack of deciophobia coming on. Um – okay – 'everything' wins.

Anyone suffering from geniophobia should clearly avoid reading the Hong Kong phone book or, indeed, looking up at John Prescott. But it pales into insignificance when measured against the fear of long words. Someone somewhere obviously pissed themselves when they named this one. Excellent. Fundamentally and undisputedly this progresses excitedly.

Being stiff (above ground) vs. being mistakenly buried as a stiff (below ground)? A hard choice but let's stick with the penis.

68

Pointless Petitions

by SIMON TREWIN

I well remember the excitement of being able to take part in the democratic process for the first time, putting that X in the box during the 1983 general election made me feel mighty proud. Had I known then that the natural conclusion of open government would be that the Number 10 website would allow anyone to post a petition online about the most ridiculous issues imaginable then perhaps I wouldn't have voted. Even though this online petition stuff is clearly a total waste of time and money, after a while you do develop a grudging respect for those tunnel-visioned nutters out there. Which current petition (of the 6,000 online at present) is the one which would have Mrs Pankhurst turning in her grave muttering, 'Blimey – was it really worth all that hassle?' Check out www.petitions. pm.gov.uk and add your own if none of these hit the mark . . .

Ensure that the 'high jump' is part of every schoolchild's P. E. (4 signatures)

Request that Ant and Dec be given knighthoods. (10 signatures)

Ant and Dec

Bring suger-filled (sic) vending machines back. (4 signatures)

Make eggs a compulsory component in our diets. (3 signatures)

suger

Ban MSN. (3 signatures)

Stop TV companies turning up the volume during commercial breaks. (181 signatures)

MSN

Save Russell T. Davies, the Executive Producer of *Doctor Who*, from the sack. (64 signatures)

Keep Christmas in Britain unchanged and stop trying to impress other religions. (300 signatures)

Russell T. Davies

Enter Ultimate Frisbee in to the 2012 Olympics. (787 signatures)

Replace the national anthem with 'Gold' by Spandau Ballet. (5,405 signatures)

'Gold'

Make horse owners pick up the horse poo. (41 signatures)

Allow the sale of elephants in pet shops in the UK. (241 signatures)

elephants

Ban Television broadcasts within a certain time period to beat the weight problem. (1 signature)

Recognize Borat as the leader of Kazakhstan. (96 signatures)

weight problem

Free the Chicken People! (disallowed)

Force house pricing down to approximately 25% of its current value. (57 signatures)

house prices

For all we know this person might be the world expert on high jump as a cure for all sorts of modern day maladies so there may be some common sense behind it. But the whole notion of someone petitioning the Prime Minister (who is a very busy man) to get Ant and Dec knighted just makes me cross. They look barely old enough to be elected Milk Monitors let alone Knights Of the Realm. Mr Ant and Mr Dec move forward.

This sounds like a sad cry for help from someone whose family communicate at the dinner table only by MSN on wireless laptops. You can almost picture the scene. Beep – CrazyGuy1 – Pass The Salt. Beep – SexEgirl2 – Piss Off. Beep – DaddyCool – Will U 2 stop fighting etc etc. Seriously there are some proper issues here about how we communicate and the fragmenting effect on society all these electronic forms of communication have and they are far far more important than who writes the scripts for *Doctor Who*. Russell T. Davies moves forward.

These are both an exceptional waste of government time and I don't know what is most worrying – that a civil servant had to devote time to processing these when they could have been doing something relevant to society or that people took time out to vote for them! Sir Ant and Sir Dec? What in the name of Jefffrey Archer is the point of honouring these little Geordie cheeky boys? But this pales into insignifance when you see that 5,405 people want to replace God Save The Queen with Tony Hadley crooning that 80s new romantic classic. You are indeed 'Gold' your majesty and I am sure you always believe in your soul but as far as a good use of government time and making a huge contribution to the democratic process this is total pants and wins our mounted Ballot Box Trophy (made of gold of course).

Yeah dude – whatever.

I have no idea what this means at all – maybe what he should be saying is 'Please make it illegal for me to sit in front of television all day and all of the night slowly turning into a huge flabby balloon filled with gloop whose only exercise is speed-dialling Domino's Pizza and ordering a fourteen inch Meat Feast with added everything'. If he had been honest it may have got more votes. That said it still beats Borat as a waste of democratic megabytes.

No. 10 did disallow this activist from trying to drum up support for the chickens because they were probably scared that he would dress up as a chicken and follow Gordon Brown around on the campaign trail. But at least this was quite clearly tongue-in-cheek, whereas the ridiculous property market idea beggars belief. Great idea, mate – plunge the whole of the UK into negative equity just so you can afford to buy a three bedroom flat instead of a bedsit. The fact that fifty-six other people have signed this demonstrates that more money needs to be spent on teaching economics at secondary school level.

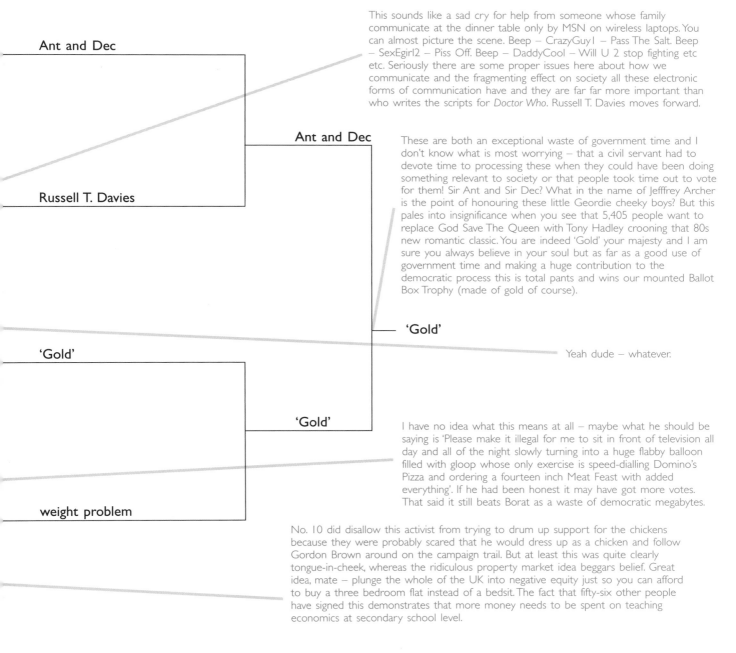

Ant and Dec

Russell T. Davies

Ant and Dec

'Gold'

'Gold'

'Gold'

weight problem

69

Pornstar Names
by SHIMMER McDIGGLE

In its pre-Murdoch days, the *News of the World* used to run under its masthead the legend 'All Human Life is Here.' Were the Internet to have such a masthead nothing could be more apposite. Whether you are a collector of nineteenth-century Australian chamber pots, a photographer of writers' garden sheds, learning the useful homeskill of taxidermy or simply looking to find out how to build a bomb, the Internet is a one-stop-shop. So when I sat down and discovered that people had spent valuable time on this planet setting up websites which randomly generated pornstar names I did stop for a while and get very cross. Shouldn't these people be trying to find a cure for cancer (or at the very least the common cold) or be trying to tackle world debt? Then I started playing with the site, www.whatisyourpornstarname.com, and I started laughing. A lot. Why pornstars can't have normal names like Barry, Joan, Peter and Hilda I don't know, but maybe it is because porn bears as much relation to what you get up to at home as TV cookery programmes do to what you do in the kitchen. But, dear reader, in the interests of science (and booksales), I have returned to the task in hand, and here follows what I hope is what the popular press will call yet another example of how Christmas humour books are sinking to an all-time low.

SHIMMER MCDIGGLE is the pseudonym of an adult entertainer currently resident in Stockholm and Penge.

Laser McCall / Cappuccino Furrby — **Cappuccino**

Cadillac Bends / Chandy Colonchowska — **Cadillac**

Craig Crutch / King Kong Rod — **Rod**

Musky Stickett / Kitten Swallows — **Kitten**

Pimp Daddy Slides / Weena Bustiere — **Pimp Daddy**

Luke Bondage / Mucky LaBouche — **Mucky**

Huge O'Toole / Candy Funkenstein — **Huge**

Dick Thrust / Annette Thong — **Dick**

Balls Fred Tuck-It / Shannon Head — **Balls**

Bonder Dick Hanger / Miss Bluebell — **Miss Bluebell**

Bunder Bob the Bandit / Maisie Bounce — **Maisie**

Jason Chuck / Dixie Bottom — **Dixie**

Ronald Diggles / Sweetly Swallows — **Sweetly**

Randy Bob the Fox / Foxy Kitten — **Foxy**

Randy Ron / Chandelier Vegas — **Chandelier**

Dirk Biggun / Chanel Ice — **Chanel**

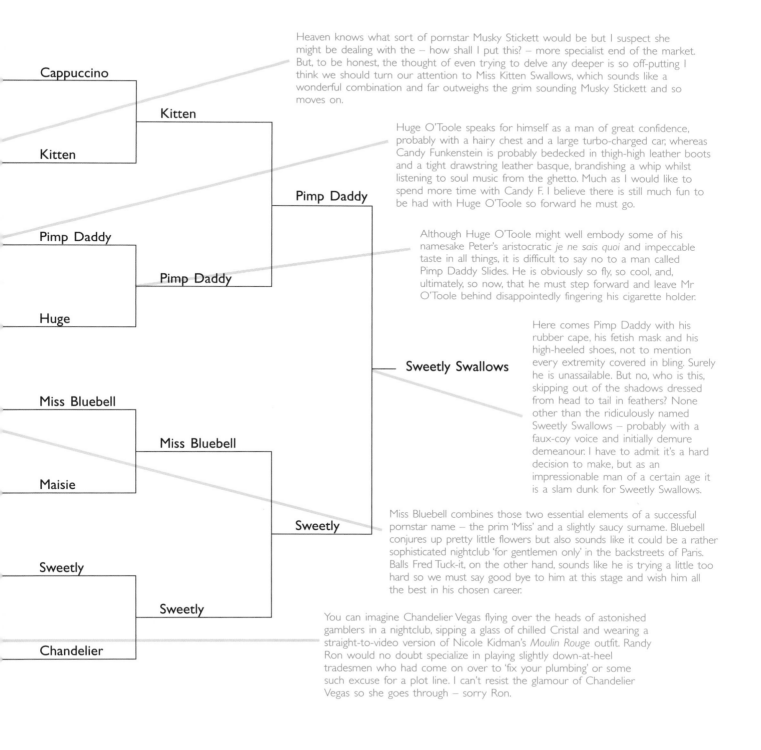

Cappuccino

Kitten

Kitten

Heaven knows what sort of pornstar Musky Stickett would be but I suspect she might be dealing with the – how shall I put this? – more specialist end of the market. But, to be honest, the thought of even trying to delve any deeper is so off-putting I think we should turn our attention to Miss Kitten Swallows, which sounds like a wonderful combination and far outweighs the grim sounding Musky Stickett and so moves on.

Pimp Daddy

Pimp Daddy

Pimp Daddy

Huge

Huge O'Toole speaks for himself as a man of great confidence, probably with a hairy chest and a large turbo-charged car, whereas Candy Funkenstein is probably bedecked in thigh-high leather boots and a tight drawstring leather basque, brandishing a whip whilst listening to soul music from the ghetto. Much as I would like to spend more time with Candy F. I believe there is still much fun to be had with Huge O'Toole so forward he must go.

Although Huge O'Toole might well embody some of his namesake Peter's aristocratic *je ne sais quoi* and impeccable taste in all things, it is difficult to say no to a man called Pimp Daddy Slides. He is obviously so fly, so cool, and, ultimately, so now, that he must step forward and leave Mr O'Toole behind disappointedly fingering his cigarette holder.

Sweetly Swallows

Here comes Pimp Daddy with his rubber cape, his fetish mask and his high-heeled shoes, not to mention every extremity covered in bling. Surely he is unassailable. But no, who is this, skipping out of the shadows dressed from head to tail in feathers? None other than the ridiculously named Sweetly Swallows – probably with a faux-coy voice and initially demure demeanour. I have to admit it's a hard decision to make, but as an impressionable man of a certain age it is a slam dunk for Sweetly Swallows.

Miss Bluebell

Miss Bluebell

Miss Bluebell

Maisie

Sweetly

Sweetly

Sweetly

Chandelier

Miss Bluebell combines those two essential elements of a successful pornstar name – the prim 'Miss' and a slightly saucy surname. Bluebell conjures up pretty little flowers but also sounds like it could be a rather sophisticated nightclub 'for gentlemen only' in the backstreets of Paris. Balls Fred Tuck-it, on the other hand, sounds like he is trying a little too hard so we must say good bye to him at this stage and wish him all the best in his chosen career.

You can imagine Chandelier Vegas flying over the heads of astonished gamblers in a nightclub, sipping a glass of chilled Cristal and wearing a straight-to-video version of Nicole Kidman's *Moulin Rouge* outfit. Randy Ron would no doubt specialize in playing slightly down-at-heel tradesmen who had come on over to 'fix your plumbing' or some such excuse for a plot line. I can't resist the glamour of Chandelier Vegas so she goes through – sorry Ron.

70

Pound Shop Treasures

by SIMON TREWIN

It is symptomatic of most high streets that vacant shop premises will soon become (even if only temporarily) those wonderful palaces of temptation and shrines to listless consumerism – Pound Shops. They can be recognized with ease as they all have the same décor – crammed windows so packed with tempting merchandise that you can't see in (or out), optimistic heaps of laundry-baskets, bin bags, Christmas decorations, candles and mops, and hoards of people buying stuff they don't need just because it is so cheap. Bit like Ikea I suppose but without the Swedish meatballs. Of course, in these inflationary times many of these exotic emporia have cleverly changed from the friendly neighbourhood 'Pound Shop' to the slightly less generous 'Pound Plus' store which, if you really think about it, means 'Nothing in this shop costs less than a pound but most costs a hell of a lot more'. I went to three pound shops in London with a single pound of my publisher's money burning a hole in my pocket to see what was the most phenomenal bit of 100 pence value that made me scream 'How do they do it for the price?' the loudest.

40g Supa goldfish flakes

eight-pack of wild bird fatballs

fatballs

tape dispenser and six rolls of Sellotape

fifteen laminating sheets

Sellotape

set of three square storage boxes (plastic)

sewing kit in a metal box

storage boxes

ladies' satin French knickers (with lace)

three-pack satin glitter pants (girls)

glitter pants

four-pack of Pepsi

ten-pack of cheesy Quavers

Pepsi

ten-pack of bristle paint brushes

four-pack of supaglue

paint brushes

Real Sound dinosaur

two-ring paddling pool

paddling pool

Agfa 24 exposure disposable camera

five-way scart splitter (twenty-one pin)

camera

Oh my God! This is a difficult choice — I am reliably informed that you could feed a family of four goldfish for upwards of two weeks with this lovingly produced 40g punnet of fish food. Not sure what it is made of but it looks like a combination of dried skin and the bits from the bottom of the cornflake packet. That works out at about two pee per day per fish which is phenomenal value and only just below what the NHS allows for patient catering. But does it win out with our valuometer against the fatball? No it doesn't — you can feed a flock of birds (not sure how big a flock is but it is a lot) for a week on one fat ball so we are talking fractions of a pence here although, for the pedants amongst you, fish ONLY eat flakes whereas the fat is only PART of the birds' diet. That said — eight balls of fat for a quid is pretty impressive and so goes through.

Both these items are designed to keep valuable items fresh and clean so they are ready to be plucked out, warmed up and put to use at a moment's notice. The pants will come and go but those tupperware-a-like boxes will outlive you so on they go.

Sellotape usually costs a quid a pop in some of the fancier stationers so this feels like some factory worker somewhere isn't get exactly pampered during the manufacturing process, especially when you see you get a handy little plastic dispenser with it. But can it win out against the summer-long pleasure provided by the joys of a TWO RING (count 'em) paddling pool on the lawn? Of course it can't — my pound is in the till and I am heading home to inflate this amazing gift. I might even pop back later and get the camera as well so I can immortalize the fun.

Not wishing to quibble here but this could be phenomenal value — unless I am mistaken there were no recording devices around during the Jurassic period so I'm not sure how accurate this 'real sound' description is. Maybe for one quid you are being let in on a secret that in a factory somewhere in Taiwan there are living dinosaurs screaming into microphones just for your pound shop pleasure. Or perhaps not.

My first camera cost about twenty pounds and came in a velvet-lined case. It felt so valuable and so precious that it was rarely taken out in case it got damaged. Nowadays you can apparently get a film AND a camera which snaps away and then gets smashed up once the film is retrieved for just one pound. Just think of all those memories you can capture — and all at the cost of just over 4 pence a snapshot. Priceless. Even in the staggering face of value the twenty-one pin five-way scary splitter offers (less than a penny a pin), those memories will live on forever so the camera goes on through.

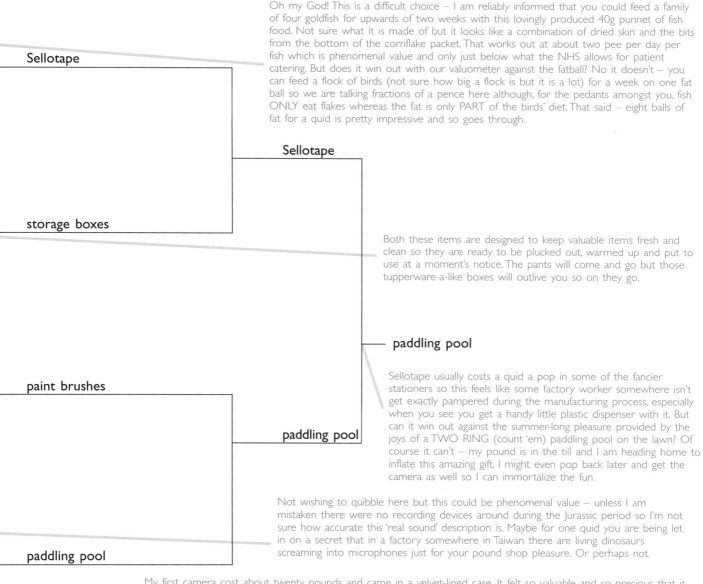

Sellotape

storage boxes

Sellotape

paint brushes

paddling pool

paddling pool

paddling pool

71

Priceless Things
by LEILA DUNBAR and Colleagues at Sotheby's

Priceless things are tangible objects that have never been sold. The buildings, landmarks, artwork, sculpture, and important documents here were all chosen for their impact on history, their longevity, their iconic standing, their sheer enormity, and their symbolism. The criterion: which is the least likely to ever come up for sale, privately or at an auction house? Most are owned by governments or the public, which suggests but doesn't guarantee that they'll never go on the block. Is there such a thing as the most priceless? According to our bracket, the answer is yes!

LEILA 'LEE' DUNBAR is senior vice president of Sotheby's Collectibles in New York. In her seven years, the Collectibles Department has been responsible for more than $60 million in sales of sports and entertainment memorabilia, including the estates of Katharine Hepburn and Johnny Cash and the bat Babe Ruth used to hit the first home run ever in Yankee Stadium. Thanks to colleagues Lisa Ladish, Hugh Hildesley, Mary Bartow, Charles Moffett, Richard Keresey, Christopher Gaillard, and the Chinese Works of Art Department.

Matchup	Winner
Statue of Liberty / Eiffel Tower	Statue of Liberty
Parthenon / Stonehenge	Parthenon
Taj Mahal / the Pyramids of Giza/Sphinx	Pyramids/Sphinx
Ka'ba in Mecca / Sistine Chapel Ceiling by Michelangelo	Sistine Chapel
Mona Lisa (La Gioconda) by Leonardo da Vinci / Birth of Venus by Sandro Botticelli	Mona Lisa
Guernica by Pablo Picasso / The Night Watch by Rembrandt van Rijn	Guernica
Impression: Sunrise by Claude Monet / Head of a Young Woman by Johannes Vermeer	Impression: Sunrise
Venus de Milo, attributed to Alexandros of Antioch / Winged Victory of Samothrace by unknown artist	Venus de Milo
Crown Jewels of Great Britain / Pope's ring	Crown Jewels
Rosetta Stone / Code of Hammurabi	Rosetta Stone
David by Michelangelo / The Thinker by Auguste Rodin	David
King Tutankhamun artifacts / Queen Nefertiti's bust	King Tut artifacts
buried city of Pompeii / Terracotta Army	Terracotta Army
Great Wall of China / Forbidden City	Great Wall of China
Magna Carta / United States Constitution	Magna Carta
Blarney Stone / Book of Kells	Blarney Stone

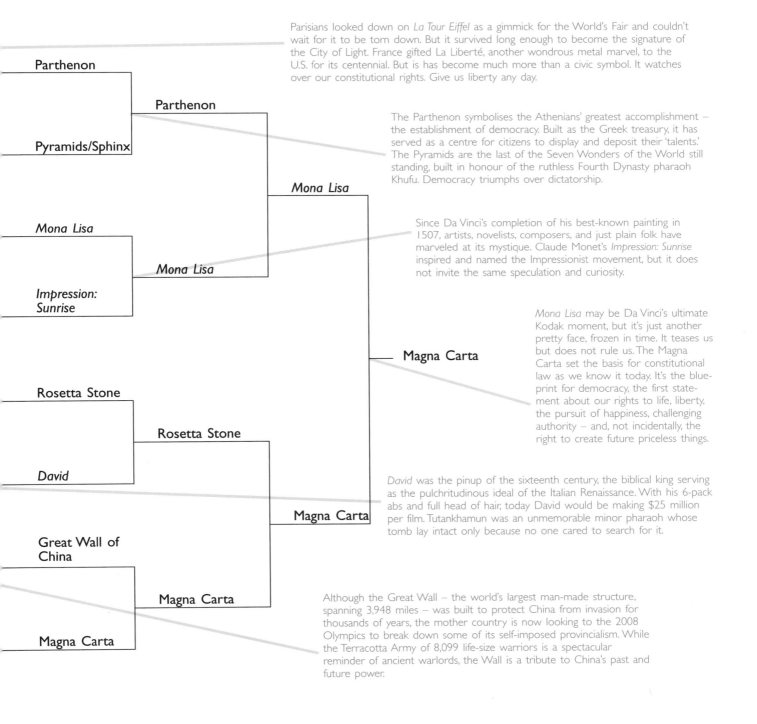

Parthenon

Pyramids/Sphinx

Mona Lisa

Impression:
Sunrise

Rosetta Stone

David

Great Wall of
China

Magna Carta

Parthenon

Mona Lisa

Rosetta Stone

Magna Carta

Mona Lisa

Magna Carta

Parisians looked down on *La Tour Eiffel* as a gimmick for the World's Fair and couldn't wait for it to be torn down. But it survived long enough to become the signature of the City of Light. France gifted *La Liberté*, another wondrous metal marvel, to the U.S. for its centennial. But is has become much more than a civic symbol. It watches over our constitutional rights. Give us liberty any day.

The Parthenon symbolises the Athenians' greatest accomplishment — the establishment of democracy. Built as the Greek treasury, it has served as a centre for citizens to display and deposit their 'talents.' The Pyramids are the last of the Seven Wonders of the World still standing, built in honour of the ruthless Fourth Dynasty pharaoh Khufu. Democracy triumphs over dictatorship.

Since Da Vinci's completion of his best-known painting in 1507, artists, novelists, composers, and just plain folk have marveled at its mystique. Claude Monet's *Impression: Sunrise* inspired and named the Impressionist movement, but it does not invite the same speculation and curiosity.

Mona Lisa may be Da Vinci's ultimate Kodak moment, but it's just another pretty face, frozen in time. It teases us but does not rule us. The Magna Carta set the basis for constitutional law as we know it today. It's the blueprint for democracy, the first statement about our rights to life, liberty, the pursuit of happiness, challenging authority — and, not incidentally, the right to create future priceless things.

David was the pinup of the sixteenth century, the biblical king serving as the pulchritudinous ideal of the Italian Renaissance. With his 6-pack abs and full head of hair, today David would be making $25 million per film. Tutankhamun was an unmemorable minor pharaoh whose tomb lay intact only because no one cared to search for it.

Although the Great Wall — the world's largest man-made structure, spanning 3,948 miles — was built to protect China from invasion for thousands of years, the mother country is now looking to the 2008 Olympics to break down some of its self-imposed provincialism. While the Terracotta Army of 8,099 life-size warriors is a spectacular reminder of ancient warlords, the Wall is a tribute to China's past and future power.

72

Proverbs
by SIMON TREWIN

Youth of today please note! There is much wisdom out there for the taking and these proverbs, found all over the world, contain enough lessons for us all to live our lives more sanely, more honestly and with more common sense than anything you are going to pick up hanging around the bus shelter in a windswept shopping centre. You can judge a nation by its proverbs, and as long as we have a healthy injection of 'Honesty is the best policy' and 'Charity begins at home' mixed in with the terrible instant credit, instant fame, instant happiness mantra that seems to be the norm at the moment then maybe, just maybe we will be alright. Here endeth the lesson.

More things belong to marriage than four bare legs in a bed. (English) — bare legs
Look down if you would know how high you stand. (Yiddish)

Look before you leap. (English) — witness
Life without a friend is death without a witness. (Spanish)

Keep a thing for seven years and you'll find a use for it. (Irish) — tomorrow
Never put off till tomorrow what may be done today. (English)

Six hours' sleep for a man, seven for a woman and eight for a fool. (English) — well fed
The well fed do not understand the lean. (Irish)

What you can not avoid, welcome. (Chinese) — avoid
With money you are a dragon; with no money, a worm. (Chinese)

You cannot unscramble eggs. (North American) — eggs
You have to kiss a lot of toads before you find a handsome prince. (North American)

A lie travels round the world while truth is putting her boots on. (French) — lie
Luck has a slender anchorage. (English)

Fame is a magnifying glass. (English) — fame
Deal with the faults of others as gently as with your own. (Chinese)

A son is a son till he gets him a wife, But a daughter's a daughter the rest of your life. (Unknown) — son/daughter
It is better to follow no saint than six. (Indian)

A little drop of water silences a boiling pot. (German) — bill
At the bottom of the bag one finds the bill. (Dutch)

A book is like a garden carried in the pocket. (Arabic) — book
A bird in the hand is worth two in a bush. (English)

A man is not honest simply because he never had a chance to steal. (Yiddish) — honest
A prudent man does not make the goat his gardener. (Hungarian)

A society grows great when old men plant trees whose shade they know they shall never sit in. (Greek) — trees
'Thank you' won't pay the fiddler. (Scottish)

Choose neither a woman nor linen by candlelight. (Italian) — candlelight
Curiosity killed the cat. (English)

Do not blame God for having created the tiger, but thank him for not having given it wings. (Indian) — evil
Evil enters like a needle and spreads like an oak tree. (Ethiopian)

He who sups with the devil has need of a long spoon. (English) — honesty
Honesty is the best policy. (English)

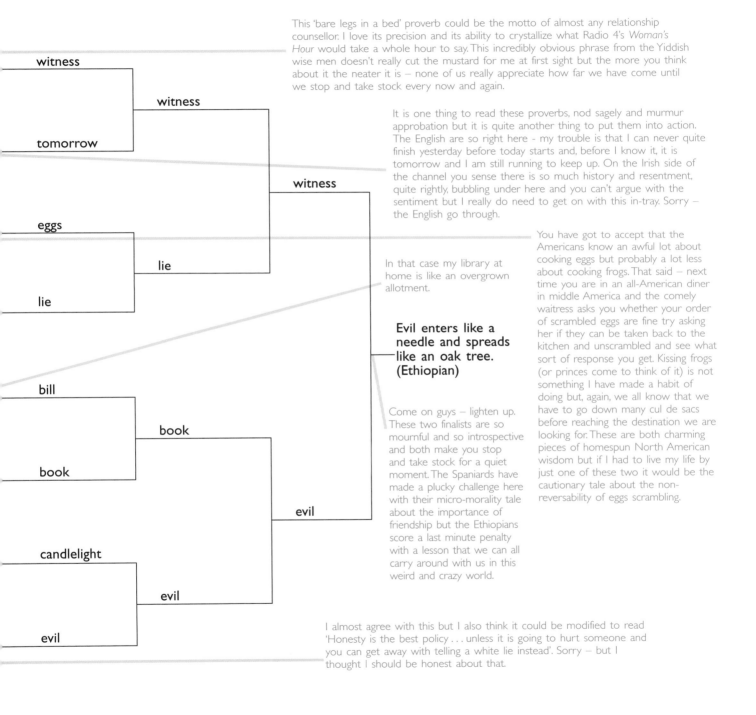

This 'bare legs in a bed' proverb could be the motto of almost any relationship counsellor. I love its precision and its ability to crystallize what Radio 4's *Woman's Hour* would take a whole hour to say. This incredibly obvious phrase from the Yiddish wise men doesn't really cut the mustard for me at first sight but the more you think about it the neater it is – none of us really appreciate how far we have come until we stop and take stock every now and again.

It is one thing to read these proverbs, nod sagely and murmur approbation but it is quite another thing to put them into action. The English are so right here - my trouble is that I can never quite finish yesterday before today starts and, before I know it, it is tomorrow and I am still running to keep up. On the Irish side of the channel you sense there is so much history and resentment, quite rightly, bubbling under here and you can't argue with the sentiment but I really do need to get on with this in-tray. Sorry – the English go through.

In that case my library at home is like an overgrown allotment.

Evil enters like a needle and spreads like an oak tree. (Ethiopian)

You have got to accept that the Americans know an awful lot about cooking eggs but probably a lot less about cooking frogs. That said – next time you are in an all-American diner in middle America and the comely waitress asks you whether your order of scrambled eggs are fine try asking her if they can be taken back to the kitchen and unscrambled and see what sort of response you get. Kissing frogs (or princes come to think of it) is not something I have made a habit of doing but, again, we all know that we have to go down many cul de sacs before reaching the destination we are looking for. These are both charming pieces of homespun North American wisdom but if I had to live my life by just one of these two it would be the cautionary tale about the non-reversability of eggs scrambling.

Come on guys – lighten up. These two finalists are so mournful and so introspective and both make you stop and take stock for a quiet moment. The Spaniards have made a plucky challenge here with their micro-morality tale about the importance of friendship but the Ethiopians score a last minute penalty with a lesson that we can all carry around with us in this weird and crazy world.

I almost agree with this but I also think it could be modified to read 'Honesty is the best policy . . . unless it is going to hurt someone and you can get away with telling a white lie instead'. Sorry – but I thought I should be honest about that.

73

Punctuation
by JESSE SHEIDLOWER

Punctuation is a system of marks used to clarify the meaning of written language by showing how words and clauses relate to each other. We can make do without much punctuation – the principal marks in modern use arose only in the fifteenth and sixteenth centuries. But punctuation is so useful that we now have a vast array of marks for various purposes, especially when the category includes other written symbols such as diacritical marks and printer's marks. Which are the ones we really need?

JESSE SHEIDLOWER is editor at large of the Oxford English Dictionary. He managed to write an entire book. The F-Word, about one word (yes, that one), and has written about language for such publications as the New York Times, Slate, Harper's, the Atlantic Monthly, and Esquire.

comma (,)
square brackets ([ ])
— ,

circumflex accent (^)
em dash (—)
— —

parentheses (())
cent sign (¢)
— ()

acute accent (´)
double quotes ("")
— ""

question mark (?)
percent sign (%)
— ?

slash (/)
the space ( )
— (the space)

asterisk (*)
number sign (#)
— *

ampersand (&)
colon (:)
— :

UPPERCASE LETTERS
exclamation mark (!)
— (UPPERCASE)

tilde (~)
at sign (@)
— @

semicolon (;)
pilcrow (¶)
— ;

euro sign (€)
pound sign (£)
— $

apostrophe (')
en dash (–)
— '

umlaut (¨)
diaeresis (¨)
— ¨ (diaeresis)

hyphen (-)
single quotes (' ')
— -

full stop (.)
grave accent (`)
— .

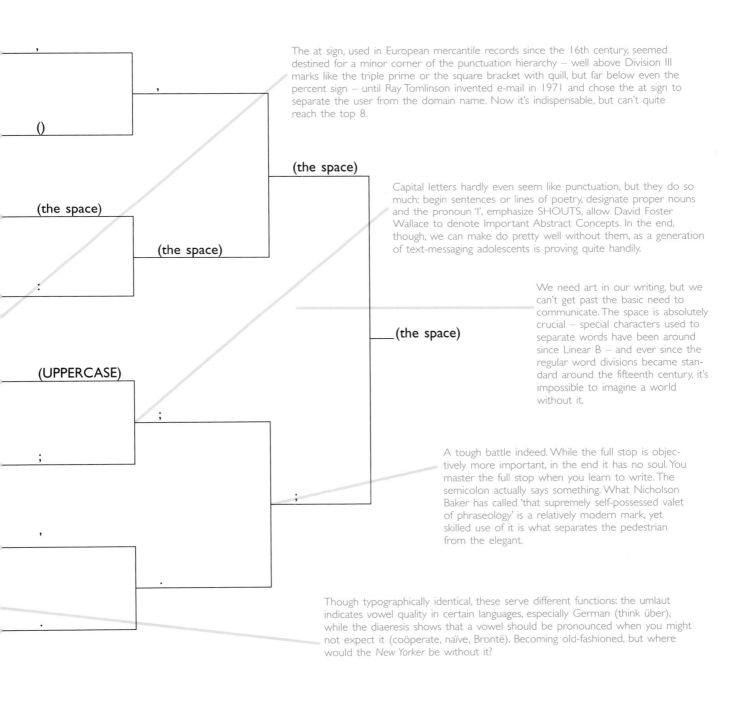

The at sign, used in European mercantile records since the 16th century, seemed destined for a minor corner of the punctuation hierarchy – well above Division III marks like the triple prime or the square bracket with quill, but far below even the percent sign – until Ray Tomlinson invented e-mail in 1971 and chose the at sign to separate the user from the domain name. Now it's indispensable, but can't quite reach the top 8.

Capital letters hardly even seem like punctuation, but they do so much: begin sentences or lines of poetry, designate proper nouns and the pronoun 'I', emphasize SHOUTS, allow David Foster Wallace to denote Important Abstract Concepts. In the end, though, we can make do pretty well without them, as a generation of text-messaging adolescents is proving quite handily.

We need art in our writing, but we can't get past the basic need to communicate. The space is absolutely crucial – special characters used to separate words have been around since Linear B – and ever since the regular word divisions became standard around the fifteenth century, it's impossible to imagine a world without it.

A tough battle indeed. While the full stop is objectively more important, in the end it has no soul. You master the full stop when you learn to write. The semicolon actually says something. What Nicholson Baker has called 'that supremely self-possessed valet of phraseology' is a relatively modern mark, yet skilled use of it is what separates the pedestrian from the elegant.

Though typographically identical, these serve different functions: the umlaut indicates vowel quality in certain languages, especially German (think über), while the diaeresis shows that a vowel should be pronounced when you might not expect it (coöperate, naïve, Brontë). Becoming old-fashioned, but where would the *New Yorker* be without it?

74

Reality Television Must-See Moments

by LOLA JAYE

While friends, family and acquaintances have been busy getting a life, I've spent the best part of the new millennium sitting through reality TV shows – like my waistline, a rapidly growing phenomenon. The intellectual in me is tempted to explain this mild addiction away pompously: 'It's a high-brow experiment in social psychology, a scholarly way of observing human behaviour.' But the sweat-pant wearing 'slouch on the couch' part of me is clearly addicted to the live (minus sixty second delay) punch-ups and the excuses to guffaw shamelessly at yet another buck-toothed auditionee, deluded into thinking he's the next Christina Aguilera. Yes, I am ready to stand up, be counted and 'fess up to the fact that I've sat through endless reality TV shows in the past – and probably will again in the future.

LOLA graduated as a psychotherapist just as the giant that is reality TV began its grip on British television. Her debut novel *The Manual* will be published by HarperCollins in the summer of 2008. Luckily, she's found a useful way of mentally blocking out the current continuous reel of such shows. How? – by switching the TV off, duh!

Leona Lewis winning *X-Factor*. (Series 3, 2006.)

Gareth Gates taking second place in *Pop Idol* (Series 1, 2002)

Leona Lewis

'Nasty' Nick Bateman finally getting rumbled by Craig Phillips in *Big Brother*. (Series 1, 2000)

Jade Goody and Shilpa Shetty arguing over chicken stock cubes in *Celebrity Big Brother*. (Series 7, 2007)

Nick Bateman

Tim Campbell winning *The Apprentice*. (Series 1, 2005)

Popstars (2001)

Tim Campbell

Helen Adams and Paul Clarke's 'will they/won't they?' in *Big Brother*. (Series 2, 2001)

Jade Goody and P. J. Ellis's 'did they/didn't they?' moment under the duvet in *Big Brother*. (Series 3, 2002)

Helen and Paul

Makosi Musambasi and Anthony Hutton's alleged copulation in the pool in *Big Brother*. (Series 6, 2005)

Natalie Appleton's endless bush tucker trials in *I'm a Celebrity, Get Me Out of Here!* (Series 4, 2004)

Makosi and Anthony

Clash between Victor Ebuwa and Emma Greenwood in *Big Brother*. (Series 5, 2004)

Lee Ottway's unrequited lust and subsequent trashing of set in *Celebrity Love Island*. (Series 2, 2006)

Victor and Emma

Katie Price (Jordan) and Peter Andre 'finding one another' in *I'm a Celebrity, Get me Out of Here!* (Series 3, 2004)

Shabhaz Chauhdry in *Big Brother*. (Series 7, 2006)

Katie and Peter

Dragons' Den (Series 3, 2006)

Helen Adams letting us know, 'I love blinking I do.' in *Big Brother*. (Series 2, 2001)

Dragons' Den

Watching the rather cute, spiky haired Gareth stutter his way into the finals was heart-warming, feel-good telly. But this round has to go to the first female winner of *X Factor*, a welcome change from the usual male pin-ups and an indication that for once the show's teeny-bopping voters managed to look beyond rapidly maturing lusts and opt for real talent.

Popstars got me all excited. It was like nothing I'd ever seen before: five youngsters plucked from obscurity and thrown into the world of showbiz right before my very eyes. Innovative television without the greedy edge it has now acquired (no phone vote for a start). Reality TV at its best, never to be seen again. Having said that, this round has to be handed to Tim because his win spoke volumes. He showed that it doesn't matter where you come from or what colour you happen to be – your dreams can still come true in corporate Blighty. Oh, and he looks like my brother.

The beautiful and pure love story that was Helen and Paul. The 'will they/won't they?' saga that had me and half the nation hooked, if not a little frustrated. With the possible risk of sounding like my Nan, those were the days.

Makosi and Anthony's alleged copulation in the pool is something I missed due to a holiday. But the ensuing furore of 'Poolgate' meant this had to win over Natalie Appleton's endless bush tucker trials, which frankly got boring after the first thousand.

Victor and Emma's massive fight scene was . . . erm . . . massive . . . at least I assume so, considering Channel Four cut the transmission mid-way. I promise, promise, promise I wasn't one of the viewers who actually rang the police. I promise. Still, Lee Ottway's unrequited lust and subsequent 'I'm a rock star, I'll trash the hotel room!' impression just doesn't compare.

As a mass of derivative reality TV shows began to overload the schedules it was great to discover a bit of an original in *Dragons' Den*, which really hit its stride in the third series. Highlights include the brewing rivalry between the dragons (Peter Jones, Richard Farleigh, Duncan Bannatyne, Theo Paphitis and Deborah Meedam) and the must-see appeal of competitors like Jackie from Inverness who came up with a disposable toilet seat cover and seat warmer? You. Are. Genius. Jackie. And we are not worthy.

Leona Lewis

Helen and Paul

Helen and Paul

Helen and Paul

Victor and Emma

Dragons' Den

Dragons' Den

75

Sandwiches
by KATE COURTENAY

The quest for the most delicious sandwich has fuelled countless moments of luxurious deliberation; and many current foodie popularity polls seem obsessed with pinpointing the perfect combination. But this can have its drawbacks. Who wants to spend hungry, wasted minutes assessing ceaseless variations on the same theme, or compete with other famished snackers, all vying to see which sandwich proffers the most generous filling? It's all too easy to get swayed by the aesthetics of a particular prawn, or waylaid computing the percentage of annoying frizzy lettuce to abundance of meat. At the end of the day, choosing the wrong sandwich, or assembling a shitty one by mistake, is akin to ruining one's hair or enduring a miserably painful paper cut. And while a whole day can be crushed by such an error, making the right sandwich choice is quite simply the bread of heaven.

KATE COURTENAY is a London-based broadcaster and writer, for many years hosting a series of half hour interview shows on the TCM channel, and previously, as Showbiz Correspondent for CNN International. She is currently completing her first novel for children called *Tree Stories*. After graduation (many moons and thousands of sandwiches ago), Kate had a short stint as a model and needed to boost her flagging income by cooking for city businesses. While the catwalk evaded as a career, her newly acquired kitchen skills ignited a lifelong passion that proved to be infinitely more nourishing.

BLT (bacon, lettuce and tomato) on brown
croque-monsieur (with béchamel sauce)
→ croque-monsieur

tomato, mozzarella and basil ciabatta
aubergine, mozzarella and basil melt
→ tomato and mozzarella

my mother's egg mayonnaise with fresh chives
Marmite and shredded lettuce
→ egg mayo

smoked salmon on thin brown (with lemon slice)
hoisin duck wrap
→ smoked salmon

greasy bacon butty on toasted white
hot sausage and mustard on white
→ hot sausage

salad niçoise wrap
crab meat and cucumber on brown
→ salad niçoise

coronation chicken & salad
cheese and pickle
→ cheese and pickle

chicken caesar wrap
toasted steak sandwich (thin fries on the side)
→ toasted steak

plain sliced tomato on white, with salt & pepper
smoked mackerel pâté on brown
→ tomato

prawn mayonnaise and avocado on brown
tuna mayonnaise and sweetcorn in pitta bread
→ prawn and avocado

toasted club sandwich
Christmas turkey, stuffing and cranberry
→ toasted club

tea time cucumber sandwich on white
sandwich spread on white
→ cucumber

roast beef and horseradish
Reuben's sandwich
→ Reuben's

doner kebab
roast beef and brie
→ doner kebab

chocolate spread
fried peanut butter and banana
→ fried peanut butter

fried egg and tomato ketchup on toasted white
chip butty
→ fried egg

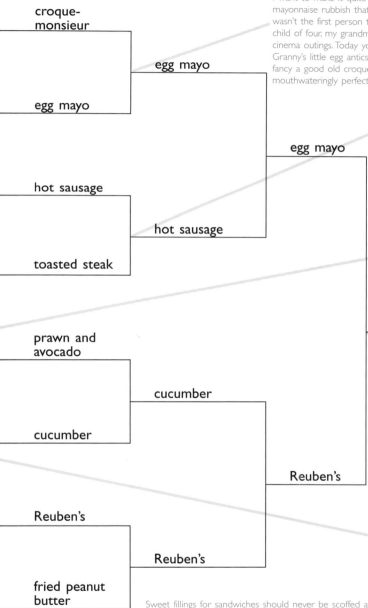

croque-monsieur

egg mayo

egg mayo

egg mayo

hot sausage

hot sausage

toasted steak

prawn and avocado

cucumber

cucumber

Reuben's

Reuben's

Reuben's

fried peanut butter

I want to make it quite clear that in this study, I am in no way alluding to the dismal, fart-worthy egg mayonnaise rubbish that frequents petrol station fridges. My mum's egg sandwiches are legendary, but she wasn't the first person to make them for such a grateful audience. When she was a wee thing and the eldest child of four, my grandmother (her mother) would always pack a whole stack of curried egg sandwiches for cinema outings. Today you can clear a row by bonking in the back seats or sucking too loudly on a fizzy drink. Granny's little egg antics fully guaranteed that Mum and her family got seats all to themselves. But still, I do fancy a good old croque-monsieur and I'm afraid to say, you cannot – cannot – get better or more mouthwateringly perfect specimens than in France. Still - not quite enough to win over an egg, *à la fin du jour*.

One of these is fodder readily dispensed from a cheap roadside caravan (sauce squirted from a plastic bottle), whilst the other denotes altogether more refined circumstances, and I quickly realize that I seem to be a bit of a truck driver at heart. I've already paid homage to the French, but a steak sandwich is always far best consumed across the channel than anywhere south of The Oval. So this choice is about the ego. Should I pretend to appear cultured and genteel, or would it be ok to sport a mullet and string vest, and go for a greasy banger? I'm bringing out the chav stick for this one.

The dilemma with both of these fishy options lies in the mayonnaise; which remains a huge problem for many a sandwich lover. Too much cheap, over-strong mayo can totally obliterate a humble sandwich. Even worse is when bargain-basement salad cream rears its vinegary head. Many sandwich shops employ the obvious trick of bulking out their fillings with mayo, thinking it'll dazzle on the generosity stakes. The sweetcorn in the tuna sandwich can really help lift such over-padding, but too much mayonnaise near an avocado and there's an instant queue for the loo. However, no one wants loose, blandly undressed prawns escaping at every angle, and a really decent mayonnaise (of the homemade Marie Rose or lemon dill variety) provides a pretty compelling transformation. The winner.

my mother's egg mayonnaise with fresh chives

It was agonizing enough having to eliminate the hot sausage sandwich, but the fresh garden chives and smooth texture of the mashed eggs (even outweighing the anti-social sulphuric smells), eventually cancelled out the grease factor. But now I have to make the final choice. You don't have to be Jewish to like a Reuben's sandwich, but you should go to New York if you want the best of the best. Which does make for rather a costly snack. Howard Jacobson once said: 'In a single salt beef sandwich is contained all of life's vicissitudes.' This could be true, but I'm not convinced that I'd be heading for a Reuben's sandwich if I'd just failed my driving test or been diagnosed with severe haemorrhoids. Surely, an easy to swallow and quick-to-assemble egg sandwich wins out during hassled moments? It's the egg mayonnaise with chive sandwich that gets the Oscar. Just gut instinct, I'm afraid.

This choice was crucifying. If I'm in starvation mode then obviously the former would win. But then who can ever deny the joyousness of a soft bread, moist cucumber sandwich, lightly sprinkled with salt and white pepper, with a cup of Earl Grey tea? I had my first club sandwich in Hong Kong and nearly spontaneously combusted with ecstasy. But does that compare to all the memories of my granny's lovely cucumber efforts, served up alongside beautiful cakey things in the garden? Wallis Simpson and Edward V11 both reputedly loved a good old club sarnie, but today, the humdrum cucumber wins out. In fact, I've just gone and made one.

Sweet fillings for sandwiches should never be scoffed at. Virtually all proper children like a bit of chocolate spread smeared around some bread, while the Americans favour peanut butter and jelly. But have you tried peanut butter and mashed banana, sandwiched between bread and quickly fried? It hits spots way beyond the most efficacious drug and is well worth loosening the belt for. And if you're going to be temporarily unhealthy, then this easily wins out on the fried egg concoction, which is only truly justifiable after a heavy night.

76

Scottish Anachronisms

by CHARLOTTE FAIRBAIRN

In the autumn of 2004, the city of Edinburgh bore witness to a small but unmistakeable sea-change. Lady X, the self-styled Coffee Morning Queen of the New Town, passed away. Lady X had been my mother's neighbour (and her predecessor's neighbour) since records began. Until her dying day (she was 101), she drove a car. Her lips pursed, her hat fastened with a pin, her stocking lines arrow-straight, she retained to the last an absence of humour and an air of frugality which sums up for me much about the Scotland of old. Then, there were no jokes (except a couple about Morningside), enjoyment of material pleasures was out of the question and hats were to be worn at all times.

Scotland seems to me vastly changed from Lady X's heyday. Devolution may not be everyone's idea of common sense but a more independent Scotland does appear to wear a lighter tone. Now in the gardens of the New Town, children are both seen and heard. Along George Street, where there were banking halls, now there are clothing emporia and – heaven forfend – 'trendy bars'. The template of a Scotsman having fun is no longer the exclusive territory of the drunken football hooligan.

For all my delight at this shift, there are still plenty of Scottishisms worth cleaving to. Food, sweets, music, vocabulary, clothing, people, myths, customs. Not long ago, I was in St Mary's Street in Edinburgh and saw that Casey's – the confectioner's – had gone. It was a sweetie shop in the best tradition with rows and rows of jars, floor to ceiling, and some very elderly people on hand to serve. In deference to the ladies of Casey's and to all my relations, herewith thirty-two Scottishisms – seen of course from the perspective of an opinionated, idiosyncratic, long-time ex-pat.

Charlotte Fairbairn is a novelist who now lives in Cumbria.

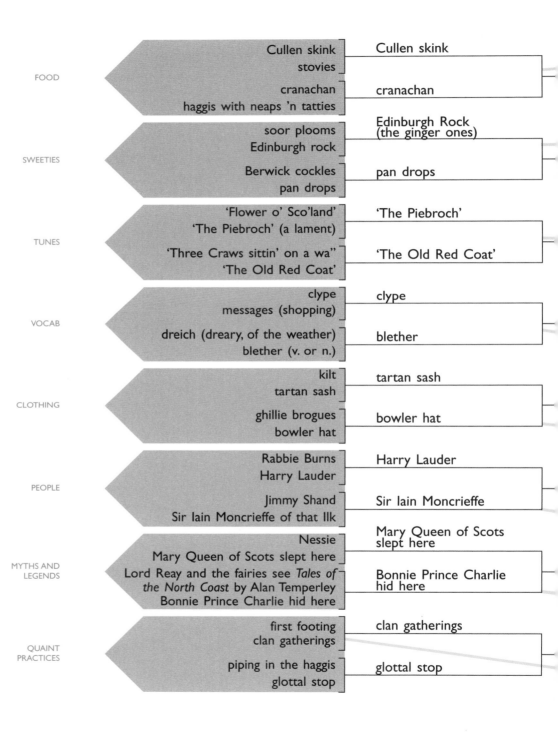

FOOD
Cullen skink
stovies
cranachan
haggis with neaps 'n tatties

Cullen skink
cranachan

SWEETIES
soor plooms
Edinburgh rock
Berwick cockles
pan drops

Edinburgh Rock (the ginger ones)
pan drops

TUNES
'Flower o' Sco'land'
'The Piebroch' (a lament)
'Three Craws sittin' on a wa''
'The Old Red Coat'

'The Piebroch'
'The Old Red Coat'

VOCAB
clype
messages (shopping)
dreich (dreary, of the weather)
blether (v. or n.)

clype
blether

CLOTHING
kilt
tartan sash
ghillie brogues
bowler hat

tartan sash
bowler hat

PEOPLE
Rabbie Burns
Harry Lauder
Jimmy Shand
Sir Iain Moncrieffe of that Ilk

Harry Lauder
Sir Iain Moncrieffe

MYTHS AND LEGENDS
Nessie
Mary Queen of Scots slept here
Lord Reay and the fairies see *Tales of the North Coast* by Alan Temperley
Bonnie Prince Charlie hid here

Mary Queen of Scots slept here
Bonnie Prince Charlie hid here

QUAINT PRACTICES
first footing
clan gatherings
piping in the haggis
glottal stop

clan gatherings
glottal stop

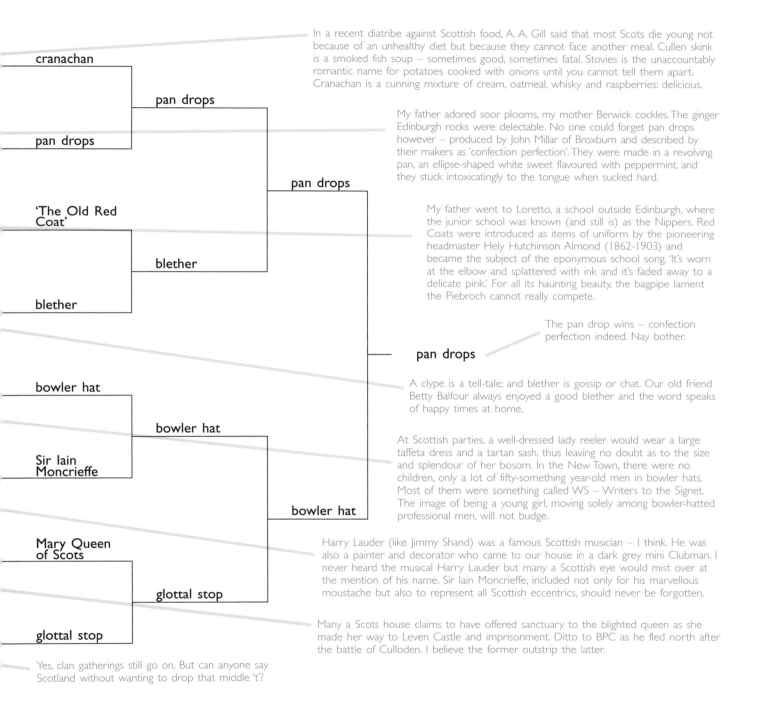

cranachan

pan drops

pan drops

'The Old Red Coat'

blether

blether

bowler hat

bowler hat

Sir Iain Moncrieffe

Mary Queen of Scots

glottal stop

glottal stop

pan drops

pan drops

bowler hat

bowler hat

pan drops

In a recent diatribe against Scottish food, A. A. Gill said that most Scots die young not because of an unhealthy diet but because they cannot face another meal. Cullen skink is a smoked fish soup — sometimes good, sometimes fatal. Stovies is the unaccountably romantic name for potatoes cooked with onions until you cannot tell them apart. Cranachan is a cunning mixture of cream, oatmeal, whisky and raspberries: delicious.

My father adored soor plooms, my mother Berwick cockles. The ginger Edinburgh rocks were delectable. No one could forget pan drops however — produced by John Millar of Broxburn and described by their makers as 'confection perfection'. They were made in a revolving pan, an ellipse-shaped white sweet flavoured with peppermint, and they stuck intoxicatingly to the tongue when sucked hard.

My father went to Loretto, a school outside Edinburgh, where the junior school was known (and still is) as the Nippers. Red Coats were introduced as items of uniform by the pioneering headmaster Hely Hutchinson Almond (1862-1903) and became the subject of the eponymous school song. 'It's worn at the elbow and splattered with ink and it's faded away to a delicate pink.' For all its haunting beauty, the bagpipe lament the Piebroch cannot really compete.

The pan drop wins — confection perfection indeed. Nay bother.

A clype is a tell-tale; and blether is gossip or chat. Our old friend Betty Balfour always enjoyed a good blether and the word speaks of happy times at home.

At Scottish parties, a well-dressed lady reeler would wear a large taffeta dress and a tartan sash, thus leaving no doubt as to the size and splendour of her bosom. In the New Town, there were no children, only a lot of fifty-something year-old men in bowler hats. Most of them were something called WS — Writers to the Signet. The image of being a young girl, moving solely among bowler-hatted professional men, will not budge.

Harry Lauder (like Jimmy Shand) was a famous Scottish musician — I think. He was also a painter and decorator who came to our house in a dark grey mini Clubman. I never heard the musical Harry Lauder but many a Scottish eye would mist over at the mention of his name. Sir Iain Moncrieffe, included not only for his marvellous moustache but also to represent all Scottish eccentrics, should never be forgotten.

Many a Scots house claims to have offered sanctuary to the blighted queen as she made her way to Leven Castle and imprisonment. Ditto to BPC as he fled north after the battle of Culloden. I believe the former outstrip the latter.

Yes, clan gatherings still go on. But can anyone say Scotland without wanting to drop that middle 't'?

77

Scrabble Words
by STEFAN FATSIS

A mind-numbing 178,691 words of two to fifteen letters are acceptable in competitive Scrabble. Though culled from several standard college dictionaries, Scrabble's lexicographic expanse is still hard for nonplayers to accept. ('That's not a word!') So is the idea of memorising, as I have, tens of thousands of weird letter strings just to play a game. How then to narrow Scrabble to 0.0179 percent of its possibilities? Pick the strategically important, the historically significant, the linguistically unusual, the creatively brilliant, the mathematically improbable (and probable), and the shots heard round the Scrabble world.

STEFAN FATSIS is the author of *Word Freak: Heartbreak, Triumph, Genius, and Obsession in the World of Competitive Scrabble Players.* He has scored 603 points in a game. He is proudest of playing OQUASSA and SWITCHEROO.

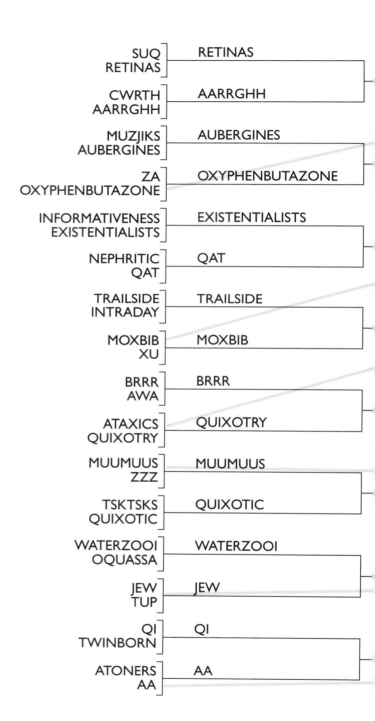

SUQ / RETINAS	RETINAS
CWRTH / AARRGHH	AARRGHH
MUZJIKS / AUBERGINES	AUBERGINES
ZA / OXYPHENBUTAZONE	OXYPHENBUTAZONE
INFORMATIVENESS / EXISTENTIALISTS	EXISTENTIALISTS
NEPHRITIC / QAT	QAT
TRAILSIDE / INTRADAY	TRAILSIDE
MOXBIB / XU	MOXBIB
BRRR / AWA	BRRR
ATAXICS / QUIXOTRY	QUIXOTRY
MUUMUUS / ZZZ	MUUMUUS
TSKTSKS / QUIXOTIC	QUIXOTIC
WATERZOOI / OQUASSA	WATERZOOI
JEW / TUP	JEW
QI / TWINBORN	QI
ATONERS / AA	AA

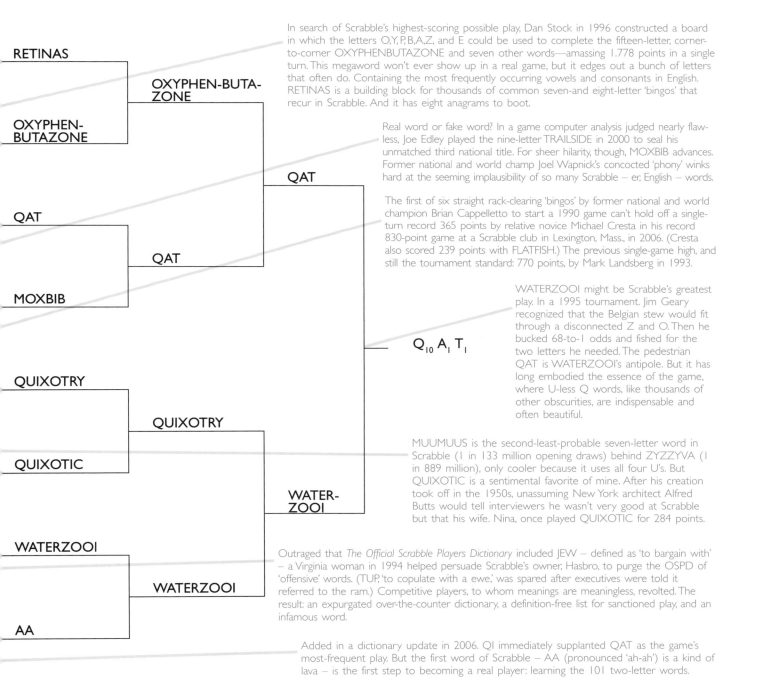

RETINAS

OXYPHEN-BUTA-ZONE

OXYPHEN-BUTAZONE

QAT

QAT

QAT

MOXBIB

Q_{10} A_1 T_1

QUIXOTRY

QUIXOTRY

QUIXOTIC

WATER-ZOOI

WATERZOOI

WATERZOOI

AA

In search of Scrabble's highest-scoring possible play, Dan Stock in 1996 constructed a board in which the letters O, Y, P, B, A, Z, and E could be used to complete the fifteen-letter, corner-to-corner OXYPHENBUTAZONE and seven other words—amassing 1,778 points in a single turn. This megaword won't ever show up in a real game, but it edges out a bunch of letters that often do. Containing the most frequently occurring vowels and consonants in English, RETINAS is a building block for thousands of common seven-and eight-letter 'bingos' that recur in Scrabble. And it has eight anagrams to boot.

Real word or fake word? In a game computer analysis judged nearly flaw-less, Joe Edley played the nine-letter TRAILSIDE in 2000 to seal his unmatched third national title. For sheer hilarity, though, MOXBIB advances. Former national and world champ Joel Wapnick's concocted 'phony' winks hard at the seeming implausibility of so many Scrabble — er, English — words.

The first of six straight rack-clearing 'bingos' by former national and world champion Brian Cappelletto to start a 1990 game can't hold off a single-turn record 365 points by relative novice Michael Cresta in his record 830-point game at a Scrabble club in Lexington, Mass., in 2006. (Cresta also scored 239 points with FLATFISH.) The previous single-game high, and still the tournament standard: 770 points, by Mark Landsberg in 1993.

WATERZOOI might be Scrabble's greatest play. In a 1995 tournament, Jim Geary recognized that the Belgian stew would fit through a disconnected Z and O. Then he bucked 68-to-1 odds and fished for the two letters he needed. The pedestrian QAT is WATERZOOI's antipole. But it has long embodied the essence of the game, where U-less Q words, like thousands of other obscurities, are indispensable and often beautiful.

MUUMUUS is the second-least-probable seven-letter word in Scrabble (1 in 133 million opening draws) behind ZYZZYVA (1 in 889 million), only cooler because it uses all four U's. But QUIXOTIC is a sentimental favorite of mine. After his creation took off in the 1950s, unassuming New York architect Alfred Butts would tell interviewers he wasn't very good at Scrabble but that his wife, Nina, once played QUIXOTIC for 284 points.

Outraged that *The Official Scrabble Players Dictionary* included JEW — defined as 'to bargain with' — a Virginia woman in 1994 helped persuade Scrabble's owner, Hasbro, to purge the OSPD of 'offensive' words. (TUP, 'to copulate with a ewe,' was spared after executives were told it referred to the ram.) Competitive players, to whom meanings are meaningless, revolted. The result: an expurgated over-the-counter dictionary, a definition-free list for sanctioned play, and an infamous word.

Added in a dictionary update in 2006. QI immediately supplanted QAT as the game's most-frequent play. But the first word of Scrabble — AA (pronounced 'ah-ah') is a kind of lava — is the first step to becoming a real player: learning the 101 two-letter words.

78

Sexy Female Cartoon Characters

by ANONYMOUS

Girls probably dream of being taken to infinity and beyond by Buzz Lightyear so time for us to weigh up the relative merits of various cartoon creations. For me a seminal moment was going to see *Who Framed Roger Rabbit?* and feeling extremely hot and bothered by Roger's wife – the ultracurvaceous Jessica Rabbit (voiced by an uncredited Kathleen Turner). She wore her sexuality on her sleeve – if she indeed owned any item of clothing that had sleeves. It was after a few minutes of appreciation of this goddess that it dawned on me that there was something very wrong going on here. After all, she was married.

ANONYMOUS started his career as a child star working for Disney and has appeared more recently in *Who Framed Roger Rabbit?*, *Shrek* and *Toy Story 2*. He lives in Toon Town, LA.

Jessica Rabbit (*Who Framed Roger Rabbit?*)
Minnie Mouse

Olive Oyl (*Popeye the Sailor Man*)
Daphne (*Scooby Doo*)

Snow White (*Snow White and the Seven Dwarves*)
Penelope Pistop (*Wacky Races*)

Mulan (*Mulan*)
Jessie (*Toy Story 2*)

Pocahontas (*Pocahontas*)
Wilma Flintstone (*The Flintstones*)

Betty Boop
Cruella De Vil (*101 Dalmations*)

Elastigirl (*The Incredibles*)
Princess Fiona (*Shrek*)

Marge Simpson (*The Simpsons*)
Betty Rubble (*The Flintstones*)

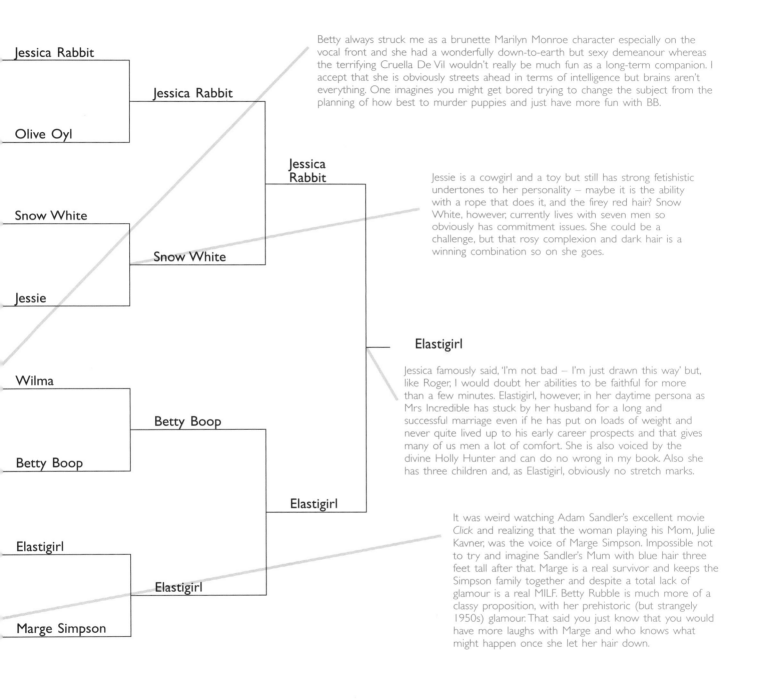

Jessica Rabbit

Olive Oyl

Jessica Rabbit

Snow White

Jessie

Snow White

Jessica Rabbit

Betty always struck me as a brunette Marilyn Monroe character especially on the vocal front and she had a wonderfully down-to-earth but sexy demeanour whereas the terrifying Cruella De Vil wouldn't really be much fun as a long-term companion. I accept that she is obviously streets ahead in terms of intelligence but brains aren't everything. One imagines you might get bored trying to change the subject from the planning of how best to murder puppies and just have more fun with BB.

Jessie is a cowgirl and a toy but still has strong fetishistic undertones to her personality – maybe it is the ability with a rope that does it, and the firey red hair? Snow White, however, currently lives with seven men so obviously has commitment issues. She could be a challenge, but that rosy complexion and dark hair is a winning combination so on she goes.

Elastigirl

Jessica famously said, 'I'm not bad – I'm just drawn this way' but, like Roger, I would doubt her abilities to be faithful for more than a few minutes. Elastigirl, however, in her daytime persona as Mrs Incredible has stuck by her husband for a long and successful marriage even if he has put on loads of weight and never quite lived up to his early career prospects and that gives many of us men a lot of comfort. She is also voiced by the divine Holly Hunter and can do no wrong in my book. Also she has three children and, as Elastigirl, obviously no stretch marks.

Wilma

Betty Boop

Betty Boop

Elastigirl

Elastigirl

Marge Simpson

Elastigirl

It was weird watching Adam Sandler's excellent movie *Click* and realizing that the woman playing his Mom, Julie Kavner, was the voice of Marge Simpson. Impossible not to try and imagine Sandler's Mum with blue hair three feet tall after that. Marge is a real survivor and keeps the Simpson family together and despite a total lack of glamour is a real MILF. Betty Rubble is much more of a classy proposition, with her prehistoric (but strangely 1950s) glamour. That said you just know that you would have more laughs with Marge and who knows what might happen once she let her hair down.

79

Shakespeare Insults

by LAWRENCE GOODMAN

Yes, the writer who brought us such great lines as 'To be or not to be' and 'Parting is such sweet sorrow' also came up with some of the greatest potty-humour put-downs and bawdy insults in the history of English literature. Whether he was remarking on the size of someone's genitals, making fun of their inexperience in the sack, or just coming up with a fancy new way to call them an idiot, Will knew how to sling the mud. Choosing the best Bard barbs is as tough as fathoming Iago's motivations or why Hamlet procrastinates. But in head-to-head face-off, it all came down to which packed the most zing per beat of iambic pentameter, which I could actually understand, and which I would most want to say to an ex-girlfriend.

LAWRENCE GOODMAN is a journalist and playwright living in Providence, RI. His plays have been produced in New York and Philadelphia, and he is a founding member of NeoShtick Theater ("What Derrida would have said if he'd ever played the Catskills").

There's no more faith in thee than in a stewed prune.
Thou art the Mars of malcontents.
— There's no more faith

They have marvelous foul linen.
Live and love thy misery.
— Live and love

Why should she live to fill the world with words?
He appears as I would wish mine enemy.
— Why should she live

I'll pray a thousand prayers for thy death.
You whoreson cullionly barbermonger!
— You whoreson

Thou art as loathsome as a toad.
If I hope well, I'll never see thee more.
— loathsome as a toad

Rump-fed ronyon!
Thou wouldst eat thy dead vomit up. And howl'st to find it.
— eat thy dead vomit

Hang! Beg! Starve! Die in the streets!
Let vultures gripe thy guts.
— Hang! Beg! Starve!

What folly I commit, I dedicate to you.
Thou cam'st on earth to make the earth my hell.
— make the earth my hell

He has not so much brain as earwax.
Pernicious bloodsucker of sleeping men!
— brain as earwax

Lean raw-boned rascal.
Thou art a boil, a plague-sore, or embossed carbuncle in my corrupted blood.
— Thou art a boil

Thou clay-brained guts, thou knotty-pated fool, thou whoreson obscene greasy tallow-catch.
Thou wert best set thy lower part where thy nose stands.
— Thou clay-brained guts

I'll beat thee, but I should infect my hands.
You breathe in vain.
— You breathe in vain

You are not worth the dust which the rude wind blows in your face.
You blocks, you stones, you worse than senseless things.
— not worth the dust

A vengeance on your crafty wither'd hide!
She's the kitchen wench, and all grease, and I know not what use to put her to but to make a lamp of her, and run from her by her own light.
— She's the kitchen wench

Irksome brawling scold.
Most excellent, accomplished lady, the heavens rain odours on you!
— Irksome brawling scold

Thou crusty botch of nature!
His brain is as dry as the remainder biscuit after a voyage.
— Thou crusty botch of nature!

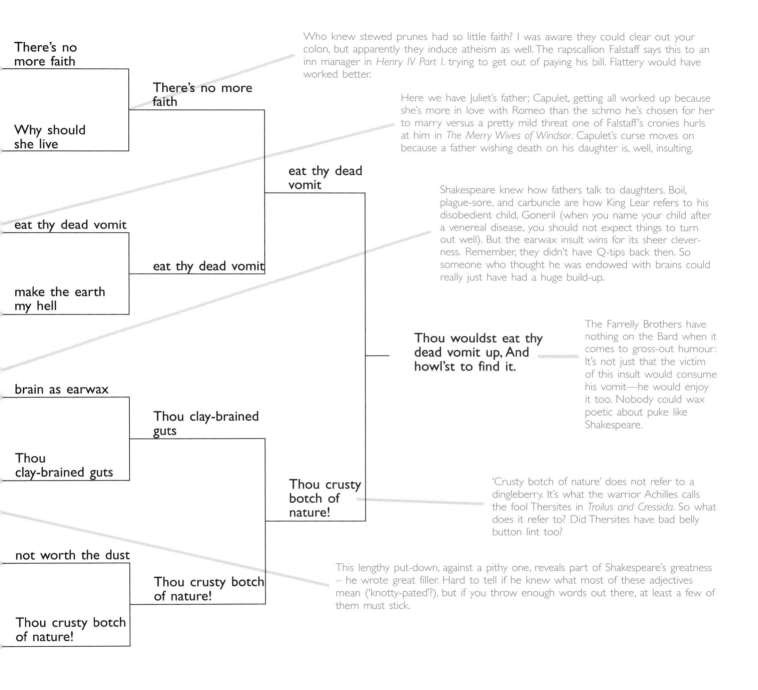

There's no more faith

Why should she live

There's no more faith

Who knew stewed prunes had so little faith? I was aware they could clear out your colon, but apparently they induce atheism as well. The rapscallion Falstaff says this to an inn manager in *Henry IV Part I*, trying to get out of paying his bill. Flattery would have worked better.

Here we have Juliet's father, Capulet, getting all worked up because she's more in love with Romeo than the schmo he's chosen for her to marry versus a pretty mild threat one of Falstaff's cronies hurls at him in *The Merry Wives of Windsor*. Capulet's curse moves on because a father wishing death on his daughter is, well, insulting.

eat thy dead vomit

make the earth my hell

eat thy dead vomit

eat thy dead vomit

Shakespeare knew how fathers talk to daughters. Boil, plague-sore, and carbuncle are how King Lear refers to his disobedient child, Goneril (when you name your child after a venereal disease, you should not expect things to turn out well). But the earwax insult wins for its sheer cleverness. Remember, they didn't have Q-tips back then. So someone who thought he was endowed with brains could really just have had a huge build-up.

Thou wouldst eat thy dead vomit up, And howl'st to find it.

The Farrelly Brothers have nothing on the Bard when it comes to gross-out humour: It's not just that the victim of this insult would consume his vomit—he would enjoy it too. Nobody could wax poetic about puke like Shakespeare.

brain as earwax

Thou clay-brained guts

Thou clay-brained guts

Thou crusty botch of nature!

'Crusty botch of nature' does not refer to a dingleberry. It's what the warrior Achilles calls the fool Thersites in *Troilus and Cressida*. So what does it refer to? Did Thersites have bad belly button lint too?

not worth the dust

Thou crusty botch of nature!

Thou crusty botch of nature!

This lengthy put-down, against a pithy one, reveals part of Shakespeare's greatness – he wrote great filler. Hard to tell if he knew what most of these adjectives mean ('knotty-pated'?), but if you throw enough words out there, at least a few of them must stick.

80

Shop Names
by SIMON TREWIN

We are British so we like a good pun. We have a possessive precision about the English language that makes us delight in tinkering with it and in bouncing off each other's verbal dexterity – all with the added bonus that it confuses foreigners who are trying to grasp why bough reads like cough but sounds like bow and why through sounds like threw. So in our humdrum commuting lives it is immensely uplifting to see some shopkeepers who have decided to have a bit of fun with their business names. Not for them Leo's Pet Shop, Mr Tumnus' Joke Emporium or Jack's Sports Shop – oh no . . . !

I am indebted to the hilarious book *Shop Horror* by the punster Guy Swillingham for many of these names. Check out his website at www.shophorror.co.uk.

SIMON thinks he once got some photographs developed in a shop called 'Someday My Prints Will Come' but he might have been mistaken.

Austin Flowers / It's Curtains For You	Austin Flowers
Beauty and The Beach / The Bitter End	Beauty and The Beach
Brief Moments / Battersea Cod's Home	Battersea Cod's Home
The Director's Cut / The Frying Scotsman	The Frying Scotsman
Junk and Disorderly / Lunatic Fringe	Junk and Disorderly
Paws For Thought / The Prawnbroker	The Prawnbroker
Sofa So Good / Spex Appeal	Sofa So Good
Suite Sensation / Tan Tropez	Suite Sensation
Wok This Way / Haircut One Hundred	Wok This Way
The Cutting Crew / Jane Armour Trading	Jane Armour Trading
Talking Heads / Fishcothèque	Fishcothèque
Only Foods and Sauces / Chainstore Massacre	Only Foods
Yew Wood Knot Believe It! / Pasta La Vista	Pasta La Vista
From Here To Maternity / Hey Pesto	From Here To Maternity
Leaning Tower Of Pizza / A Fish Called Rhondda	A Fish Called Rhondda
Wheelie Serious / Cake Expectations	Wheelie Serious

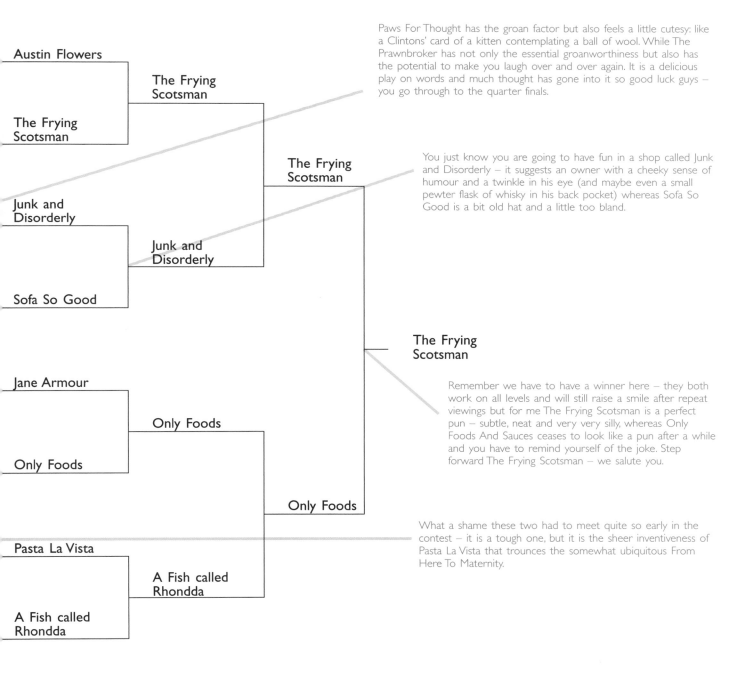

Austin Flowers

The Frying Scotsman

The Frying Scotsman

Junk and Disorderly

Sofa So Good

Jane Armour

Only Foods

Only Foods

Pasta La Vista

A Fish called Rhondda

A Fish called Rhondda

The Frying Scotsman

Junk and Disorderly

Only Foods

The Frying Scotsman

Paws For Thought has the groan factor but also feels a little cutesy: like a Clintons' card of a kitten contemplating a ball of wool. While The Prawnbroker has not only the essential groanworthiness but also has the potential to make you laugh over and over again. It is a delicious play on words and much thought has gone into it so good luck guys — you go through to the quarter finals.

You just know you are going to have fun in a shop called Junk and Disorderly — it suggests an owner with a cheeky sense of humour and a twinkle in his eye (and maybe even a small pewter flask of whisky in his back pocket) whereas Sofa So Good is a bit old hat and a little too bland.

Remember we have to have a winner here — they both work on all levels and will still raise a smile after repeat viewings but for me The Frying Scotsman is a perfect pun — subtle, neat and very very silly, whereas Only Foods And Sauces ceases to look like a pun after a while and you have to remind yourself of the joke. Step forward The Frying Scotsman — we salute you.

What a shame these two had to meet quite so early in the contest — it is a tough one, but it is the sheer inventiveness of Pasta La Vista that trounces the somewhat ubiquitous From Here To Maternity.

81

Sins Against the Language
by BEN YAGODA

Tsk-tsking about declining grammatical standards has been a popular pastime since the early seventeenth century and shows no sign of going away. Much of the hand-wringing can be chalked up to retrograde nostalgia and an insufficient recognition that the protocol of the language is continuously changing. (Not very long ago, we were taught that the first-person future tense is *shall*, remember?) On the other hand, the use of language is a good representation — maybe the best — of the condition of a speaker's or writer's thought. Judging from what I read in the papers (my students', and the ones published on newsprint and online), that condition is currently serious but could swerve toward critical at any moment.

BEN YAGODA directs the journalism program at the University of Delaware and is the author of *About Town: The New Yorker and the World it Made*, *The Sound on the Page: Style and Voice in Writing*, and, most recently, *When You Catch an Adjective, Kill it: The Parts of Speech, for Better and/or Worse*.

mixed metaphors	wordiness
wordiness	
clichés	clichés
bogus apostrophes, as in 'Apple's—$1.19 lb'	
journalese	it's/its
it's/its, who's/whose, you're/your confusion	
dangling modifiers	dangling modifiers
double negatives	
no comma after parenthetical phrase	no comma
commas or full stops outside quotation marks	
verbing nouns	nouning verbs
nouning verbs	
'that'/'which' confusion	vagueness
vagueness and abstraction	
'less' instead of 'fewer'	disagreement
antecedent-pronoun disagreement	
'of' in clauses like 'I didn't have that good of a time'	hypercorrection
hypercorrection, e.g., 'between you and I'	
sesquipedality	sesquipedality
'presently' to mean 'currently'	
spellcheck errors like 'pour over' to mean 'pore over'	spellcheck errors
faux ebonic diction, e.g., 'My bad'	
semicolon abuse	semicolon abuse
elegant variation	
comma splices	comma splices
subjunctive errors, such as 'If I was rich'	
incorrect or imprecise word choice	poor word choice
using 'who' instead of 'whom'	
'myself' to mean 'me' or 'I'	'myself'
e-mail abuse like emoticons and acronyms (LOL)	
vocalisms like 'um,' 'uh,' 'er,' and 'ew' in print	vocalisms
faulty parallelism	

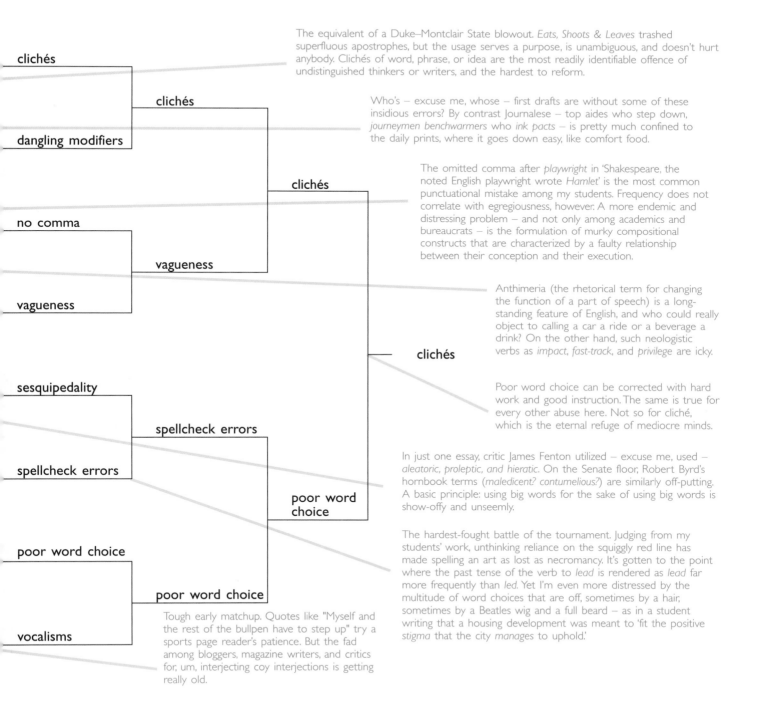

clichés

clichés

dangling modifiers

clichés

no comma

vagueness

vagueness

clichés

sesquipedality

spellcheck errors

spellcheck errors

clichés

poor word choice

poor word choice

poor word choice

vocalisms

The equivalent of a Duke–Montclair State blowout. *Eats, Shoots & Leaves* trashed superfluous apostrophes, but the usage serves a purpose, is unambiguous, and doesn't hurt anybody. Clichés of word, phrase, or idea are the most readily identifiable offence of undistinguished thinkers or writers, and the hardest to reform.

Who's – excuse me, whose – first drafts are without some of these insidious errors? By contrast Journalese – top aides who step down, *journeymen benchwarmers* who *ink pacts* – is pretty much confined to the daily prints, where it goes down easy, like comfort food.

The omitted comma after *playwright* in 'Shakespeare, the noted English playwright wrote *Hamlet*' is the most common punctuational mistake among my students. Frequency does not correlate with egregiousness, however. A more endemic and distressing problem – and not only among academics and bureaucrats – is the formulation of murky compositional constructs that are characterized by a faulty relationship between their conception and their execution.

Anthimeria (the rhetorical term for changing the function of a part of speech) is a long-standing feature of English, and who could really object to calling a car a ride or a beverage a drink? On the other hand, such neologistic verbs as *impact*, *fast-track*, and *privilege* are icky.

Poor word choice can be corrected with hard work and good instruction. The same is true for every other abuse here. Not so for cliché, which is the eternal refuge of mediocre minds.

In just one essay, critic James Fenton utilized – excuse me, used – *aleatoric, proleptic,* and *hieratic*. On the Senate floor, Robert Byrd's hornbook terms (*maledicent? contumelious?*) are similarly off-putting. A basic principle: using big words for the sake of using big words is show-offy and unseemly.

The hardest-fought battle of the tournament. Judging from my students' work, unthinking reliance on the squiggly red line has made spelling an art as lost as necromancy. It's gotten to the point where the past tense of the verb to *lead* is rendered as *lead* far more frequently than *led*. Yet I'm even more distressed by the multitude of word choices that are off, sometimes by a hair, sometimes by a Beatles wig and a full beard – as in a student writing that a housing development was meant to 'fit the positive *stigma* that the city *manages* to uphold.'

Tough early matchup. Quotes like "Myself and the rest of the bullpen have to step up" try a sports page reader's patience. But the fad among bloggers, magazine writers, and critics for, um, interjecting coy interjections is getting really old.

82

Slanguage of Sex
by SIMON TREWIN

I don't know why we are a little bit shy about sexual intercourse – everyone does it (apart from your parents of course) and everyone enjoys it so why do we hide behind so many different phrases to describe it? I suppose you could argue that not all sex is the same and so you need gradations to indicate how important each occasion is – no one could feasibly describe a drunken encounter round the back of Chantelle's Night Club and Exclusive Wine Bar in Basildon as warranting the phrase 'making love' and I am certain that our beloved monarch and her consort never indulge in a 'drunken shag'. These phrases are here for a reason and long may they continue. Some are funny, some are misogynistic, some are crude and some are just weird. Anyway – time to shut your eyes and think of England as we strip the sheets back and see what the nation get up to.

Phrases	Answer
going at it like a rat up a drainpipe / spearing the bearded clam	clam
playing hide the salami / knowing in the biblical sense	salami
driving the pink bus to tuna town / playing doctors and nurses	doctors and nurses
slipping someone the hot beef injection / putting Percy in the playpen	Percy
making the beast with two backs / storming the pearly gates with your purple-headed devil	beast
polishing the love javelin / sleeping together	sleeping together
kicking a sausage down the high street / a bit of the other	sausage
humping / stabbing the trout	humping
bumping uglies / parting the pink sea	bumping
burping the worm in the mole hole / screwing	burping
growling at the badger / shagging	shagging
Ugandan discussions / making love	Ugandan
horizontal jogging / going at it like hammers and tongs	jogging
sinking the middle pin / giving the old one-gun salute	middle pin
riding the pink pony / freeing your willy	pink pony
jumping someone's bones / driving the train through the tunnel	tunnel

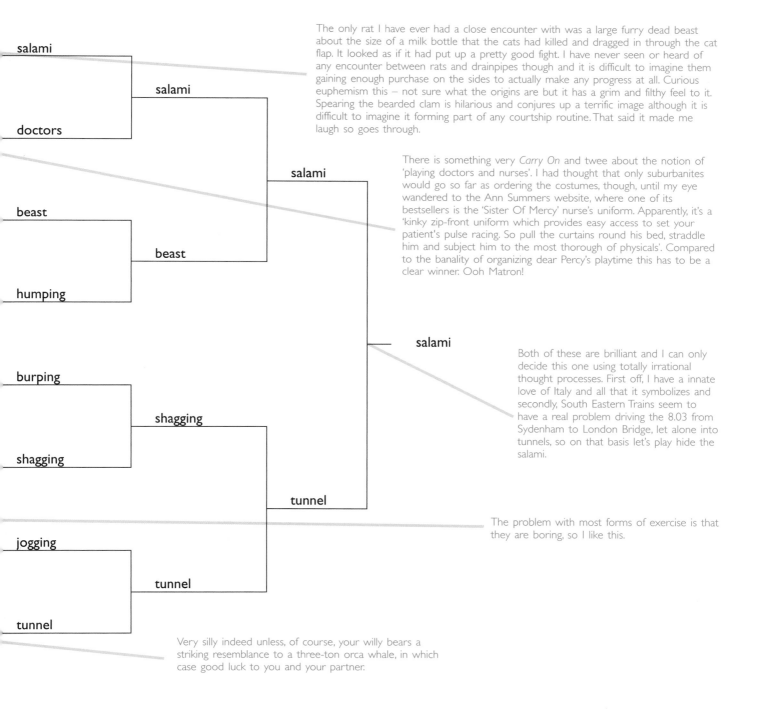

salami

doctors

salami

beast

humping

beast

burping

shagging

shagging

jogging

tunnel

tunnel

salami

salami

salami

tunnel

The only rat I have ever had a close encounter with was a large furry dead beast about the size of a milk bottle that the cats had killed and dragged in through the cat flap. It looked as if it had put up a pretty good fight. I have never seen or heard of any encounter between rats and drainpipes though and it is difficult to imagine them gaining enough purchase on the sides to actually make any progress at all. Curious euphemism this – not sure what the origins are but it has a grim and filthy feel to it. Spearing the bearded clam is hilarious and conjures up a terrific image although it is difficult to imagine it forming part of any courtship routine. That said it made me laugh so goes through.

There is something very *Carry On* and twee about the notion of 'playing doctors and nurses'. I had thought that only suburbanites would go so far as ordering the costumes, though, until my eye wandered to the Ann Summers website, where one of its bestsellers is the 'Sister Of Mercy' nurse's uniform. Apparently, it's a 'kinky zip-front uniform which provides easy access to set your patient's pulse racing. So pull the curtains round his bed, straddle him and subject him to the most thorough of physicals'. Compared to the banality of organizing dear Percy's playtime this has to be a clear winner. Ooh Matron!

Both of these are brilliant and I can only decide this one using totally irrational thought processes. First off, I have a innate love of Italy and all that it symbolizes and secondly, South Eastern Trains seem to have a real problem driving the 8.03 from Sydenham to London Bridge, let alone into tunnels, so on that basis let's play hide the salami.

The problem with most forms of exercise is that they are boring, so I like this.

Very silly indeed unless, of course, your willy bears a striking resemblance to a three-ton orca whale, in which case good luck to you and your partner.

83

Snigger-Worthy Place Names

by SIMON TREWIN

When we were on our honeymoon at the Gardone Riviera we stayed at a rather grand but now faded hotel and one night when studying the menu my new wife, *la belle Hélène*, called the waiter over and asked him to explain what a 'galetto' was. He paused, cleared his throat, leant forward and said, quite loudly in broken English, 'It is a cock madam . . . it is a BIG cock'. Needless to say, it took a long time before we were sufficiently composed enough to place our order. It isn't of course just menus that can appeal to the double-entendre obsessed schoolkid inside all of us – British place names have a lot to answer for and have brightened up many a dull car journey in the Trewin family. They are all good, some of them very naughty indeed, but one has to win out.

Upper Dicker (Sussex) / Great Snoring (Norfolk) — **Dicker**

Sandy Balls (Hampshire) / Cockshutt (Shropshire) — **Balls**

Tarty (Aberdeenshire) / Six Mile Bottom (Cambridgeshire) — **Bottom**

Mincing Lane (London) / Bummers Hill (Cambridgeshire) — **Bummers**

Herbert's Hole (Buckinghamshire) / Crapham Down (Sussex) — **Crapham**

Claggy Cott (Herefordshire) / Thong (Kent) — **Thong**

Feltwell (Norfolk) / Poke Holes (Lincolnshire) — **Holes**

Bottom Head (Lancashire) / Lickfold (West Sussex) — **Bottom**

Nob End (South Lancashire) / Brown Willy (Cornwall) — **Willy**

Flushdyke (Yorkshire) / Horton Cum Studley (Oxfordshire) — **Flushdyke**

Lower Piddle (Worcestershire) / Pennycomequick (Devon) — **Piddle**

Twatt (Orkney Islands) / Wetwang (North Yorkshire) — **Wetwang**

Lord Hereford's Knob (Wales) / Ugley (Essex) — **Knob**

Twathats (Dumfries and Galloway) / Cockermouth (Cumbria) — **Cockermouth**

Foul End (Warwickshire) / Shittington (Warwickshire) — **Shittington**

Staines (Surrey) / Three Cocks (Powys) — **Cocks**

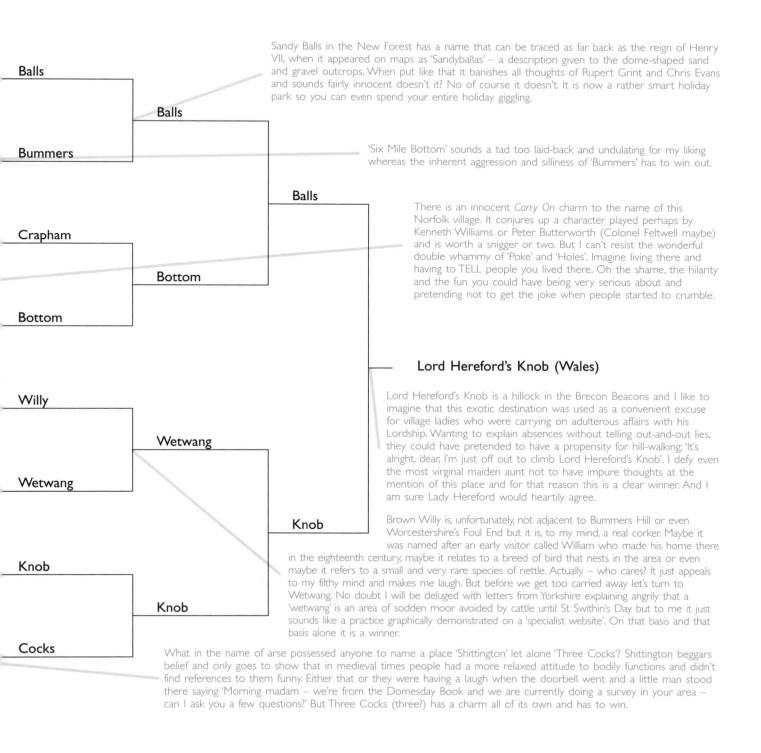

Balls

Bummers

Balls

Balls

Crapham

Bottom

Bottom

Sandy Balls in the New Forest has a name that can be traced as far back as the reign of Henry VII, when it appeared on maps as 'Sandyballas' – a description given to the dome-shaped sand and gravel outcrops. When put like that it banishes all thoughts of Rupert Grint and Chris Evans and sounds fairly innocent doesn't it? No of course it doesn't. It is now a rather smart holiday park so you can even spend your entire holiday giggling.

'Six Mile Bottom' sounds a tad too laid-back and undulating for my liking whereas the inherent aggression and silliness of 'Bummers' has to win out.

There is an innocent *Carry On* charm to the name of this Norfolk village. It conjures up a character played perhaps by Kenneth Williams or Peter Butterworth (Colonel Feltwell maybe) and is worth a snigger or two. But I can't resist the wonderful double whammy of 'Poke' and 'Holes'. Imagine living there and having to TELL people you lived there. Oh the shame, the hilarity and the fun you could have being very serious about and pretending not to get the joke when people started to crumble.

Lord Hereford's Knob (Wales)

Willy

Wetwang

Wetwang

Knob

Knob

Cocks

Knob

Lord Hereford's Knob is a hillock in the Brecon Beacons and I like to imagine that this exotic destination was used as a convenient excuse for village ladies who were carrying on adulterous affairs with his Lordship. Wanting to explain absences without telling out-and-out lies, they could have pretended to have a propensity for hill-walking: 'It's alright, dear, I'm just off out to climb Lord Hereford's Knob'. I defy even the most virginal maiden aunt not to have impure thoughts at the mention of this place and for that reason this is a clear winner. And I am sure Lady Hereford would heartily agree.

Brown Willy is, unfortunately, not adjacent to Bummers Hill or even Worcestershire's Foul End but it is, to my mind, a real corker. Maybe it was named after an early visitor called William who made his home there in the eighteenth century, maybe it relates to a breed of bird that nests in the area or even maybe it refers to a small and very rare species of nettle. Actually – who cares? It just appeals to my filthy mind and makes me laugh. But before we get too carried away let's turn to Wetwang. No doubt I will be deluged with letters from Yorkshire explaining angrily that a 'wetwang' is an area of sodden moor avoided by cattle until St Swithin's Day but to me it just sounds like a practice graphically demonstrated on a 'specialist website'. On that basis and that basis alone it is a winner.

What in the name of arse possessed anyone to name a place 'Shittington' let alone 'Three Cocks'? Shittington beggars belief and only goes to show that in medieval times people had a more relaxed attitude to bodily functions and didn't find references to them funny. Either that or they were having a laugh when the doorbell went and a little man stood there saying 'Morning madam – we're from the Domesday Book and we are currently doing a survey in your area – can I ask you a few questions?' But Three Cocks (three?) has a charm all of its own and has to win.

84

Special Powers
by CLARE BENNETT

'Invisible or invincible?' This is a great debate currently between my two nephews Henry (aged eight) and Caspar (aged five) who are real connoisseurs of the superhero world. Henry is a great admirer of Superman, and his take on Batman is that he 'doesn't really have special powers, he's just a man,' which is factually true but *appalls* Caspar in its lack of respect. A lot of these powers look totally cool in theory, like being invisible or having super hearing – but in reality I'm not sure I want to be privy to things people don't want to say to my face, let alone barge in on the private lives of those I admire and be disappointed by how normal they are. What if Kiefer Sutherland isn't like Jack Bauer? What if Sarah Jessica Parker actually dresses really badly? What if there is no Father Christmas and it's just your Mum? I don't want to know, frankly.

There is a character in the US series *Heroes* called Claire Bennet, who is a cheerleader with the power to spontaneously regenerate herself when injured and who can't die. She does not feel pain like normal people, can heal herself in seconds and 'did not complain when her head got twisted 180 degrees.' She first discovered this great gift when she was wrestling with another cheerleader (that sounds like a different show altogether) and almost certainly has foundations in this CLARE BENNETT's life and times on the netball team at Putney High.

invincible
super hearing

invisible
self duplicate

fly
crawl up anything

breathe fire
breathe ice

time travel
run at super human speed

X-ray vision
super fast reflexes

Jedi mind tricks
shrink

change your clothes by spinning around
breathe underwater

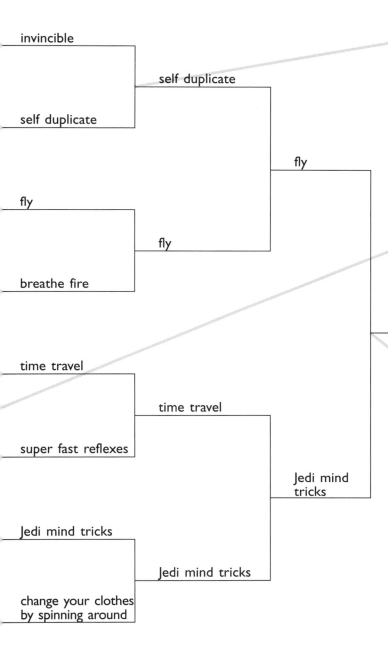

invincible

self duplicate

self duplicate

fly

fly

breathe fire

fly

time travel

super fast reflexes

time travel

Jedi mind tricks

Jedi mind tricks

change your clothes by spinning around

Jedi mind tricks

fly

Not being one for throwing myself in front of lorries or wrestling someone off the top of a tall building, I don't know that being invincible particularly appeals to me. Self duplication, on the other hand, would be marvellous for the days when you don't want to go to work or you just can't face spending an evening with your boyfriend/girlfriend's boring parents, and it's particularly attractive as an antidote for my pathetic and immature habit of double-booking.

X-ray vision would be useful if you were allergic to Kryptonite and needed to look into a box your enemy had given you before you opened it and went all weird – but I'm not aware that I suffer from this particular problem, so I'd like to have it to look at my own internal organs to self diagnose and also just for fun. Presumably having super fast reflexes would mean that you'd never break anything, crash your car, spend ages tidying your house ever again. This has to win, because ultimately, X-ray vision would make birthdays and Christmas totally rubbish.

Jedi mind tricks

Think of the money you'd save being able to fly, let alone the carbon footprint you'd eradicate. Yet, however useful the ability to just zip around like a bluebottle would be, I can imagine it would be terrible for one's hair: as bad as driving in an open top car, so the fun would be taken out of it for all of us who aren't bald. At first I thought Jedi mind tricks were for people who don't know how to get their own way – but however astute you are at making people bend to your will, no one can influence the cast iron resolve of the traffic warden. Had I been a Jedi master, my conversation with the traffic warden who gave me a ticket TOTALLY UNNECESSARILY last week might have gone more like this:

Me: *'You don't want to give me a ticket.'*
TW: *'I don't want to give you a ticket.'*
Me: *'This is not the car you're looking for.'*
TW: *'This is not the car I'm looking for.'*
Me: *'Move along.'*
TW: *'Move along.'*

The conversation we actually had is not really repeatable, suffice to say that Jedi mind tricks win due to their ability to keep you from losing your cool, your command of the English language and your money. And presumably you'd also get a light sabre too so you could laser their head off if they were to say 'I *am* your father – but you're still too late because I've already keyed it into the system.'

85

Sport Films
by RICHARD SANDOMIR

Ever notice that the best sports films are about baseball and boxing? Fourteen were invited to this year's tournament, and one from each sport moved to the final. Pool, horse racing, and even swordplay in the Roman Colosseum got invites too, but major sports like football and basketball (*The Fish That Saved Pittsburgh* couldn't make a Division III tourney) rarely achieve greatness. Comedies are rare; *Coddyshack* advanced because Bill Murray's Carl Spackler played golf with the Dalai Lama. To make it beyond round I, a sports film must follow rule 1: The actors must look like they could actually play the sport. *Pride of the Yankees*, with Gary Cooper's lame at-bats and fielding, is the exception that proves the rule.

A De Niro faceoff. His wussy, dim-witted, dying catcher in *Bang* proves the young Don Corleone could do 'sensitive,' but his Oscar-winning portrayal of the nasty, relentless boxer Jake LaMotta is the signature De Niro character.

A matchup of athletes dying young: one by incurable disease (Gary Cooper's Lou Gehrig in *Pride*), the other Hilary Swank's paralysed boxer who begs her trainer to end it all. *Pride* goes to the next round on dignity points. Gehrig dies off-screen while *Baby*'s Maggie bites her tongue.

RICHARD SANDOMIR, the coeditor of this book, watches sports on television for a living as a columnist for the *New York Times*. He has watched one film in the tournament more than any other: *A League of Their Own*.

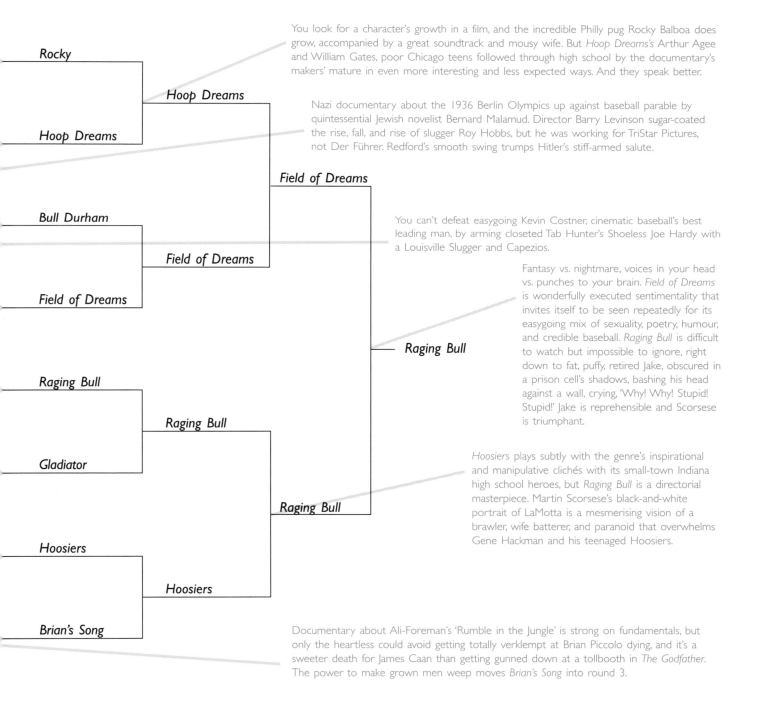

Rocky

Hoop Dreams

Hoop Dreams

Bull Durham

Field of Dreams

Field of Dreams

Field of Dreams

Raging Bull

Raging Bull

Gladiator

Raging Bull

Raging Bull

Hoosiers

Hoosiers

Brian's Song

You look for a character's growth in a film, and the incredible Philly pug Rocky Balboa does grow, accompanied by a great soundtrack and mousy wife. But *Hoop Dreams's* Arthur Agee and William Gates, poor Chicago teens followed through high school by the documentary's makers' mature in even more interesting and less expected ways. And they speak better.

Nazi documentary about the 1936 Berlin Olympics up against baseball parable by quintessential Jewish novelist Bernard Malamud. Director Barry Levinson sugar-coated the rise, fall, and rise of slugger Roy Hobbs, but he was working for TriStar Pictures, not Der Führer. Redford's smooth swing trumps Hitler's stiff-armed salute.

You can't defeat easygoing Kevin Costner, cinematic baseball's best leading man, by arming closeted Tab Hunter's Shoeless Joe Hardy with a Louisville Slugger and Capezios.

Fantasy vs. nightmare, voices in your head vs. punches to your brain. *Field of Dreams* is wonderfully executed sentimentality that invites itself to be seen repeatedly for its easygoing mix of sexuality, poetry, humour, and credible baseball. *Raging Bull* is difficult to watch but impossible to ignore, right down to fat, puffy, retired Jake, obscured in a prison cell's shadows, bashing his head against a wall, crying, 'Why! Why! Stupid! Stupid!' Jake is reprehensible and Scorsese is triumphant.

Hoosiers plays subtly with the genre's inspirational and manipulative clichés with its small-town Indiana high school heroes, but *Raging Bull* is a directorial masterpiece. Martin Scorsese's black-and-white portrait of LaMotta is a mesmerising vision of a brawler, wife batterer, and paranoid that overwhelms Gene Hackman and his teenaged Hoosiers.

Documentary about Ali-Foreman's 'Rumble in the Jungle' is strong on fundamentals, but only the heartless could avoid getting totally verklempt at Brian Piccolo dying, and it's a sweeter death for James Caan than getting gunned down at a tollbooth in *The Godfather*. The power to make grown men weep moves *Brian's Song* into round 3.

86

Sporting Moments

by ADAM GILL

Sports fans seem to have an amazing ability to 'remember' events they weren't there for at the time. How many thirty-year-olds are able to picture Bobby Moore holding the World Cup trophy aloft in 1966? How many teenage football fans seem to recall Gazza's tears in Italia 90? Some moments, it seems, leave such an indelible mark on the public consciousness that they don't fade in people's memories from one generation to the next. Indeed, they seem to gain importance the further away from them we get. What self-respecting Formula One fan doesn't know about Ayrton Senna's tragic accident? And how can you fully appreciate Freddie Flintoff's performance in the 2005 Ashes without comparing it to Ian Botham's tour de force in 1981? But what is the most significant moment in the English sporting fans' psyche?

ADAM GILL works in the City having enjoyed a spectacularly unsuccessful career in sports' journalism. His vast knowledge of sporting trivia compensates for his lack of prowess on the field/green/pitch/court.

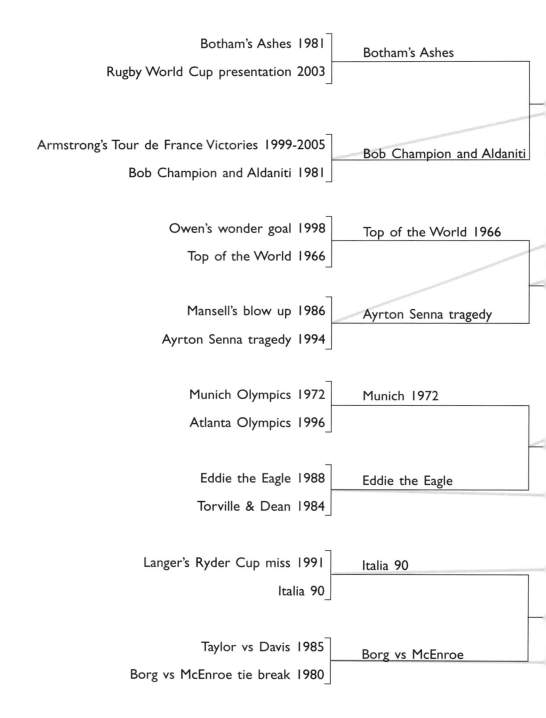

Botham's Ashes 1981
Rugby World Cup presentation 2003
Botham's Ashes

Armstrong's Tour de France Victories 1999-2005
Bob Champion and Aldaniti 1981
Bob Champion and Aldaniti

Owen's wonder goal 1998
Top of the World 1966
Top of the World 1966

Mansell's blow up 1986
Ayrton Senna tragedy 1994
Ayrton Senna tragedy

Munich Olympics 1972
Atlanta Olympics 1996
Munich 1972

Eddie the Eagle 1988
Torville & Dean 1984
Eddie the Eagle

Langer's Ryder Cup miss 1991
Italia 90
Italia 90

Taylor vs Davis 1985
Borg vs McEnroe tie break 1980
Borg vs McEnroe

Nothing pulls at the heart strings more than underdogs and both Bob Champion and Aldaniti were write-offs until the 1981 Grand National.

Botham's Ashes

Poor Nigel. A whole season up in smoke along with the nation's dreams. But the tragedy of Ayrton Senna has to win through on the ground that it shouldn't really be 'up against' anything. Sport's equivalent to JFK's assassination.

Top of the World 1966

We sympathised with the tragedy of a supremely talented man driven by personal ambition, but that 1966 team was driven by pride and patriotism . . . it gets you every time.

Top of the World 1966

The Eagle made bold attempts to promote an Olympian spirit but only restored a little of the flame that was so spectacularly destroyed by the darkness of Black September. I am afraid that dear Eddie is slightly out of his depth in comparison with the historical and political gravitas of a terrible act of international terrorism which will never be forgotten.

Top of the World 1966

All competitions should end with a worthy winner, and this is no exception. Let's conjure up that magical image of Bobby on his team-mates' shoulders, triumphantly holding the Jules Rimet aloft as he, I must admit effortlessly, wins this competition as well.

Munich 1972

Well he really was the most glorious of losers, Eddie from Cheltenham. A short-sighted man on a ski-jump – almost unwatchable! And as for T & D with those dresses, those tens and that terrible smiling . . . To me, no contest, Eddie flies through.

Italia 90

Both definitive 'pin-drop' moments, and Langer's agony was pretty painful to see. But those penalties? Even your Aunt Beryl remembers Pearce and Waddle.

Italia 90

With a staggering eighteen million people staying tuned in until one o'clock on a Sunday night this was snooker's finest hour, but surely a drop volley is far harder than potting a black. The only good thing about rain at Wimbledon today is the replaying of this sublime duel. Sure as hell knocks the socks off any of today's matches.

87

Swear Words
by S**** T*****

In 1976 Johnny Rotten swore in front of a television audience of millions when he was being interviewed by ITV teatime presenter Bill Grundy. This incident, reported by the tabloids under the headline 'The Filth and the Fury', effectively ended Grundy's career and propelled The Sex Pistols higher and higher. I don't think I have ever heard my parents swear and it is still very rare to hear anything other than the very mildest of swearwords on Radio 4. I think I once heard Ruth Archer say 'shit' but that may have been an aural illusion. The television, however, is very different. Turn on *Mock the Week, Have I Got News for You, Eight out of Ten Cats*, or any number of post-watershed programmes and the f-word will be there in abundance. That is why I was surprised to see in a recent survey by the broadcasting standards agency that 'fuck' still ranks as the third most offensive swearword. So I decided to ignore this survey and have a look at the words myself. This section is not to be read by my parents.

arse	arse
balls	
f*ck	f*ck
shit	
wanker	wanker
twat	
c*nt	c*nt
prick	
motherf*cker	motherf*cker
bloody	
dickhead	dickhead
bugger	
slag	slag
whore	
spastic	spastic
bastard	

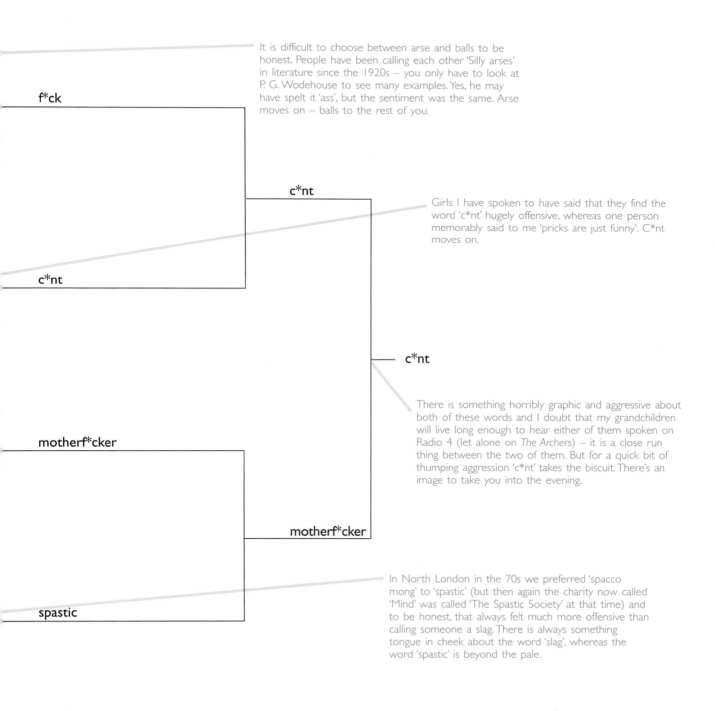

f*ck

c*nt

c*nt

It is difficult to choose between arse and balls to be honest. People have been calling each other 'Silly arses' in literature since the 1920s – you only have to look at P. G. Wodehouse to see many examples. Yes, he may have spelt it 'ass', but the sentiment was the same. Arse moves on – balls to the rest of you.

Girls I have spoken to have said that they find the word 'c*nt' hugely offensive, whereas one person memorably said to me 'pricks are just funny'. C*nt moves on.

c*nt

There is something horribly graphic and aggressive about both of these words and I doubt that my grandchildren will live long enough to hear either of them spoken on Radio 4 (let alone on *The Archers*) – it is a close run thing between the two of them. But for a quick bit of thumping aggression 'c*nt' takes the biscuit. There's an image to take you into the evening.

motherf*cker

motherf*cker

spastic

In North London in the 70s we preferred 'spacco mong' to 'spastic' (but then again the charity now called 'Mind' was called 'The Spastic Society' at that time) and to be honest, that always felt much more offensive than calling someone a slag. There is always something tongue in cheek about the word 'slag', whereas the word 'spastic' is beyond the pale.

88

Tabloid Headlines
by SIMON TREWIN

The days of 'STOP PRESS! READ ALL ABOUT IT!' have long gone and it is very rare to hear the hard news first through print media. The smart broadsheets are all investing gazillions of pounds in creating their online counterparts in a scramble to keep their brand value high and their advertisers happy. But luckily for us the grubby tabloids are much as they used to be – maybe a little bit more celebrity gossip and scandal but still as opinionated, shouty and in-yer-face as ever and we love them for it. Who can fail to laugh at 'It's Paddy Pantsdown' or 'Zip Me Up Before You Go Go'? Who would not be impressed by the encapsulation of a serious news story into one easy bite-sized headline? I have resisted the temptation to include overseas headlines or UK magazines which sadly means my all-time US classic headline – HEADLESS BODY IN TOPLESS BAR is omitted as is the headline I saw on a glossy women's mag this morning. It simply said 'DOES YOUR POSTCODE AFFECT YOUR ORGASM?' No answer to that really.

It's Paddy Pantsdown (1993/*Sun*) – Paddy Ashdown's extra-marital affair is revealed.

Gotcha! (1982/*Sun*) – British ships sink Argentine destroyer *The Belgrano*.

> Gotcha!

Freddie Starr Ate My Hamster (1986/*Sun*) – Story fabricated by Max Clifford.

So Where Are They Mr Blair? (2003/*Sun*) – The hunt for weapons of mass destruction.

> Freddie Starr

Super Caley Go Ballistic Celtic Are Atrocious (2000/*Sun*) – Caley Thistle knocks Celtic out of the Scottish Cup.

The Truth (1989/*Sun*) – The alleged misconduct of Liverpool fans at the Hillsborough disaster.

> Super Caley

Stick It Up Your Junta (1982/*Sun*) – Characteristic response to a possible compromise agreement being reached over the Falkland Islands.

It's The Sun Wot Won It (1992/*Sun*) – After the surprise Tory victory under John Major

> It's The Sun Wot Won It

From Hitler Youth To Papa Razi (2005/*Sun*) – The election of Pope Benedict XVI and his German past.

'How Can 59,054,087 People Be So DUMB?' (2004/*Daily Mirror*) – The re-election of George Bush Jnr as President of the U.S.A.

> 59,054,087 people

Zip me up before you go go (1998/*Sun*) – George Michael's arrest in a public toilet for 'engaging in a lewd act' after propositioning an off-duty cop.

'Elton Takes David Up The Aisle' (2005/*Sun*) – The civil partnership of Elton John and David Furnish.

> Zip Me Up

Two Shags (2006/*Sun*) – Diary secretary Tracey Temple reveals her affair with John Prescott.

Chuck A Khan (2007/*Sun*) – Hugh Grant leaves his girlfriend Jemima Khan.

> Two Shags

How Do You Solve A Problem Like Korea? (2007/*Sun*) – North Korea breaches nuclear testing rules.

Up Yours Delors (1990/*Sun*) – Britain's relationship with France reaches a new low.

> Up Yours Delors

Freddie Starr

You can picture the scene in the Ashdown household when this little beauty plopped on the mat – a joyous play on words and a nickname that will haunt him forever even if he is now, of course, Lord Pantsdown. The 'Gotcha' headline teetered on the edge of poor taste by displaying the worst jingoistic 'Our Boys' tendencies of the red tops and, indeed, it was rescinded in later editions but it still works for me – it captured a moment in time and moves forward to round two. Pants stay down but Gotcha moves on.

Freddie Starr

Doesn't matter whether you enjoy football, know anything about the ins-and-outs of Scottish rivalry or, frankly, have ever seen Mary Poppins – this is a headline to read, read again and tell your friends about. As you will now.

Super Caley

Freddie Starr Ate My Hamster

Washed-up F list celebrity Freddie Starr (represented by Max Clifford) received a huge publicity boost thanks to this front-page Sun story about his late night snack attack. He admitted many years later that it never happened (Really? Gosh! But it was in the papers so it must be true . . .) but in a sense we don't mind and we don't care – it is British tabloid genius and easily thrashes Sun's anti-French flash in the pan. Freddie Starr reigns supreme.

Zip Me Up

This Whamtastic little beauty perfectly made light of an ultimately unimportant story with wit and panache. American friends of mine asked me to send them real copies of this anti-Bush edition of the Daily Mirror as they thought it was an online photoshop spoof – it is a headline worthy of the Guardian and the Independent but no one would have noticed it unless it was splashed in a blaze of tabloid glory. However, you can't sing 'How Can 59,054,087 People Be So Dumb?' so the George Michael headline moves onwards.

Delors

Up Yours Delors

89

Text Message Abbreviations

by SIMON TREWIN

WU? God knows why people can't just pick up the phone and talk to each other. All this instant messaging, text messaging and emailing is fine and very twenty-first century I'm sure but when I were nobbut a lad we found it perfectly convenient to go round to our friends' houses, knock on the door and say to their mums, 'Can Michael/Jimmy/Orlando come out to play for a bit?' Occasionally we were allowed to pick up the phone but only if it was a local number – now there are billions of text messages sent a month, whole TV programmes are funded on the back of text voting and teenagers are communicating to their heart's content about all sorts of wrong-doing without parents having a clue. Disgraceful! And what is worse is that the youth of today have created a ridiculous language to speed the process and pack as much as possible into each message. Hilariously, in 2006, Britney Spears reportedly told her husband Kevin Federline that she wanted a divorce by text and a Ms Chuang Yang of Singapore managed to get into the *Guinness Book Of Records* by sending the following text message in 41.52 seconds: 'The razor-toothed piranhas of the genera Serrasalmus and Pygocentrus are the most ferocious freshwater fish in the world. In reality they seldom attack a human.' WE! WAN2TLK?

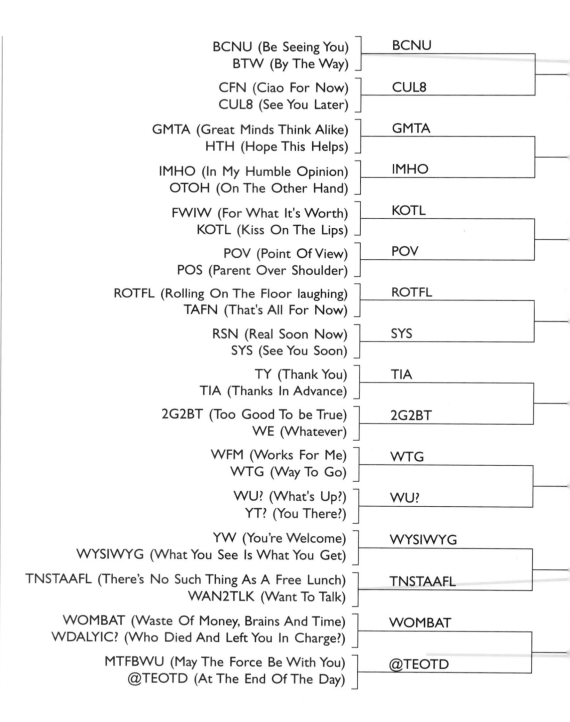

BCNU (Be Seeing You)
BTW (By The Way)

CFN (Ciao For Now)
CUL8 (See You Later)

GMTA (Great Minds Think Alike)
HTH (Hope This Helps)

IMHO (In My Humble Opinion)
OTOH (On The Other Hand)

FWIW (For What It's Worth)
KOTL (Kiss On The Lips)

POV (Point Of View)
POS (Parent Over Shoulder)

ROTFL (Rolling On The Floor laughing)
TAFN (That's All For Now)

RSN (Real Soon Now)
SYS (See You Soon)

TY (Thank You)
TIA (Thanks In Advance)

2G2BT (Too Good To be True)
WE (Whatever)

WFM (Works For Me)
WTG (Way To Go)

WU? (What's Up?)
YT? (You There?)

YW (You're Welcome)
WYSIWYG (What You See Is What You Get)

TNSTAAFL (There's No Such Thing As A Free Lunch)
WAN2TLK (Want To Talk)

WOMBAT (Waste Of Money, Brains And Time)
WDALYIC? (Who Died And Left You In Charge?)

MTFBWU (May The Force Be With You)
@TEOTD (At The End Of The Day)

BCNU

CUL8

GMTA

IMHO

KOTL

POV

ROTFL

SYS

TIA

2G2BT

WTG

WU?

WYSIWYG

TNSTAAFL

WOMBAT

@TEOTD

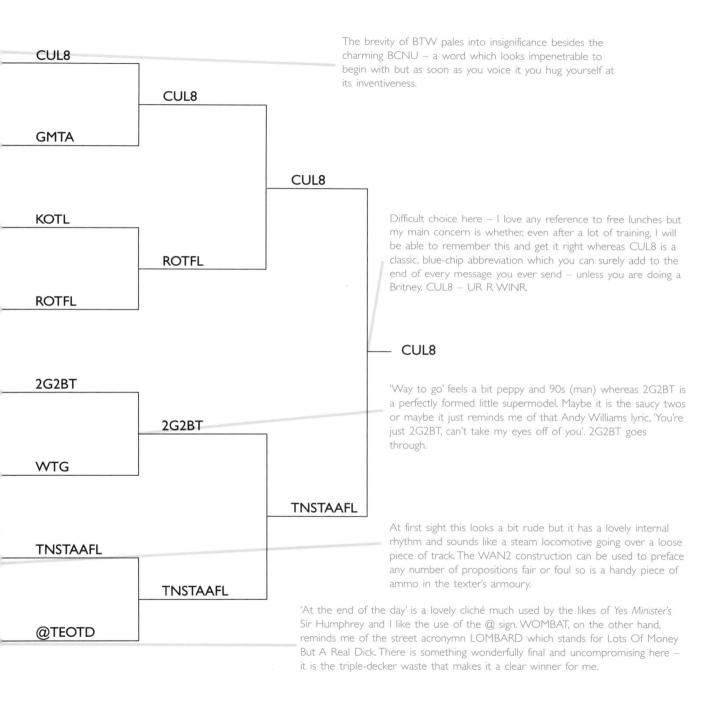

CUL8

GMTA

CUL8

KOTL

ROTFL

ROTFL

CUL8

CUL8

The brevity of BTW pales into insignificance besides the charming BCNU – a word which looks impenetrable to begin with but as soon as you voice it you hug yourself at its inventiveness.

Difficult choice here – I love any reference to free lunches but my main concern is whether, even after a lot of training, I will be able to remember this and get it right whereas CUL8 is a classic, blue-chip abbreviation which you can surely add to the end of every message you ever send – unless you are doing a Britney. CUL8 – UR R WINR.

CUL8

2G2BT

WTG

2G2BT

2G2BT

TNSTAAFL

'Way to go' feels a bit peppy and 90s (man) whereas 2G2BT is a perfectly formed little supermodel. Maybe it is the saucy twos or maybe it just reminds me of that Andy Williams lyric, 'You're just 2G2BT, can't take my eyes off of you'. 2G2BT goes through.

TNSTAAFL

@TEOTD

TNSTAAFL

At first sight this looks a bit rude but it has a lovely internal rhythm and sounds like a steam locomotive going over a loose piece of track. The WAN2 construction can be used to preface any number of propositions fair or foul so is a handy piece of ammo in the texter's armoury.

'At the end of the day' is a lovely cliché much used by the likes of *Yes Minister's* Sir Humphrey and I like the use of the @ sign. WOMBAT, on the other hand, reminds me of the street acronymn LOMBARD which stands for Lots Of Money But A Real Dick. There is something wonderfully final and uncompromising here – it is the triple-decker waste that makes it a clear winner for me.

90

Things I Wish I'd Known When I Was Younger

by JANIE HAMPTON

The trouble with totting up the years is that one can't help totting up wisdom too; and then wishing that the wisdom had been there a bit earlier. So I hope that these rays of sunny wise things will help all you young readers. But I doubt it. The only way anyone learnt the importance of filling the car with petrol is by running out on a blasted heath, in the dark. Most of the things I wish I'd known when I was younger involve saving effort, and creating an effect with little trouble. None of them will make you rich or famous.

JANIE HAMPTON is the author of fifteen books including the first biography of entertainer Joyce Grenfell, and *The Austerity Olympics, London 1948*. She has worked as a journalist on four continents, travelling by bus, boat and bicycle. Now her four grown-up children have flown the nest, she lives with her husband, three lodgers, six bantams and 24 quails. She enjoys lying in her hammock under the apple tree contemplating her accumulated wisdom.

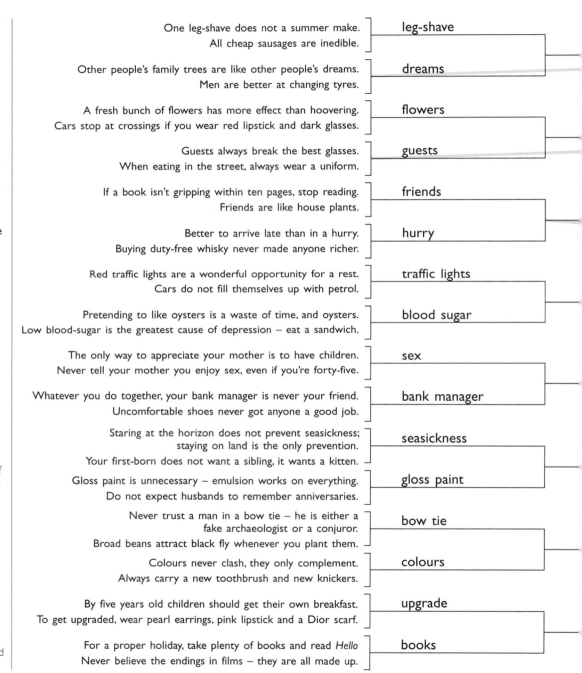

One leg-shave does not a summer make.
All cheap sausages are inedible.

Other people's family trees are like other people's dreams.
Men are better at changing tyres.

A fresh bunch of flowers has more effect than hoovering.
Cars stop at crossings if you wear red lipstick and dark glasses.

Guests always break the best glasses.
When eating in the street, always wear a uniform.

If a book isn't gripping within ten pages, stop reading.
Friends are like house plants.

Better to arrive late than in a hurry.
Buying duty-free whisky never made anyone richer.

Red traffic lights are a wonderful opportunity for a rest.
Cars do not fill themselves up with petrol.

Pretending to like oysters is a waste of time, and oysters.
Low blood-sugar is the greatest cause of depression – eat a sandwich.

The only way to appreciate your mother is to have children.
Never tell your mother you enjoy sex, even if you're forty-five.

Whatever you do together, your bank manager is never your friend.
Uncomfortable shoes never got anyone a good job.

Staring at the horizon does not prevent seasickness; staying on land is the only prevention.
Your first-born does not want a sibling, it wants a kitten.

Gloss paint is unnecessary – emulsion works on everything.
Do not expect husbands to remember anniversaries.

Never trust a man in a bow tie – he is either a fake archaeologist or a conjuror.
Broad beans attract black fly whenever you plant them.

Colours never clash, they only complement.
Always carry a new toothbrush and new knickers.

By five years old children should get their own breakfast.
To get upgraded, wear pearl earrings, pink lipstick and a Dior scarf.

For a proper holiday, take plenty of books and read *Hello*
Never believe the endings in films – they are all made up.

leg-shave

dreams

flowers

guests

friends

hurry

traffic lights

blood sugar

sex

bank manager

seasickness

gloss paint

bow tie

colours

upgrade

books

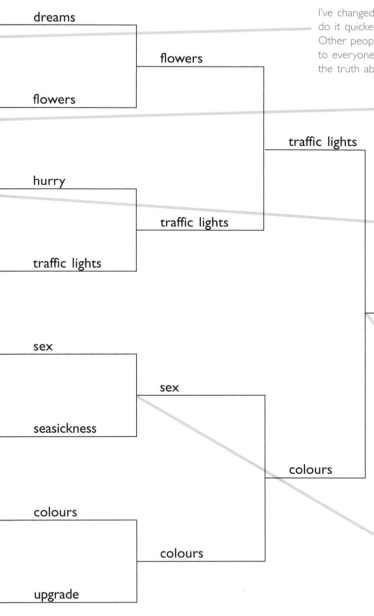

I've changed hundreds of tyres in my life, and I've noticed that men always do it quicker, and seem to enjoy it. So look helpless and leave it to them. Other people's family trees are fascinating to the owner, and boring as hell to everyone else. And like dreams, nobody knows whether you are telling the truth about your fascinating genealogy, and neither do they care.

As a child I was taught it was very bad manners to eat in the street, especially ice cream. So if you wear a uniform, then the school/RAF/Police will get a bad name, and not you. It's nice if guests offer to wash up, but they always break the glasses – decide which is more important to you, and either separate them or stop worrying.

Arriving late obviously applies only to meetings (social or professional) and not to trains. Arriving at any destination in a state of sweat and 'I'm so sorry I'm late' never impressed anyone, whether a potential employer or your Great Aunt Sally. But friends are delicate creatures, they need nurturing with love, tender phone calls and frequent cocktails. Friends are more important than employers, so they win.

Red traffic lights are a wonderful opportunity for a rest.

These are both about optical illusions, and gaining otherwise wasted time. Colours never clash, they only complement. Years of one's life can be spent looking for the T-shirt that coordinates beautifully with a new pair of trousers, or searching for a paint to match your curtains, completely unnecessarily. But enjoying the break that a red traffic light affords you is an aspect of 'Positive Thinking Philosophy' (PTP) – always looking for the good in any occasion, however dire it may seem. This is an attractive, twenty-first century attitude and so I'm going to stick with it. Red traffic lights win.

Seasickness is a problem one can avoid by simply not going to sea. Most of us have mothers, but they cannot be avoided. They love us dearly but do not want to imagine their darlings doing certain things. So 'Never Tell your mother' wins, as it applies to many other aspects of an adult's life.

91

Tongue Twisters
by SIMON TREWIN

I decided I wanted to go into the theatre when I left school so applied to a number of universities that offered degrees in drama and theatre studies. I was called for interview at a number of places, but the letter back from Kent looked rather worrying – it was not just an interview but also 'an informal audition workshop'. Yikes! Anyway, I duly turned up for my audition, and the first hurdle was a vocal warm-up consisting of many different tongue twisters. Things were not looking good for me as I stumbled through 'Peggy Babcock' and 'Red Lorry, Yellow Lorry', but amazingly I was eventually offered a place. I secretly think this may have been because I was standing next to someone with such a spectacular lisp that the examiners were all but donning rain coats as he struggled through 'She Sells Sea Shells On the Sea Shore'. Next to him I probably looked quite good! Welcome to the magical world of the tongue-twister – at first sight curiously simple but oh, how wrong you are.

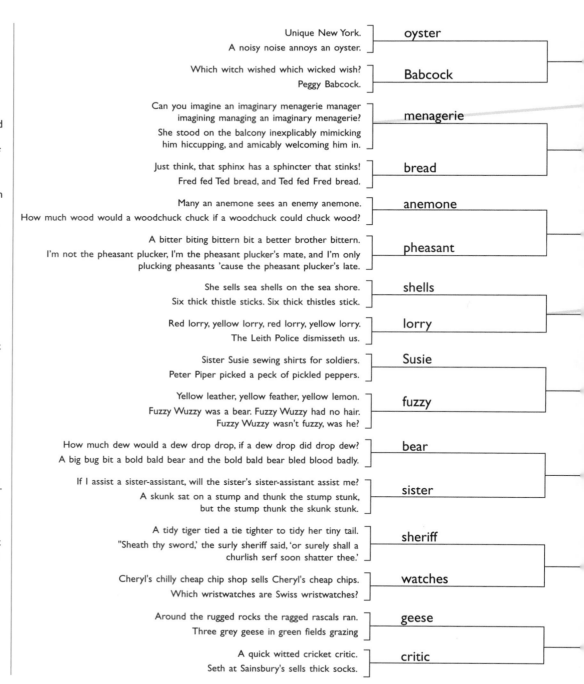

Unique New York.
A noisy noise annoys an oyster.

oyster

Which witch wished which wicked wish?
Peggy Babcock.

Babcock

Can you imagine an imaginary menagerie manager imagining managing an imaginary menagerie?
She stood on the balcony inexplicably mimicking him hiccupping, and amicably welcoming him in.

menagerie

Just think, that sphinx has a sphincter that stinks!
Fred fed Ted bread, and Ted fed Fred bread.

bread

Many an anemone sees an enemy anemone.
How much wood would a woodchuck chuck if a woodchuck could chuck wood?

anemone

A bitter biting bittern bit a better brother bittern.
I'm not the pheasant plucker, I'm the pheasant plucker's mate, and I'm only plucking pheasants 'cause the pheasant plucker's late.

pheasant

She sells sea shells on the sea shore.
Six thick thistle sticks. Six thick thistles stick.

shells

Red lorry, yellow lorry, red lorry, yellow lorry.
The Leith Police dismisseth us.

lorry

Sister Susie sewing shirts for soldiers.
Peter Piper picked a peck of pickled peppers.

Susie

Yellow leather, yellow feather, yellow lemon.
Fuzzy Wuzzy was a bear. Fuzzy Wuzzy had no hair.
Fuzzy Wuzzy wasn't fuzzy, was he?

fuzzy

How much dew would a dew drop drop, if a dew drop did drop dew?
A big bug bit a bold bald bear and the bold bald bear bled blood badly.

bear

If I assist a sister-assistant, will the sister's sister-assistant assist me?
A skunk sat on a stump and thunk the stump stunk, but the stump thunk the skunk stunk.

sister

A tidy tiger tied a tie tighter to tidy her tiny tail.
"Sheath thy sword,' the surly sheriff said, 'or surely shall a churlish serf soon shatter thee.'

sheriff

Cheryl's chilly cheap chip shop sells Cheryl's cheap chips.
Which wristwatches are Swiss wristwatches?

watches

Around the rugged rocks the ragged rascals ran.
Three grey geese in green fields grazing

geese

A quick witted cricket critic.
Seth at Sainsbury's sells thick socks.

critic

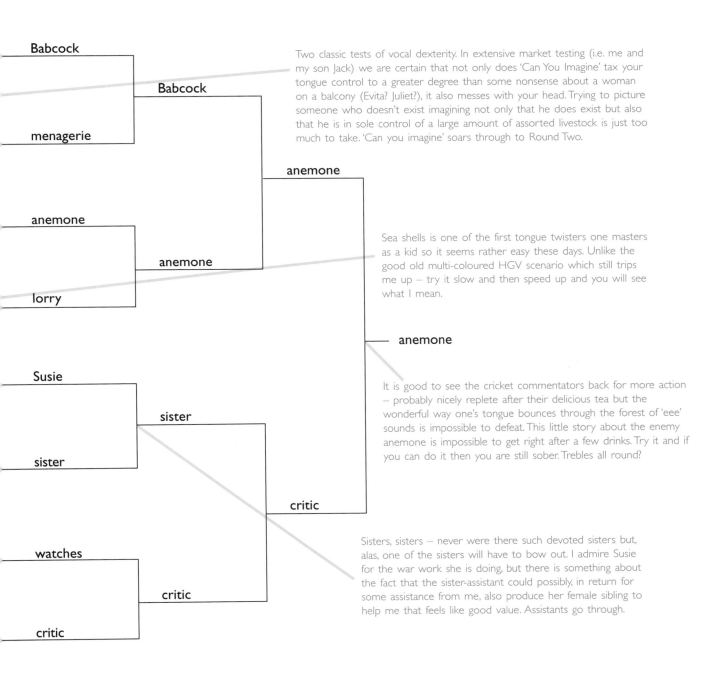

Babcock

menagerie

Babcock

Two classic tests of vocal dexterity. In extensive market testing (i.e. me and my son Jack) we are certain that not only does 'Can You Imagine' tax your tongue control to a greater degree than some nonsense about a woman on a balcony (Evita? Juliet?), it also messes with your head. Trying to picture someone who doesn't exist imagining not only that he does exist but also that he is in sole control of a large amount of assorted livestock is just too much to take. 'Can you imagine' soars through to Round Two.

anemone

anemone

lorry

anemone

Sea shells is one of the first tongue twisters one masters as a kid so it seems rather easy these days. Unlike the good old multi-coloured HGV scenario which still trips me up — try it slow and then speed up and you will see what I mean.

anemone

Susie

sister

sister

It is good to see the cricket commentators back for more action — probably nicely replete after their delicious tea but the wonderful way one's tongue bounces through the forest of 'eee' sounds is impossible to defeat. This little story about the enemy anemone is impossible to get right after a few drinks. Try it and if you can do it then you are still sober. Trebles all round?

critic

watches

critic

critic

Sisters, sisters — never were there such devoted sisters but, alas, one of the sisters will have to bow out. I admire Susie for the war work she is doing, but there is something about the fact that the sister-assistant could possibly, in return for some assistance from me, also produce her female sibling to help me that feels like good value. Assistants go through.

92

Unseen Characters

by SIMON TREWIN

I remember my joy at school in an English lesson at school when our teacher, Mr Hartley, said that not only were we going to be reading Samuel Beckett's *Waiting for Godot* in class (a play I had heard much about but never seen or read) but that he had decided to award me the honour of playing the eponymous hero. This was certainly a step up from my last triumph of 'the porter' in *Macbeth* and 'a lord' in *Richard III* so I was naturally thrilled. As I swelled with pride I noticed a few knowing boys at the back of the class sniggering and winking in the direction of the teacher. Assuming it was an in-joke I eagerly turned the pages of Beckett's masterpiece looking for my entrance, my opening line and my big scene. After a while I began to feel apprehensive – I hoped I could live up to the build-up to my first appearance – the build-up was certainly unceasing. And then it dawned on me – I was the victim of a cruel joke and something inside me has hated Beckett ever since. I was sure this is a trick that has been played on many people throughout the years and not just through the medium of this play. There are a whole plethora of characters that are never seen or heard in literature and the performing arts but which one will win the coveted trophy as Best Invisible Performance In An Invisible Role?

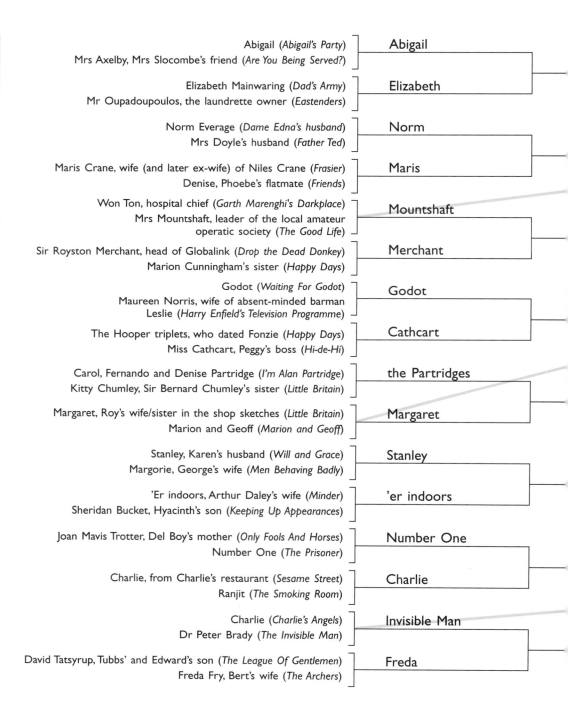

Abigail (*Abigail's Party*)
Mrs Axelby, Mrs Slocombe's friend (*Are You Being Served?*)

Abigail

Elizabeth Mainwaring (*Dad's Army*)
Mr Oupadoupoulos, the laundrette owner (*Eastenders*)

Elizabeth

Norm Everage (*Dame Edna's husband*)
Mrs Doyle's husband (*Father Ted*)

Norm

Maris Crane, wife (and later ex-wife) of Niles Crane (*Frasier*)
Denise, Phoebe's flatmate (*Friends*)

Maris

Won Ton, hospital chief (*Garth Marenghi's Darkplace*)
Mrs Mountshaft, leader of the local amateur operatic society (*The Good Life*)

Mountshaft

Sir Royston Merchant, head of Globalink (*Drop the Dead Donkey*)
Marion Cunningham's sister (*Happy Days*)

Merchant

Godot (*Waiting For Godot*)
Maureen Norris, wife of absent-minded barman Leslie (*Harry Enfield's Television Programme*)

Godot

The Hooper triplets, who dated Fonzie (*Happy Days*)
Miss Cathcart, Peggy's boss (*Hi-de-Hi*)

Cathcart

Carol, Fernando and Denise Partridge (*I'm Alan Partridge*)
Kitty Chumley, Sir Bernard Chumley's sister (*Little Britain*)

the Partridges

Margaret, Roy's wife/sister in the shop sketches (*Little Britain*)
Marion and Geoff (*Marion and Geoff*)

Margaret

Stanley, Karen's husband (*Will and Grace*)
Margorie, George's wife (*Men Behaving Badly*)

Stanley

'Er indoors, Arthur Daley's wife (*Minder*)
Sheridan Bucket, Hyacinth's son (*Keeping Up Appearances*)

'er indoors

Joan Mavis Trotter, Del Boy's mother (*Only Fools And Horses*)
Number One (*The Prisoner*)

Number One

Charlie, from Charlie's restaurant (*Sesame Street*)
Ranjit (*The Smoking Room*)

Charlie

Charlie (*Charlie's Angels*)
Dr Peter Brady (*The Invisible Man*)

Invisible Man

David Tatsyrup, Tubbs' and Edward's son (*The League Of Gentlemen*)
Freda Fry, Bert's wife (*The Archers*)

Freda

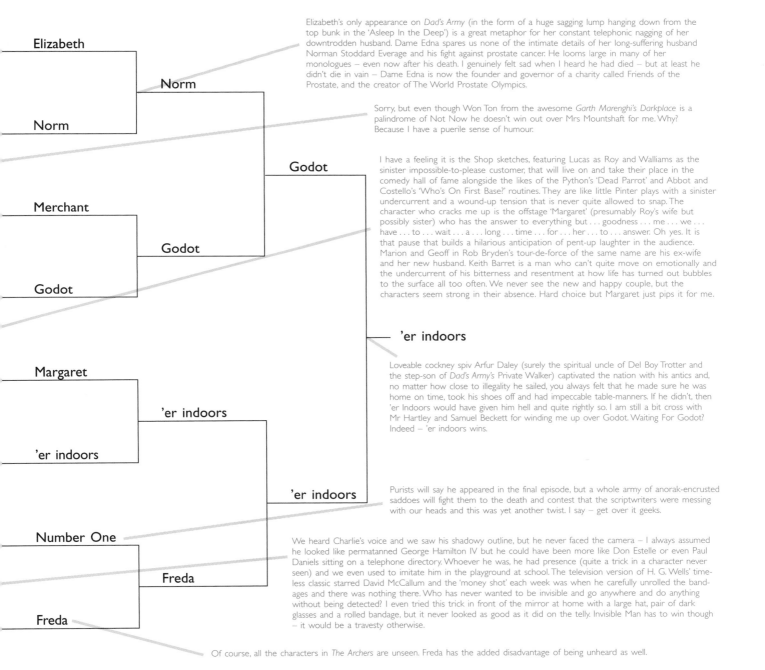

Elizabeth

Norm

Norm

Merchant

Godot

Godot

Godot

Margaret

'er indoors

'er indoors

Number One

Freda

Freda

Godot

'er indoors

'er indoors

'er indoors

Elizabeth's only appearance on *Dad's Army* (in the form of a huge sagging lump hanging down from the top bunk in the 'Asleep In the Deep') is a great metaphor for her constant telephonic nagging of her downtrodden husband. Dame Edna spares us none of the intimate details of her long-suffering husband Norman Stoddard Everage and his fight against prostate cancer. He looms large in many of her monologues – even now after his death. I genuinely felt sad when I heard he had died – but at least he didn't die in vain – Dame Edna is now the founder and governor of a charity called Friends of the Prostate, and the creator of The World Prostate Olympics.

Sorry, but even though Won Ton from the awesome *Garth Marenghi's Darkplace* is a palindrome of Not Now he doesn't win out over Mrs Mountshaft for me. Why? Because I have a puerile sense of humour.

I have a feeling it is the Shop sketches, featuring Lucas as Roy and Walliams as the sinister impossible-to-please customer, that will live on and take their place in the comedy hall of fame alongside the likes of the Python's 'Dead Parrot' and Abbot and Costello's 'Who's On First Base?' routines. They are like little Pinter plays with a sinister undercurrent and a wound-up tension that is never quite allowed to snap. The character who cracks me up is the offstage 'Margaret' (presumably Roy's wife but possibly sister) who has the answer to everything but . . . goodness . . . me . . . we . . . have . . . to . . . wait . . . a . . . long . . . time . . . for . . . her . . . to . . . answer. Oh yes. It is that pause that builds a hilarious anticipation of pent-up laughter in the audience. Marion and Geoff in Rob Bryden's tour-de-force of the same name are his ex-wife and her new husband. Keith Barret is a man who can't quite move on emotionally and the undercurrent of his bitterness and resentment at how life has turned out bubbles to the surface all too often. We never see the new and happy couple, but the characters seem strong in their absence. Hard choice but Margaret just pips it for me.

Loveable cockney spiv Arfur Daley (surely the spiritual uncle of Del Boy Trotter and the step-son of *Dad's Army's* Private Walker) captivated the nation with his antics and, no matter how close to illegality he sailed, you always felt that he made sure he was home on time, took his shoes off and had impeccable table-manners. If he didn't, then 'er Indoors would have given him hell and quite rightly so. I am still a bit cross with Mr Hartley and Samuel Beckett for winding me up over Godot. Waiting For Godot? Indeed – 'er indoors wins.

Purists will say he appeared in the final episode, but a whole army of anorak-encrusted saddoes will fight them to the death and contest that the scriptwriters were messing with our heads and this was yet another twist. I say – get over it geeks.

We heard Charlie's voice and we saw his shadowy outline, but he never faced the camera – I always assumed he looked like permatanned George Hamilton IV but he could have been more like Don Estelle or even Paul Daniels sitting on a telephone directory. Whoever he was, he had presence (quite a trick in a character never seen) and we even used to imitate him in the playground at school. The television version of H. G. Wells' time-less classic starred David McCallum and the 'money shot' each week was when he carefully unrolled the band-ages and there was nothing there. Who has never wanted to be invisible and go anywhere and do anything without being detected? I even tried this trick in front of the mirror at home with a large hat, pair of dark glasses and a rolled bandage, but it never looked as good as it did on the telly. Invisible Man has to win though – it would be a travesty otherwise.

Of course, all the characters in *The Archers* are unseen. Freda has the added disadvantage of being unheard as well.

93

Urban Legends
by SIMON TREWIN

A friend of a friend told me that his friend's mother's cleaner was on the tube in London and saw a bearded, swarthy man dropping his wallet. She ran after him and kindly returned the wallet to him. He thanked her profusely and then whispered in her ear, 'Avoid London this coming Saturday. A bomb attack is planned.' What an amazing stroke of luck, I hear you cry. What are the chances that my friend's friend's friend's mother's cleaner should get this invaluable piece of life-saving intelligence, and thank goodness she thought to tell her boss who then decided to tell her whole family who then each sent an email to their friends who then sent it to everyone they knew. I am certainly avoiding London this coming Saturday and hopefully you will too. Isn't the Internet a great thing? Wow! Not sure why some people out there believe all the total piffle in this chart but maybe there is part of us all which just wants to believe the extraordinary because it brings a much-needed lustre to our otherwise ordinary lives. Anyway – must dash – I have to get on a plane to Nigeria because a man there is going to give me $50,000,000 in return for my bank details. There IS a god.

The Great Wall Of China is visible from the moon.
Ships still disappear in the Bermuda Triangle.

Great Wall Of China

'Paul Is Dead' is hidden in 'Getting Better' on *Sgt Pepper's Lonely Hearts Club Band*.
Colouring the edge of CDs green improves the sound quality.

'Paul Is Dead'

Walt Disney has been cryogenically frozen.
A bonsai kitten craze is sweeping America.

bonsai kittens

There is a gangland initiation ritual that involves killing motorists who flash their headlights.
Queen Victoria's grandson Prince Albert Victor was Jack the Ripper

headlights

Alligators live in New York's sewers.
Sharks can attack helicopters (and there's a photo to prove it).

shark

The Loch Ness Monster.
The moon landing was faked.

moon landing

Richard Gere has an unhealthy fondness for gerbils.
Celebrity X had to have his/her stomach pumped and it was full of semen.

gerbils

Elvis is alive.
An alien spaceship crashed at Roswell.

Elvis

Great Wall Of
China

                    headlights

headlights

                                    headlights

The original, much-forwarded bonsai kitten website caused outrage across the Internet – people really seem to believe that a company was forcing newborn kittens into glass jars to shape them then selling them as knick-knacks. Of course this was total nonsense but even now people accidentally come across www.shorty.com/bonsaikitten/ and believe it – some even try to order their own furry ornaments. The site is hilariously straight-laced and easily beats stories of Walt being in a big freezer somewhere (probably with Mickey Mouse). Who cares really? We don't – all we want for Christmas is a bonsai kitten. Ahhh!

Reading this viral email about not flashing headlights at anyone in case they follow you and kill you did make me pause and think for a bit. Of course I then re-started my regular practice of indiscriminate flashing, but I can't help but worry that life could imitate art on this one. Maybe it's been secretly adopted by a gang who liked the urban legend so much they thought they would give it a go. As a great example of a bit of modern myth-making that's really got under people's skin, it has to win out.

moonlanding

                    Elvis

Elvis

Both have a medical theme and both have been circulating ever since I was in school. The name of the celebrity in the semen story changes frequently (though, worryingly, it is never anyone but Gere in the animal hospital anecdote), and the story is always prefaced with something along the lines of, 'My cousin's best friend worked in the casualty department of hospital X,' which gives the whole thing a false sense of veracity. The semen story is a bit graphic for my taste and so Gere has to win out. All we need now is for Uncle Rolf to pop up and say 'Sadly the little gerbil didn't make it through the night.'

94

Video Games

by JACK TREWIN and FREDDIE MICKSHIK

When our dads were our age their idea of 'gaming' involved a bat, a ball and a net. Times, thank God, have changed and millions of us gaming enthusiasts around the world have bundles of fun trying out the latest technology, from the Xbox 360 and the PS3 to the must-have Xmas gift for 2006 – the Wii. These days it seems like there are no limits to the imagination of those games inventors and we can't wait to try out, in time, the inevitable PS14 and the Nintendo Puu – probably some time in 2034.

JACK and FREDDIE are fourteen-year-old classmates in London and have been game enthusiasts ever since they each acquired their first Game Boys. Between them they have ten consoles, ninety-seven games and four square eyes.

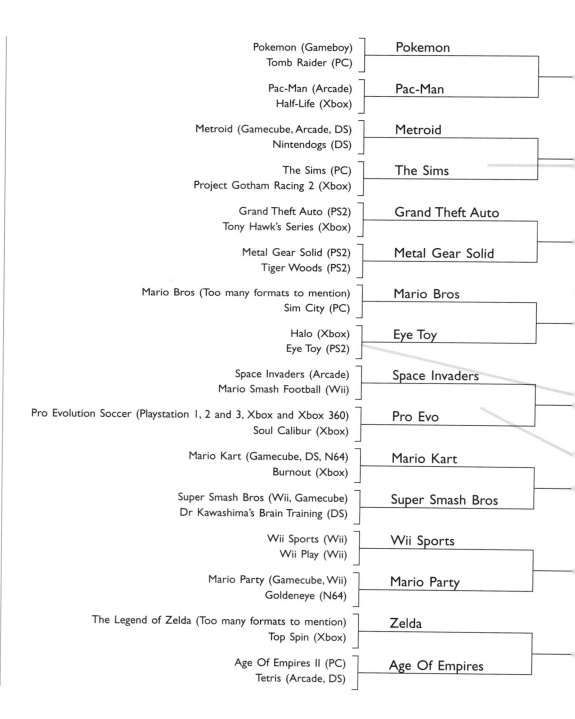

Pokemon (Gameboy)
Tomb Raider (PC)
Pokemon

Pac-Man (Arcade)
Half-Life (Xbox)
Pac-Man

Metroid (Gamecube, Arcade, DS)
Nintendogs (DS)
Metroid

The Sims (PC)
Project Gotham Racing 2 (Xbox)
The Sims

Grand Theft Auto (PS2)
Tony Hawk's Series (Xbox)
Grand Theft Auto

Metal Gear Solid (PS2)
Tiger Woods (PS2)
Metal Gear Solid

Mario Bros (Too many formats to mention)
Sim City (PC)
Mario Bros

Halo (Xbox)
Eye Toy (PS2)
Eye Toy

Space Invaders (Arcade)
Mario Smash Football (Wii)
Space Invaders

Pro Evolution Soccer (Playstation 1, 2 and 3, Xbox and Xbox 360)
Soul Calibur (Xbox)
Pro Evo

Mario Kart (Gamecube, DS, N64)
Burnout (Xbox)
Mario Kart

Super Smash Bros (Wii, Gamecube)
Dr Kawashima's Brain Training (DS)
Super Smash Bros

Wii Sports (Wii)
Wii Play (Wii)
Wii Sports

Mario Party (Gamecube, Wii)
Goldeneye (N64)
Mario Party

The Legend of Zelda (Too many formats to mention)
Top Spin (Xbox)
Zelda

Age Of Empires II (PC)
Tetris (Arcade, DS)
Age Of Empires

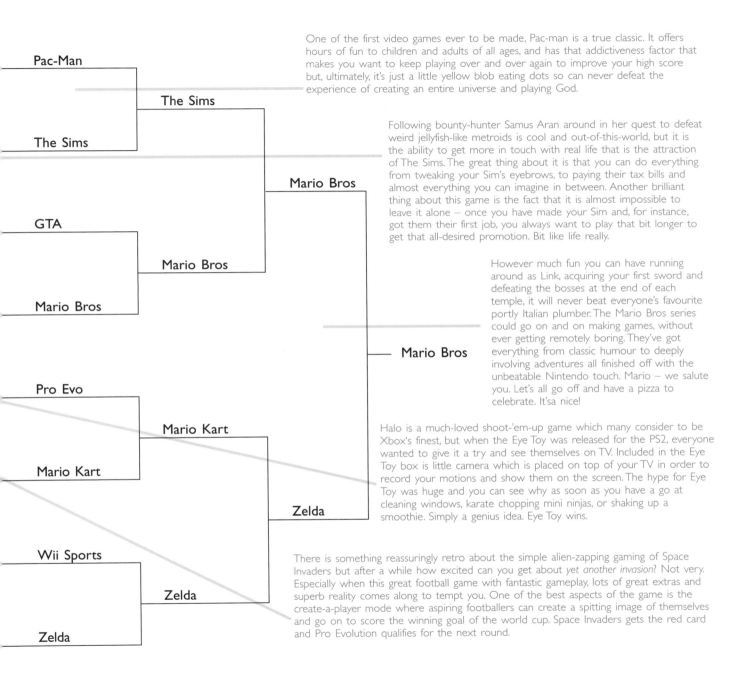

Pac-Man

The Sims

The Sims

Mario Bros

GTA

Mario Bros

Mario Bros

Mario Bros

Pro Evo

Mario Kart

Mario Kart

Zelda

Wii Sports

Zelda

Zelda

One of the first video games ever to be made, Pac-man is a true classic. It offers hours of fun to children and adults of all ages, and has that addictiveness factor that makes you want to keep playing over and over again to improve your high score but, ultimately, it's just a little yellow blob eating dots so can never defeat the experience of creating an entire universe and playing God.

Following bounty-hunter Samus Aran around in her quest to defeat weird jellyfish-like metroids is cool and out-of-this-world, but it is the ability to get more in touch with real life that is the attraction of The Sims. The great thing about it is that you can do everything from tweaking your Sim's eyebrows, to paying their tax bills and almost everything you can imagine in between. Another brilliant thing about this game is the fact that it is almost impossible to leave it alone – once you have made your Sim and, for instance, got them their first job, you always want to play that bit longer to get that all-desired promotion. Bit like life really.

However much fun you can have running around as Link, acquiring your first sword and defeating the bosses at the end of each temple, it will never beat everyone's favourite portly Italian plumber. The Mario Bros series could go on and on making games, without ever getting remotely boring. They've got everything from classic humour to deeply involving adventures all finished off with the unbeatable Nintendo touch. Mario – we salute you. Let's all go off and have a pizza to celebrate. It'sa nice!

Halo is a much-loved shoot-'em-up game which many consider to be Xbox's finest, but when the Eye Toy was released for the PS2, everyone wanted to give it a try and see themselves on TV. Included in the Eye Toy box is little camera which is placed on top of your TV in order to record your motions and show them on the screen. The hype for Eye Toy was huge and you can see why as soon as you have a go at cleaning windows, karate chopping mini ninjas, or shaking up a smoothie. Simply a genius idea. Eye Toy wins.

There is something reassuringly retro about the simple alien-zapping gaming of Space Invaders but after a while how excited can you get about *yet another invasion*? Not very. Especially when this great football game with fantastic gameplay, lots of great extras and superb reality comes along to tempt you. One of the best aspects of the game is the create-a-player mode where aspiring footballers can create a spitting image of themselves and go on to score the winning goal of the world cup. Space Invaders gets the red card and Pro Evolution qualifies for the next round.

95

What Men Want Women to Understand

by SIMON TREWIN

I was summoned to meet a very successful female client once who SAID she had something to tell me face to face. I said to my (female) assistant, 'I am SO going to get fired,' who replied, 'Don't be silly.' I turned up and was, of course, duly fired. On hearing the news I said, 'That's a shame, but just drop me a letter and we can get the formalities underway. I hope it all works out well for you.' The client then burst into tears and cried and cried until I found myself comforting her and telling her everything was going to be alright. She then broke away and banged her fists on the table (and against my arm) and screamed (across a packed but now strangely silent Starbucks), 'What is it with men? Why aren't you more upset?' She then gave me a present of a tie. What she needs to understand about me (and men in general) is that even though I was gutted I wasn't going to give her the satisfaction of seeing that and, secondly, I was never going to choose to wear a tie that would remind me all day that I had been fired. What was she thinking? We both stumbled out of Starbucks and off in different directions scratching our heads in utter bemusement at the opposite sex. Anyway, for female readers out there **PLEASE READ THIS AND DON'T ASK QUESTIONS UNTIL YOU HAVE FINISHED.**

That we enjoy spending hours wandering the aisles of Homebase in a trance looking at stuff.

That we don't enjoy reading instruction manuals.

That we don't like asking for directions – it emasculates us.

That we only need asking once to do things – if you ask us twice we won't do them.

That we don't like being presented with problems if we are not allowed to provide solutions.

That we have simple needs.

That we CAN multi-task.

That we don't want to be asked for our opinion on what you are wearing.

That we don't want you to walk into a room we have been decorating all day and start the conversation with 'you've missed a bit'.

That by the age of thirty-five we have enough friends.

That we like catchphrases.

That we use the telephone as a business tool not a social one.

That we need our egos stroking more than we might let on.

That we will buy you flowers when we want to.

That if you think you are fat then you probably are – don't ask.

That if you say you are 'fine' then we will believe you.

instruction
manuals

asking
directions

asking directions

A tricky challenge here – we don't read instructions manuals UNLESS we realize that our instinctive mastering of technology has for some reason failed us. Our job is to remove new gadget from box, plug it in and then play with it mercilessly for evenings on end until we have broken the little bugger in (rather like taming a lion or a wild horse) and it sits next to us obeying our every need. Same goes for directions – it is a well known fact that us men have a highly developed pineal gland (truly) and an innate sense of direction. It may look like we are hopelessly lost and we go a bit quiet for a while but we are just trying to work it all out in Nietzschean terms as we drive around. Asking passers by just destroys our cunning plan. Tough call this but directions win.

problems/solutions

problems/
solutions

problems/solutions

what you are
wearing

Men take things at face value – if you are crying, your wrists are bandaged and you are carrying what looks like the contents of your desk in a black sack when you get back from the office and, in reply to the innocent question 'How was your day darling?' you say 'Fine' then we will BELIEVE you and talk about what's on the telly and whether we should get a take-away or not. Simple really. And if, at 11pm, when we are feeling sleepy you start talking about how you hate our house/car/location/wardrobes/wallpaper/holiday plans/sex-life then, as men, we will then try to resolve all these issues until you are happy and we can sleep. Please understand that this is what we do and if you don't want solutions don't bring up problems. This is fundamental and has to win. As long as that's okay with you sweetheart?

problems/ solutions

enough friends

telephone

telephone

Women want to endlessly make new friends and go to parties, arrange parties, talk about parties whereas quite a lot of the time men want to be allowed to go into their multi-media caves, put on comfortable clothing and just mooch around a bit. We aren't ill – it is just what we do. As far as the telephone is concerned we might ring you at work and say 'Drink? Pub. 9pm? Cool' and that doesn't mean anything other than we can do the whole conversation thing when we meet and not pre-empt it all during the arrangement stage. It doesn't mean we aren't interested in your day – we would just rather prefer to talk it about when the day is almost over. This is important and wins out.

egos

fine

fine

Nothing annoys a man more than hearing, 'why don't you buy me flowers anymore?' It usually happens just after we have made the spontaneous decision to actually purchase some aforesaid blooms and to present them in a romantic gesture (honest). Of course, once we have been whined at there is no way we can follow through with this plan without it looking as if we are only doing it because you complained that we never do it. Duhh! And on the ego front every now and again, like well-behaved pets, we just need a little pat on the head and to be told that we are the greatest/sexiest/cleverest/ handsomest/biggest. Not rocket science. On balance the whole ego thing solves so many problems it has to go through. Please stroke us more and – who knows? – you might even get some flowers as a result.

fine

96

What Women Want Men to Understand

by SARAH BALLARD

When I was sixteen and some foolish boy's misdemeanours had unwittingly made me furious and a little bit tearful, a wise crone gave me a piece of advice which has haunted me ever since. She (my mother) said, 'The thing about boys is: they don't mean to be hurtful, they're just thoughtless.' And oh, how right she was. In the years since then when I've had cause to relay this piece of advice to crumpled friends, I've often wished that Mother Nature, or some other canny female relative, had taken the whole of mankind to one side in a timely manner, and explained a few simple facts to them. Once upon a time I'd have liked to correct them all myself – clean them up and just sort the bastards out. These days, I'm not so sure. On a good day, I think perhaps the differences between us are to be celebrated. On a bad day, the whole bunch are clearly just a lost cause. Either way – and since popular wisdom has it that it's the female of the species who do the communicating, I think I'm qualified enough to say this – some oiling of the wheels would really help us all get through the day. It's dangerous conducting research on this subject, it turns out, but I've braved the waves of vitriol to assemble something I hope is genuinely useful. It's not too much to hope for a revolution, is it? The ONE thing women want men to understand? Let's see . . .

SARAH BALLARD is thirty-two, works as an editor for a literary agency and lives very happily in Richmond with her boyfriend of two years. She hasn't let him read this entry ahead of publication (since he doesn't need correcting on any of these fronts, obviously).

How to white lie well. I know I look bad in it. You know I look bad in it. I know you know I look bad in it. But if you claim – convincingly enough – that I look *as beautiful as I always do*, I'll love you for it. (I might change my outfit another five times though.)

That sometimes having a bath, going to bed early with pyjamas, hot water bottle and a book is better than sex. Sometimes it's not. We don't know why.

That romance isn't dependent on the element of surprise. It doesn't matter how many times I've asked you to send me flowers – it will *never* spoil it when you do it.

That physical discomfort doesn't impress the ladies. No to futons and the cold, yes to clean sheets, cushions and low level lighting.

How to give a great massage.

Romance is easy. No to swathes of red velour and swimming through shark-infested waters. Yes to daily small (or not so small . . .) gestures of thoughtfulness.

How not to solve my problems. When I get in at the end of a bad day, and I want to let off steam, I don't want to hear any smart-arse solutions, I just want him to listen.

That buying flowers costs nothing (metaphorically speaking).

To err on the side of chivalry. We understand the path between political correctness and good old-fashioned manners is heavily mined, but really . . . Open the door. Offer your seat. Carry my bags. Pay for dinner once in a while. And teach all your sons to do likewise.

A kiss is just a kiss. It needn't be a warm up.

The truth about 'let's not do Valentine's/birthday/Christmas this year' agreements. We don't mean it. Even if we think we do.

That chocolate always helps.

What crying means and how to respond to it. DON'T panic, run away, shout, or start crying too; DO listen, ponder, carry a clean handkerchief and prepare to get wet.

That we'd like perfectly matching underwear too.

That men need to groom too. We really can smell your trainers/see your untamed body or facial hair, and it really does make you grim.

We don't care about the offside rule. It's boring AND it's easy. We play ball games too, you know.

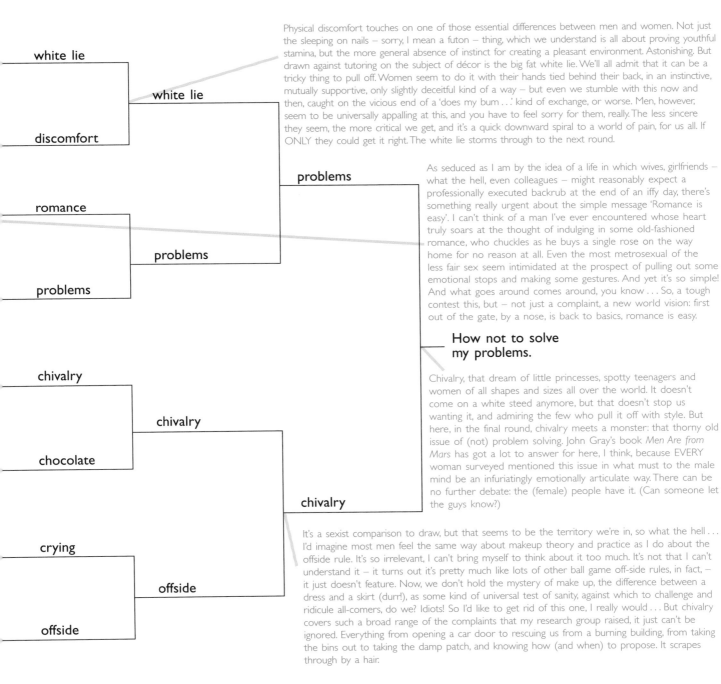

white lie

discomfort

white lie

romance

problems

problems

problems

chivalry

chocolate

chivalry

crying

offside

offside

problems

chivalry

How not to solve my problems.

Physical discomfort touches on one of those essential differences between men and women. Not just the sleeping on nails – sorry, I mean a futon – thing, which we understand is all about proving youthful stamina, but the more general absence of instinct for creating a pleasant environment. Astonishing. But drawn against tutoring on the subject of décor is the big fat white lie. We'll all admit that it can be a tricky thing to pull off. Women seem to do it with their hands tied behind their back, in an instinctive, mutually supportive, only slightly deceitful kind of a way – but even we stumble with this now and then, caught on the vicious end of a 'does my bum …' kind of exchange, or worse. Men, however, seem to be universally appalling at this, and you have to feel sorry for them, really. The less sincere they seem, the more critical we get, and it's a quick downward spiral to a world of pain, for us all. If ONLY they could get it right. The white lie storms through to the next round.

As seduced as I am by the idea of a life in which wives, girlfriends – what the hell, even colleagues – might reasonably expect a professionally executed backrub at the end of an iffy day, there's something really urgent about the simple message 'Romance is easy'. I can't think of a man I've ever encountered whose heart truly soars at the thought of indulging in some old-fashioned romance, who chuckles as he buys a single rose on the way home for no reason at all. Even the most metrosexual of the less fair sex seem intimidated at the prospect of pulling out some emotional stops and making some gestures. And yet it's so simple! And what goes around comes around, you know … So, a tough contest this, but – not just a complaint, a new world vision: first out of the gate, by a nose, is back to basics, romance is easy.

Chivalry, that dream of little princesses, spotty teenagers and women of all shapes and sizes all over the world. It doesn't come on a white steed anymore, but that doesn't stop us wanting it, and admiring the few who pull it off with style. But here, in the final round, chivalry meets a monster: that thorny old issue of (not) problem solving. John Gray's book *Men Are from Mars* has got a lot to answer for here, I think, because EVERY woman surveyed mentioned this issue in what must to the male mind be an infuriatingly emotionally articulate way. There can be no further debate: the (female) people have it. (Can someone let the guys know?)

It's a sexist comparison to draw, but that seems to be the territory we're in, so what the hell … I'd imagine most men feel the same way about makeup theory and practice as I do about the offside rule. It's so irrelevant, I can't bring myself to think about it too much. It's not that I can't understand it – it turns out it's pretty much like lots of other ball game off-side rules, in fact, – it just doesn't feature. Now, we don't hold the mystery of make up, the difference between a dress and a skirt (durr!), as some kind of universal test of sanity, against which to challenge and ridicule all-comers, do we? Idiots! So I'd like to get rid of this one, I really would … But chivalry covers such a broad range of the complaints that my research group raised, it just can't be ignored. Everything from opening a car door to rescuing us from a burning building, from taking the bins out to taking the damp patch, and knowing how (and when) to propose. It scrapes through by a hair.

97

'Where Were You When?' Moments

by SIMON TREWIN

It is difficult to remember a world before Wi-Fi, before email, before digital radio, before 24/7 newsfeeds on two hundred satellite channels available in the majority of homes. Now if something happens you hear about it within seconds, and with a click of a mouse, you can monitor an international story without even having to leave your computer. In earlier times, certainly when I was growing up, you could spend an entire day doing ordinary things, unaware that extraordinary events were taking place on the other side of the world. It was only when you went home and turned on *Newsround* or the *Six O'clock News* that this blissful ignorance was shattered. With so much access to news now, it is sometimes difficult to sort through the stories to discover what is truly important, but every now and again an event comes along that is so memorable that an office of disparate individuals are suddenly united around a television set, a computer terminal, or a radio. Our criteria here is simple, how deeply has the event singed itself on your memory? For an older generation the death of Churchill, VE day, Hiroshima and the Great Train Robbery are surely indelible, so we have established a cut-off date here of 1963, that marking the beginning of the baby-boomer generation.

A truly momentous occasion many thought we would never see. Having travelled through Checkpoint Charlie myself in 1982 this moment had a particular resonance for me.

I had only recently discovered the music of John Lennon (through the *Double Fantasy* album) and remember coming back from my paper round to turn on the radio and hear the news of John Lennon's shooting. It took me a while to realize the cultural significance of the death of one of the Fab Four.

Berlin Wall comes tumbling down (1989) — Katrina
Hurricane Katrina hits New Orleans (2005)

Saddam found (2003) — Ashes
England win The Ashes (2005)

9/11 (2001) — 9/11
7 July bombing in London (2005)

Thatcher resigns (1990) — O J
O. J. Verdict (1995)

Argentinian bombing of Port Stanley (1982) — Port Stanley
England football team wins World Cup (1966)

Richard Hammond crashes (2006) — Tsunami
Asian Tsunami (2004)

Elvis Presley dies (1977) — Nasty Nick
Nasty Nick Bateman's expulsion from *Big Brother* (2000)

Titanic found (1985) — John Lennon
John Lennon shot (1980)

Diana dies (1997) — Diana
Jade vs Shilpa on *Big Brother* (2007)

Tiananmen Square (1989) — Tiananmen
Windsor Castle burns (1992)

Lockerbie (1988) — Lockerbie
Jill Dando murdered (1999)

Dunblane massacre (1996) — Dunblane
Munich Olympics terrorist attack (1972)

Chernobyl nuclear reaction explosion (1986) — Chernobyl
Canary Wharf bombing (1996)

Man on the Moon (1969) — Live Aid
Live Aid (1985)

JFK assassinated (1963) — Hillsborough
Hillsborough (1989)

Shuttle Challenger explodes on takeoff (1986) — Shuttle
Yorkshire Ripper arrested (1981)

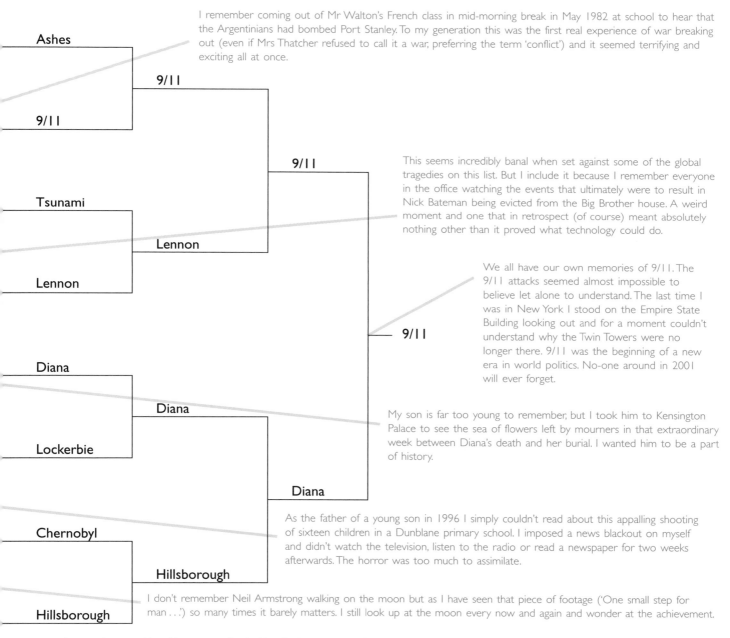

I remember coming out of Mr Walton's French class in mid-morning break in May 1982 at school to hear that the Argentinians had bombed Port Stanley. To my generation this was the first real experience of war breaking out (even if Mrs Thatcher refused to call it a war, preferring the term 'conflict') and it seemed terrifying and exciting all at once.

Ashes

9/11

9/11

9/11

Tsunami

Lennon

Lennon

9/11

This seems incredibly banal when set against some of the global tragedies on this list. But I include it because I remember everyone in the office watching the events that ultimately were to result in Nick Bateman being evicted from the Big Brother house. A weird moment and one that in retrospect (of course) meant absolutely nothing other than it proved what technology could do.

We all have our own memories of 9/11. The 9/11 attacks seemed almost impossible to believe let alone to understand. The last time I was in New York I stood on the Empire State Building looking out and for a moment couldn't understand why the Twin Towers were no longer there. 9/11 was the beginning of a new era in world politics. No-one around in 2001 will ever forget.

9/11

Diana

Diana

Lockerbie

My son is far too young to remember, but I took him to Kensington Palace to see the sea of flowers left by mourners in that extraordinary week between Diana's death and her burial. I wanted him to be a part of history.

Diana

As the father of a young son in 1996 I simply couldn't read about this appalling shooting of sixteen children in a Dunblane primary school. I imposed a news blackout on myself and didn't watch the television, listen to the radio or read a newspaper for two weeks afterwards. The horror was too much to assimilate.

Chernobyl

Hillsborough

Hillsborough

I don't remember Neil Armstrong walking on the moon but as I have seen that piece of footage ('One small step for man . . .') so many times it barely matters. I still look up at the moon every now and again and wonder at the achievement.

I remember watching this on a small television backstage at the Birmingham Rep after a matinee of Thomas Middleton's *Women Beware Women*. Suddenly, football commentators were commentating on real tragedy.

98

Women's Magazine Sex Clichés

by STEPHANIE DOLGOFF

To men, sex is like pizza: even when it's bad it's pretty good. Not so for women. Fortunately, there are women's magazines, which provide euphemistic how-tos for the easily embarrassed and explicit road maps for the insatiably curious. As long as you're going for better sex, how about amazing, seismic, glass-shattering, chandelier-swinging, earthmoving, life-altering, exponentially orgasmic sex? Women's magazines are unrivaled when it comes to new ways to say the same thing (i.e., buy this magazine, and you, too, will experience the stove-hot passion known only to bodice-ripped heroines), and that includes titles from *Cosmo* to *Ladies' Home Journal*. The result, despite the cumulative efforts of sharp Ivy League minds, is phrasemaking worthy of the Cliché Hall of Fame. The promise has to be real and the language surreal for winners to keep advancing.

STEPHANIE DOLGOFF, the health director of *Self* magazine, has observed, employed, and even tested a few of the promises on this page at home during the course of nearly two decades writing and editing for *Glamour, Cosmopolitan*, and *Seventeen*, among many others.

The words 'mother' and 'sex' should never appear in the same sentence.

20 Ways to Spice Up Your Sex Life
Recharge Your Relationship in One Weekend — **Recharge Weekend**

Six Secrets of Highly Orgasmic Women
Sex Secrets of Really Happy Couples — **Six Secrets**

Banish Boredom in Bed
Are You Sex Smart? — **Banish Boredom in Bed**

Seven Secrets of Sexually Satisfied Women
Realize Your Full Passion Potential — **Seven Secrets**

Are You Sabotaging Your Sex Life?
12 Secrets of Sensational Solo Sex — **Sabotaging?**

10 Hot New Sex Positions to Try Tonight
Supersize Your Sex Life – Tonight! — **Supersize Tonight!**

The Good Girls' Guide to Talking Dirty
Are You Sexually in Sync? — **Talking Dirty**

The Good Girls' Guide to Bad-Girl Sex
Love: What Makes It Last — **Bad-Girl Sex**

Get in Touch with Your Inner Sex Goddess
What Your Mother Never Told You About Sex — **Inner Goddess**

What Does He Really Want in Bed? Find Out – Now!
Unleash Your Inner Sex Kitten — **Inner Kitten**

Your Burning Sex Questions – Answered!
Are You Boring in Bed? How to Tell — **Burning Questions**

The Ultimate Guide to Bedroom Bliss – Revealed!
What Really Makes Men Cheat — **Bedroom Bliss**

Thrill Every Inch of Him – Tonight!
How to Blow His Mind in Bed — **Thrill Every Inch**

Go from Oh to OOOOOO!
Great Sexpectations! Make Long-Term Sex Sizzle — **Oh to OOOOOO!**

Is He Cheating? How to Tell
25 Ways to Rev Up Your Romance — **Is He Cheating?**

30 Sizzling Ideas for Mind-Blowing Sex
7 Ways to Make Him Ache for You — **Make Him Ache**

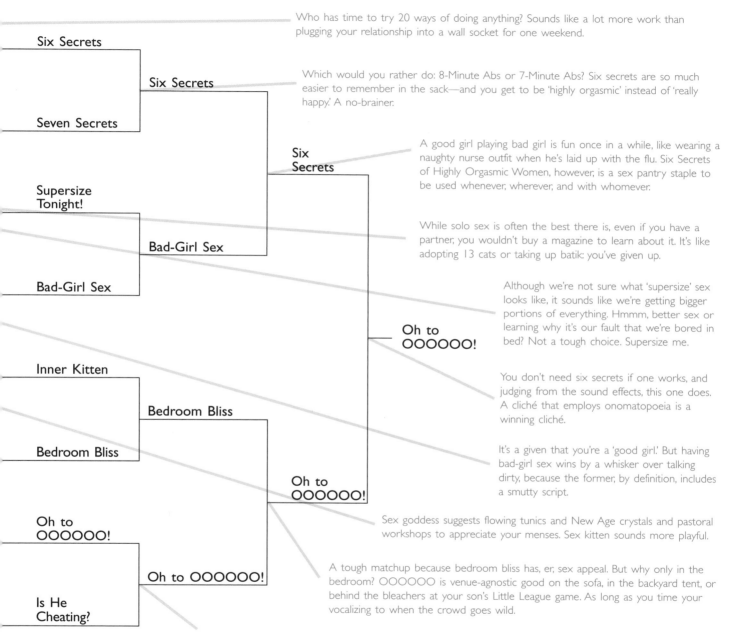

Six Secrets

Six Secrets

Seven Secrets

Supersize
Tonight!

Bad-Girl Sex

Bad-Girl Sex

Inner Kitten

Bedroom Bliss

Bedroom Bliss

Oh to
OOOOOO!

Oh to OOOOOO!

Is He
Cheating?

Six
Secrets

Oh to
OOOOOO!

Oh to
OOOOOO!

Who has time to try 20 ways of doing anything? Sounds like a lot more work than plugging your relationship into a wall socket for one weekend.

Which would you rather do: 8-Minute Abs or 7-Minute Abs? Six secrets are so much easier to remember in the sack—and you get to be 'highly orgasmic' instead of 'really happy.' A no-brainer.

A good girl playing bad girl is fun once in a while, like wearing a naughty nurse outfit when he's laid up with the flu. Six Secrets of Highly Orgasmic Women, however, is a sex pantry staple to be used whenever, wherever, and with whomever.

While solo sex is often the best there is, even if you have a partner, you wouldn't buy a magazine to learn about it. It's like adopting 13 cats or taking up batik: you've given up.

Although we're not sure what 'supersize' sex looks like, it sounds like we're getting bigger portions of everything. Hmmm, better sex or learning why it's our fault that we're bored in bed? Not a tough choice. Supersize me.

You don't need six secrets if one works, and judging from the sound effects, this one does. A cliché that employs onomatopoeia is a winning cliché.

It's a given that you're a 'good girl.' But having bad-girl sex wins by a whisker over talking dirty, because the former, by definition, includes a smutty script.

Sex goddess suggests flowing tunics and New Age crystals and pastoral workshops to appreciate your menses. Sex kitten sounds more playful.

A tough matchup because bedroom bliss has, er, sex appeal. But why only in the bedroom? OOOOOO is venue-agnostic good on the sofa, in the backyard tent, or behind the bleachers at your son's Little League game. As long as you time your vocalizing to when the crowd goes wild.

If he's cheating, you'll eventually find out, with or without this article—and dump him. What you learn from OOOOOO ensures your own happy ending, with or without him.

99

Yiddish Phrases
by MICHAEL WEX

If even people who speak nothing but Yiddish sometimes sit around discussing their favourite words and arguing about which ones are the most deeply Yiddish, who are we not to do likewise? Given the fact that Yiddish speakers would rather vent their feelings than share them, the language is full of colourful locutions that are meant to be remembered forever. Words that made the cut did so on the basis of euphony, utility, and frequency of use. They're all typically Yiddish; the ones that wouldn't come up in a Yiddish-language discussion of the same topic would be overlooked only because they'd be driving the conversation.

MICHAEL WEX was once paid to translate *The Threepenny Opera* from German to Yiddish so that someone else could be paid to do surtitles in English. He is the author of *Born to Kvetch* and the forthcoming *Wex's Shmooze Essentials*.

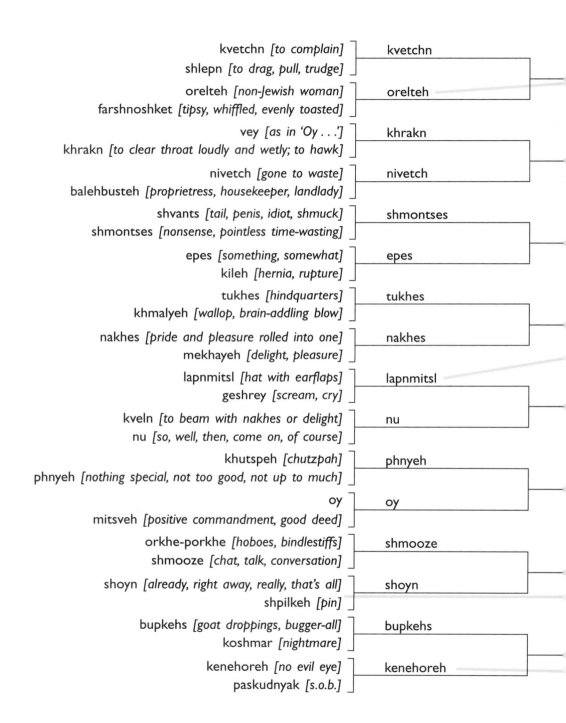

kvetchn [to complain] — kvetchn
shlepn [to drag, pull, trudge]

orelteh [non-Jewish woman] — orelteh
farshnoshket [tipsy, whiffled, evenly toasted]

vey [as in 'Oy . . .'] — khrakn
khrakn [to clear throat loudly and wetly; to hawk]

nivetch [gone to waste] — nivetch
balehbusteh [proprietress, housekeeper, landlady]

shvants [tail, penis, idiot, shmuck] — shmontses
shmontses [nonsense, pointless time-wasting]

epes [something, somewhat] — epes
kileh [hernia, rupture]

tukhes [hindquarters] — tukhes
khmalyeh [wallop, brain-addling blow]

nakhes [pride and pleasure rolled into one] — nakhes
mekhayeh [delight, pleasure]

lapnmitsl [hat with earflaps] — lapnmitsl
geshrey [scream, cry]

kveln [to beam with nakhes or delight] — nu
nu [so, well, then, come on, of course]

khutspeh [chutzpah] — phnyeh
phnyeh [nothing special, not too good, not up to much]

oy — oy
mitsveh [positive commandment, good deed]

orkhe-porkhe [hoboes, bindlestiffs] — shmooze
shmooze [chat, talk, conversation]

shoyn [already, right away, really, that's all] — shoyn
shpilkeh [pin]

bupkehs [goat droppings, bugger-all] — bupkehs
koshmar [nightmare]

kenehoreh [no evil eye] — kenehoreh
paskudnyak [s.o.b.]

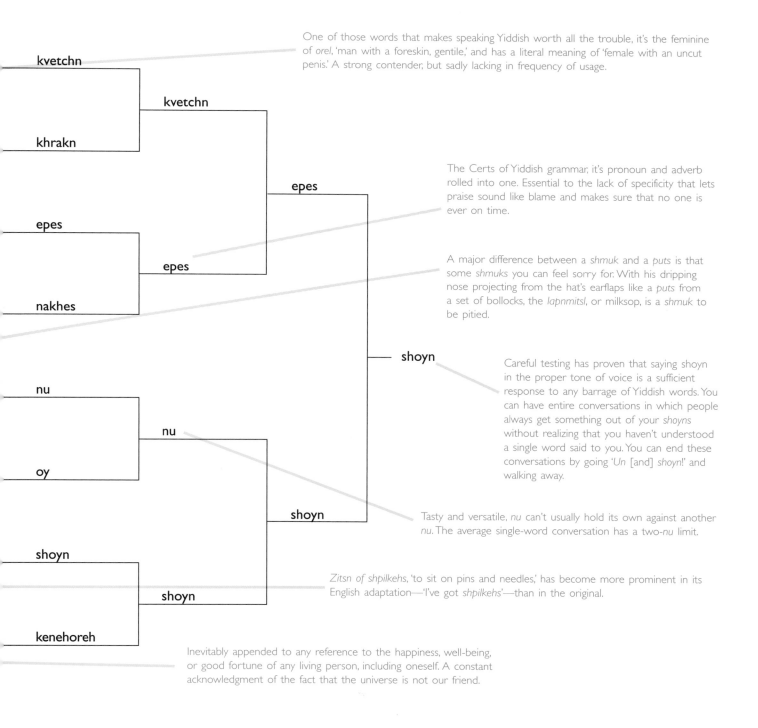

kvetchn

kvetchn

khrakn

One of those words that makes speaking Yiddish worth all the trouble, it's the feminine of *orel*, 'man with a foreskin, gentile,' and has a literal meaning of 'female with an uncut penis.' A strong contender, but sadly lacking in frequency of usage.

epes

epes

nakhes

epes

The Certs of Yiddish grammar, it's pronoun and adverb rolled into one. Essential to the lack of specificity that lets praise sound like blame and makes sure that no one is ever on time.

A major difference between a *shmuk* and a *puts* is that some *shmuks* you can feel sorry for. With his dripping nose projecting from the hat's earflaps like a *puts* from a set of bollocks, the *lapnmitsl*, or milksop, is a *shmuk* to be pitied.

shoyn

nu

nu

oy

Careful testing has proven that saying shoyn in the proper tone of voice is a sufficient response to any barrage of Yiddish words. You can have entire conversations in which people always get something out of your *shoyns* without realizing that you haven't understood a single word said to you. You can end these conversations by going '*Un* [and] *shoyn!*' and walking away.

shoyn

Tasty and versatile, *nu* can't usually hold its own against another *nu*. The average single-word conversation has a two-*nu* limit.

shoyn

shoyn

kenehoreh

Zitsn of shpilkehs, 'to sit on pins and needles,' has become more prominent in its English adaptation—'I've got *shpilkehs*'—than in the original.

Inevitably appended to any reference to the happiness, well-being, or good fortune of any living person, including oneself. A constant acknowledgment of the fact that the universe is not our friend.

And now it's your turn
by YOU

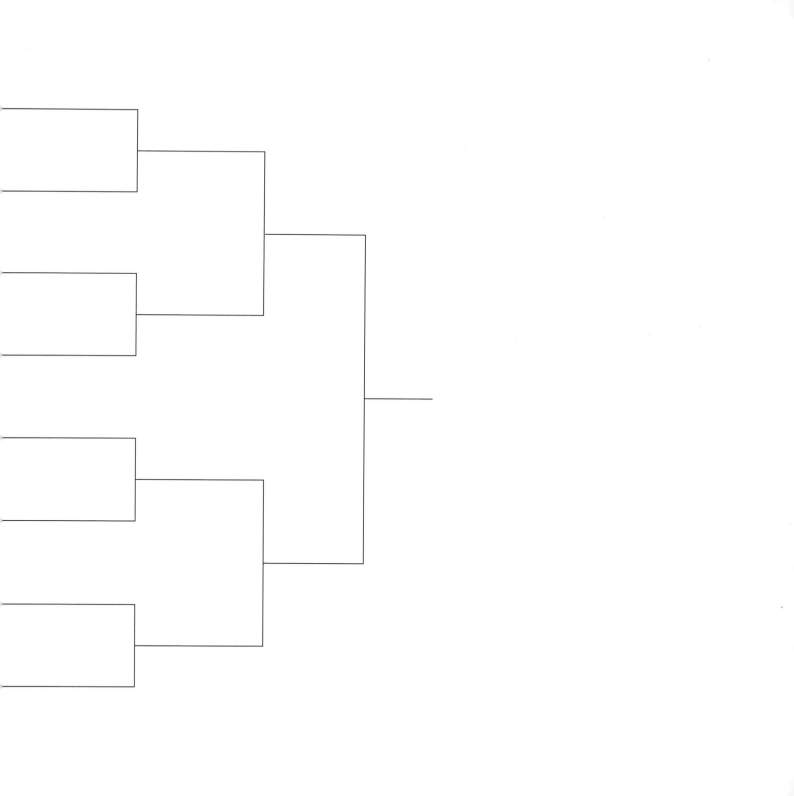

ACKNOWLEDGEMENTS

I would like to thank Mark Reiter, Richard Sandomir and Nigel Holmes who created the wonderful American book *The Enlightened Bracketologist* which inspired and contributed to this edition. Without them I would not have had five highly enjoyable months arguing with friends, colleagues and family over the contents and the ultimate winners of many of the lists you have just read. I would also like to thank my guest contributors who have come aboard with their own eccentricities, opinions and voices. They are all fine people and you should rush out and buy their books/attend their live shows/dine at their restaurants/buy their underwear/employ them as therapists/pat them on the head and say nice things/laugh at their jokes etc*. Thanks to my wonderful editrice Sophie Lazar, to Team Trewin: Helen, Jack, Teddy and Leo for putting up with yet another list-based obsession, my excellent support team – Emily Sklar, Claire Gill, Sarah Ballard, Ariella Feiner, James Gill, publicist Louise Campbell and my literary rock band members Messrs Bromley and Moran for allowing me time off for this solo album. May the gods of bracketology shine on you all.

Simon Trewin, University Of Bracketology (Secure Unit). October 2007

*delete as applicable